MENTAL CAUSATION
AND THE METAPHYSICS OF MIND

MENTAL CAUSATION
AND THE METAPHYSICS OF MIND

A READER

edited by NEIL CAMPBELL

broadview press

National Library of Canada Cataloguing in Publication

Mental causation and the metaphysics of mind : a reader / edited by Neil Campbell.

Includes bibliographical references.
ISBN 1-55111-509-3

1. Philosophy of mind.   2. Mind and body.   3. Causation.   I. Campbell, Neil, 1967–   .

BD418.3.M46 2002   128'.2   C2002-905034-0

Broadview Press Ltd. is an independent, international publishing house, incorporated in 1985. Broadview believes in shared ownership, both with its employees and with the general public; since the year 2000 Broadview shares have traded publicly on the Toronto Venture Exchange under the symbol BDP.

We welcome comments and suggestions regarding any aspect of our publications – please feel free to contact us at the addresses below or at broadview@broadviewpress.com.

North America
Post Office Box 1243, Peterborough, Ontario, Canada K9J 7H5
3576 California Road, Orchard Park, NY, USA 14127
Tel: (705) 743-8990; Fax: (705) 743-8353;
e-mail: customerservice@broadviewpress.com

UK, Ireland, and continental Europe
Thomas Lyster Ltd., Units 3 & 4a, Old Boundary Way,
Burscough Rd, Ormskirk, Lancashire L39 2YW
Tel: (1695) 575112; Fax: (1695) 570120
email: books@tlyster.co.uk

Australia and New Zealand
UNIREPS, University of New South Wales
Sydney, NSW, 2052
Tel: 61 2 9664 0999; Fax: 61 2 9664 5420
email: info.press@unsw.edu.au

www.broadviewpress.com

Broadview Press Ltd. gratefully acknowledges the financial support of the Government of Canada through the Book Publishing Industry Development Program for our publishing activities.

Typesetting and assembly: True to Type Inc., Mississauga, Canada.

PRINTED IN CANADA

In loving memory of my father, Colin

CONTENTS

Part III: Qualia

Part IV: Supervenience

INTRODUCTION

You feel thirsty. You decide you would like a drink and get up and go to the refrigerator to liberate a beer. This is an example of a simple intentional action. You are doing something for a reason, and the reason, among other things, is made up of a cluster of mental states, including the *feeling* of dryness in your mouth, the *desire* for a drink, the *belief* that there is a cold beer in the fridge, and so on. Nothing could be more familiar, yet nothing could be more mysterious. What is the relationship between these mental states and your getting up? The natural thing to say is that the reasons together *caused* your getting up, which is why referring to these mental states *explains* why you went to the refrigerator. That seems simple enough, but now consider how a physiologist might explain the above action. Your getting up is a matter of your muscles expanding and contracting in a particular way. The movement of your muscles is caused by electrochemical signals sent from your brain, which were in turn caused by extremely complex events in your neurons, which were caused by even more complex microphysical events, and so on. An increasingly detailed physiological story about the causal origins of your getting up is possible, but nowhere in this story do we see any mention of your desires or other mental states. This isn't just because we haven't looked hard enough. There is every reason to think that no matter how far back we go in the physiological explanation we will encounter nothing but increasingly more complicated physical processes. If we cannot find the point at which your reasons enter the causal sequence of events that produce your actions, then just what is the relationship between your reasons and your actions? How is it that your reasons explain what you do?

This is the problem of mental causation. The problem has its origins in the philosophy of René Descartes and is perhaps best regarded as a component of the "mind-body problem" which deals generally with the nature of the relationship between our mental lives and our physical being. In any account of mental causation, then, it is inevitable that one will draw on quite specific metaphysical views about the nature of mental states. Thus, while the focus of this book is on the problem of mental causation, the issues and views investigated are intimately connected to philosophical discussions of the nature of mind, its relation to the physical world, and the nature of causation and causal explanation.

In the seventeenth century Descartes argued that human beings are a composite of material and immaterial substance. On the one hand, he claimed, we are physical beings whose behaviour can often be explained in completely physiological terms. On the other hand, however, we also have minds. In his view, the mind or soul is the seat of all mental operations, such as willing, thinking, feeling, believing, and so on, and is connected to the body by means of a causal relationship. This causal interaction, Descartes claimed, occurs in a small gland near the centre of the brain called the "pineal gland" (sometimes also called the "conarion" or "common sense"). Historically, Descartes's view was criticized on the grounds that there is something inherently mysterious, and perhaps even incoherent, about the idea of a causal interaction between two such radically distinct types of substance. How could such an interaction occur? Since the pineal gland is itself a physical part of the brain, appealing to it as a go-between does not explain anything; for the question then arises, "How does the pineal gland interact with a non-physical soul?" Descartes, then, does not appear to provide a satisfactory account of mental causation. Nevertheless, Descartes has left us the problem as a legacy, and with it the tendency to think of ourselves as beings with both physical and mental characteristics.

One solution to the problem is to deny that there is any causal interaction between mind and body. In this case, there really is no such thing as mental causation; there only seems to be. There are two possibilities here. The first, adopted by Leibniz and Malbranche, accepted Descartes's dualism but claimed that mind and body run along parallel courses, making it *seem* as though our mental states cause our actions. The synchronization of mental and bodily events is attributed to acts of God. Our bodies make their way in the world in accordance with the laws of physics without any intervention by our minds. When we formulate an intention to act in our souls, our bodies are unaffected by those intentions. It just happens (through God's direct intervention, or according to God's divine plan) that our bodies perform the act intended.

Parallelism is not a very popular theory among contemporary philosophers of mind. Appealing to God to account for the appearance of mental causation is, to many, no less mysterious than Descartes's appeal to the pineal gland. Thus, others have adopted what is called "epiphenomenalism" as an alternative theory. Like the parallelists, epiphenomenalists claim that mental causation is an illusion; it only seems as though mental states cause actions. According to epiphenomenalism, mental states are by-products of brain states and are completely without causal powers of their own. Let's look back to our example of getting up because you want a drink. An epiphenomenalist would say that your desire is completely without effects in the world. You did not get up because you had a desire for a drink; you got up because of the occurrence of the kind of events in your body the physiologist talks about. Somewhere in that causal sequence, however, there is a physical event that has two effects. One effect is a link in the causal chain of physical events that leads to your getting up. The other effect is mental: it is the production in you of your desire. On this view, then, our mental states, such as beliefs, desires, reasons, and so on, are simply by-products of physiological processes and, as such, are completely without any power to influence our bodies.

Epiphenomenalism has become an important theory in contemporary discussions of mental causation. This is not because it is widely accepted (though some philosophers do accept it), or even because it is a plausible theory (most find it quite *implausible*). Epiphenomenalism is important because it represents a threat. It is the theory to avoid at all costs, yet it is a theory that is notoriously difficult to avoid. An assortment of philosophical views of the mind and various attempts to account for mental causation raise the spectre of epiphenomenalism. This is undesirable because epiphenomenalism fails to do justice to our firm conviction that we act the way we do because our beliefs, desires, and reasons cause us to act. Since epiphenomenalism represents the failure to provide an adequate account of mental causation, the theme of epiphenomenalism will figure prominently in the articles within this collection. In what follows we will see arguments for and against epiphenomenalism in a variety of attempts to explain—sometimes to explain the illusion of—mental causation. Our exploration of these issues is divided into four parts.

Part one provides the historical background and development of the problem of mental causation and the concept of epiphenomenalism. We will begin with Descartes's *Sixth Meditation* and some excerpts from *Passions of the Soul*. It is in the *Meditations* that Descartes gives birth to the mind-body problem in general, and the problem of mental causation in particular. Here he argues that human beings are a composite of physical and non-physical substances. The nature of the connection between these distinct substances is elaborated in *Passions of the Soul*. According to Descartes, your desire for a drink is a state of your soul. Using your free will, your soul decides to get a drink. This causes your pineal gland to move in a particular manner, which causes pores in your brain to open, releasing "animal spirits" that flow through your body to the muscles, causing them to expand and contract in the manner necessary for the movement of your body toward the refrigerator. Descartes's views are contrasted in this section with those of T.H. Huxley. Although Huxley described his view as "automatism" (the philosophical term "epiphenomenalism" was introduced later by William James), he is usually credited with defining and providing the first arguments for epiphenomenalism. Hence, these two works, along with William James's critique of Huxley's position, provide the historical backdrop for the rest of the articles in this collection.

Part two focuses on Donald Davidson's theory of mind: anomalous monism. Davidson's is a materialist theory, according to which every mental event, such as having a desire, is identical to a physical event, such as a neurological process. His means of accounting for mental causation is entirely dependent on his unique brand of identity theory. Going back to the example of feeling thirsty and getting a beer, Davidson would say that the desire for a drink is identical to some stage in the physiological causal antecedents of the action. For Davidson, then, the desire just *is* a part of that physiological process, but it has been described using a different vocabulary. The bulk of Part two is devoted to discussions among Davidson and his defenders and detractors. The point of contention is whether or not Davidson's theory of mind entails a form of epiphenomenalism. Generally, his critics think that on his view, mental *properties* are without any causal efficacy. Basically, the idea is this: While it is true that the desire for a drink caused your getting up, it did so only in virtue of its physical properties, the properties picked out in the physiological explanation. The mental properties of the event (i.e., the fact it was the desire it was) seem to contribute nothing to your getting up. If this is so, then Davidson fails to provide an adequate account of mental causation because our reasons, *as reasons*, contribute nothing to our actions.

Part three deals with an argument that purports to show that a certain category of mental state is epiphenomenal. The group of mental states in question are called "qualia." Qualia are the subjective elements in experience. They denote the intrinsic "feel" of sensory experiences: how colours look, how lemons taste, how roses smell, and so on. The argument about qualia is Frank Jackson's *knowledge argument*. Learn everything physical there is to know about colour vision, he claims, and there is something that will forever elude you unless you experience colours first hand: what it is like to see colours. He proposes that this conclusion implies that qualia are non-physical and epiphenomenal. If they weren't, then you would have known what colours are like from the physical information alone. The rest of part three is taken up with the various responses to Jackson's argument. Most claim that Jackson is guilty of an equivocation of one sort or another, while others question the very cogency of the thought experiment itself. If Jackson is correct, his conclusion has serious ramifications for the concept of mental causation. Ordinarily we would agree that we say a meal is delicious because of the way it tastes. It is on the basis of a complex series of gustatory qualia that we offer this evaluation. If qualia are, in fact, epiphenomenal, then our words of praise are not in any way caused by our taste sensations, but by their physical antecedents.

In part four we examine some of the most recent attempts to account for mental causation. At centre stage in these discussions is the concept of supervenience. Jaegwon Kim has been the most vocal philosopher about its advantages and its shortcomings alike. Supervenience describes a relationship of determination and dependence between two sets of properties. Kim and others have suggested that mental properties supervene on physical properties. This means that the mental properties an object has are dependent on, and determined by, the object's physical properties; however, the mental properties in question cannot be reduced to their physical base properties. This is analogous to other kinds of property relations. For instance, it has been suggested that aesthetic properties supervene on non-aesthetic properties, that moral properties supervene on descriptive properties, and that social properties supervene on economic properties. Kim proposes that the concept of supervenience can be used to describe a special species of causation, which he calls "supervenient causation." In his view, we might be able to account for mental causation by regarding it as an instance of supervenient causation. The rest of the selections in part four challenge the effectiveness of Kim's use of supervenient causation and question the accuracy of his account of the relationship between physiological and psychological explanations.

My hope is that this anthology will give the reader an accurate sense of the problem of mental causation, its relationship to the mind-body problem, and the intricacies of the issue. Many important contributions to this discussion could not be included in this volume, but the most important and influential ones are. I trust the papers collected here will stimulate further thought about that very deepest of mysteries: our own nature.

PART I
⇥ HISTORICAL BACKGROUND ⇤

1

Sixth Meditation*

René Descartes

THE EXISTENCE OF MATERIAL THINGS, AND THE REAL DISTINCTION BETWEEN MIND AND BODY[1]

It remains for me to examine whether material things exist. And at least I now know they are capable of existing, in so far as they are the subject-matter of pure mathematics, since I perceive them clearly and distinctly. For there is no doubt that God is capable of creating everything that I am capable of perceiving in this manner; and I have never judged that something could not be made by him except on the grounds that there would be a contradiction in my perceiving it distinctly. The conclusion that material things exist is also suggested by the faculty of imagination, which I am aware of using when I turn my mind to material things. For when I give more attentive consideration to what imagination is, it seems to be nothing else but an application of the cognitive faculty to a body which is intimately present to it, and which therefore exists.

To make this clear, I will first examine the difference between imagination and pure understanding. When I imagine a triangle, for example, I do not merely understand that it is a figure bounded by three lines, but at the same time I also see the three lines with my mind's eye as if they were present before me; and this is what I call imagining. But if I want to think of a chiliagon, although I understand that it is a figure consisting of a thousand sides just as well as I understand the triangle to be a three-sided figure, I do not in the same way imagine the thousand sides or see them as if they were present before me. It is true that since I am in the habit of imagining something whenever I think of a corporeal thing, I may construct in my mind a confused representation of some figure; but it is clear that this is not a chiliagon. For it

---

*   This translation is taken from *Descartes: Selected Philosophical Writings*, translated by John Cottingham, Robert Stoothoff, and Dugald Murdoch (Cambridge: Cambridge University Press, 1988). Reprinted with the permission of Cambridge University Press.

differs in no way from the representation I should form if I were thinking of a myriagon, or any figure with very many sides. Moreover, such a representation is useless for recognizing the properties which distinguish a chiliagon from other polygons. But suppose I am dealing with a pentagon: I can of course understand the figure of a pentagon, just as I can the figure of a chiliagon, without the help of the imagination; but I can also imagine a pentagon, by applying my mind's eye to its five sides and the area contained within them. And in doing this I notice quite clearly that imagination requires a peculiar effort of mind which is not required for understanding; this additional effort of mind clearly shows the difference between imagination and pure understanding.

Besides this, I consider that this power of imagining which is in me differing as it does from the power of understanding, is not a necessary constituent of my own essence, that is, of the essence of my mind. For if I lacked it, I should undoubtedly remain the same individual as I now am; from which it seems to follow that it depends on something distinct from myself. And I can easily understand that, if there does exist some body to which the mind is so joined that it can apply itself to contemplate it, as it were, whenever it pleases, then it may possibly be this very body that enables me to imagine corporeal things. So the difference between this mode of thinking and pure understanding may simply be this: when the mind understands, it in some way turns towards itself and inspects one of the ideas which are within it; but when it imagines, it turns towards the body and looks at something in the body which conforms to an idea understood by the mind or perceived by the senses. I can, as I say, easily understand that this is how imagination comes about, if the body exists; and since there is no other equally suitable way of explaining imagination that comes to mind, I can make a probable conjecture that the body exists. But this is only a probability; and despite a careful and comprehensive investigation, I do not yet see how the distinct idea of corporeal nature which I find in my imagination can provide any basis for a necessary inference that some body exists.

But besides that corporeal nature which is the subject-matter of pure mathematics, there is much else that I habitually imagine, such as colours, sounds, tastes, pain and so on—though not so distinctly. Now I perceive these things much better by means of the senses, which is how, with the assistance of memory, they appear to have reached the imagination. So in order to deal with them more fully, I must pay equal attention to the senses, and see whether the things which are perceived by means of that mode of thinking which I call "sensory perception" provide me with any sure argument for the existence of corporeal things.

To begin with, I will go back over all the things which I previously took to be perceived by the senses, and reckoned to be true; and I will go over my reasons for thinking this. Next, I will set out my reasons for subsequently calling these things into doubt. And finally I will consider what I should now believe about them.

First of all then, I perceived by my senses that I had a head, hands, feet and other limbs making up the body which I regarded as part of myself, or perhaps even as my whole self. I also perceived by my senses that this body was situated among many other bodies which could affect it in various favourable or unfavourable ways; and I gauged the favourable effects by a sensation of pleasure, and the unfavourable ones by a sensation of pain. In addition to pain and pleasure, I also had sensations within me of hunger, thirst, and other such appetites, and also of physical propensities towards cheerfulness, sadness, anger and similar emotions. And outside me, besides the extension, shapes and movements of bodies, I also had sensations of their hardness and heat, and of the other tactile qualities. In addition, I had sensations of light, colours, smells, tastes and sounds, the variety of which enabled me to distinguish the sky, the earth, the seas, and all other bodies, one from another. Considering the ideas of all these qualities which presented themselves to my thought, although the ideas were, strictly speaking, the only immediate objects of my sensory awareness, it was not unreasonable for me to think that the items which I was perceiving through the senses were things quite distinct from my thought, namely bodies which produced the ideas. For my experience was that these ideas came to me quite without my consent, so that I could not have sensory awareness of any object, even if I wanted to, unless it was present to my sense organs; and I could not avoid having sensory awareness of it when it was present. And since the ideas perceived by the senses were much more lively and vivid and even, in their own way, more distinct than any of those which I deliberately formed through meditating or which I found impressed on my memory, it seemed impossible that they should have come from within me; so the only alternative was that they came from other things. Since the sole source of my knowledge of these things was the ideas themselves, the supposition that the things resembled the ideas was bound to occur to me. In addition, I remembered that the use of my senses had come first, while the use of my reason came only later; and I saw that the ideas which I formed myself were less vivid than those which I perceived with the senses and were, for the most part, made up of elements of sensory ideas. In this way I easily convinced myself that I had nothing at all in the intellect which I had not previously had in sensation. As for the body which by some special right I called "mine," my belief that this body, more than any other, belonged to me had some justification. For I could never be separated from it, as I could from other bodies; and I felt all my appetites and emotions in, and on account of, this body; and finally, I was aware of pain and pleasurable ticklings in parts of this body, but not in other bodies external to it. But why should that curious sensation of pain give rise to a particular distress of mind; or why should a certain kind of delight follow on a tickling sensation? Again, why should that curious tugging in the stomach which I call hunger tell me that I should eat, or a dryness of the throat tell me to drink, and so on? I was not able to give any explanation of all this, except that nature taught me so. For there is absolutely no connection (at least that I can understand) between the tugging sensation and the decision to take food, or between the sensation of something causing pain and the mental apprehension of distress that arises from that sensation. These and other judgements that I made concerning sensory objects, I was apparently taught to make by nature; for I had already made up my mind that this was how things were, before working out any arguments to prove it.

Later on, however, I had many experiences which gradually undermined all the faith I had had in the senses. Sometimes towers which had looked round from a distance appeared square from close up; and enormous statues standing on their pediments did not seem large when observed from the ground. In these and countless other such cases, I found that the judgements of the external senses were mistaken. And this applied not just to the external senses but to the internal senses as well. For what can be more internal than pain? And yet I had heard that those who had had a leg or an arm amputated sometimes still seemed to feel pain intermittently in the missing part of the body. So even in my own case it was apparently not quite certain that a particular limb was hurting, even if I felt pain in it. To these reasons for doubting, I recently added two very general ones. The first was that every sensory experience I have ever thought I was having while awake I can also think of myself as sometimes having while asleep; and since I do not believe that what I seem to perceive in sleep comes from things located outside me, I did not see why I should be any more inclined to believe this of what I think I perceive while awake. The second reason for doubt was that since I did not know the author of my being (or at least was pretending not to), I saw nothing to rule out the possibility that my natural constitution made me prone to error even in matters which seemed to me most true. As for the reasons for my previous confident belief in the truth of the things perceived by the senses, I had no trouble in refuting them. For since I apparently had natural impulses towards many things which reason told me to avoid, I reckoned that a great deal of confidence should not be placed in what I was taught by nature. And despite the fact that the perceptions of the senses were not dependent on my will, I did not think that I should on that account infer that they proceeded from things distinct from myself, since I might perhaps have a faculty not yet known to me which produced them.

But now, when I am beginning to achieve a better knowledge of myself and the author of my being, although I do not think I should heedlessly accept everything I seem to have acquired from the senses, neither do I think that everything should be called into doubt.

First, I know that everything which I clearly and distinctly understand is capable of being created by God so as to correspond exactly with my understanding of it. Hence the fact that I can clearly and distinctly understand one thing apart from another is enough to make me certain that the two things are distinct, since they are capable of being separated, at least by God. The question of what kind of power is required to bring about such a separation does not affect the judgement that the two things are distinct. Thus, simply by knowing that I exist and seeing at the same time that absolutely nothing else belongs to my nature or essence except that I am a thinking thing, I can infer correctly that my essence consists solely in the fact that I am a thinking thing. It is true that I may have (or, to anticipate, that I certainly have) a body that is very closely joined to me. But nevertheless, on the one hand I have a clear and distinct idea of myself, in so far as I am simply a thinking, non-extended thing; and on the other hand I have a distinct idea of body,[2] in so far as this is simply an extended, non-thinking thing. And accordingly, it is certain that I[3] am really distinct from my body, and can exist without it.

Besides this, I find in myself faculties for certain special modes of thinking,[4] namely imagination and sensory perception. Now I can clearly and distinctly understand myself as a whole without these faculties; but I cannot, conversely, understand these faculties without me, that is, without an intellectual substance to inhere in. This is because there is an intellectual act included in their essential definition; and hence I perceive that the distinction between them and myself corresponds to the distinction between the modes of a thing and the thing itself.[5] Of course I also recognize that there are other faculties (like those of changing position, of taking on various shapes, and so on) which, like sensory perception and imagination, cannot be understood apart from some substance for them to inhere in, and hence cannot exist without it. But it is clear that these other faculties, if they exist, must be in a corporeal or extended substance and not an intellectual one; for the clear and distinct conception of them includes extension, but does not include any intellectual act whatsoever. Now there is in me a passive faculty of sensory perception, that is, a faculty for receiving and recognizing the ideas of sensible objects; but I could not make use of it unless there was also an active faculty, either in me or in something else, which produced or brought about these ideas. But this faculty cannot be in me, since clearly it presupposes no intellectual act on my part,[6] and the ideas in question are produced without my cooperation and often even against my will. So the only alternative is that it is in another substance distinct from me—a substance which contains either formally or eminently all the reality which exists objectively in the ideas produced by this faculty (as I have just noted). This substance is either a body, that is, a corporeal nature, in which case it will contain formally <and in fact> everything which is to be found objectively <or representatively> in the ideas;

or else it is God, or some creature more noble than a body, in which case it will contain eminently whatever is to be found in the ideas. But since God is not a deceiver, it is quite clear that he does not transmit the ideas to me either directly from himself, or indirectly, via some creature which contains the objective reality of the ideas not formally but only eminently. For God has given me no faculty at all for recognizing any such source for these ideas; on the contrary, he has given me a great propensity to believe that they are produced by corporeal things. So I do not see how God could be understood to be anything but a deceiver if the ideas were transmitted from a source other than corporeal things. It follows that corporeal things exist. They may not all exist in a way that exactly corresponds with my sensory grasp of them, for in many cases the grasp of the senses is very obscure and confused. But at least they possess all the properties which I clearly and distinctly understand, that is, all those which, viewed in general terms, are comprised within the subject-matter of pure mathematics.

What of the other aspects of corporeal things which are either particular (for example that the sun is of such and such a size or shape), or less clearly understood, such as light or sound or pain, and so on? Despite the high degree of doubt and uncertainty involved here, the very fact that God is not a deceiver, and the consequent impossibility of there being any falsity in my opinions which cannot be corrected by some other faculty supplied by God, offers me a sure hope that I can attain the truth even in these matters. Indeed, there is no doubt that everything that I am taught by nature contains some truth. For if nature is considered in its general aspect, then I understand by the term nothing other than God himself, or the ordered system of created things established by God. And by my own nature in particular I understand nothing other than the totality of things bestowed on me by God.

There is nothing that my own nature teaches me more vividly than that I have a body, and that when I feel pain there is something wrong with the body, and that when I am hungry or thirsty the body needs food and drink, and so on. So I should not doubt that there is some truth in this.

Nature also teaches me, by these sensations of pain, hunger, thirst and so on, that I am not merely present in my body as a sailor is present in a ship,[7] but that I am very closely joined and, as it were, intermingled with it, so that I and the body form a unit. If this were not so, I, who am nothing but a thinking thing, would not feel pain when the body was hurt, but would perceive the damage purely by the intellect, just as a sailor perceives by sight if anything in his ship is broken. Similarly, when the body needed food or drink, I should have an explicit understanding of the fact, instead of having confused sensations of hunger and thirst. For these sensations of hunger, thirst, pain and so on are nothing but confused modes of thinking which arise from the union and, as it were, intermingling of the mind with the body.

I am also taught by nature that various other bodies exist in the vicinity of my body, and that some of these are to be sought out and others avoided. And from the fact that I perceive by my senses a great variety of colours, sounds, smells and tastes, as well as differences in heat, hardness and the like, I am correct in inferring that the bodies which are the source of these various sensory perceptions possess differences corresponding to them, though perhaps not resembling them. Also, the fact that some of the perceptions are agreeable to me while others are disagreeable makes it quite certain that my body, or rather my whole self, in so far as I am a combination of body and mind, can be affected by the various beneficial or harmful bodies which surround it.

There are, however, many other things which I may appear to have been taught by nature, but which in reality I acquired not from nature but from a habit of making ill-considered judgements; and it is therefore quite possible that these are false. Cases in point are the belief that any space in which nothing is occurring to stimulate my senses must be empty; or that the heat in a body is something exactly resembling the idea of heat which is in me; or that when a body is white or green, the selfsame whiteness or greenness which I perceive through my senses is present in the body; or that in a body which is bitter or sweet there is the selfsame taste which I experience, and so on; or, finally, that stars and towers and other distant bodies have the same size and shape which they present to my senses, and other examples of this kind. But to make sure that my perceptions in this matter are sufficiently distinct, I must more accurately define exactly what I mean when I say that I am taught something by nature. In this context I am taking nature to be something more limited than the totality of things bestowed on me by God. For this includes many things that belong to the mind alone—for example my perception that what is done cannot be undone, and all other things that are known by the natural light;[8] but at this stage I am not speaking of these matters. It also includes much that relates to the body alone, like the tendency to move in a downward direction, and so on; but I am not speaking of these matters either. My sole concern here is with what God has bestowed on me as a combination of mind and body. My nature, then, in this limited sense, does indeed teach me to avoid what induces a feeling of pain and to seek out what induces feelings of pleasure, and so on. But it does not appear to teach us to draw any conclusions from these sensory perceptions about things located outside us without waiting until the intellect has examined[9] the matter. For knowledge of the truth about such things seems to belong to the mind alone, not to the combination of mind and body. Hence, although a star has no greater effect on my eye than the flame of a small light, that does not mean that there is any real or positive inclination in me to believe that the star is no bigger than the light; I have simply made this judgement from childhood onwards without any rational basis. Similarly, although I feel heat when I go near a fire and feel pain when I go too near, there is no convincing argument for supposing that there is something in the fire which resembles the heat, any more than for supposing that there is something which resembles the pain. There is simply reason to suppose that there is something in the fire, whatever it may eventually turn out to be, which produces in us the feelings of heat or pain. And likewise, even though there is nothing in any given space that stimulates the senses, it does not follow that there is no body there. In these cases and many others I see that I have been in the habit of misusing the order of nature. For the proper purpose of the sensory perceptions given me by nature is simply to inform the mind of what is beneficial or harmful for the composite of which the mind is a part; and to this extent they are sufficiently clear and distinct. But I misuse them by treating them as reliable touchstones for immediate judgements about the essential nature of the bodies located outside us; yet this is an area where they provide only very obscure information.

I have already looked in sufficient detail at how, notwithstanding the goodness of God, it may happen that my judgements are false. But a further problem now comes to mind regarding those very things which nature presents to me as objects which I should seek out or avoid, and also regarding the internal sensations, where I seem to have detected errors[10]—e.g. when someone is tricked by the pleasant taste of some food into eating the poison concealed inside it. Yet in this case, what the man's nature urges him to go for is simply what is responsible for the pleasant taste, and not the poison, which his nature knows nothing about. The only inference that can be drawn from this is that his nature is not omniscient. And this is not surprising, since man is a limited thing, and so it is only fitting that his perfection should be limited.

And yet it is not unusual for us to go wrong even in cases where nature does urge us towards something. Those who are ill, for example, may desire food or drink that will shortly afterwards turn out to be bad for them. Perhaps it may be said that they go wrong because their nature is disordered, but this does not remove the difficulty. A sick man is no less one of God's creatures than a healthy one, and it seems no less a contradiction to suppose that he has received from God a nature which deceives him. Yet a clock constructed with wheels and weights observes all the laws of its nature just as closely when it is badly made and tells the wrong time as when it completely fulfils the wishes of the clockmaker. In the same way, I might consider the body of a man as a kind of machine equipped with and made up of bones, nerves, muscles, veins, blood and skin in such a way that, even if there were no mind in it, it would still perform all the same movements as it now does in those cases where movement is not under the control of the will or, consequently, of the mind.[11] I can easily see that if such a body suffers from dropsy, for example, and is affected by the dryness of the throat which normally produces in the mind the sensation of thirst, the resulting condition of the nerves and other parts will dispose the body to take a drink, with the result that the disease will be aggravated. Yet this is just as natural as the body's being stimulated by a similar dryness of the throat to take a drink when there is no such illness and the drink is beneficial. Admittedly, when I consider the purpose of the clock, I may say that it is departing from its nature when it does not tell the right time; and similarly when I consider the mechanism of the human body, I may think that, in relation to the movements which normally occur in it, it too is deviating from its nature if the throat is dry at a time when drinking is not beneficial to its continued health. But I am well aware that "nature" as I have just used it has a very different significance from "nature" in the other sense. As I have just used it, "nature" is simply a label which depends on my thought; it is quite extraneous to the things to which it is applied, and depends simply on my comparison between the idea of a sick man and a badly-made clock, and the idea of a healthy man and a well-made clock. But by "nature" in the other sense I understand something which is really to be found in the things themselves; in this sense, therefore, the term contains something of the truth.

When we say, then, with respect to the body suffering from dropsy, that it has a disordered nature because it has a dry throat and yet does not need drink, the term "nature" is here used merely as an extraneous label. However, with respect to the composite, that is, the mind united with this body, what is involved is not a mere label, but a true error of nature, namely that it is thirsty at a time when drink is going to cause it harm. It thus remains to inquire how it is that the goodness of God does not prevent nature, in this sense, from deceiving us.

The first observation I make at this point is that there is a great difference between the mind and the body, inasmuch as the body is by its very nature always divisible, while the mind is utterly indivisible. For when I consider the mind, or myself in so far as I am merely a thinking thing, I am unable to distinguish any parts within myself; I understand myself to be something quite single and complete. Although the whole mind seems to be united to the whole body, I recognize that if a foot or arm or any other part of the body is cut off, nothing has thereby been taken away from the mind. As for the faculties of willing, of understanding, of sensory perception and so on, these cannot be termed parts of the mind, since it is one and the same mind that wills, and understands and has sensory perceptions. By contrast, there is no corporeal or extended thing that I can think of which in my thought I cannot easily divide into parts; and this very fact makes me understand that it is divisible. This one argument would be enough to show me that the mind is completely different from the body, even if I did not already know as much from other considerations.

My next observation is that the mind is not immediately affected by all parts of the body, but only by the brain, or perhaps just by one small part of the brain, namely the part which is said to contain the "common" sense.[12] Every time this part of the brain is in a given state, it presents the same signals to the mind, even though the other parts of the body may be in a different condition at the time. This is established by countless observations, which there is no need to review here.

I observe, in addition, that the nature of the body is such that whenever any part of it is moved by another part which is some distance away, it can always be moved in the same fashion by any of the parts which lie in between, even if the more distant part does nothing. For example, in a cord ABCD, if one end D is pulled so that the other end A moves, the exact same movement could have been brought about if one of the intermediate points B or C had been pulled, and D had not moved at all. In similar fashion, when I feel a pain in my foot, physiology tells me that this happens by means of nerves distributed throughout the foot, and that these nerves are like cords which go from the foot right up to the brain. When the nerves are pulled in the foot, they in turn pull on inner parts of the brain to which they are attached, and produce a certain motion in them; and nature has laid it down that this motion should produce in the mind a sensation of pain, as occurring in the foot. But since these nerves, in passing from the foot to the brain, must pass through the calf, the thigh, the lumbar region, the back and the neck, it can happen that, even if it is not the part in the foot but one of the intermediate parts which is being pulled, the same motion will occur in the brain as occurs when the foot is hurt, and so it will necessarily come about that the mind feels the same sensation of pain. And we must suppose the same thing happens with regard to any other sensation.

My final observation is that any given movement occurring in the part of the brain that immediately affects the mind produces just one corresponding sensation; and hence the best system that could be devised is that it should produce the one sensation which, of all possible sensations, is most especially and most frequently conducive to the preservation of the healthy man. And experience shows that the sensations which nature has given us are all of this kind; and so there is absolutely nothing to be found in them that does not bear witness to the power and goodness of God. For example, when the nerves in the foot are set in motion in a violent and unusual manner, this motion, by way of the spinal cord, reaches the inner parts of the brain, and there gives the mind its signal for having a certain sensation, namely the sensation of a pain as occurring in the foot. This stimulates the mind to do its best to get rid of the cause of the pain, which it takes to be harmful to the foot. It is true that God could have made the nature of man such that this particular motion in the brain indicated something else to the mind; it might, for example, have made the mind aware of the actual motion occurring in the brain, or in the foot, or in any of the intermediate regions; or it might have indicated something else entirely. But there is nothing else which would have been so conducive to the continued well-being of the body. In the same way, when we need drink, there arises a certain dryness in the throat; this sets in motion the nerves of the throat, which in turn move the inner parts of the brain. This motion produces in the mind a sensation of thirst, because the most useful thing for us to know about the whole business is that we need drink in order to stay healthy. And so it is in the other cases.

It is quite clear from all this that, notwithstanding the immense goodness of God, the nature of man as a combination of mind and body is such that it is bound to mislead him from time to time. For there may be some occurrence, not in the foot but in one of the other areas through which the nerves travel in their route from the foot to the brain, or even in the brain itself; and if this cause produces the same motion which is generally produced by injury to the foot, then pain will be felt as if it were in the foot. This deception of the senses is natural, because a given motion in the brain must always produce the same sensation in the mind; and the origin of the motion in question is much more often going to be something which is hurting the foot, rather than something existing elsewhere. So it is reasonable that this motion should always indicate to the mind a pain in the foot rather than in any other part of the body. Again, dryness of the throat may sometimes arise not, as it normally does, from the fact that a drink is necessary to the health of the body, but from some quite opposite cause, as happens in the case of the man with dropsy. Yet it is much better that it should mislead on this occasion than that it should always mislead when the body is in good health. And the same goes for the other cases.

This consideration is the greatest help to me, not only for noticing all the errors to which my nature is liable, but also for enabling me to correct or avoid them without difficulty. For I know that in matters regarding the well-being of the body, all my senses report the truth much more frequently than not. Also, I can almost always make use of more than one sense to investigate the same thing; and in addition, I can use both my memory, which connects present experiences with preceding ones, and my intellect, which has by now examined all the causes of error. Accordingly, I should not have any further fears about the falsity of what my senses tell me every day; on the contrary, the exaggerated doubts of the last few days should be dismissed as laughable. This applies especially to the principal reason for doubt, namely my inability to distinguish between being asleep and being awake. For I now notice that there is a vast difference between the two, in that dreams are never linked by memory with all the other actions of life as waking experiences are. If, while I am awake, anyone were suddenly to appear to me and then disappear immediately, as happens in sleep, so that I could not see where he had come from or where he had gone to, it would not be unreasonable for me to judge that he was a ghost, or a vision created in my brain,[13] rather than a real man. But when I distinctly see where things come from and where and when they come to me, and when I can connect my perceptions of them with the whole of the rest of my life without a break, then I am quite certain that when I encounter these things I am not asleep but awake. And I ought not to have even the slightest doubt of their reality if, after calling upon all the senses as well as my memory and my intellect in order to check them, I receive no conflicting reports from any of these sources. For from the fact that God is not a deceiver it follows that in cases like these I am completely free from error. But since the pressure of things to be done does not always allow us to stop and make such a meticulous check, it must be admitted that in this human life we are often liable to make mistakes about particular things, and we must acknowledge the weakness of our nature.

Notes

1 "... between the soul and body of man" (French version).

2 The Latin term *corpus* as used here by Descartes is ambiguous as between "body" (i.e. corporeal matter in general) and "the body" (i.e. this particular body of mine). The French version preserves the ambiguity.

3 "... that is, my soul, by which I am what I am" (added in French version).

4 "... certain modes of thinking which are quite special and distinct from me" (French version).

5 "... between the shapes, movements and other modes or accidents of a body and the body which supports them" (French version).

6 "... cannot be in me in so far as I am merely a thinking thing, since it does not presuppose any thought on my part" (French version).

7 "... as a pilot in his ship" (French version).

8 "... without any help from the body" (added in French version).

9 "... carefully and maturely examined" (French version).

10 "... and thus seem to have been directly deceived by my nature" (added in French version).

11 "... but occurs merely as a result of the disposition of the organs" (French version).

12 The supposed faculty which integrates the data from the five specialized senses (the notion goes back ultimately to Aristotle). "The seat of the common sense must be very mobile, to receive all the impressions coming from the senses, but must be moveable only by the spirits which transmit these impressions. Only the *conarion* [pineal gland] fits these conditions" (letter to Mersenne, 21 April 1641).

13 "... like those that are formed in the brain when I sleep" (added in French version).

2

Passions of the Soul[*]

René Descartes

10. HOW THE ANIMAL SPIRITS
ARE PRODUCED IN THE BRAIN

What is, however, more worthy of consideration here is that all the most lively and finest parts of the blood, which have been rarefied by the heat in the heart, constantly enter the cavities of the brain in large numbers. What makes them go there rather than elsewhere is that all the blood leaving the heart through the great artery follows a direct route towards this place, and since not all this blood can enter there because the passages are too narrow, only the most active and finest parts pass into it while the rest spread out into the other regions of the body. Now these very fine parts of the blood make up the animal spirits. For them to do this the only change they need to undergo in the brain is to be separated from the other less fine parts of the blood. For what I am calling "spirits" here are merely bodies: they have no property other than that of being extremely small bodies which move very quickly, like the jets of flame that come from a torch. They never stop in any place, and as some of them enter the brain's cavities, others leave it through the pores in its substance. These pores conduct them into the nerves, and then to the muscles. In this way the animal spirits move the body in all the various ways it can be moved.

11. HOW THE MOVEMENTS OF THE MUSCLES
TAKE PLACE

For, as already mentioned, the sole cause of all the movements of the limbs is the shortening of certain muscles and the lengthening of the opposed muscles. What causes one muscle to become shorter rather than its opposite is simply that fractionally more spirits from the brain come to it than to the other.

---

[*] This translation is taken from *Descartes: Selected Philosophical Writings*, translated by John Cottingham, Robert Stoothoff, and Dugald Murdoch (Cambridge: Cambridge University Press, 1988). Reprinted with the permission of Cambridge University Press.

Not that the spirits which come directly from the brain are sufficient by themselves to move the muscles; but they cause the other spirits already in the two muscles to leave one of them very suddenly and pass into the other. In this way the one they leave becomes longer and more relaxed, and the one they enter, being suddenly swollen by them, becomes shorter and pulls the limb to which it is attached. This is easy to understand, provided one knows that very few animal spirits come continually from the brain to each muscle, and that any muscle always contains a quantity of its own spirits. These move very quickly, sometimes merely eddying in the place where they are located (that is, when they find no passages open for them to leave from), and sometimes flowing into the opposed muscle. In each of the muscles there are small openings through which the spirits may flow from one into the other, and which are so arranged that when the spirits coming from the brain to one of the muscles are slightly more forceful than those going to the other, they open all the passages through which the spirits in the latter can pass into the former, and at the same time they close all the passages through which the spirits in the former can pass into the latter. In this way all the spirits previously contained in the two muscles are gathered very rapidly in one of them, thus making it swell and become shorter, while the other lengthens and relaxes.

12. HOW EXTERNAL OBJECTS ACT
UPON THE SENSE ORGANS

We still have to know what causes the spirits not to flow always in the same way from the brain to the muscles, but to come sometimes more to some muscles than to others. In our case, indeed, one of these causes is the activity of the soul (as I shall explain further on). But in addition we must note two other causes, which depend solely on the body. The first consists in differences in the movements produced in the sense organs by their objects. I have already explained this quite fully in the *Optics*.[1] But in order that readers of this work should not need to consult any other, I shall say once again that there are three things to consider in the nerves. First, there is the marrow, or internal substance, which extends in the form of tiny fibres from the brain, where they originate, to the extremities of the parts of the body to which they are attached. Next, there are the membranes surrounding the fibres, which are continuous with those surrounding the brain and form little tubes in which the fibres are enclosed. Finally, there are the animal spirits which, being carried by these tubes from the brain to the muscles, cause the fibres to remain so completely free and extended that if anything causes the slightest motion in the part of the body where one of the fibres terminates, it thereby causes a movement in the part of the brain where the fibre originates, just as we make one end of a cord move by pulling the other end.

13. THIS ACTION OF EXTERNAL OBJECTS MAY DIRECT THE SPIRITS INTO THE MUSCLES IN VARIOUS DIFFERENT WAYS

I explained in the *Optics* how the objects of sight make themselves known to us simply by producing, through the medium of the intervening transparent bodies, local motions in the optic nerve-fibres at the back of our eyes, and then in the regions of the brain where these nerves originate.[2] I explained too that the objects produce as much variety in these motions as they cause us to see in the things, and that it is not the motions occurring in the eye, but those occurring in the brain, which directly represent these objects to the soul. By this example, it is easy to conceive how sounds, smells, tastes, heat, pain, hunger, thirst and, in general, all the objects both of our external senses and of our internal appetites, also produce some movement in our nerves, which passes through them into the brain. Besides causing our soul to have various different sensations, these various movements in the brain can also act without the soul, causing the spirits to make their way to certain muscles rather than others, and so causing them to move our limbs. I shall prove this here by one example only. If someone suddenly thrusts his hand in front of our eyes as if to strike us, then even if we know that he is our friend, that he is doing this only in fun, and that he will take care not to harm us, we still find it difficult to prevent ourselves from closing our eyes. This shows that it is not through the mediation of our soul that they close, since this action is contrary to our volition, which is the only, or at least the principal, activity of the soul. They close rather because the mechanism of our body is so composed that the movement of the hand towards our eyes produces another movement in our brain, which directs the animal spirits into the muscles that make our eyelids drop.

14. DIFFERENCES AMONG THE SPIRITS MAY ALSO CAUSE THEM TO TAKE VARIOUS DIFFERENT COURSES

The other cause which serves to direct the animal spirits to the muscles in various different ways is the unequal agitation of the spirits and differences in their parts. For when some of their parts are coarser and more agitated than others, they penetrate more deeply in a straight line into the cavities and pores of the brain, and in this way they are directed to muscles other than those to which they would go if they had less force.

15. THE CAUSES OF THESE DIFFERENCES

And this inequality may arise from the different materials of which the spirits are composed. One sees this in the case of those who have drunk a lot of wine: the vapours of the wine enter the blood rapidly and rise from the heart to the brain, where they turn into spirits which, being stronger and more abundant than those normally present there, are capable of moving the body in many strange ways. Such an inequality of the spirits may also arise from various conditions of the heart, liver, stomach, spleen and all the other organs that help to produce them. In this connection we must first note certain small nerves embedded in the base of the heart, which serve to enlarge and contract the openings to its cavities, thus causing the blood, according to the strength of its expansion, to produce spirits having various different dispositions. It must also be observed that even though the blood entering the heart comes there from every other place in the body, it often happens nevertheless that it is driven there more from some parts than from others, because the nerves and muscles responsible for these parts exert more pressure on it or make it more agitated. And differences in these parts are matched by corresponding differences in the expansion of the blood in the heart, which results in the production of spirits having different qualities. Thus, for example, the blood coming from the lower part of the liver, where the gall is located, expands in the heart in a different manner from the blood coming from the spleen; the latter expands differently from the blood coming from the veins of the arms or legs; and this expands differently again from the alimentary juices when, just after leaving the stomach and bowels, they pass rapidly to the heart through the liver.

16. HOW ALL THE LIMBS CAN BE MOVED BY THE OBJECTS OF THE SENSES AND BY THE SPIRITS WITHOUT THE HELP OF THE SOUL

Finally it must be observed that the mechanism of our body is so composed that all the changes occurring in the movement of the spirits may cause them to open some pores in the brain more than others. Conversely, when one of the pores is opened somewhat more or less than usual by an action of the sensory nerves, this brings about a change in the movement of the spirits and directs them to the muscles which serve to move the body in the way it is usually moved on the occasion of such an action. Thus every movement we make without any contribution from our will—as often happens when we breathe, walk, eat and, indeed, when we perform any action which is common to us and the beasts— depends solely on the arrangement of our limbs and on the route which the spirits, produced by the heat of the heart, follow naturally in the brain, nerves and muscles. This occurs in the same way that the movement of a watch is produced merely by the strength of its spring and the configuration of its wheels.

17. THE FUNCTIONS OF THE SOUL

Having thus considered all the functions belonging solely to the body, it is easy to recognize that there is nothing in us which we must attribute to our soul except our thoughts. These are of two principal kinds, some being actions of the soul and others its passions. Those I call its actions are all our volitions, for we experience them as proceeding directly from our soul and as seeming to depend on it alone. On the other hand, the various perceptions or modes of knowledge present in us may be called its passions, in a general sense, for it is often not our soul which makes them such as they are, and the soul always receives them from the things that are represented by them.

18. THE WILL

Our volitions, in turn, are of two sorts. One consists of the actions of the soul which terminate in the soul itself, as when we will to love God or, generally speaking, to apply our mind to some object which is not material. The other consists of actions which terminate in our body, as when our merely willing to walk has the consequence that our legs move and we walk.

19. PERCEPTION

Our perceptions are likewise of two sorts: some have the soul as their cause, others the body. Those having the soul as their cause are the perceptions of our volitions and of all the imaginings or other thoughts which depend on them. For it is certain that we cannot will anything without thereby perceiving that we are willing it. And although willing something is an action with respect to our soul, the perception of such willing may be said to be a passion in the soul. But because this perception is really one and the same thing as the volition, and names are always determined by whatever is most noble, we do not normally call it a "passion," but solely an "action."

20. IMAGININGS AND OTHER THOUGHTS FORMED BY THE SOUL

When our soul applies itself to imagine something non-existent—as in thinking about an enchanted palace or a chimera—and also when it applies itself to consider something that is purely intelligible and not imaginable—for example, in considering its own nature—the perceptions it has of these things depend chiefly on the volition which makes it aware of them. That is why we usually regard these perceptions as actions rather than passions.

21. IMAGININGS WHICH ARE CAUSED SOLELY BY THE BODY

Among the perceptions caused by the body, most of them depend on the nerves. But there are some which do not and which, like those I have just described, are called "imaginings." These differ from the others, however, in that our will is not used in forming them. Accordingly they cannot be numbered among the actions of the soul, for they arise simply from the fact that the spirits, being agitated in various different ways and coming upon the traces of various impressions which have preceded them in the brain, make their way by chance through certain pores rather than others. Such are the illusions of our dreams and also the day-dreams we often have when we are awake and our mind wanders idly without applying itself to anything of its own accord. Now some of these imaginings are passions of the soul, taking the word "passion" in its proper and more exact sense, and all may be regarded as such if the word is understood in a more general sense. Nonetheless, their cause is not so conspicuous and determinate as that of the perceptions which the soul receives by means of the nerves, and they seem to be mere shadows and pictures of these perceptions. So before we can characterize them satisfactorily we must consider how these other perceptions differ from one another.

22. HOW THESE OTHER PERCEPTIONS DIFFER FROM ONE ANOTHER

All the perceptions which I have not yet explained come to the soul by means of the nerves. They differ from one another in so far as we refer some to external objects which strike our senses, others to our body or to certain of its parts, and still others to our soul.

23. THE PERCEPTIONS WE REFER TO OBJECTS OUTSIDE US

The perceptions we refer to things outside us, namely to the objects of our senses, are caused by these objects, at least when our judgements are not false. For in that case the objects produce certain movements in the organs of the external senses and, by means of the nerves, produce other movements in the brain, which cause the soul to have sensory perception of the objects. Thus, when we see the light of a torch and hear the sound of a bell, the sound and the light are two different actions which, simply by producing two different movements in some of our nerves, and through them in our brain, give to the soul two different sensations. And we refer these sensations to the subjects we suppose to be their causes in such a way that we think that we see the torch itself and hear the bell, and not that we have sensory perception merely of movements that come from these objects.

24. THE PERCEPTIONS WE REFER TO OUR BODY

The perceptions we refer to our body or to certain of its parts are those of hunger, thirst and other natural appetites. To these we may add pain, heat and the other states we feel as being in our limbs, and not as being in objects outside us. Thus, at the same time and by means of the same nerves we can feel the cold of our hand and the heat of a nearby flame or, on the other hand, the heat of our hand and the cold of the air to which it is exposed. This happens without there being any difference between the actions which make us feel the heat or cold in our hand and those which make us feel the heat or cold outside us, except that since one of these actions succeeds the other, we judge that the first is already in us, and that its successor is not yet there but in the object which causes it.

25. THE PERCEPTIONS WE REFER TO OUR SOUL

The perceptions we refer only to the soul are those whose effects we feel as being in the soul itself, and for which we do not normally know any proximate cause to which we can refer them. Such are the feelings of joy, anger and the like, which are aroused in us sometimes by the objects which stimulate our nerves and sometimes also by other causes. Now all our perceptions, both those we refer to objects outside us and those we refer to the various states of our body, are indeed passions with respect to our soul, so long as we use the term "passion" in its most general sense; nevertheless we usually restrict the term to signify only perceptions which refer to the soul itself. And it is only the latter that I have undertaken to explain here under the title "passions of the soul"....

26. THE IMAGININGS WHICH DEPEND SOLELY ON
THE FORTUITOUS MOVEMENT OF THE SPIRITS MAY BE PASSIONS
JUST AS TRULY AS THE PERCEPTIONS WHICH DEPEND ON THE NERVES

It remains to be noted that everything the soul perceives by means of the nerves may also be represented to it through the fortuitous course of the spirits. The sole difference is that the impressions which come into the brain through the nerves are normally more lively and more definite than those produced there by the spirits—a fact that led me to say in article 21 that the latter are, as it were, a shadow or picture of the former. We must also note that this picture is sometimes so similar to the thing it represents that it may mislead us regarding the perceptions which refer to objects outside us, or even regarding those which refer to certain parts of our body. But we cannot be misled in the same way regarding the passions, in that they are so close and so internal to our soul that it cannot possibly feel them unless they are truly as it feels them to be. Thus often when we sleep, and sometimes even when we are awake, we imagine certain things so vividly that we think we see them before us, or feel them in our body, although they are not there at all. But even if we are asleep and dreaming, we cannot feel sad, or moved by any other passion, unless the soul truly has this passion within it.

27. DEFINITION OF THE PASSIONS OF THE SOUL

After having considered in what respects the passions of the soul differ from all its other thoughts, it seems to me that we may define them generally as those perceptions, sensations or emotions of the soul which we refer particularly to it, and which are caused, maintained and strengthened by some movement of the spirits.

28. EXPLANATION OF THE FIRST PART OF THIS DEFINITION

We may call them "perceptions" if we use this term generally to signify all the thoughts which are not actions of the soul or volitions, but not if we use it to signify only evident knowledge. For experience shows that those who are the most strongly agitated by their passions are not those who know them best, and that the passions are to be numbered among the perceptions which the close alliance between the soul and the body renders confused and obscure. We may also call them "sensations," because they are received into the soul in the same way as the objects of the external senses, and they are not known by the soul any differently. But it is even better to call them "emotions" of the soul, not only because this term may be applied to all the changes which occur in the soul—that is, to all the various thoughts which come to it—but more particularly because, of all the kinds of thought which the soul may have, there are none that agitate and disturb it so strongly as the passions.

29. EXPLANATION OF THE OTHER PART OF THE DEFINITION

I add that they refer particularly to the soul, in order to distinguish them from other sensations, some referred to external objects (e.g. smells, sounds and colours) and others to our body (e.g. hunger, thirst and pain). I also add that they are caused, maintained and strengthened by some movement of the spirits, both in order to distinguish them from our volitions (for these too may be called "emotions of the soul which refer to it," but they are caused by the soul itself), and also in order to explain their ultimate and most proximate cause, which distinguishes them once again from other sensations.

30. THE SOUL IS UNITED TO ALL THE PARTS OF THE BODY CONJOINTLY

But in order to understand all these things more perfectly, we need to recognize that the soul is really joined to the whole body, and that we cannot properly say that it exists in any one part of the body to the exclusion of the others. For the body is a unity which is in a sense indivisible because of the arrangement of its organs, these being so related to one another that the removal of any one of them renders the whole body defective. And the soul is of such a nature that it has no relation to extension, or to the dimensions or other properties of the matter of which the body is composed: it is related solely to the whole assemblage of the body's organs. This is obvious from our inability to conceive of a half or a third of a soul, or of the extension which a soul occupies. Nor does the soul become any smaller if we cut off some part of the body, but it becomes completely separate from the body when we break up the assemblage of the body's organs.

31. THERE IS A LITTLE GLAND[3] IN THE BRAIN WHERE THE SOUL EXERCISES ITS FUNCTIONS MORE PARTICULARLY THAN IN THE OTHER PARTS OF THE BODY

We need to recognize also that although the soul is joined to the whole body, nevertheless there is a certain part of the body where it exercises its functions more particularly than in all the others. It is commonly held that this part is the brain, or perhaps the heart—the brain because the sense organs are related to it, and the heart because we feel the passions as if they were in it. But on carefully examining the matter I think I have clearly established that the part of the body in which the soul directly exercises its functions is not the heart at all, or the whole of the brain. It is rather the innermost part of the brain, which is a certain very small gland situated in the middle of the brain's substance and suspended above the passage through which the spirits in the brain's anterior cavities communicate with those in its posterior cavities. The slightest movements on the part of this gland may alter very greatly the course of these spirits, and conversely any change, however slight, taking place in the course of the spirits may do much to change the movements of the gland.

32. HOW WE KNOW THAT THIS GLAND IS THE PRINCIPAL SEAT OF THE SOUL

Apart from this gland, there cannot be any other place in the whole body where the soul directly exercises its functions. I am convinced of this by the observation that all the other parts of our brain are double, as also are all the organs of our external senses—eyes, hands, ears and so on. But in so far as we have only one simple thought about a given object at any one time, there must necessarily be some place where the two images coming through the two eyes, or the two impressions coming from a single object through the double organs of any other sense, can come together in a single image or impression before reaching the soul, so that they do not present to it two objects instead of one. We can easily understand that these images or other impressions are unified in this gland by means of the spirits which fill the cavities of the brain. But they cannot exist united in this way in any other place in the body except as a result of their being united in this gland.

33. THE SEAT OF THE PASSIONS IS NOT IN THE HEART

As for the opinion of those who think that the soul receives its passions in the heart, this is not worth serious consideration, since it is based solely on the fact that the passions make us feel some change in the heart. It is easy to see that the only reason why this change is felt as occurring in the heart is that there is a small nerve which descends to it from the brain—just as pain is felt as in the foot by means of the nerves in the foot, and the stars are perceived as in the sky by means of their light and the optic nerves. Thus it is no more necessary that our soul should exercise its functions directly in the heart in order to feel its passions there, than that it should be in the sky in order to see the stars there.

34. HOW THE SOUL AND THE BODY ACT ON EACH OTHER

Let us therefore take it that the soul has its principal seat in the small gland located in the middle of the brain. From there it radiates through the rest of the body by means of the animal spirits, the nerves, and even the blood, which can take on the impressions of the spirits and carry them through the arteries to all the limbs. Let us recall what we said previously about the mechanism of our body. The nerve-fibres are so distributed in all the parts of the body that when the objects of the senses produce various different movements in these parts, the fibres are occasioned to open the pores of the brain in various different ways. This, in turn, causes the animal spirits contained in these cavities to enter the muscles in various different ways. In this manner the spirits can move the limbs in all the different ways they are capable of being moved. And all the other causes that can move the spirits in different ways are sufficient to direct them into different muscles. To this we may now add that the small gland which is the principal seat of the soul is suspended within the cavities containing these spirits, so that it can be moved by them in as many different ways as there are perceptible differences in the objects. But it can also be moved in various different ways by the soul, whose nature is such that it receives as many different impressions—that is, it has as many different perceptions as there occur different movements in this gland. And conversely, the mechanism of our body is so constructed that simply by this gland's being moved in any way by the soul or by any other cause, it drives the surrounding spirits towards the pores of the brain, which direct them through the nerves to the muscles; and in this way the gland makes the spirits move the limbs.

35. EXAMPLE OF THE WAY IN WHICH THE IMPRESSIONS OF OBJECTS ARE UNITED IN THE GLAND IN THE MIDDLE OF THE BRAIN

Thus, for example, if we see some animal approaching us, the light reflected from its body forms two images, one in each of our eyes; and these images form two others, by means of the optic nerves, on the internal surface of the brain facing its cavities. Then, by means of the spirits that fill these cavities, the images radiate towards the little gland which the spirits surround: the movement forming each point of one of the images tends towards the same point on the gland as the movement forming the corresponding point of the other image, which represents the same part of the animal. In this way, the two images in the brain form only one image on the gland, which acts directly upon the soul and makes it see the shape of the animal.

36. EXAMPLE OF THE WAY IN WHICH THE PASSIONS ARE AROUSED IN THE SOUL

If, in addition, this shape is very strange and terrifying—that is, if it has a close relation to things which have previously been harmful to the body—this arouses the passion of anxiety in the soul, and then that of courage or perhaps fear and terror, depending upon the particular temperament of the body or the strength of the soul, and upon whether we have protected ourselves previously by defence or by flight against the harmful things to which the present impression is related. Thus in certain persons these factors dispose their brain in such a way that some of the spirits reflected from the image formed on the gland proceed from there to the nerves which serve to turn the back and move the legs in order to flee. The rest of the spirits go to nerves which expand or constrict the orifices of the heart, or else to nerves which agitate other parts of the body from which blood is sent to the heart, so that the blood is rarefied in a different manner from usual and spirits are sent to the brain which are adapted for maintaining and strengthening the passion of fear—that is, for holding open or reopening the pores of the brain which direct the spirits into these same nerves. For merely by entering into these pores they produce in the gland a particular movement which is ordained by nature to make the soul feel this passion. And since these pores are related mainly to the little nerves which serve to contract or expand the orifices of the heart, this makes the soul feel the passion chiefly as if it were in the heart.

37. HOW ALL THE PASSIONS APPEAR TO BE CAUSED BY SOME MOVEMENT OF THE SPIRITS

Something similar happens with all the other passions. That is, they are caused chiefly by the spirits contained in the cavities of the brain making their way to nerves which serve to expand or constrict the orifices of the heart, or to drive blood towards the heart in a distinctive way from other parts of the body, or to maintain the passion in some other way. This makes it clear why I included in my definition of the passions that they are caused by some particular movement of the spirits.

38. EXAMPLE OF MOVEMENTS OF THE BODY WHICH ACCOMPANY THE PASSIONS AND DO NOT DEPEND ON THE SOUL

Moreover, just as the course which the spirits take to the nerves of the heart suffices to induce a movement in the gland through which fear enters the soul, so too the mere fact that some spirits at the same time proceed to the nerves which serve to move the legs in flight causes another movement in the gland through which the soul feels and perceives this action. In this way, then, the body may be moved to take flight by the mere disposition of the organs, without any contribution from the soul.

39. HOW ONE AND THE SAME CAUSE MAY EXCITE DIFFERENT PASSIONS IN DIFFERENT PEOPLE

The same impression which the presence of a terrifying object forms on the gland, and which causes fear in some people, may excite courage and bold-ness in others. The reason for this is that brains are not all constituted in the same way. Thus the very same movement of the gland which in some excites fear, in others causes the spirits to enter the pores of the brain which direct them partly into nerves which serve to move the hands in self-defence and partly into those which agitate the blood and drive it towards the heart in the manner required to produce spirits appropriate for continuing this defence and for maintaining the will to do so.

40. THE PRINCIPAL EFFECT OF THE PASSIONS

For it must be observed that the principal effect of all the human passions is that they move and dispose the soul to want the things for which they prepare the body. Thus the feeling of fear moves the soul to want to flee, that of courage to want to fight, and similarly with the others.

41. THE POWER OF THE SOUL WITH RESPECT TO THE BODY

But the will is by its nature so free that it can never be constrained. Of the two kinds of thought I have distinguished in the soul—the first its actions, i.e. its volitions, and the second its passions, taking this word in its most general sense to include every kind of perception—the former are absolutely within its power and can be changed only indirectly by the body, whereas the latter are absolutely dependent on the actions which produce them, and can be changed by the soul only indirectly, except when it is itself their cause. And the activity of the soul consists entirely in the fact that simply by willing some-thing it brings it about that the little gland to which it is closely joined moves in the manner required to produce the effect corresponding to this volition.

42. HOW WE FIND IN OUR MEMORY THE THINGS WE WANT TO REMEMBER

Thus, when the soul wants to remember something, this volition makes the gland lean first to one side and then to another, thus driving the spirits towards different regions of the brain until they come upon the one containing traces left by the object we want to remember. These traces consist simply in the fact that the pores of the brain through which the spirits previously made their way owing to the presence of this object have thereby become more apt than the others to be opened in the same way when the spirits again flow towards them. And so the spirits enter into these pores more easily when they come upon them, thereby producing in the gland that special movement which represents the same object to the soul, and makes it recognize the object as the one it wanted to remember.

43. HOW THE SOUL CAN IMAGINE, BE ATTENTIVE, AND MOVE THE BODY

When we want to imagine something we have never seen, this volition has the power to make the gland move in the way required for driving the spirits towards the pores of the brain whose opening enables the thing to be represented. Again, when we want to fix our attention for some time on some particular object, this volition keeps the gland leaning in one particular direction during that time. And finally, when we want to walk or move our body in some other way, this volition makes the gland drive the spirits to the muscles which serve to bring about this effect.

44. EACH VOLITION IS NATURALLY JOINED TO SOME MOVEMENT OF THE GLAND, BUT THROUGH EFFORT OR HABIT WE MAY JOIN IT TO OTHERS

Yet our volition to produce some particular movement or other effect does not always result in our producing it; for that depends on the various ways in which nature or habit has joined certain movements of the gland to certain thoughts. For example, if we want to adjust our eyes to look at a far-distant object, this volition causes the pupils to grow larger; and if we want to adjust them to look at a very near object, this volition makes the pupils contract. But if we think only of enlarging the pupils, we may indeed have such a volition, but we do not thereby enlarge them. For the movement of the gland, whereby the spirits are driven to the optic nerve in the way required for enlarging or contracting the pupils, has been joined by nature with the volition to look at distant or nearby objects, rather than with the volition to enlarge or contract the pupils. Again, when we speak, we think only of the meaning of what we want to say, and this makes us move our tongue and lips much more readily and effectively than if we thought of moving them in all the ways required for uttering the same words. For the habits acquired in learning to speak have made us join the action of the soul (which, by means of the gland, can move the tongue and lips) with the meaning of the words which follow upon these movements, rather than with the movements themselves.

45. THE POWER OF THE SOUL WITH RESPECT TO ITS PASSIONS

Our passions, too, cannot be directly aroused or suppressed by the action of our will, but only indirectly through the representation of things which are usually joined with the passions we wish to have and opposed to the passions we wish to reject. For example, in order to arouse boldness and suppress fear in ourselves, it is not sufficient to have the volition to do so. We must apply ourselves to consider the reasons, objects, or precedents which persuade us that the danger is not great; that there is always more security in defence than in flight; that we shall gain glory and joy if we conquer, whereas we can expect nothing but regret and shame if we flee; and so on.

46. WHAT PREVENTS THE SOUL FROM HAVING FULL CONTROL OVER ITS PASSIONS

There is one special reason why the soul cannot readily change or suspend its passions, which is what led me to say in my definition that the passions are not only caused but also maintained and strengthened by some particular movement of the spirits. The reason is that they are nearly all accompanied by some disturbance which takes place in the heart and consequently also throughout the blood and the animal spirits. Until this disturbance ceases they remain present to our mind in the same way as the objects of the senses are present to it while they are acting upon our sense organs. The soul can prevent itself from hearing a slight noise or feeling a slight pain by attending very closely to some other thing, but it cannot in the same way prevent itself from hearing thunder or feeling a fire that burns the hand. Likewise it can easily overcome the lesser passions, but not the stronger and more violent ones, except after the disturbance of the blood and spirits has died down. The most the will can do while this disturbance is at its full strength is not to yield to its effects and to inhibit many of the movements to which it disposes the body. For example, if anger causes the hand to rise to strike a blow, the will can usually restrain it; if fear moves the legs in flight, the will can stop them; and similarly in other cases ...

Notes

1   See *Optics*, p. 62 of *Descartes: Selected Philosophical Writings*, translated by John Cottingham, Robert Stoothoff, and Dugald Murdoch (Cambridge: Cambridge University Press, 1988).

2   See Ibid., p. 64.

3   The pineal gland, which Descartes had identified as the seat of the imagination and the common sense in the *Treatise on Man*, in *The Philosophical Writings of Descartes*, Vol. I, translated by John Cottingham, Robert Stoothoff, and Dugald Murdoch (Cambridge: Cambridge University Press, 1985).

3

ON THE HYPOTHESIS THAT
ANIMALS ARE AUTOMATA, AND ITS HISTORY*

T.H. Huxley

The first half of the seventeenth century is one of the great epochs of biological science. For though suggestions and indications of the conceptions which took definite shape, at that time, are to be met with in works of earlier date, they are little more than the shadows which coming truth casts forward; men's knowledge was neither extensive enough nor exact enough to show them the solid body of fact which threw these shadows.

But, in the seventeenth century, the idea that the physical processes of life are capable of being explained in the same way as other physical phenomena, and, therefore, that the living body is a mechanism, was proved to be true for certain classes of vital actions; and, having thus taken firm root in irrefragable fact, this conception has not only successfully repelled every assault which has been made upon it, but has steadily grown in force and extent of application, until it is now the expressed or implied fundamental proposition of the whole doctrine of scientific Physiology.

If we ask to whom mankind are indebted for this great service, the general voice will name William Harvey. For, by his discovery of the circulation of the blood in the higher animals, by his explanation of the nature of the mechanism by which that circulation is effected and by his no less remarkable, though less known, investigations of the process of development, Harvey solidly laid the foundations of all those physical explanations of the functions of sustentation and reproduction which modern physiologists have achieved.

But the living body is not only sustained and reproduced: it adjusts itself to external and internal changes; it moves and feels. The attempt to reduce the endless complexities of animal motion and feeling to law and order is, at least, as important a part of the task of the physiologist as the elucidation of what are sometimes called the vegetative processes. Harvey did not make this attempt himself; but the influence of his work upon the man who did make it is patent and unquestionable. This man was René Descartes, who, though by many years Harvey's junior, died before him; and yet in his short span of

---

* Taken from *Methods and Results: Essays*, edited by Leonard Huxley (London: MacMillan, 1902).

fifty-four years, took an undisputed place, not only among the chiefs of philosophy, but amongst the greatest and most original of mathematicians; while, in my belief, he is no less certainly entitled to the rank of a great and original physiologist; inasmuch as he did for the physiology of motion and sensation that which Harvey had done for the circulation of the blood, and opened up that road to the mechanical theory of these processes, which has been followed by all his successors.

Descartes was no more speculator, as some would have us believe: but a man who knew of his own knowledge what was to be known of the facts of anatomy and physiology in his day. He was an unwearied dissector and observer; and it is said, that, on a visitor once asking to see his library, Descartes led him into a room set aside for dissections, and full of specimens under examination. "There," said he, "is my library."

I anticipate a smile of incredulity when I thus champion Descartes's claim to be considered a physiologist of the first rank. I expect to be told that I have read into his works what I find there, and to be asked, Why is it that we are left to discover Descartes's deserts at this time of day, more than two centuries after his death? How is it that Descartes is utterly ignored in some of the latest works which treat expressly of the subject in which he is said to have been so great?

It is much easier to ask such questions than to answer them, especially if one desires to be on good terms with one's contemporaries; but, if I must give an answer, it is this: The growth of physical science is now so prodigiously rapid, that those who are actively engaged in keeping up with the present, have much ado to find time to look at the Past, and even grow into the habit of neglecting it. But, natural as this result may be, it is none the less detrimental. The intellect loses, for there is assuredly no more effectual method of clearing up one's own mind on any subject than by talking it over, so to speak, with men of real power and grasp, who have considered it from a totally different point of view. The parallax of time helps us to the true position of a conception, as the parallax of space helps us to that of a star. And the moral nature loses no less. It is well to turn aside from the fretful stir of the present and to dwell with gratitude and respect upon the services of those "mighty men of old who have gone down to the grave with their weapons of war," but who, while they yet lived, won splendid victories over ignorance. It is well, again, to reflect that the fame of Descartes filled all Europe, and his authority overshadowed it, for a century; while now, most of those who know his name think of him, either as a person who had some preposterous notions about vortices and was deservedly annihilated by the great Sir Isaac Newton; or as the apostle of an essentially vicious method of deductive speculation; and that, nevertheless, neither the chatter of shifting opinion, nor the silence of personal oblivion, has in the slightest degree affected the growth of the great ideas of which he was the instrument and the mouthpiece.

It is a matter of fact that the greatest physiologist of the eighteenth century, Haller, in treating of the functions of nerve does little more than reproduce and enlarge upon the ideas of Descartes. It is a matter of fact that David Hartley, in his remarkable work the "Essay on Man," expressly, though still insufficiently, acknowledges the resemblance of his fundamental conceptions to those of Descartes; and I shall now endeavour to show that a series of propositions, which constitute the foundation and essence of the modern physiology of the nervous system, are fully expressed and illustrated in the works of Descartes.

I. The brain is the organ of sensation, thought, and emotion; that is to say, some change in the condition of the matter of this organ is the invariable antecedent of the state of consciousness to which each of these terms is applied.

In the "Principes de la Philosophie" [*Principles of Philosophy*] (§ 169), Descartes says:—[1]

> Although the soul is united to the whole body, its principal functions are, nevertheless, performed in the brain; it is here that it not only understands and imagines, but also feels; and this is effected by the intermediation of the nerves, which extend in the form of delicate threads from the brain to all parts of the body, to which they are attached in such a manner, that we can hardly touch any part of the body without setting the extremity of some nerve in motion. This motion passes along the nerve to that part of the brain which is the common sensorium as I have sufficiently explained in my "Treatise of Dioptrics"; and the movements which thus travel along the nerves, as far as that part of the brain with which the soul is closely joined and united, cause it, by reason of their diverse characters, to have different thoughts. And it is these different thoughts of the soul, which arise immediately from the movements that are excited by the nerves in the brain, which we properly term our feelings, or the perceptions of our senses.

Elsewhere,[2] Descartes, in arguing that the seat of the passions is not (as many suppose) the heart, but the brain, uses the following remarkable language:—

> The opinion of those who think that the soul receives its passions in the heart, is of no weight, for it is based upon the fact that the passions cause a change to be felt in that organ; and it is easy to see that this change is felt, as if it were in the heart, only by the intermediation of a little nerve which descends from the brain to it; just as pain is felt, as if it were in the foot, by the intermediation of the nerves of the foot; and

the stars are perceived, as if they were in the heavens, by the intermediation of their light and of the optic nerves. So that it is no more necessary for the soul to exert its functions immediately in the heart, to feel its passions there, than it is necessary that it should be in the heavens to see the stars there.

This definite allocation of all the phenomena of consciousness to the brain as their organ was a step the value of which it is difficult for us to appraise, so completely has Descartes's view incorporated itself with every-day thought and common language. A lunatic is said to be "crack-brained" or "touched in the head," a confused thinker is "muddle-headed," while a clever man is said to have "plenty of brains"; but it must be remembered that at the end of the last century a considerable, though much over-estimated, anatomist, Bichat, so far from having reached the level of Descartes, could gravely argue that the apparatuses of organic life are the sole seat of the passions, which in no way affect the brain, except so far as it is the agent by which the influence of the passions is transmitted to the muscles.[3]

Modern physiology, aided by pathology, easily demonstrates that the brain is the seat of all forms of consciousness, and fully bears out Descartes's explanation of the reference of those sensations in the viscera which accompany intense emotion, to these organs. It proves, directly, that those states of consciousness which we call sensations are the immediate consequent of a change in the brain excited by the sensory nerves; and, on the well-known effects of injuries, of stimulants, and of narcotics, it bases the conclusion that thought and emotion are, in like manner, the consequents of physical antecedents.

II. The movements of animals are due to the change of form of muscles, which shorten and become thicker; and this change of form in a muscle arises from a motion of the substance contained within the nerves which go to the muscle.

In the "Passions de l'Âme" [*Passions of the Soul*], Art. vii., Descartes writes:

Moreover, we know that all the movements of the limbs depend on the muscles, and that these muscles are opposed to one another in such a manner, that when one of them shortens, it draws along the part of the body to which it is attached, and so gives rise to a simultaneous elongation of the muscle which is opposed to it. Then, if it happens, afterwards, that the latter shortens, it causes the former to elongate, and draws towards itself the part to which it is attached. Lastly, we know that all these movements of the muscles, as all the senses, depend on the nerves, which are like little threads or tubes, which all come from the brain, and, like it, contain a certain very subtle air or wind, termed the animal spirits.

The property of muscle mentioned by Descartes now goes by the general name of contractility, but his definition of it remains untouched. The long-continued controversy whether contractile substance, speaking generally, has an inherent power of contraction, or whether it contracts only in virtue of an influence exerted by nerve, is now settled in Haller's favour; but Descartes's statement of the dependence of muscular contraction on nerve holds good for the higher forms of muscle, under normal circumstances; so that, although the structure of the various modifications of contractile matter has been worked out with astonishing minuteness—although the delicate physical and chemical changes which accompany muscular contraction have been determined to an extent of which Descartes could not have dreamed, and have quite upset his hypothesis that the cause of the shortening and thickening of the muscle is the flow of animal spirits into it from the nerves—the important and fundamental part of his statement remains perfectly true.

The like may be affirmed of what he says about nerve. We know now that nerves are not exactly tubes, and that "animal spirits" are myths; but the exquisitely refined methods of investigation of Dubois-Reymond and of Helmholz have no less clearly proved that the antecedent of ordinary muscular contraction is a motion of the molecules of the nerve going to the muscle; and that this motion is propagated with a measurable, and by no means great, velocity, through the substance of the nerve towards the muscle.

With the progress of research, the term "animal spirits" gave way to "nervous fluid," and "nervous fluid" has now given way to "molecular motion of nerve-substance." Our conceptions of what takes place in nerve have altered in the same way as our conceptions of what takes place in a conducting wire have altered, since electricity was shown to be not a fluid, but a mode of molecular motion. The change is of vast importance, but it does not affect Descartes's fundamental idea, that a change in the substance of a motor nerve propagated towards a muscle is the ordinary cause of muscular contraction.

III. The sensations of animals are due to a motion of the substance of the nerves which connect the sensory organs with the brain.

In "La Dioptrique" (Discours Quatrième) [Optics, Discourse Four], Descartes explains, more fully than in the passage cited above, his hypothesis of the mode of action of sensory nerves:—

It is the little threads of which the inner substance of the nerves is composed which subserve sensation. You must conceive that these little threads, being enclosed in tubes, which are always distended and kept open by the animal spirits which they contain, neither press upon nor interfere with one another and are extended from the brain to the extremities of all the members which are sensitive—in such a manner, that the slightest touch which excites the part of one of the members to which a thread is attached, gives rise to a motion of the part of the brain whence it arises, just as by pulling one of the ends of a stretched cord, the other end is instantaneously moved.... And we must take care not to imagine that, in order to feel, the soul needs to behold certain images sent by the objects of sense to the brain, as our philosophers commonly suppose; or, at least, we must conceive these images to be something quite different from what they suppose them to be. For, as all they suppose is that these images ought to resemble the objects which they represent, it is impossible for them to show how they can be formed by the objects received by the organs of the external senses; and transmitted to the brain. And they have had no reason for supposing the existence of these images except this; seeing that the mind is readily excited by a picture to conceive the object which is depicted, they have thought that it must be excited in the same way to conceive those objects which affect our senses by little pictures of them formed in the head; instead of which we ought to recollect that there are many things besides images which may excite the mind, as, for example, signs and words, which have not the least resemblance to the objects which they signify.[4]

Modern physiology amends Descartes's conception of the mode of action of sensory nerves in detail, by showing that their structure is the same as that of motor nerves; and that the changes which take place in them, when the sensory organs with which they are connected are excited, are of just the same nature as those which occur in motor nerves, when the muscles to which they are distributed are made to contract: there is a molecular change which, in the case of the sensory nerve, is propagated towards the brain. But the great fact insisted upon by Descartes, that no likeness of external things is, or can be, transmitted to the mind by the sensory organs; on the contrary, that, between the external cause of a sensation and the sensation, there is interposed a mode of motion of nervous matter, of which the state of consciousness is no likeness, but a mere symbol, is of the profoundest importance. It is the physiological foundation of the doctrine of the relativity of knowledge, and a more or less complete idealism is a necessary consequence of it.

For of two alternatives one must be true. Either consciousness is the function of a something distinct from the brain which we call the soul, and a sensation is the mode in which this soul is affected by a motion of a part of the brain; or there is no soul, and a sensation is something generated by the mode of motion of a part of the brain. In the former case, the phenomena of the senses are purely spiritual affections; in the latter, they are something manufactured by the mechanism of the body and as unlike the causes which set that mechanism in motion as the sound of a repeater is unlike the pushing of the spring which gives rise to it.

The nervous system stands between consciousness and the assumed external world, as an interpreter who can talk with his fingers stands between a hidden speaker and a man who is stone deaf—and Realism is equivalent to a belief on the part of the deaf man, that the speaker must also be talking with his fingers. "Les extrêmes se touchent;" the shibboleth of materialists that "thought is a secretion of the brain," is the Fichtean doctrine that "the phenomenal universe is the creation of the Ego," expressed in other language.

IV. The motion of the matter of a sensory nerve may be transmitted through the brain to motor nerves, and thereby give rise to contraction of the muscles to which these motor nerves are distributed; and this reflection of motion from a sensory into a motor nerve may take place without volition, or even contrary to it.

In stating these important truths, Descartes defined that which we now term "reflex action." Indeed he almost uses the term itself, as he talks of the "animal spirits" as "réfléchis,"[5] from the sensory into the motor nerves....

Nothing can be clearer in statement, or in illustration, than the view of reflex action which Descartes gives in the "Passions de l'Âme," Art. xiii [*Passions of the Soul*, 13]. After recapitulating the manner in which sensory impressions transmitted by the sensory nerves to the brain give rise to sensation, he proceeds:—

> And in addition to the different feelings excited in the soul by these different motions of the brain, the animal spirits, without the intervention of the soul, may take their course towards certain muscles, rather than towards others, and thus move the limbs, as I shall prove by an example. If some one moves his hand rapidly towards our eyes, as if he were going to strike us, although we know that he is a friend, that he does it only in jest, and that he will be very careful to do us no harm, nevertheless it will be hard to keep from winking. And this shows, that it is not by the agency of the soul that the eyes shut, since this action is contrary to that volition which is the only, or at least the chief, function of the soul; but it is because the mechanism of our body is so disposed, that the motion of the hand towards our eyes excites another movement in our brain, and this sends the animal spirits into those muscles which cause the eyelids to close.

Since Descartes's time, experiment has eminently enlarged our knowledge of the details of reflex action. The discovery of Bell has enabled us to follow the tracks of the sensory and motor impulses, along distinct bundles of nerve fibres; and the spinal cord, apart from the brain, has been proved to be a great centre of reflex action; but the fundamental conception remains as Descartes left it, and it is one of the pillars of nerve physiology at the present day.

V. The motion of any given portion of the matter of the brain excited by the motion of a sensory nerve, leaves behind a readiness to be moved in the same way, in that part. Anything which resuscitates the motion gives rise to the appropriate feeling. This is the physical mechanism of memory.

Descartes imagined that the pineal body (a curious appendage to the upper side of the brain, the function of which, if it have any, is wholly unknown) was the instrument through which the soul received impressions from, and communicated them to, the brain. And he thus endeavours to explain what happens when one tries to recollect something:—

> Thus when the soul wills to remember anything, this volition, causing the [pineal] gland to incline itself in different directions, drives the [animal] spirits towards different regions of the brain, until they reach that part in which are the traces, which the object which it desires to remember has left. These traces are produced thus—those pores of the brain through which the [animal] spirits have previously been driven, by reason of the presence of the object, have thereby acquired a tendency to be opened by the animal spirits which return towards them more easily than other pores, so that the animal spirits, impinging on these pores, enter them more readily than others. By this means they excite a particular movement in the pineal gland, which represents the object to the soul, and causes it to know what it is which it desired to recollect.[6]

That memory is dependent upon some condition of the brain is a fact established by many considerations—among the most important of which are the remarkable phenomena of aphasia. And that the condition of the brain on which memory depends, is largely determined by the repeated occurrence of that condition of its molecules, which gives rise to the idea of the thing remembered, is no less certain. Every boy who learns his lesson by repeating it exemplifies the fact. Descartes, as we have seen, supposes that the pores of a given part of the brain are stretched by the animal spirits, on the occurrence of a sensation, and that the part of the brain thus stretched, being imperfectly elastic, does not return to exactly its previous condition, but remains more distensible than it was before.... Physiology is, at present, incompetent to say anything positively about the matter, or to go farther than the expression of the high probability, that every molecular change which gives rise to a state of consciousness, leaves a more or less persistent structural modification, through which the same molecular change may be regenerated by other agencies than the cause which first produced it.

Thus far, the propositions respecting the physiology of the nervous system which are stated by Descartes have simply been more clearly defined, more fully illustrated, and, for the most part, demonstrated, by modern physiological research. But there remains a doctrine to which Descartes attached great weight so that full acceptance of it became a sort of note of a thoroughgoing Cartesian, but which, nevertheless, is so opposed to ordinary prepossessions that it attained more general notoriety, and gave rise to more discussion, than almost any other Cartesian hypothesis. It is the doctrine that brute animals are mere machines or automata, devoid not only of reason, but of any kind of consciousness, which is stated briefly in the "Discours de la Méthode" [*Discourse on Method*], and more fully in the "Réponses aux Quatrièmes Objections" [Response to the Fourth Set of Objections], and in the correspondence with Henry More.[7]

The process of reasoning by which Descartes arrived at this startling conclusion is well shown in the following passage of the "Réponses:"—

> But as regards the souls of beasts, although this is not the place for considering them, and though, without a general exposition of physics, I can say no more on this subject than I have already said in the fifth Part of my Treatise on Method; yet, I will further state, here, that it appears to me to be a very remarkable circumstance that no movement can take place, either in the bodies of beasts, or even in our own, if these bodies have not in themselves all the organs and instruments by means of which the very same movements would be accomplished in a machine. So that, even in us, the spirit, or the soul, does not directly move the limbs, but only determines the course of that very subtle liquid which is called the animal spirits, which, running continually from the heart by the brain into the muscles, is the cause of all the movements of our limbs, and often may cause many different motions, one as easily as the other.
>
> And it does not even always exert this determination; for among the movements which take place in us, there are many which do not depend on the mind at all, such as the beating of the heart, the digestion of food, the nutrition, the respiration of those who sleep; and even in those who are awake, walking, singing, and other similar actions, when they are performed without the mind thinking about them. And, when one who falls from a height throws his hands forward to save his head, it is in virtue of no ratiocination that he performs this action; it does not depend upon his mind, but takes place merely because his senses being affected by the present danger, some change arises in his brain which determines the animal spirits to pass

thence into the nerves, in such a manner as is required to produce this motion, in the same way as in a machine, and without the mind being able to hinder it. Now since we observe this in ourselves, why should we be so much astonished if the light reflected from the body of a wolf into the eye of a sheep, has the same force to excite in it the motion of flight?

After having observed this, if we wish to learn by reasoning, whether certain movements of beasts are comparable to those which are effected in us by the operation of the mind, or, on the contrary, to those which depend only on the animal spirits and the disposition of the organs, it is necessary to consider the difference between the two, which I have explained in the fifth part of the Discourse on Method (for I do not think that any others are discoverable), and then it will easily be seen, that all the actions of beasts are similar only to those which we perform without the help of our minds. For which reason we shall be forced to conclude, that we know of the existence in them of no other principle of motion than the disposition of their organs and the continual affluence of animal spirits produced by the heat of the heart, which attenuates and subtilises the blood; and, at the same time, we shall acknowledge that we have had no reason for assuming any other principle, except that, not having distinguished these two principles of motion, and seeing that the one, which depends only on the animal spirits and the organs, exists in beasts as well as in us, we have hastily concluded that the other, which depends on mind and on thought, was also possessed by them.

Descartes's line of argument is perfectly clear. He starts from reflex action in man, from the unquestionable fact that, in ourselves, co-ordinate, purposive, actions may take place, without the intervention of consciousness or volition, or even contrary to the latter. As actions of a certain degree of complexity are brought about by mere mechanism, why may not actions of still greater complexity be the result of a more refined mechanism? What proof is there that brutes are other than a superior race of marionettes, which eat without pleasure, cry without pain, desire nothing, know nothing, and only simulate intelligence as a bee simulates a mathematician?[8]

The Port Royalists adopted the hypothesis that brutes are machines, and are said to have carried its practical applications so far as to treat domestic animals with neglect, if not with actual cruelty. As late as the middle of the eighteenth century, the problem was discussed very fully and ably by Bouillier, in his "Essai philosophique sur L'Âme des Bêtes" [*Philosophical Essay on the Soul of Animals*], while Condillac deals with it in his "Traité des Animaux" [*Treatise on Animals*]; but since then it has received little attention. Nevertheless, modern research has brought to light a great multitude of facts, which not only show that Descartes's view is defensible, but render it far more defensible than it was in his day.

It must be premised that it is wholly impossible absolutely to prove the presence or absence of consciousness in anything but one's own brain, though, by analogy, we are justified in assuming its existence in other men. Now if, by some accident, a man's spinal cord is divided, his limbs are paralysed, so far as his volition is concerned, below the point of injury; and he is incapable of experiencing all those states of consciousness which, in his uninjured state, would be excited by irritation of those nerves which come off below the injury. If the spinal cord is divided in the middle of the back, for example, the skin of the feet may be cut, or pinched, or burned, or wetted with vitriol, without any sensation of touch, or of pain, arising in consciousness. So far as the man is concerned, therefore, the part of the central nervous system which lies beyond the injury is cut off from consciousness. It must indeed be admitted, that, if any one think fit to maintain that the spinal cord below the injury is conscious, but that it is cut off from any means of making its consciousness known to the other consciousness in the brain, there is no means of driving him from his position by logic. But assuredly there is no way of proving it, and in the matter of consciousness, if in anything, we may hold by the rule, "*De non apparentibus et de non existentibus eadem est ratio.*"[9] However near the brain the spinal cord is injured, consciousness remains intact, except that the irritation of parts below the injury is no longer represented by sensation. On the other hand, pressure upon the interior division of the brain, or extensive injuries to it, abolish consciousness. Hence, it is a highly probable conclusion, that consciousness in man depends upon the integrity of the anterior division of the brain, while the middle and hinder divisions of the brain,[10] and the rest of the nervous centres, have nothing to do with it. And it is further highly probable, that what is true for man is true for other vertebrated animals.

We may assume, then, that in a living vertebrated animal, any segment of the cerebro-spinal axis (or spinal cord and brain) separated from that anterior division of the brain which is the organ of consciousness, is as completely incapable of giving rise to consciousness as we know it to be incapable of carrying out volitions. Nevertheless, this separated segment of the spinal cord is not passive and inert. On the contrary, it is the seat of extremely remarkable powers. In our imaginary case of injury, the man would, as we have seen, be devoid of sensation in his legs, and would have not the least power of moving them. But, if the soles of his feet were tickled, the legs would be drawn up just as vigorously as they would have been before the injury. We know exactly what happens when the soles of the feet are tickled; a molecular change takes place in the sensory nerves of the skin, and is propagated along them and through the posterior roots of the spinal nerves, which are constituted by them, to the grey matter of the spinal cord. Through that grey matter the molecular motion is reflected into the anterior roots of the same nerves, constituted by the filaments which supply the muscles of the legs, and, travelling along these motor filaments, reaches the muscles, which at once contract, and cause the limbs to be drawn up.

In order to move the legs in this way, a definite coordination of muscular contractions is necessary; the muscles must contract in a certain order and with duly proportioned force; and moreover, as the feet are drawn away from the source of irritation, it may be said that the action has a final cause, or is purposive.

Thus it follows, that the grey matter of the segment of the man's spinal cord, though it is devoid of consciousness, nevertheless responds to a simple stimulus by giving rise to a complex set of muscular contractions, co-ordinated towards a definite end, and serving an obvious purpose.

If the spinal cord of a frog is cut across, so as to provide us with a segment separated from the brain, we shall have a subject parallel to the injured man, on which experiments can be made without remorse; as we have a right to conclude that a frog's spinal cord is not likely to be conscious, when a man's is not.

Now the frog behaves just as the man did. The legs are utterly paralysed, so far as voluntary movement is concerned; but they are vigorously drawn up to the body when any irritant is applied to the foot. But let us study our frog a little farther. Touch the skin of the side of the body with a little acetic acid, which gives rise to all the signs of great pain in an uninjured frog. In this case, there can be no pain, because the application is made to a part of the skin supplied with nerves which come off from the cord below the point of section; nevertheless, the frog lifts up the limb of the same side, and applies the foot to rub off the acetic acid; and, what is still more remarkable, if the limb be held so that the frog cannot use it, it will, by and by, move the limb of the other side, turn it across the body, and use it for the same rubbing process. It is impossible that the frog, if it were in its entirety and could reason, should perform actions more purposive than these: and yet we have most complete assurance that, in this case, the frog is not acting from purpose, has no consciousness, and is a mere insensible machine.

But now suppose that, instead of making a section of the cord in the middle of the body, it had been made in such a manner as to separate the hindermost division of the brain from the rest of the organ, and suppose the foremost two-thirds of the brain entirely taken away. The frog is then absolutely devoid of any spontaneity; it sits upright in the attitude which a frog habitually assumes; and it will not stir unless it is touched; but it differs from the frog which I have just described in this, that, if it be thrown into the water, it begins to swim, and swims just as well as the perfect frog does. But swimming requires the combination and successive co-ordination of a great number of muscular actions. And we are forced to conclude, that the impression made upon the sensory nerves of the skin of the frog by the contact with the water into which it is thrown, causes the transmission to the central nervous apparatus of an impulse which sets going a certain machinery by which all the muscles of swimming are brought into play in due coordination. If the frog be stimulated by some irritating body, it jumps or walks as well as the complete frog can do. The simple sensory impression, acting through the machinery of the cord, gives rise to these complex combined movements.

It is possible to go a step farther. Suppose that only the anterior division of the brain—so much of it as lies in front of the "optic lobes"—is removed. If that operation is performed quickly and skilfully, the frog may be kept in a state of full bodily vigour for months, or it may be for years; but it will sit unmoved. It sees nothing: it hears nothing. It will starve sooner than feed itself, although food put into its mouth is swallowed. On irritation, it jumps or walks; if thrown into the water it swims. If it be put on the hand it sits there, crouched, perfectly quiet, and would sit there for ever. If the hand be inclined very gently and slowly, so that the frog would naturally tend to slip off, the creature's fore paws are shifted on to the edge of the hand, until he can just prevent himself from falling. If the turning of the hand be slowly continued, he mounts up with great care and deliberation, putting first one leg forward and then another, until he balances himself with perfect precision upon the edge; and if the turning of the hand is continued, he goes through the needful set of muscular operations, until he comes to be seated in security, upon the back of the hand. The doing of all this requires a delicacy of coordination, and a precision of adjustment of the muscular apparatus of the body, which are only comparable to those of a ropedancer. To the ordinary influences of light, the frog, deprived of its cerebral hemispheres, appears to be blind. Nevertheless, if the animal be put upon a table, with a book at some little distance between it and the light, and the skin of the hinder part of its body is then irritated, it will jump forward, avoiding the book by passing to the right or left of it. Therefore, although the frog appears to have no sensation of light, visible objects act through its brain upon the motor mechanism its body.[11]

It is obvious that had Descartes been acquainted with these remarkable results of modern research, they would have furnished him with far more powerful arguments than he possessed in favour of his view of the automatism of brutes. The habits of a frog, leading its natural life, involve such simple adaptations to surrounding conditions, that the machinery which is competent to do so much without the intervention of consciousness, might well do all. And this argument is vastly strengthened by what has been learned in recent times of the marvellously complex operations which are performed mechanically, and to all appearance without consciousness, by men, when, in consequence of injury or disease, they are reduced to a condition more or less comparable to that of a frog, in which the anterior part of the brain has been removed. A case has recently been published by an eminent French physician, Dr. Mesnet, which illustrates this condition so remarkably, that I make no apology for dwelling upon it at considerable length.[12]

A sergeant of the French army, F——, twenty-seven years of age, was wounded during the battle of Bazeilles, by a ball which fractured his left parietal bone. He ran his bayonet through the Prussian soldier who wounded him, but almost immediately his right arm became paralysed; after walking about two hundred yards, his right leg became similarly affected, and he lost his senses. When he recovered them, three weeks afterwards, in hospital at Mayence, the right half of the body was completely paralysed, and remained in this condition for a year. At present, the only trace of the paralysis which remains is a slight weakness of the right half of the body. Three or four months after the wound was inflicted, periodical disturbances of the functions of the brain made their appearance, and have continued ever since. The disturbances last from fifteen to thirty hours; the intervals at which they occur being from fifteen to thirty days.

For four years, therefore, the life of this man has been divided into alternating phases—short abnormal states intervening between long normal states.

In the periods of normal life, the ex-sergeant's health is perfect; he is intelligent and kindly, and performs, satisfactorily, the duties of a hospital attendant. The commencement of the abnormal state is ushered in by uneasiness and a sense of weight about the forehead, which the patient compares to the constriction of a circle of iron; and, after its termination, he complains, for some hours, of dullness and heaviness of the head. But the transition from the normal to the abnormal state takes place in a few minutes, without convulsions or cries, and without anything to indicate the change to a bystander. His movements remain free and his expression calm, except for a contraction of the brow, an incessant movement of the eyeballs, and a chewing motion of the jaws. The eyes are wide open, and their pupils dilated. If the man happens to be in a place to which he is accustomed, he walks about as usual; but, if he is in a new place, or if obstacles are intentionally placed in his way, he stumbles gently against them, stops, and then, feeling over the objects with his hands, passes on one side of them. He offers no resistance to any change of direction which may be impressed upon him, or to the forcible acceleration or retardation of his movements. He eats, drinks, smokes, walks about, dresses and undresses himself, rises and goes to bed at the accustomed hours. Nevertheless, pins may be run into his body, or strong electric shocks sent through it without causing the least indication of pain; no odorous substance, pleasant or unpleasant, makes the least impression; he eats and drinks with avidity whatever is offered, and takes asafœtida, or vinegar, or quinine, as readily as water; no noise affects him; and light influences him only under certain conditions. Dr. Mesnet remarks, that the sense of touch alone seems to persist, and indeed to be more acute and delicate than in the normal state: and it is by means of the nerves of touch, almost exclusively, that his organism is brought into relation with the external world. Here a difficulty arises. It is clear from the facts detailed, that the nervous apparatus by which, in the normal state, sensations of touch are excited, is that by which external influences determine the movements of the body, in the abnormal state. But does the state of consciousness, which we term a tactile sensation, accompany the operation of this nervous apparatus in the abnormal state? or is consciousness utterly absent, the man being reduced to an insensible mechanism?

It is impossible to obtain direct evidence in favour of the one conclusion or the other; all that can be said is, that the case of the frog shows that the man may be devoid of any kind of consciousness.

A further difficult problem is this. The man is insensible to sensory impressions made through the ear, the nose, the tongue and, to a great extent, the eye; nor is he susceptible of pain from causes operating during his abnormal state. Nevertheless, it is possible so to act upon his tactile apparatus, as to give rise to those molecular changes in his sensorium, which are ordinarily the causes of associated trains of ideas...

The ex-sergeant has a good voice, and had, at one time, been employed as a singer at a café. In one of his abnormal states he was observed to begin humming a tune. He then went to his room, dressed himself carefully, and took up some parts of a periodical novel, which lay on his bed, as if he were trying to find something. Dr. Mesnet, suspecting that he was seeking his music, made up one of these into a roll and put it into his hand. He appeared satisfied, took his cane and went down stairs to the door. Here Dr. Mesnet turned him round, and he walked quite contentedly, in the opposite direction, towards the room of the concierge. The light of the sun shining through a window now happened to fall upon him, and seemed to suggest the footlights of the stage on which he was accustomed to make his appearance. He stopped, opened his roll of imaginary music, put himself into the attitude of a singer, and sang with perfect execution, three songs, one after the other. After which he wiped his face with his handkerchief and drank, without a grimace, a tumbler of strong vinegar and water which was put into his hand.

An experiment which may be performed upon the frog deprived of the fore part of its brain, well known as Göltz's "Quak-versuch," affords a parallel to this performance. If the skin of a certain part of the back of such a frog is gently stroked with the finger, it immediately croaks. It never croaks unless it is so stroked, and the croak always follows the stroke, just as the sound of a repeater follows the touching of the spring. In the frog, this "song" is innate—so to speak *à priori*—and depends upon a mechanism in the brain governing the vocal apparatus, which is set at work by the molecular change set up in the sensory nerves of the skin of the back by the contact of a foreign body.

In man there is also a vocal mechanism, and the cry of an infant is in the same sense innate and *à priori*, inasmuch as it depends on an organic relation between its sensory nerves and the nervous mechanism which governs the vocal apparatus. Learning to speak, and learning to sing, are processes by which the vocal mechanism is set to new tunes. A song which has been learned has its molecular equivalent, which potentially represents it in the brain, just as a musical box, wound up, potentially represents an overture. Touch the stop and the overture begins; send a molecular impulse along the proper afferent nerve and the singer begins his song.

Again, the manner in which the frog, though apparently insensible to light, is yet, under some circumstances, influenced by visual images, finds a singular parallel in the case of the ex-sergeant.

Sitting at a table, in one of his abnormal states, he took up a pen, felt for paper and ink, and began to write a letter to his general, in which he recommended himself for a medal, on account of his good conduct and courage. It occurred to Dr. Mesnet to ascertain experimentally how far vision was concerned in this act of writing. He therefore interposed a screen between the man's eyes and his hands; under these circumstances he went on writing for a short time, but the words became illegible, and he finally stopped, without manifesting any discontent. On the withdrawal of the screen he began to write again where he had left off. The substitution of water for ink in the inkstand had a similar result. He stopped, looked at his pen, wiped it on his coat, dipped it in the water, and began again with the same effect.

On one occasion, he began to write upon the topmost of ten superimposed sheets of paper. After he had written a line or two, this sheet was suddenly drawn away. There was a slight expression of surprise, but he continued his letter on the second sheet exactly as if it had been the first. This operation was repeated five times, so that the fifth sheet contained nothing but the writer's signature at the bottom of the page. Nevertheless, when the signature was finished, his eyes turned to the top of the blank sheet, and he went through the form of reading over what he had written, a movement of the lips accompanying each word; moreover, with his pen, he put in such corrections as were needed, in that part of the blank page which corresponded with the position of the words which required correction, in the sheets which had been taken away. If the five sheets had been transparent, therefore, they would, when superposed, have formed a properly written and corrected letter.

Immediately after he had written his letter, F—— got up, walked down to the garden, made himself a cigarette, lighted and smoked it. He was about to prepare another, but sought in vain for his tobacco-pouch, which had been purposely taken away. The pouch was now thrust before his eyes and put under his nose, but he neither saw nor smelt it; yet, when it was placed in his hand, he at once seized it, made a fresh cigarette, and ignited a match to light the latter. The match was blown out, and another lighted match placed close before his eyes, but he made no attempt to take it; and, if his cigarette was lighted for him, he made no attempt to smoke. All this time the eyes were vacant, and neither winked, nor exhibited any contraction of the pupils. From those and other experiments, Dr. Mesnet draws the conclusion that his patient sees some things and not others; that the sense of sight is accessible to all things which are brought into relation with him by the sense of touch, and, on the contrary, insensible to things which lie outside this relation. He sees the match he holds and does not see any other.

Just so the frog "sees" the book which is in the way of his jump at the same time that isolated visual impressions take no effect upon him.[13]

As I have pointed out, it is impossible to prove that F—— is absolutely unconscious in his abnormal state, but it is no less impossible to prove the contrary; and the case of the frog goes a long way to justify the assumption that, in the abnormal state, the man is a mere insensible machine.

If such facts as these had come under the knowledge of Descartes, would they not have formed an apt commentary upon that remarkable passage in the "Traité de l'Homme" [*Treatise on Man*], which I have quoted elsewhere, but which is worth repetition?——

All the functions which I have attributed to this machine (the body), as the digestion of food, the pulsation of the heart and of the arteries; the nutrition and the growth of the limbs; respiration, wakefulness, and sleep; the reception of light, sounds, odours, flavours, heat, and such like qualities, in the organs of the external senses; the impression of the ideas of these in the organ of common sensation and in the imagination; the retention or the impression of these ideas on the memory; the internal movements of the appetites and the passions; and lastly the external movements of all the limbs, which follow so aptly, as well the action of the objects which are presented to the senses, as the impressions which meet in the memory, that they imitate as nearly as possible those of a real man; I desire, I say, that you should consider that those functions in the machine naturally proceed from the mere arrangement of its organs, neither more nor less than do the movements of a clock, or other automaton, from that of its weights and its wheels; so that, so far as these are concerned, it is not necessary to conceive any other vegetative or sensitive soul, nor any other principle of motion or of life, than the blood and the spirits agitated by the fire which burns continually in the heart and which is no wise essentially different from all the fires which exist in inanimate bodies.

And would Descartes not have been justified in asking why we need deny that animals are machines, when men, in a state of unconsciousness, perform, mechanically, actions as complicated and as seemingly rational as those of any animals?

But though I do not think that Descartes's hypothesis can be positively refuted, I am not disposed to accept it. The doctrine of continuity is too well established for it to be permissible to me to suppose that any complex natural phenomenon comes into existence suddenly, and without being preceded by simpler modifications; and very strong arguments would be needed to prove that such complex phenomena as those of consciousness, first make their appearance in man. We know, that, in the individual man, consciousness grows from a dim glimmer to its full light, whether we consider the infant advancing in years, or the adult emerging from slumber and swoon. We know, further, that the lower animals possess, though less developed, that part of the brain which we have every reason to believe to be the organ of consciousness in man; and as, in other cases, function and organ are proportional, so we have a right to conclude it is with the brain; and that the brutes, though they may not possess our intensity of consciousness, and though, from the absence of language, they can have no trains of thoughts, but only trains of feelings, yet have a consciousness which, more or less distinctly, foreshadows our own.

I confess that, in view of the struggle for existence which goes on in the animal world, and of the frightful quantity of pain with which it must be accompanied, I should be glad if the probabilities were in favour of Descartes's hypothesis; but, on the other hand, considering the terrible practical consequences to domestic animals which might ensue from any error on our part, it is as well to err on the right side, if we err at all, and deal with them as weaker brethren, who are bound, like the rest of us, to pay their toll for living, and suffer what is needful for the general good. As Hartley finely says, "We seem to be in the place of God to them"; and we may justly follow the precedents He sets in nature in our dealings with them.

But though we may see reason to disagree with Descartes's hypothesis that brutes are unconscious machines, it does not follow that he was wrong in regarding them as automata. They may be more or less conscious, sensitive, automata; and the view that they are such conscious machines is that which is implicitly, or explicitly, adopted by most persons. When we speak of the actions of the lower animals being guided by instinct and not by reason, what we really mean is that, though they feel as we do, yet their actions are the results of their physical organisation. We believe, in short, that they are machines, one part of which (the nervous system) not only sets the rest in motion, and co-ordinates its movements in relation with changes in surrounding bodies, but is provided with special apparatus, the function of which is the calling into existence of those states of consciousness which are termed sensations, emotions, and ideas. I believe that this generally accepted view is the best expression of the facts at present known.

It is experimentally demonstrable—any one who cares to run a pin into himself may perform a sufficient demonstration of the fact—that a mode of motion of the nervous system is the immediate antecedent of a state of consciousness. All but the adherents of "Occasionalism," or of the doctrine of "Pre-established Harmony" (if any such now exist), must admit that we have as much reason for regarding the mode of motion of the nervous system as the cause of the state of consciousness, as we have for regarding any event as the cause of another. How the one phenomenon causes the other we know, as much or as little, as in any other case of causation; but we have as much right to believe that the sensation is an effect of the molecular change, as we have to believe that motion is an effect of impact; and there is as much propriety in saying that the brain evolves sensation, as there is in saying that an iron rod, when hammered, evolves heat.

As I have endeavoured to show, we are justified in supposing that something analogous to what happens in ourselves takes place in the brutes, and that the affections of their sensory nerves give rise to molecular changes in the brain, which again give rise to, or evolve, the corresponding states of consciousness. Nor can there be any reasonable doubt that the emotions of brutes, and such ideas as they possess, are similarly dependent upon molecular brain changes. Each sensory impression leaves behind a record in the structure of the brain—an "ideagenous" molecule, so to speak, which is competent, under certain conditions, to reproduce, in a fainter condition, the state of consciousness which corresponds with that sensory impression; and it is these "ideagenous molecules" which are the physical basis of memory.

It may be assumed, then, that molecular changes in the brain are the causes of all the states of consciousness of brutes. Is there any evidence that these states of consciousness may, conversely, cause those molecular changes which give rise to muscular motion? I see no such evidence. The frog walks, hops, swims, and goes through his gymnastic performances quite as well without consciousness, and consequently without volition, as with it; and, if a frog, in his natural state, possesses anything corresponding with what we call volition, there is no reason to think that it is anything but a concomitant of the molecular changes in the brain which form part of the series involved in the production of motion.

The consciousness of brutes would appear to be related to the mechanism of their body simply as a collateral product of its working, and to be as completely without any power of modifying that working as the steam-whistle which accompanies the work of a locomotive engine is without influence upon its machinery. Their volition, if they have any, is an emotion indicative of physical changes, not a cause of such changes.

This conception of the relations of states of consciousness with molecular changes in the brain—of psychoses with neuroses—does not prevent us from ascribing free will to brutes. For an agent is free when there is nothing to prevent him from doing that which he desires to do. If a greyhound chases a hare, he is a free agent, because his action is in entire accordance with his strong desire to catch the hare; while so long as he is held back by the leash he is not free, being prevented by external force from following his inclination. And the ascription of freedom to the greyhound under the former circumstances is by no means inconsistent with the other aspect of the facts of the case— that he is a machine impelled to the chase, and caused, at the same time, to have the desire to catch the game by the impression which the rays of light proceeding from the hare make upon his eyes, and through them upon his brain.

Much ingenious argument has at various times been bestowed upon the question: How is it possible to imagine that volition, which is a state of consciousness, and, as such, has not the slightest community of nature with matter in motion, can act upon the moving matter of which the body is composed, as it is assumed to do in voluntary acts? But if, as is here suggested, the voluntary acts of brutes—or, in other words, the acts which they desire to perform—are as purely mechanical as the rest of their actions and are simply accompanied by the state of consciousness called volition, the inquiry, so far as they are concerned, becomes superfluous. Their volitions do not enter into the chain of causation of their actions at all.

The hypothesis that brutes are conscious automata is perfectly consistent with any view that may be held respecting the often discussed and curious question whether they have souls or not; and, if they have souls, whether those souls are immortal or not. It is obviously harmonious with the most literal adherence to the text of Scripture concerning "the beast that perisheth"; but it is not inconsistent with the amiable conviction ascribed by Pope to his "untutored savage," that when he passes to the happy hunting-grounds in the sky, "his faithful dog shall bear him company." If the brutes have consciousness and no souls, then it is clear that, in them, consciousness is a direct function of material changes; while, if they possess immaterial subjects of consciousness, or souls, then, as consciousness is brought into existence only as the consequence of molecular motion of the brain, it follows that it is an indirect product of material changes. The soul stands related to the body as the bell of a clock to the works, and consciousness answers to the sound which the bell gives out when it is struck.

Thus far I have strictly confined myself to the problem with which I proposed to deal at starting—the automatism of brutes. The question is, I believe, a perfectly open one, and I feel happy in running no risk of either Papal or Presbyterian condemnation for the views which I have ventured to put forward. And there are so very few interesting questions which one is, at present, allowed to think out scientifically—to go as far as reason leads, and stop where evidence comes to an end without speedily being deafened by the tattoo of "the drum ecclesiastic" that I have luxuriated in my rare freedom, and would now willingly bring this disquisition to an end if I could hope that other people would go no farther. Unfortunately, past experience debars me from entertaining any such hope, even if

> "…. that drum's discordant sound
> Parading round and round and round,"

were not, at present, as audible to me as it was to the mild poet who ventured to express his hatred of drums in general, in that well-known couplet.

It will be said, that I mean that the conclusions deduced from the study of the brutes are applicable to man, and that the logical consequences of such application are fatalism, materialism, and atheism—whereupon the drums will beat the *pas de charge*.

One does not do battle with drummers; but I venture to offer a few remarks for the calm consideration of thoughtful persons, untrammelled by foregone conclusions, unpledged to shore-up tottering dogmas, and anxious only to know the true bearings of the case.

It is quite true that, to the best of my judgment, the argumentation which applies to brutes holds equally good of men; and, therefore, that all states of consciousness in us, as in them, are immediately caused by molecular changes of the brain-substance. It seems to me that in men, as in brutes, there is no proof that any consciousness is the cause of change in the motion of the matter of the organism. If these positions are well based, it follows that our mental conditions are simply the symbols in consciousness of the changes which take place automatically in the organism; and that, to take an extreme illustration, the feeling we call volition is not the cause of a voluntary act, but the symbol of that state of the brain which is the immediate cause of that act. We are conscious automata, endowed with free will in the only intelligible sense of that much-abused term—inasmuch as in many respects we are able to do as we like—but none the less parts of the great series of causes and effects which, in unbroken continuity, composes that which is, and has been, and shall be—the sum of existence.

As to the logical consequences of this conviction of mine, I may be permitted to remark that logical consequences are the scarecrows of fools and the beacons of wise men. The only question which any wise man can ask himself, and which any honest man will ask himself, is whether a doctrine is true or false. Consequences will take care of themselves; at most their importance can only justify us in testing with extra care the reasoning process from which they result.

So that if the view I have taken did really and logically lead to fatalism, I should profess myself a fatalist, materialist, and atheist; and I should look upon those who, while they believed in my honesty of purpose and intellectual competency, should raise a hue and cry against me, as people who by their own admission preferred lying to truth, and whose opinions therefore were unworthy of the smallest attention.

But, as I have endeavoured to explain on other occasions, I really have no claim to rank myself among fatalistic, materialistic, or atheistic philosophers. Not among fatalists, for I take the conception of necessity to have a logical, and not a physical foundation; not among materialists, for I am utterly incapable of conceiving the existence of matter if there is no mind in which to picture that existence; not among atheists, for the problem of the ultimate cause of existence is one which seems to me to be hopelessly out of reach of my poor powers. Of all the senseless babble I have ever had occasion to read, the demonstrations of these philosophers who undertake to tell us all about the nature of God would be the worst, if they were not surpassed by the still greater absurdities of the philosophers who try to prove that there is no God.

And if this personal disclaimer should not be enough, let me further point out that a great many persons whose acuteness and learning will not be contested, and whose Christian piety, and, in some cases, strict orthodoxy, are above suspicion, have held more or less definitely the view that man is a conscious automaton.

It is held, for example, in substance, by the whole school of predestinarian theologians, typified by St. Augustine, Calvin, and Jonathan Edwards—the great work of the latter on the will showing in this, as in other cases, that the growth of physical science has introduced no new difficulties of principle into theological problems, but has merely given visible body, as it were, to those already existed.

Among philosophers, the pious Geulinex and the whole school of occasionalist Cartesians hold this view; the orthodox Leibnitz invented the term "automate spirituel," and applied it to man; the fervent Christian, Hartley, was one of the chief advocates and best expositors of the doctrine; while another zealous apologist of Christianity in a sceptical age, and a contemporary of Hartley, Charles Bonnet, the Genevese naturalist, has embodied the doctrine in language of such precision and simplicity, that I will quote the little-known passage of his "Essai de Psychologie" at length:—

ANOTHER HYPOTHESIS CONCERNING THE MECHANISM OF IDEAS[14]

Philosophers accustomed to judge of things by that which they are in themselves, and not by their relation to received ideas, would not be shocked if they met with the proposition that the soul is a mere spectator of the movements of its body; that the latter performs of itself all that series of actions which constitutes life: that it moves of itself: that it is the body alone which reproduces ideas, compares and arranges them; which forms reasonings, imagines and executes plans of all kinds, etc. This hypothesis, though perhaps of an excessive boldness, nevertheless deserves some consideration.

It is not to be denied that Supreme Power could create an automaton which should exactly imitate all the external and internal actions of man.

I understand by external actions, all those movements which pass under our eyes: I term internal actions, all the motions which in the natural state cannot be observed because they take place in the interior of the body—such as the movements of digestion, circulation, sensation, etc. Moreover, I include in this category the movements which give rise to ideas, whatever be their nature.

In the automaton which we are considering everything would be precisely determined. Everything would occur according to the rules of the most admirable mechanism: one state would succeed another state, one operation would lead to another operation, according to invariable laws; motion would become alternately cause and effect, effect and cause; reaction would answer to action, and reproduction to production.

Constructed with definite relations to the activity of the beings which compose the world, the automaton would receive impressions from it, and, in faithful correspondence thereto, it would execute a corresponding series of motions.

Indifferent towards any determination, it would yield equally to all, if the first impressions did not, so to speak, wind up the machine and decide its operations and its course.

The series of movements which this automaton could execute would distinguish it from all others formed of the same model, but which, not having been placed in similar circumstances, would not have experienced the same impressions, or would not have experienced them in the same order.

The senses of the automaton, set in motion by the objects presented to it, would communicate their motion to the brain, the chief motor apparatus of the machine. This would put in action the muscles of the hands and feet in virtue of their secret connection with the senses. These muscles, alternately contracted and dilated, would approximate or remove the automaton from the objects, in the relation which they would bear to the conservation or the destruction of the machine.

The motions of perception and sensation which the objects would have impressed on the brain, would be preserved in it by the energy of its mechanism. They would become more vivid according to the actual condition of the automaton, considered in itself and relatively to the objects.

Words being only the motions impressed on the organ of hearing and that of voice, the diversity of these movements, their combination, the order in which they would succeed one another, would represent judgments, reasoning, and all the operations of the mind.

A close correspondence between the organs of the senses, either by the opening into one another of their nervous ramifications or by interposed springs (*ressorts*), would establish such a connection in their working, that, on the occasion of the movements impressed on one of these organs, other movements would be excited, or would become more vivid in some of the other senses.

Give the automaton a soul which contemplates its movements, which believes itself to be the author of them, which has different volitions on the occasion of the different movements, and you will on this hypothesis construct a man.

But would this man be free? Can the feeling of our liberty, this feeling which is so clear and so distinct and so vivid as to persuade us that we are the authors of our actions, be conciliated with this hypothesis? If it removes the difficulty which attends the conception of the action of the soul on the body, on the other hand and it leaves untouched that which meets us in endeavouring to conceive the action of the body on the soul.

But if Leibnitz, Jonathan Edwards, and Hartley—men who rank among the giants of the world of thought—could see no antagonism between the doctrine under discussion and Christian orthodoxy, is it not just possible that smaller folk may be wrong in making such a coil about "logical consequences"? And, seeing how large a share of this clamour is raised by the clergy of one denomination or another, may I say, in conclusion, that it really would be well if ecclesiastical persons would reflect that ordination, whatever deep-seated graces it may confer, has never been observed to be followed by any visible increase in the learning or the logic of its subject. Making a man a Bishop, or entrusting him with the office of ministering to even the largest of Presbyterian congregations, or setting him up to lecture to a Church congress, really does not in the smallest degree augment such title to respect as his opinions may intrinsically possess. And when such a man presumes on an authority which was conferred upon him for other purposes to sit in judgment upon matters his incompetence to deal with which is patent, it is permissible to ignore his sacerdotal pretensions, and to tell him, as one would tell a mere common, unconsecrated, layman: that it is not necessary for any man to occupy himself with problems of this kind unless he so choose; life is filled full enough by the performance of its ordinary and obvious duties. But that, if a man elect to become a judge of these grave questions; still more, if he assume the responsibility of attaching praise or blame to his fellow-men for the conclusions at which they arrive touching them, he will commit a sin more grievous than most breaches of the Decalogue, unless he avoid a lazy reliance upon the information that is gathered by prejudice and filtered through passion, unless he go back to the prime sources of knowledge—the facts of Nature, and the thoughts of those wise men who for generations past have been her best interpreters.

Notes

1   I quote, here and always, Cousin's edition of the works of Descartes, as most convenient for reference. It is entitled *Œuvres complètes de Descartes*, publiées par Victor Cousin. 1824.

2   *Les Passions de l'Âme*, Art. xxxiii [*Passions of the Soul*, 33, this volume, XX].

3   *Recherches physiologiques sur la Vie et la Mort*. Par Xav. Bichat. Art. Sixième.

4   Locke (*Human Understanding*, Book II, chap. viii, 37) uses Descartes's illustration for the same purpose, and warns us that "most of the ideas of sensation are no more the likeness of something existing without us than the names that stand for them are the likeness of our ideas, which yet, upon hearing, they are apt to excite in us," a declaration which paved the way for Berkeley.

5   *Les Passions de l'Âme*, Art. xxxvi [*Passions of the Soul*, 36, this volume, XX].

6   *Les Passions de l'Âme*, Art. xlii [*Passions of the Soul*, 42, this volume, XX].

7   *Réponse de M. Descartes à M. Morus*, 1649. *Œuvres*, tome x. p. 204. "Mais le plus grand de tous les préjugés que nous ayons retenus de notre enfance, est celui de croire que les bêtes pensent," etc. ["But the greatest of all the prejudices we have retained from our childhood, is that of believing that animals think."]

8   Malebranche states the view taken by orthodox Cartesians in 1689 very forcibly: "Ainsi dans les chiens, les chats, et les autres animaux, il n'y a ny intelligence, ny âme spirituelle comme on l'entend ordinairement. Ils mangent sans plaisir; ils crient sans douleur; ils croissent sans le sçavoir; ils ne désirent rien; ils ne connoissent rien; et s'ils agissent avec adresse et d'une manière qui marque l'intelligence, c'est que Dieu les faisant pour les conserver, il a conformé leurs corps de telle manière, qu'ils évitent organiquement, sans le sçavoir, tout ce qui peut les detruire et qu'ils semblent craindre." (*Feuillet de Conches, Méditations Métaphysiques et Correspondance de N. Malebranche, Neuvième Méditation*, 1841.) [Thus in dogs, cats and other animals there is neither intelligence nor spiritual soul as ordinarily understood. They eat without pleasure; they cry without pain; they believe without knowing; they desire nothing; they know nothing; and if they act with dexterity and a manner which suggests intelligence, it is God who makes them do so for their preservation; he has so formed their bodies that they avoid organically, without knowledge, everything which could destroy them and which they seem to fear."]

9   "The same account is for that which is not visible and that which does not exist."

10   Not to be confounded with the anterior middle and hinder parts of the hemispheres of the cerebrum.

11   See the remarkable essay of. Göltz, *Beiträge zur Lehre von den Functionen der Ner-*

vencentren des Frosches [*Contributions to the Theory of the Functions of the Nerve-centres of Frogs*], published in 1869. I have repeated Göltz's experiments, and obtained the same results.

12   "De l'Automatisme de la Mémoire et du Souvenir, dans le Somnambulisme pathologique." ["Concerning the Automatism of Memory in Pathological Sleep-walkers"] Par le Dr. E. Mesnet, Médecin de l'Hôpital Saint-Antoine. *L'Union Médicale,* Juillet 21 et 23, 1874. My attention was first called to a summary of this remarkable case, which appeared in the *Journal des Débats* for the 7th of August, 1874, by my friend General Strachey, F.R.S.

13   Those who have had occasion to become acquainted with the phenomena of somnambulism and of mesmerism will be struck with the close parallel which they present to the proceedings of F. in his abnormal state. But the great value of Dr. Mesnet's observations lies in the fact that the abnormal condition is traceable to a definite injury to the brain, and that the circumstances are such as to keep us clear of the cloud of voluntary and involuntary fictions in which the truth is too often smothered in such cases. In the unfortunate subjects of such abnormal conditions of the brain, the disturbance of the sensory and intellectual faculties is not unfrequently accompanied by a perturbation of the moral nature, which may manifest itself in a most astonishing love of lying for its own sake. And, in this respect, also, F.'s case is singularly instructive, for though, in his normal state, he is a perfectly honest man, in his abnormal condition he is an inveterate thief, stealing and hiding away whatever he can lay hands on, with much dexterity, and with all absurd indifference as to whether the property is his own or not. Hoffman's terrible conception of the "Doppelt-gänger" is realized by men in this state—who live two lives, in the one of which they may be guilty of the most criminal acts, while, in the other, they are eminently virtuous and respectable. Neither life knows anything of the other. Dr. Mesnet states that he has watched a man in his abnormal state elaborately prepare to hang himself, and has let him go on until asphyxia set in, when he cut him down. But on passing into the normal state the would-be suicide was wholly ignorant of what had happened. The problem of responsibility is here as complicated as that of the prince-bishop, who swore as a prince and not as a bishop. "But, highness, if the prince is damned, what will become of the bishop?" said the peasant.

14   *Essai de Psychologie* [*Essay of Psychology*], chap. xxvii.

4

THE AUTOMATON-THEORY[*]

William James

In describing the functions of the hemispheres a short way back, we used language derived from both the bodily and the mental life, saying now that the animal made indeterminate and unforeseeable reactions, and anon that he was swayed by considerations of future good and evil; treating his hemispheres sometimes as the seat of memory and ideas in the psychic sense, and sometimes talking of them as simply a complicated addition to his reflex machinery. This sort of vacillation in the point of view is a fatal incident of all ordinary talk about these questions; but I must now settle my scores with those readers to whom I already dropped a word in passing ... and who have probably been dissatisfied with my conduct ever since.

Suppose we restrict our view to facts of one and the same plane, and let that be the bodily plane: cannot all the outward phenomena of intelligence still be exhaustively described? Those mental images, those "considerations," whereof we spoke—presumably they do not arise without neural processes arising simultaneously with them, and presumably each consideration corresponds to a process *sui generis*, and unlike all the rest. In other words, however numerous and delicately differentiated the train of ideas may be, the train of brain-events that runs alongside of it must in both respects be exactly its match, and we must postulate a neural machinery that offers a living counterpart for every shading, however fine, of the history of its owner's mind. Whatever degree of complication the latter may reach, the complication of the machinery must be quite as extreme, otherwise we should have to admit that there may be mental events to which no brain-events correspond. But such an admission as this the physiologist is reluctant to make. It would violate all his beliefs. "No psychosis without neurosis," is one form which the principle of continuity takes in his mind.

But this principle forces the physiologist to make still another step. If neural action is as complicated as mind; and if in the sympathetic system and lower spinal cord we see what, so far as we know, is unconscious neural action executing deeds that to all outward intent may be called intelligent; what is there to hinder us from supposing that even where we know consciousness to be there, the still more complicated neural action which we believe to be its

---

[*] Taken from William James, *The Principles of Psychology* (New York: Holt, 1890).

inseparable companion is alone and of itself the real agent of whatever intelligent deeds may appear? "As actions of a certain degree of complexity are brought about by mere mechanism, why may not actions of a still greater degree of complexity be the result of a more refined mechanism?" The conception of reflex action is surely one of the best conquests of physiological theory; why not be radical with it? Why not say that just as the spinal cord is a machine with few reflexes, so the hemispheres are a machine with many, and that that is all the difference? The principle of continuity would press us to accept this view.

But what on this view could be the function of the consciousness itself? *Mechanical* function it would have none. The sense-organs would awaken the brain-cells; these would awaken each other in rational and orderly sequence, until the time for action came; and then the last brain-vibration would discharge downwards into the motor tracts. But this would be a quite autonomous chain of occurrences, and whatever mind went with it would be there only as an "epiphenomenon," an inert spectator, a sort of foam, aura, or melody as Mr. Hodgson says, whose opposition or whose furtherance would be alike powerless over the occurrences themselves. When talking, some time ago, we ought not, accordingly, as *physiologists*, to have said anything about "considerations" as guiding the animal. We ought to have said "paths left in the hemispherical cortex by former currents," and nothing more.

Now so simple and attractive is this conception from the consistently physiological point of view, that it is quite wonderful to see how late it was stumbled on in philosophy, and how few people, even when it has been explained to them, fully and easily realize its import. Much of the polemic writing against it is by men who have as yet failed to take it into their imaginations. Since this has been the case, it seems worth while to devote a few more words to making it plausible, before criticising it ourselves.

To Descartes belongs the credit of having first been bold enough to conceive of a completely self-sufficing nervous mechanism which should be able to perform complicated and apparently intelligent acts. By a singularly arbitrary restriction, however, Descartes stopped short at man, and while contending that in beasts the nervous machinery was all, he held that the higher acts of man were the result of the agency of his rational soul. The opinion that beasts have no consciousness at all was of course too paradoxical to maintain itself long as anything more than a curious item in the history of philosophy. And with its abandonment the very notion that the nervous system *per se* might work the work of intelligence, which was an integral, though detachable part of the whole theory, seemed also to slip out of men's conception, until, in this century, the elaboration of the doctrine of reflex action made it possible and natural that it should again arise. But it was not till 1870, I believe, that Mr. Hodgson made the decisive step, by saying that feelings, no matter how intensely they may be present, can have no causal efficacy whatever, and comparing them to the colors laid on the surface of a mosaic, of which the events in the nervous system are represented by the stones.[1] Obviously the stones are held in place by each other and not by the several colors which they support.

About the same time Mr. Spalding, and a little later Messrs. Huxley and Clifford, gave great publicity to an identical doctrine, though in their case it was backed by less refined metaphysical considerations.[2]

A few sentences from Huxley and Clifford may be subjoined to make the matter entirely clear. Professor Huxley says:

> The consciousness of brutes would appear to be related to the mechanism of their body simply as a collateral product of its working, and to be as completely without any power of modifying that working, as the steam-whistle which accompanies the work of a locomotive engine is without influence upon its machinery. Their volition, if they have any, is an emotion *indicative* of physical changes, not a *cause* of such changes.... The soul stands related to the body as the bell of a clock to the works, and consciousness answers to the sound which the bell gives out when it is struck. Thus far I have strictly confined myself to ... the automatism of brutes.... It is quite true that, to the best of my judgment, the argumentation which applies to brutes holds equally good of men; and, therefore, that all states of consciousness in us, as in them, are immediately caused by molecular changes of the brain-substance. It seems to me that in men, as in brutes, there is no proof that any state of consciousness is the cause of change in the motion of the matter of the organism. If these positions are well based, it follows that our mental conditions are simply the symbols in consciousness of the changes which take place automatically in the organism; and that, to take an extreme illustration, the feeling we call volition is not the cause of a voluntary act, but the symbol of that state of the brain which is the immediate cause of that act. We are conscious automata.

Professor Clifford writes:

> All the evidence that we have goes to show that the physical world gets along entirely by itself, according to practically universal rules.... The train of physical facts between the stimulus sent into the eye, or to any one of our senses, and the exertion which follows it, and the train of physical facts which goes on in the brain, even when there is no stimulus and no exertion,—these are perfectly complete physical trains, and every step is fully accounted for by mechanical conditions.... The two things are on utterly different platforms—the physical facts go along by

themselves, and the mental facts go along by themselves. There is a parallelism between them, but there is no interference of one with the other. Again, if anybody says that the will influences matter, the statement is not untrue, but it is nonsense.... Such an assertion belongs to the crude materialism of the savage. The only thing which influences matter is the position of surrounding matter or the motion of surrounding matter.... The assertion that another man's volition, a feeling in his consciousness which I cannot perceive, is part of the train of physical facts which I may perceive,—this is neither true nor untrue, but nonsense; it is a combination of words whose corresponding ideas will not go together.... Sometimes one series is known better, and sometimes the other; so that in telling a story we speak sometimes of mental and sometimes of material facts. A feeling of chill made a man run; strictly speaking, the nervous disturbance which coexisted with that feeling of chill made him run, if we want to talk about material facts; or the feeling of chill produced the form of sub-consciousness which coexists with the motion of legs, if we want to talk about mental facts.... When, therefore, we ask, "What is the physical link between the ingoing message from chilled skin and the outgoing message which moves the leg?" and the answer is, "A man's Will," we have as much right to be amused as if we had asked our friend with the picture what pigment was used in painting the cannon in the foreground, and received the answer, "Wrought iron." It will be found excellent practice in the mental operations required by this doctrine to imagine a train, the fore part of which is an engine and three carriages linked with iron couplings, and the hind part three other carriages linked with iron couplings; the bond between the two parts being made out of the sentiments of amity subsisting between the stoker and the guard.

To comprehend completely the consequences of the dogma so confidently enunciated, one should unflinchingly apply it to the most complicated examples. The movements of our tongues and pens, the flashings of our eyes in conversation, are of course events of a material order, and as such their causal antecedents must be exclusively material. If we knew thoroughly the nervous system of Shakespeare, and as thoroughly all his environing conditions, we should be able to show why at a certain period of his life his hand came to trace on certain sheets of paper those crabbed little black marks which we for shortness's sake call the manuscript of *Hamlet*. We should understand the rationale of every erasure and alteration therein, and we should understand all this without in the slightest degree acknowledging the existence of the thoughts in Shakespeare's mind. The words and sentences would be taken, not as signs of anything beyond themselves, but as little outward facts, pure and simple. In like manner we might exhaustively write the biography of those two hundred pounds, more or less, of warmish albuminoid matter called Martin Luther, without ever implying that it felt.

But, on the other hand, nothing in all this could prevent us from giving an equally complete account of either Luther's or Shakespeare's spiritual history, an account in which every gleam of thought and emotion should find its place. The mind-history would run alongside of the body-history of each man, and each point in the one would correspond to, but not react upon, a point in the other. So the melody floats from the harp-string, but neither checks nor quickens its vibrations; so the shadow runs alongside the pedestrian, but in no way influences his steps.

Another inference, apparently more paradoxical still, needs to be made, though, as far as I am aware, Dr. Hodgson is the only writer who has explicitly drawn it. That inference is that feelings, not causing nerve-actions, cannot even cause each other. To ordinary common-sense, felt pain is, as such, not only the cause of outward tears and cries, but also the cause of such inward events as sorrow, compunction, desire, or inventive thought. So the consciousness of good news is the direct producer of the feeling of joy, the awareness of premises that of the belief in conclusions. But according to the automaton-theory, each of the feelings mentioned is only the correlate of some nerve-movement whose *cause* lay wholly in a previous nerve-movement. The first nerve-movement called up the second; whatever feeling was attached to the second consequently found itself following upon the feeling that was attached to the first. If, for example, good news was the consciousness correlated with the first movement, then joy turned out to be the correlate in consciousness of the second. But all the while the items of the nerve series were the only ones in causal continuity; the items of the conscious series, however inwardly rational their sequence, were simply juxtaposed.

REASONS FOR THE THEORY

The "conscious automaton-theory," as this conception is generally called, is thus a radical and simple conception of the manner in which certain facts may possibly occur. But between conception and belief, proof ought to lie. And when we ask, "What proves that all this is more than a mere conception of the possible?" it is not easy to get a sufficient reply. If we start from the frog's spinal cord and reason by continuity, saying, as that acts so intelligently, *though unconscious*, so the higher centres, *though conscious*, may have the intelligence they show quite as mechanically based; we are immediately met by the exact counter-argument from continuity, an argument actually urged by such writers as Pflüger and Lewes, which starts from the acts of the hemispheres, and says: "As *these* owe *their* intelligence to the consciousness which we know to be there, so the intelligence of the spinal cord's acts must really be due to the invisible presence of a consciousness lower in degree." All arguments from continuity work in two ways: you can either level up or level down by their means. And it is clear that such arguments as these can eat each other up to all eternity.

There remains a sort of philosophic faith, bred like most faiths from an aesthetic demand. Mental and physical events are, on all hands, admitted to present the strongest contrast in the entire field of being. The chasm which yawns between them is less easily bridged over by the mind than any interval we know. Why, then, not call it an absolute chasm, and say not only that the two worlds are different, but that they are independent? This gives us the comfort of all simple and absolute formulas, and it makes each chain homogeneous to our consideration. When talking of nervous tremors and bodily actions, we may feel secure against intrusion from an irrelevant mental world. When, on the other hand, we speak of feelings, we may with equal consistency use terms always of one denomination, and never be annoyed by what Aristotle calls "slipping into another kind." The desire on the part of men educated in laboratories not to have their physical reasonings mixed up with such incommensurable factors as feelings is certainly very strong. I have heard a most intelligent biologist say: "It is high time for scientific men to protest against the recognition of any such thing as consciousness in a scientific investigation." In a word, feeling constitutes the "unscientific" half of existence, and anyone who enjoys calling himself a "scientist" will be too happy to purchase an untrammelled homogeneity of terms in the studies of his predilection, at the slight cost of admitting a dualism which, in the same breath that it allows to mind an independent status of being, banishes it to a limbo of causal inertness, from whence no intrusion or interruption on its part need ever be feared.

Over and above this great postulate that matters must be kept simple, there is, it must be confessed, still another highly abstract reason for denying causal efficacity to our feelings. We can form no positive image of the *modus operandi* of a volition or other thought affecting the cerebral molecules.

Let us try to imagine an idea—say of food, producing a movement, say of carrying food to the mouth.... What is the method of its action? Does it assist the decomposition of the molecules of the gray matter, or does it retard the process, or does it alter the direction in which the shocks are distributed? Let us imagine the molecules of the gray matter combined in such a way that they will fall into simpler combinations on the impact of an incident force. Now, suppose the incident force, in the shape of a shock from some other centre, to impinge upon these molecules. By hypothesis, it will decompose them, and they will fall into the simpler combination. How is the idea of food to prevent this decomposition? Manifestly it can do so only by increasing the force which binds the molecules together. Good! Try to imagine the idea of a beefsteak binding two molecules together. It is impossible. Equally impossible is it to imagine a similar idea loosening the attractive force between two molecules.[3]

This passage from an exceedingly clever writer expresses admirably the difficulty to which I allude. Combined with a strong sense of the "chasm" between the two worlds, and with a lively faith in reflex machinery, the sense of this difficulty can hardly fail to make one turn consciousness out of the door as a superfluity so far as one's explanations go. One may bow her out politely, allow her to remain as an "epiphenomenon" (invaluable word!), but one insists that matter shall hold all the power.

Having thoroughly recognised the fathomless abyss that separates mind from matter, and having so blended the notion into his very nature, that there is no chance of his ever forgetting it, or failing to saturate with it all his meditations, the student of psychology has next to appreciate the association between these two orders of phenomena.... They are associated in a manner so intimate that some of the greatest thinkers consider them different aspects of the same process.... When the re-arrangement of molecules takes place in the higher regions of the brain, a change of consciousness simultaneously occurs.... The change of consciousness never takes place without the change in the brain; the change in the brain never ... without the change in consciousness. But why the two occur together, or what the link is which connects them, we do not know, and most authorities believe that we never shall and never can know. Having firmly and tenaciously grasped these two notions, of the absolute separateness of mind and matter, and of the invariable concomitance of a mental change with a bodily change, the student will enter on the study of psychology with half his difficulties surmounted.[4]

Half his difficulties ignored, I should prefer to say. For this "concomitance" in the midst of "absolute separateness" is an utterly irrational notion. It is to my mind quite inconceivable that consciousness should have *nothing to do* with a business which it so faithfully attends. And the question, "What has it to do?" is one which psychology has no right to "surmount," for it is her plain duty to consider it. The fact is that the whole question of interaction and influence between things is a metaphysical question, and cannot be discussed at all by those who are unwilling to go into matters thoroughly. It is truly enough hard to imagine the "idea of a beef-steak binding two molecules together"; but since Hume's time it has been equally hard to imagine *anything* binding them together. The whole notion of "binding" is a mystery, the first step towards the solution of which is to clear scholastic rubbish out of the way. Popular science talks of "forces," "attractions" or "affinities" as binding the molecules; but clear science, though she may use such words to abbreviate discourse, has no use for the conceptions, and is satisfied when she can express in simple "laws" the bare space-relations of the molecules as functions of each other and of time. To the more curiously inquiring mind, however, this simplified expression of the bare facts is not enough; there must be a "reason" for them, and something must "determine" the laws. And when one seriously sits down to consider what sort of a thing one *means* when one asks for a "reason," one is led so far afield, so far away from popular science and its scholasticism, as to see that even such a fact as the existence or non-existence in the universe of "the idea of a beef-steak" may not be wholly indifferent to other facts in the same universe, and in particular may have something to do with determining the distance at which two molecules in that universe shall lie apart. If this is so, then common-sense, though the intimate nature of causality and of the connection of things in the universe lies beyond her pitifully bounded horizon, has the root and gist of the truth in her hands when she obstinately holds to it that feelings and ideas are causes. However inadequate our ideas of causal efficacy may be, we are less wide of the mark when we say that our ideas and feelings have it, than the Automatists are when they say they haven't it. As in the night all cats are gray, so in the darkness of metaphysical criticism all causes are obscure. But one has no right to pull the pall over the psychic half of the subject only, as the automatists do, and to say that *that* causation is unintelligible, whilst in the same breath one dogmatizes about *material* causation as if Hume, Kant, and Lotze had never been born. One cannot thus blow hot and cold. One must be impartially *naif* or impartially critical. If the latter, the reconstruction must be thoroughgoing or "metaphysical," and will probably preserve the common-sense view that ideas are forces, in some translated form. But Psychology is a mere natural science, accepting certain terms uncritically as her data, and stopping short of metaphysical reconstruction. Like physics, she must be *naïve*, and if she finds that in her very peculiar field of study ideas *seem* to be causes, she had better continue to talk of them as such. She gains absolutely nothing by a breach with common-sense in this matter, and she loses, to say the least, all naturalness of speech. If feelings are causes, of course their effects must be furtherances and checkings of internal cerebral motions, of which in themselves we are entirely without knowledge. It is probable that for years to come we shall have to infer what happens in the brain either from our feelings or from motor effects which we observe. The organ will be for us a sort of vat in which feelings and motions somehow go on stewing together, and in which innumerable things happen of which we catch but the statistical result. Why, under these circumstances, we should be asked to forswear the language of our childhood I cannot well imagine, especially as it is perfectly compatible with the language of physiology. The feelings can produce nothing absolutely new, they can only reinforce and inhibit reflex currents which already exist, and the original organization of these by physiological forces must always be the ground-work of the psychological scheme.

My conclusion is that to urge the automaton-theory upon us, as it is now urged, on purely *a priori* and *quasi*-metaphysical grounds, is an *unwarrantable impertinence in the present state of psychology.*

REASONS AGAINST THE THEORY

But there are much more positive reasons than this why we ought to continue to talk in psychology as if consciousness had causal efficacy. The *particulars of the distribution of consciousness*, so far as we know them, *point to its being efficacious.* Let us trace some of them.

It is very generally admitted, though the point would be hard to prove, that consciousness grows the more complex and intense the higher we rise in the animal kingdom. That of a man must exceed that of an oyster. From this point of view it seems an organ, superadded to the other organs which maintain the animal in the struggle for existence; and the presumption of course is that it helps him in some way in the struggle, just as they do. But it cannot help him without being in some way efficacious and influencing the course of his bodily history. If now it could be shown in what way consciousness *might* help him, and if, moreover, the defects of his other organs (where consciousness is most developed) are such as to make them need just the kind of help that consciousness would bring provided it *were* efficacious; why, then the plausible inference would be that it came just *because* of its efficacy—in other words, its efficacy would be inductively proved.

Now the study of the phenomena of consciousness ... will show us that consciousness is at all times primarily *a selecting agency.* Whether we take it in the lowest sphere of sense, or in the highest of intellection, we find it always doing one thing, choosing one out of several of the materials so presented to its notice, emphasizing and accentuating that and suppressing as far as possible all the rest. The item emphasized is always in close connection with some *interest* felt by consciousness to be paramount at the time.

But what are now the defects of the nervous system in those animals whose consciousness seems most highly developed? Chief among them must be *instability.* The cerebral hemispheres are the characteristically "high" nerve-centres, and we saw how indeterminate and unforeseeable their performances were in comparison with those of the basal ganglia and the cord. But this very vagueness constitutes their advantage. They allow their possessor to adapt his conduct to the minutest alterations in the environing circumstances, any one of which may be for him a sign, suggesting distant motives more powerful than any present solicitations of sense. It seems as if certain mechanical conclusions should be drawn from this state of things. An organ swayed by slight impressions is an organ whose natural state is one of unstable equilibrium. We may imagine the various lines of discharge in the cerebrum to be almost on a par in point of permeability—what discharge a given small impression will produce may be called *accidental,* in the sense in which we say it is a matter of accident whether a raindrop falling on a mountain ridge descend the eastern or the western slope. It is in this sense that we may call it a matter of accident whether a child be a boy or a girl. The ovum is so unstable a body that certain causes too minute for our apprehension may at a certain moment tip it one way or the other. The natural law of an organ constituted after this fashion can be nothing but a law of caprice. I do not see how one could reasonably expect from it any certain pursuance of useful lines of reaction, such as the few and fatally determined performances of the lower centres constitute within their narrow sphere. The dilemma in regard to the nervous system seems, in short, to be of the following kind. We may construct one which will react infallibly and certainly, but it will then be capable of reacting to very few changes in the environment—it will fail to be adapted to all the rest. We may, on the other hand, construct a nervous system potentially adapted to respond to an infinite variety of minute features in the situation; but its fallibility will then be as great as its elaboration. We can never be sure that its equilibrium will be upset in the appropriate direction. In short, a high brain may do many things, and may do each of them at a very slight hint. But its hair-trigger organization makes of it a happy-go-lucky, hit-or-miss affair. It is as likely to do the crazy as the sane thing at any given moment. A low brain does few things, and in doing them perfectly forfeits all other use. The performances of a high brain are like dice thrown forever on a table. Unless they be loaded, what chance is there that the highest number will turn up oftener than the lowest?

All this is said of the brain as a physical machine pure and simple. *Can consciousness increase its efficiency by loading its dice?* Such is the problem.

Loading its dice would mean bringing a more or less constant pressure to bear in favor of *those* of its performances which make for the most permanent interests of the brain's owner; it would mean a constant inhibition of the tendencies to stray aside.

Well, just such pressure and such inhibition are what consciousness *seems* to be exerting all the while. And the interests in whose favor it seems to exert them are its interests and its alone, interests which it *creates,* and which, but for it, would have no status in the realm of being whatever. We talk, it is true, when we are darwinizing, as if the mere *body* that owns the brain had interests; we speak about the utilities of its various organs and how they help or hinder the body's survival; and we treat the survival as if it were an absolute end, existing as such in the physical world, a sort of actual *should-be,* presiding over the animal and judging his reactions, quite apart from the presence of any commenting intelligence outside. We forget that in the absence of some such superadded commenting intelligence (whether it be that of the animal itself, or only ours or Mr. Darwin's), the reactions cannot be properly talked of as "useful" or "hurtful" at all. Considered merely physically, all that can be said of them is that *if* they occur in a certain way survival will as a matter of fact prove to be their incidental consequence. The organs themselves, and all the rest of the physical world, will, however, all the time be quite indifferent to this consequence, and would quite as cheerfully, the circumstances changed, compass the animal's destruction. In a word, survival can enter into a purely physiological discussion only as an *hypothesis made by an onlooker* about the future. But the moment you bring a consciousness into the midst, survival ceases to be a mere hypothesis. No longer is it, "*if* survival is to occur, then so and so must brain and other organs work." It has now become an imperative decree: "Survival *shall* occur, and therefore organs *must* so work!" *Real* ends appear for the first time now upon the world's stage. The conception of consciousness as a purely cognitive form of being, which is the pet way of regarding it in many idealistic schools, modern as well as ancient, is thoroughly antipsychological ... Every actually existing consciousness seems to itself at any rate to be a *fighter for ends*, of which many, but for its presence, would not be ends at all. Its powers of cognition are mainly subservient to these ends, discerning which facts further them and which do not.

Now let consciousness only be what it seems to itself, and it will help an instable brain to compass its proper ends. The movements of the brain *per se* yield the means of attaining these ends mechanically, but only out of a lot of other ends, if so they may be called, which are not the proper ones of the animal, but often quite opposed. The brain is an instrument of possibilities, but of no certainties. But the consciousness, with its own ends present to it, and knowing also well which possibilities lead thereto and which away, will, if endowed with causal efficacy, reinforce the favorable possibilities and repress the unfavorable or indifferent ones. The nerve-currents, coursing through the cells and fibres, must in this case be supposed strengthened by the fact of their awaking one consciousness and dampened by awaking another. How such reaction of the consciousness upon the currents may occur must remain at present unsolved: it is enough for my purpose to have shown that it may not uselessly exist, and that the matter is less simple than the brain-automatists hold.

All the facts of the natural history of consciousness lend color to this view. Consciousness, for example, is only intense when nerve-processes are hesitant. In rapid, automatic, habitual action it sinks to a minimum. Nothing could be more fitting than this, if consciousness have the teleological function we suppose; nothing more meaningless, if not. Habitual actions are certain, and being in no danger of going astray from their end, need no extraneous help. In hesitant action, there seem many alternative possibilities of final nervous discharge. The feeling awakened by the nascent excitement of each alternative nerve-tract seems by its attractive or repulsive quality to determine whether the excitement shall abort or shall become complete. Where indecision is great, as before a dangerous leap, consciousness is agonizingly intense. Feeling, from this point of view, may be likened to a cross-section of the chain of nervous discharge, ascertaining the links already laid down, and groping among the fresh ends presented to it for the one which seems best to fit the case.

The phenomena of "vicarious function" ... seem to form another bit of circumstantial evidence. A machine in working order acts fatally in one way. Our consciousness calls this the right way. Take out a valve, throw a wheel out of gear or bend a pivot, and it becomes a different machine, acting just as fatally in another way which we call the wrong way. But the machine itself knows nothing of wrong or right: matter has no ideals to pursue. A locomotive will carry its train through an open drawbridge as cheerfully as to any other destination.

A brain with part of it scooped out is virtually a new machine, and during the first days after the operation functions in a thoroughly abnormal manner. As a matter of fact, however, its performances become from day to day more normal, until at last a practised eye may be needed to suspect anything wrong. Some of the restoration is undoubtedly due to "inhibitions" passing away. But if the consciousness which goes with the rest of the brain, be there not only in order to take cognizance of each functional error, but also to exert an efficient pressure to check it if it be a sin of commission, and to lend a strengthening hand if it be a weakness or sin of omission,—nothing seems more natural than that the remaining parts, assisted in this way, should by virtue of the principle of habit grow back to the old teleological modes of exercise for which they were at first incapacitated. Nothing, on the contrary, seems at first sight more unnatural than that they should vicariously take up the duties of a part now lost without those *duties as such* exerting any persuasive or coercive force....

There is yet another set of facts which seem explicable on the supposition that consciousness has causal efficacy. *It is a well-known fact that pleasures are generally associated with beneficial, pains with detrimental, experiences.* All the fundamental vital processes illustrate this law. Starvation, suffocation, privation of food, drink and sleep, work when exhausted, burns, wounds, inflammation, the effects of poison, are as disagreeable as filling the hungry stomach, enjoying rest and sleep after fatigue, exercise after rest, and a sound skin and unbroken bones at all times, are pleasant. Mr. Spencer and others have suggested that these coincidences are due, not to any pre-established harmony, but to the mere action of natural selection which would certainly kill off in the long-run any breed of creatures to whom the fundamentally noxious experience seemed enjoyable. An animal that should take pleasure in a feeling of suffocation would, if that pleasure were efficacious enough to make him immerse his head in water, enjoy a longevity of four or five minutes. But if pleasures and pains have no efficacy, one does not see (without some such *a priori* rational harmony as would be scouted by the "scientific" champions of the automaton-theory) why the most noxious acts, such as burning, might not give thrills of delight, and the most necessary ones, such as breathing, cause agony. The exceptions to the law are, it is true, numerous, but relate to experiences that are either not vital or not universal. Drunkenness, for instance, which though noxious, is to many persons delightful, is a very exceptional experience. But, as the excellent physiologist Fick remarks, if all rivers and springs ran alcohol instead of water either all men would now be born to hate it or our nerves would have been selected so as to drink it with impunity. The only considerable attempt, in fact, that has been made to explain the *distribution* of our feelings is that of Mr. Grant Allen in his suggestive little work *Physiological Æsthetics*; and his reasoning is based exclusively on that causal efficacy of pleasures and pains which the "double-aspect" partisans so strenuously deny.

Thus, then, from every point of view the circumstantial evidence against that theory is strong. *A priori* analysis of both brain-action and conscious action shows us that if the latter were efficacious it would, by its selective emphasis, make amends for the indeterminateness of the former; whilst the study *a posteriori* of the *distribution* of consciousness shows it to be exactly such as we might expect in an organ added for the sake of steering a nervous system grown too complex to regulate itself. The conclusion that it is useful is, after all this, quite justifiable. But, if it is useful, it must be so through its causal efficaciousness, and the automaton-theory must succumb to the theory of common-sense. I, at any rate (pending metaphysical reconstructions not yet successfully achieved), shall have no hesitation in using the language of commonsense....

Notes

1   S.H. Hodgson, *The Theory of Practice* (London: Longman, Green, and Co., 1870) vol. I, 416 *ff.*

2   The present writer recalls how in 1869, when still a medical student, he began to write an essay showing how almost everyone who speculated about brain-processes illicitly interpolated into his account of them links derived from the entirely heterogeneous universe of Feeling. Spencer, Hodgson (in his *Time and Space* [London: Longman, Green and Co., 1865]), Maudsley, Lockhart Clarke, Bain, Dr. Carpenter, and other authors were cited as having been guilty of the confusion. The writing was soon stopped because he perceived that the view which he was upholding against these authors was a pure conception, with no proofs to be adduced of its reality. Later it seemed to him that whatever proofs existed really told in favor of their view.

3   Charles Mercier, *The Nervous System and the Mind* (London: Macmillan, 1888), 8.

4   Ibid., 10.

PART II
Anomalous Monism

5

MENTAL EVENTS*

Donald Davidson

Mental events such as perceivings, rememberings, decisions, and actions resist capture in the nomological net of physical theory. How can this fact be reconciled with the causal role of mental events in the physical world? Reconciling freedom with causal determinism is a special case of the problem if we suppose that causal determinism entails capture in, and freedom requires escape from, the nomological net. But the broader issue can remain alive even for someone who believes a correct analysis of free action reveals no conflict with determinism. *Autonomy* (freedom, self-rule) may or may not clash with determinism; *anomaly* (failure to fall under a law) is, it would seem, another matter.

I start from the assumption that both the causal dependence, and the anomalousness, of mental events are undeniable facts. My aim is therefore to explain, in the face of apparent difficulties, how this can be. I am in sympathy with Kant when he says,

> it is as impossible for the subtlest philosophy as for the commonest reasoning to argue freedom away. Philosophy must therefore assume that no true contradiction will be found between freedom and natural necessity in the same human actions, for it cannot give up the idea of nature any more than that of freedom. Hence even if we should never be able to conceive how freedom is possible, at least this apparent contradiction must be convincingly eradicated. For if the thought of freedom contradicts itself or nature ... it would have to be surrendered in competition with natural necessity.[1]

Generalize human actions to mental events, substitute anomaly for freedom, and this is a description of my problem. And of course the connection is closer, since Kant believed freedom entails anomaly.

* Taken from Donald Davidson, *Essays on Actions and Events* (Oxford: Clarendon Press, 1980). Reprinted with kind permission of the author. Originally published in L. Foster and J. Swanson, eds., *Experience and Theory* (Amherst: University of Massachusetts Press, 1970).

Now let me try to formulate a little more carefully the "apparent contradiction" about mental events that I want to discuss and finally dissipate. It may be seen as stemming from three principles.

The first principle asserts that at least some mental events interact causally with physical events. (We could call this the Principle of Causal Interaction.) Thus for example if someone sank the *Bismarck*, then various mental events such as perceivings, notings, calculations, judgements, decisions, intentional actions, and changes of belief played a causal role in the sinking of the *Bismarck*. In particular, I would urge that the fact that someone sank the *Bismarck* entails that he moved his body in a way that was caused by mental events of certain sorts, and that this bodily movement in turn caused the *Bismarck* to sink. Perception illustrates how causality may run from the physical to the mental: if a man perceives that a ship is approaching, then a ship approaching must have caused him to come to believe that a ship is approaching. (Nothing depends on accepting these as examples of causal interaction.)

Though perception and action provide the most obvious cases where mental and physical events interact causally, I think reasons could be given for the view that all mental events ultimately, perhaps through causal relations with other mental events, have causal intercourse with physical events. But if there are mental events that have no physical events as causes or effects, the argument will not touch them.

The second principle is that where there is causality, there must be a law: events related as cause and effect fall under strict deterministic laws. (We may term this the Principle of the Nomological Character of Causality.) This principle, like the first, will be treated here as an assumption, though I shall say something by way of interpretation.[2]

The third principle is that there are no strict deterministic laws on the basis of which mental events can be predicted and explained (the Anomalism of the Mental).

The paradox I wish to discuss arises for someone who is inclined to accept these three assumptions or principles, and who thinks they are inconsistent with one another. The inconsistency is not, of course, formal unless more premises are added. Nevertheless it is natural to reason that the first two principles, that of causal interaction and that of the nomological character of causality, together imply that at least some mental events can be predicted and explained on the basis of laws, while the principle of the anomalism of the mental denies this. Many philosophers have accepted, with or without argument, the view that the three principles do lead to a contradiction. It seems to me, however, that all three principles are true, so that what must be done is to explain away the appearance of contradiction; essentially the Kantian line.

The rest of this paper falls into three parts. The first part describes a version of the identity theory of the mental and the physical that shows how the three principles may be reconciled. The second part argues that there cannot be strict psychophysical laws; this is not quite the principle of the anomalism of the mental, but on reasonable assumptions entails it. The last part tries to show that from the fact that there can be no strict psychophysical laws, and our other two principles, we can infer the truth of a version of the identity theory, that is, a theory that identifies at least some mental events with physical events. It is clear that this "proof" of the identity theory will be at best conditional, since two of its premises are unsupported, and the argument for the third may be found less than conclusive. But even someone unpersuaded of the truth of the premises may be interested to learn how they can be reconciled and that they serve to establish a version of the identity theory of the mental. Finally, if the argument is a good one, it should lay to rest the view, common to many friends and some foes of identity theories, that support for such theories can come only from the discovery of psychophysical laws.

I

The three principles will be shown consistent with one another by describing a view of the mental and the physical that contains no inner contradiction and that entails the three principles. According to this view, mental events are identical with physical events. Events are taken to be unrepeatable, dated individuals such as the particular eruption of a volcano, the (first) birth or death of a person, the playing of the 1968 World Series, or the historic utterance of the words, "You may fire when ready, Gridley." We can easily frame identity statements about individual events; examples (true or false) might be:

The death of Scott = the death of the author of *Waverley*;

The assassination of the Archduke Ferdinand = the event that started the First World War;

The eruption of Vesuvius in A.D. 79 = the cause of the destruction of Pompeii.

The theory under discussion is silent about processes, states, and attributes if these differ from individual events.

What does it mean to say that an event is mental or physical? One natural answer is that an event is physical if it is describable in a purely physical vocabulary, mental if describable in mental terms. But if this is taken to suggest that an event is physical, say, if some physical predicate is true of it, then there is the following difficulty. Assume that the predicate "x took place at Noosa

Heads" belongs to the physical vocabulary; then so also must the predicate "x did not take place at Noosa Heads" belong to the physical vocabulary. But the predicate "x did or did not take place at Noosa Heads" is true of every event, whether mental or physical.[3] We might rule out predicates that are tautologically true of every event, but this will not help since every event is truly describable either by "x took place at Noosa Heads" or by "x did not take place at Noosa Heads." A different approach is needed.[4]

We may call those verbs mental that express propositional attitudes like believing, intending, desiring, hoping, knowing, perceiving, noticing, remembering, and so on. Such verbs are characterized by the fact that they sometimes feature in sentences with subjects that refer to persons, and are completed by embedded sentences in which the usual rules of substitution appear to break down. This criterion is not precise, since I do not want to include these verbs when they occur in contexts that are fully extensional ("He knows Paris," "He perceives the moon" may be cases), nor exclude them whenever they are not followed by embedded sentences. An alternative characterization of the desired class of mental verbs might be that they are psychological verbs as used when they create apparently nonextensional contexts.

Let us call a description of the form "the event that is M" or an open sentence of the form "event x is M" a *mental description* or a *mental open sentence* if and only if the expression that replaces "M" contains at least one mental verb essentially. (Essentially, so as to rule out cases where the description or open sentence is logically equivalent to one not containing mental vocabulary.) Now we may say that an event is mental if and only if it has a mental description, or (the description operator not being primitive) if there is a mental open sentence true of that event alone. Physical events are those picked out by descriptions or open sentences that contain only the physical vocabulary essentially. It is less important to characterize a physical vocabulary because relative to the mental it is, so to speak, recessive in determining whether a description is mental or physical. (There will be some comments presently on the nature of a physical vocabulary, but these comments will fall far short of providing a criterion.)

On the proposed test of the mental, the distinguishing feature of the mental is not that it is private, subjective, or immaterial, but that it exhibits what Brentano called intentionality. Thus intentional actions are clearly included in the realm of the mental along with thoughts, hopes, and regrets (or the events tied to these). What may seem doubtful is whether the criterion will include events that have often been considered paradigmatic of the mental. Is it obvious, for example, that feeling a pain or seeing an after-image will count as mental? Sentences that report such events seem free from taint of nonextensionality, and the same should be true of reports of raw feels, sense data, and other uninterpreted sensations, if there are any.

However, the criterion actually covers not only the havings of pains and after-images, but much more besides. Take some event one would intuitively accept as physical, let's say the collision of two stars in distant space. There must be a purely physical predicate "*Px*" true of this collision, and of others, but true of only this one at the time it occurred. This particular time, though, may be pinpointed as the same time that Jones notices that a pencil starts to roll across his desk. The distant stellar collision is thus the event *x* such that *Px* and *x* is simultaneous with Jones's noticing that a pencil starts to roll across his desk. The collision has now been picked out by a mental description and must be counted as a mental event.

This strategy will probably work to show every event to be mental; we have obviously failed to capture the intuitive concept of the mental. It would be instructive to try to mend this trouble, but it is not necessary for present purposes. We can afford Spinozistic extravagance with the mental since accidental inclusions can only strengthen the hypothesis that all mental events are identical with physical events. What would matter would be failure to include bona fide mental events, but of this there seems to be no danger.

I want to describe, and presently to argue for, a version of the identity theory that denies that there can be strict laws connecting the mental and the physical. The very possibility of such a theory is easily obscured by the way in which identity theories are commonly defended and attacked. Charles Taylor, for example, agrees with protagonists of identity theories that the sole "ground" for accepting such theories is the supposition that correlations or laws can be established linking events described as mental with events described as physical. He says, "It is easy to see why this is so: unless a given mental event is invariably accompanied by a given, say, brain process, there is no ground for even mooting a general identity between the two."[5] Taylor goes on (correctly, I think) to allow that there may be identity without correlating laws, but my present interest is in noticing the invitation to confusion in the statement just quoted. What can "a given mental event" mean here? Not a particular, dated, event, for it would not make sense to speak of an individual event being "invariably accompanied" by another. Taylor is evidently thinking of events of a given *kind*. But if the only identities are of kinds of events, the identity theory presupposes correlating laws.

One finds the same tendency to build laws into the statements of the identity theory in these typical remarks:

When I say that a sensation is a brain process or that lightning is an electrical discharge, I am using "is" in the sense of strict identity ... there are not two things: a flash of lightning and an electrical discharge. There is one thing, a flash of lightning, which is described scientifically as an electrical discharge to the earth from a cloud of ionized water molecules.[6]

The last sentence of this quotation is perhaps to be understood as saying that for every lightning flash there exists an electrical discharge to the earth from a cloud of ionized water molecules with which it is identical. Here we have an honest ontology of individual events and can make literal sense of identity. We can also see how there could be identities without correlating laws. It is possible, however, to have an ontology of events with the conditions of individuation specified in such a way that any identity implies a correlating law. Kim, for example, suggests that *Fa* and *Gb* "describe or refer to the same event" if and only if $a = b$ and the property of being $F =$ the property of being G. The identity of the properties in turn entails that (x) $(Fx \leftrightarrow Gx)$.[7] No wonder Kim says:

> If pain is identical with brain state *B*, there must be a concomitance between occurrences of pain and occurrences of brain state *B*.... Thus, a necessary condition of the pain-brain state *B* identity is that the two expressions "being in pain" and "being in brain state *B*" have the same extension.... There is no conceivable observation that would confirm or refute the identity but not the associated correlation.[8]

It may make the situation clearer to give a fourfold classification of theories of the relation between mental and physical events that emphasizes the independence of claims about laws and claims of identity. On the one hand there are those who assert, and those who deny, the existence of psychophysical laws; on the other hand there are those who say mental events are identical with physical and those who deny this. Theories are thus divided into four sorts: *nomological monism*, which affirms that there are correlating laws and that the events correlated are one (materialists belong in this category); *nomological dualism*, which comprises various forms of parallelism, interactionism, and epiphenomenalism; *anomalous dualism*, which combines ontological dualism with the general failure of laws correlating the mental and the physical (Cartesianism). And finally there is *anomalous monism*, which classifies the position I wish to occupy.[9]

Anomalous monism resembles materialism in its claim that all events are physical, but rejects the thesis, usually considered essential to materialism, that mental phenomena can be given purely physical explanations. Anomalous monism shows an ontological bias only in that it allows the possibility that not all events are mental, while insisting that all events are physical. Such a bland monism, unbuttressed by correlating laws or conceptual economies, does not seem to merit the term "reductionism"; in any case it is not apt to inspire the nothing-but reflex ("Conceiving the *Art of the Fugue* was nothing but a complex neural event," and so forth).

Although the position I describe denies there are psychophysical laws, it is consistent with the view that mental characteristics are in some sense dependent, or supervenient, on physical characteristics. Such supervenience might be taken to mean that there cannot be two events alike in all physical respects but differing in some mental respect, or that an object cannot alter in some mental respect without altering in some physical respect. Dependence or supervenience of this kind does not entail reducibility through law or definition: if it did, we could reduce moral properties to descriptive, and this there is good reason to *believe* cannot be done; and we might be able to reduce truth in a formal system to syntactical properties, and this we *know* cannot in general be done.

This last example is a useful analogy with the sort of lawless monism under consideration. Think of the physical vocabulary as the entire vocabulary of some language L with resources adequate to express a certain amount of mathematics, and its own syntax. L' is L augmented with the truth predicate "true-in-L," which is "mental." In L (and hence L') it is possible to pick out, with a definite description or open sentence, each sentence in the extension of the truth predicate, but if L is consistent there exists no predicate of syntax (of the "physical" vocabulary), no matter how complex, that applies to all and only the true sentences of L. There can be no "psychophysical law" in the form of a biconditional, "(x) (x is true-in-L if and only if x is ϕ)" where "ϕ" is replaced by a "physical" predicate (a predicate of L). Similarly, we can pick out each mental event using the physical vocabulary alone, but no purely physical predicate, no matter how complex, has, as a matter of law, the same extension as a mental predicate.

It should now be evident how anomalous monism reconciles the three original principles. Causality and identity are relations between individual events no matter how described. But laws are linguistic; and so events can instantiate laws, and hence be explained or predicted in the light of laws, only as those events are described in one or another way. The principle of causal interaction deals with events in extension and is therefore blind to the mental-physical dichotomy. The principle of the anomalism of the mental concerns events described as mental, for events are mental only as described. The principle of the nomological character of causality must be read carefully: it says that when events are related as cause and effect, they have descriptions that instantiate a law. It does not say that every true singular statement of causality instantiates a law.[10]

II

The analogy just bruited, between the place of the mental amid the physical, and the place of the semantical in a world of syntax, should not be strained. Tarski proved that a consistent language cannot (under some natural assumptions) contain an open sentence "Fx" true of all and only the true sentences of that language. If our analogy were pressed, then we would expect a proof that there can be no physical open sentence "*Px*" true of all and only the events having some mental property. In fact, however, nothing I can say about the irreducibility of the mental deserves to be called a proof; and the kind of irreducibility is different. For if anomalous monism is correct, not only can every mental event be uniquely singled out using only physical concepts, but since the number of events that falls under each mental predicate may, for all we know, be finite, there may well exist a physical open sentence coextensive with each mental predicate, though to construct it might involve the tedium of a lengthy and uninstructive alternation. Indeed, even if finitude is not assumed, there seems no compelling reason to deny that there could be coextensive predicates, one mental and one physical.

The thesis is rather that the mental is nomologically irreducible: there may be *true* general statements relating the mental and the physical, statements that have the logical form of a law; but they are not *lawlike* (in a strong sense to be described). If by an absurdly remote chance we were to stumble on a nonstochastic true psychophysical generalization, we would have no reason to believe it more than roughly true.

Do we, by declaring that there are no (strict) psychophysical laws, poach on the empirical preserves of science—a form of *hubris* against which philosophers are often warned? Of course, to judge a statement lawlike or illegal is not to decide its truth outright; relative to the acceptance of a general statement on the basis of instances, ruling it lawlike must be a priori. But such relative apriorism does not in itself justify philosophy, for in general the grounds for deciding to trust a statement on the basis of its instances will in turn be governed by theoretical and empirical concerns not to be distinguished from those of science. If the case of supposed laws linking the mental and the physical is different, it can only be because to allow the possibility of such laws would amount to changing the subject. By changing the subject I mean here: deciding not to accept the criterion of the mental in terms of the vocabulary of the propositional attitudes. This short answer cannot prevent further ramifications of the problem, however, for there is no clear line between changing the subject and changing what one says on an old subject, which is to admit, in the present context at least, that there is no clear line between philosophy and science. Where there are no fixed boundaries only the timid never risk trespass.

It will sharpen our appreciation of the anomological character of mental-physical generalizations to consider a related matter, the failure of definitional behaviourism. Why are we willing (as I assume we are) to abandon the attempt to give explicit definitions of mental concepts in terms of behavioural ones? Not, surely, just because all actual tries are conspicuously inadequate. Rather it is because we are persuaded, as we are in the case of so many other forms of definitional reductionism (naturalism in ethics, instrumentalism and operationalism in the sciences, the causal theory of meaning, phenomenalism, and so on—the catalogue of philosophy's defeats), that there is system in the failures. Suppose we try to say, not using any mental concepts, what it is for a man to believe there is life on Mars. One line we could take is this: when a certain sound is produced in the man's presence ("Is there life on Mars?") he produces another ("Yes"). But of course this shows he believes there is life on Mars only if he understands English, his production of the sound was intentional, and was a response to the sounds as meaning something in English; and so on. For each discovered deficiency, we add a new proviso. Yet no matter how we patch and fit the non-mental conditions, we always find the need for an additional condition (provided he *notices, understands,* etc.) that is mental in character.[11]

A striking feature of attempts at definitional reduction is how little seems to hinge on the question of synonymy between definiens and definiendum. Of course, by imagining counterexamples we do discredit claims of synonymy. But the pattern of failure prompts a stronger conclusion: if we were to find an open sentence couched in behavioural terms and exactly coextensive with some mental predicate, nothing could reasonably persuade us that we had found it. We know too much about thought and behaviour to trust exact and universal statements linking them. Beliefs and desires issue in behaviour only as modified and mediated by further beliefs and desires, attitudes and attendings, without limit. Clearly this holism of the mental realm is a clue both to the autonomy and to the anomalous character of the mental.

These remarks apropos definitional behaviourism provide at best hints of why we should not expect nomological connections between the mental and the physical. The central case invites further consideration.

Lawlike statements are general statements that support counterfactual and subjunctive claims, and are supported by their instances. There is (in my view) no non-question-begging criterion of the lawlike, which is not to say there are no reasons in particular cases for a judgement. Lawlikeness is a matter of degree, which is not to deny that there may be cases beyond debate. And within limits set by the conditions of communication, there is room for much variation between individuals in the pattern of statements to which various degrees of nomologicality are assigned. In all these respects nomologicality is much like analyticity, as one might expect since both are linked to meaning.

"All emeralds are green" is lawlike in that its instances confirm it, but "all emeralds are grue" is not, for "grue" means "observed before time t and green, otherwise blue," and if our observations were all made before t and uniformly revealed green emeralds, this would not be a reason to expect other emeralds to be blue. Nelson Goodman has suggested that this shows that some predicates, "grue" for example, are unsuited to laws (and thus a criterion of suitable predicates could lead to a criterion of the lawlike). But it seems to me the anomalous character of "All emeralds are grue" shows only that the predicates "is an emerald" and "is grue" are not suited to one another: grueness is not an inductive property of emeralds. Grueness *is* however an inductive property of entities of other sorts, for instance of emerires. (Something is an emerire if it is examined before *t* and is an emerald, and otherwise is a sapphire.) Not only is "All emerires are grue" entailed by the conjunction of lawlike statements "All emeralds are green" and "All sapphires are blue," but there is no reason, as far as I can see, to reject the deliverance of intuition, that it is itself lawlike.[12] Nomological statements bring together predicates that we know a priori are made for each other—know, that is, independently of knowing whether the evidence supports a connection between them. "Blue," "red," and green" are made for emeralds, sapphires, and roses; "grue," "bleen," and "gred" are made for sapphalds, emerires, and emeroses.

The direction in which the discussion seems headed is this: mental and physical predicates are not made for one another. In point of lawlikeness, psychophysical statements are more like "All emeralds are grue" than like "All emeralds are green."

Before this claim is plausible, it must be seriously modified. The fact that emeralds examined before *t* are grue not only is no reason to believe all emeralds are grue; it is not even a reason (if we know the time) to believe *any* unobserved emeralds are grue. But if an event of a certain mental sort has usually been accompanied by an event of a certain physical sort, this often is a good reason to expect other cases to follow suit roughly in proportion. The generalizations that embody such practical wisdom are assumed to be only roughly true, or they are explicitly stated in probabilistic terms, or they are insulated from counterexample by generous escape clauses. Their importance lies mainly in the support they lend singular causal claims and related explanations of particular events. The support derives from the fact that such a generalization, however crude and vague, may provide good reason to believe that underlying the particular case there is a regularity that could be formulated sharply and without caveat.

In our daily traffic with events and actions that must be foreseen or understood, we perforce make use of the sketchy summary generalization, for we do not know a more accurate law, or if we do, we lack a description of the particular events in which we are interested that would show the relevance of the law. But there is an important distinction to be made within the category of the rude rule of thumb. On the one hand, there are generalizations whose positive instances give us reason to believe the generalization itself could be improved by adding further provisos and conditions stated in the same general vocabulary as the original generalization. Such a generalization points to the form and vocabulary of the finished law: we may say that it is a *homonomic* generalization. On the other hand there are generalizations which when instantiated may give us reason to believe there is a precise law at work, but one that can be stated only by shifting to a different vocabulary. We may call such generalizations *heteronomic*.

I suppose most of our practical lore (and science) is heteronomic. This is because a law can hope to be precise, explicit, and as exceptionless as possible only if it draws its concepts from a comprehensive closed theory. This ideal theory may or may not be deterministic, but it is if any true theory is. Within the physical sciences we do find homonomic generalizations, generalizations such that if the evidence supports them, we then have reason to believe they may be sharpened indefinitely by drawing upon further physical concepts: there is a theoretical asymptote of perfect coherence with all the evidence, perfect predictability (under the terms of the system), total explanation (again under the terms of the system). Or perhaps the ultimate theory is probabilistic, and the asymptote is less than perfection; but in that case there will be no better to be had.

Confidence that a statement is homonomic, correctible within its own conceptual domain, demands that it draw its concepts from a theory with strong constitutive elements. Here is the simplest possible illustration; if the lesson carries, it will be obvious that the simplification could be mended.

The measurement of length, weight, temperature, or time depends (among many other things, of course) on the existence in each case of a two-place relation that is transitive and asymmetric: warmer than, later than, heavier than, and so forth. Let us take the relation *longer than* as our example. The law or postulate of transitivity is this:

(L) $L(x,y)$ and $L(y,z) \rightarrow L(x,z)$

Unless this law (or some sophisticated variant) holds, we cannot easily make sense of the concept of length. There will be no way of assigning numbers to register even so much as ranking in length, let alone the more powerful demands of measurement on a ratio scale. And this remark goes not only for any three items directly involved in an intransitivity: it is easy to show (given a few more assumptions essential to measurement of length) that there is no consistent assignment of a ranking to any item unless (L) holds in full generality.

Clearly (L) alone cannot exhaust the import of "longer than"—otherwise it would not differ from "warmer than" or "later than." We must suppose there is some empirical content, however difficult to formulate in the available vocabulary, that distinguishes "longer than" from the other two-place transitive predicates of measurement and on the basis of which we may assert that one thing is longer than another. Imagine this empirical content to be partly given by the predicate "$O(x,y)$." So we have this "meaning postulate":

(M) $O(x,y) \rightarrow L(x,y)$

that partly interprets (L). But now (L) and (M) together yield an empirical theory of great strength, for together they entail that there do not exist three objects a, b, and c such that $O(a,b)$, $O(b,c)$, and $O(c,a)$. Yet what is to prevent this happening if "$O(x,y)$" is a predicate we can ever, with confidence, apply? Suppose we *think* we observe an intransitive triad; what do we say? We could count (L) false, but then we would have no application for the concept of length. We could say (M) gives a wrong test for length; but then it is unclear what we thought was the *content* of the idea of one thing being longer than another. Or we could say that the objects under observation are not, as the theory requires, *rigid* objects. It is a mistake to think we are forced to accept some one of these answers. Concepts such as that of length are sustained in equilibrium by a number of conceptual pressures, and theories of fundamental measurement are distorted if we force the decision, among such principles as (L) and (M): analytic or synthetic. It is better to say the whole set of axioms, laws, or postulates for the measurement of length is partly constitutive of the idea of a system of macroscopic, rigid, physical objects. I suggest that the existence of lawlike statements in physical science depends upon the existence of constitutive (or synthetic a priori) laws like those of the measurement of length within the same conceptual domain.

Just as we cannot intelligibly assign a length to any object unless a comprehensive theory holds of objects of that sort, we cannot intelligibly attribute any propositional attitude to an agent except within the framework of a viable theory of his beliefs, desires, intentions, and decisions.

There is no assigning beliefs to a person one by one on the basis of his verbal behaviour, his choices, or other local signs no matter how plain and evident, for we make sense of particular beliefs only as they cohere with other beliefs, with preferences, with intentions, hopes, fears, expectations, and the rest. It is not merely, as with the measurement of length, that each case tests a theory and depends upon it, but that the content of a propositional attitude derives from its place in the pattern.

Crediting people with a large degree of consistency cannot be counted mere charity: it is unavoidable if we are to be in a position to accuse them meaningfully of error and some degree of irrationality. Global confusion, like universal mistake, is unthinkable, not because imagination boggles, but because too much confusion leaves nothing to be confused about and massive error erodes the background of true belief against which alone failure can be construed. To appreciate the limits to the kind and amount of blunder and bad thinking we can intelligibly pin on others is to see once more the inseparability of the question what concepts a person commands and the question what he does with those concepts in the way of belief, desire, and intention. To the extent that we fail to discover a coherent and plausible pattern in the attitudes and actions of others we simply forego the chance of treating them as persons.

The problem is not bypassed but given centre stage by appeal to explicit speech behaviour. For we could not begin to decode a man's sayings if we could not make out his attitudes towards his sentences, such as holding, wishing, or wanting them to be true. Beginning from these attitudes, we must work out a theory of what he means, thus simultaneously giving content to his attitudes and to his words. In our need to make him make sense, we will try for a theory that finds him consistent, a believer of truths, and a lover of the good (all by our own lights, it goes without saying). Life being what it is, there will be no simple theory that fully meets these demands. Many theories will effect a more or less acceptable compromise, and between these theories there may be no objective grounds for choice.

The heteronomic character of general statements linking the mental and the physical traces back to this central role of translation in the description of all propositional attitudes, and to the indeterminacy of translation.[13] There are no strict psychophysical laws because of the disparate commitments of the mental and physical schemes. It is a feature of physical reality that physical change can be explained by laws that connect it with other changes and conditions physically described. It is a feature of the mental that the attribution of mental phenomena must be responsible to the background of reasons, beliefs, and intentions of the individual. There cannot be tight connections between the realms if each is to retain allegiance to its proper source of evidence. The nomological irreducibility of the mental does not derive merely from the seamless nature of the world of thought, preference, and intention, for such interdependence is common to physical theory, and is compatible with there being a single right way of interpreting a man's attitudes without relativization to a scheme of translation. Nor is the irreducibility due simply to the possibility of many equally eligible schemes, for this is compatible with an arbitrary choice of one scheme relative to which assignments of mental traits are made. The point is rather that when we use the concepts of belief, desire, and the rest, we must stand prepared as the evidence accumulates, to adjust our theory in the light of considerations of overall cogency: the constitutive ideal of rationality partly controls each phase in the evolution of what must be an evolving theory. An arbitrary choice of translation scheme would preclude such opportunistic tempering of theory; put differently, a right arbitrary choice of a translation manual would be of a manual acceptable in the light of all possible evidence, and this is a choice we cannot make. We must conclude, I think, that nomological slack between the mental and the physical is essential as long as we conceive of man as a rational animal.

III

The gist of the foregoing discussion, as well as its conclusion, will be familiar. That there is a categorial difference between the mental and the physical is a commonplace. It may seem odd that I say nothing of the supposed privacy of the mental, or the special authority an agent has with respect to his own propositional attitudes, but this appearance of novelty would fade if we were to investigate in more detail the grounds for accepting a scheme of translation. The step from the categorial difference between the mental and the physical to the impossibility of strict laws relating them is less common, but certainly not new. If there is a surprise, then, it will be to find the lawlessness of the mental serving to help establish the identity of the mental with that paradigm of the lawlike, the physical.

The reasoning is this. We are assuming, under the Principle of the Causal Dependence of the Mental, that some mental events at least are causes or effects of physical events; the argument applies only to these. A second Principle (of the Nomological Character of Causality) says that each true singular causal statement is backed by a strict law connecting events of kinds to which events mentioned as cause and effect belong. Where there are rough, but homonomic, laws, there are laws drawing on concepts from the same conceptual domain and upon which there is no improving in point of precision and comprehensiveness. We urged in the last section that such laws occur in the physical sciences. Physical theory promises to provide a comprehensive closed system guaranteed to yield a standardized, unique description of every physical event couched in a vocabulary amenable to law.

It is not plausible that mental concepts alone can provide such a framework, simply because the mental does not, by our first principle, constitute a closed system. Too much happens to affect the mental that is not itself a systematic part of the mental. But if we combine this observation with the conclusion that no psychophysical statement is, or can be built into, a strict law, we have the Principle of the Anomalism of the Mental: there are no strict laws at all on the basis of which we can predict and explain mental phenomena.

The demonstration of identity follows easily. Suppose m, a mental event, caused p, a physical event; then, under some description m and p instantiate a strict law. This law can only be physical, according to the previous paragraph. But if m falls under a physical law, it has a physical description; which is to say it is a physical event. An analogous argument works when a physical event causes a mental event. So every mental event that is causally related to a physical event is a physical event. In order to establish anomalous monism in full generality it would be sufficient to show that every mental event is cause or effect of some physical event; I shall not attempt this.

If one event causes another, there is a strict law which those events instantiate when properly described. But it is possible (and typical) to know of the singular causal relation without knowing the law or the relevant descriptions. Knowledge requires reasons, but these are available in the form of rough heteronomic generalizations, which are lawlike in that instances make it reasonable to expect other instances to follow suit without being lawlike in the sense of being indefinitely refinable. Applying these facts to knowledge of identities, we see that it is possible to know that a mental event is identical with some physical event without knowing which one (in the sense of being able to give it a unique physical description that brings it under a relevant law). Even if someone knew the entire physical history of the world, and every mental event were identical with a physical, it would not follow that he could predict or explain a single mental event (so described, of course).

Two features of mental events in their relation to the physical—causal dependence and nomological independence—combine, then, to dissolve what has often seemed a paradox, the efficacy of thought and purpose in the material world, and their freedom from law. When we portray events as perceivings, rememberings, decisions and actions, we necessarily locate them amid physical happenings through the relation of cause and effect; but as long as we do not change the idiom that same mode of portrayal insulates mental events from the strict laws that can in principle be called upon to explain and predict physical phenomena.

Mental events as a class cannot be explained by physical science; particular mental events can when we know particular identities. But the explanations of mental events in which we are typically interested relate them to other mental events and conditions. We explain a man's free actions, for example, by appeal to his desires, habits, knowledge and perceptions. Such accounts of intentional behaviour operate in a conceptual framework removed from the direct reach of physical law by describing both cause and effect, reason and action, as aspects of a portrait of a human agent. The anomalism of the mental is thus a necessary condition for viewing action as autonomous. I conclude with a second passage from Kant:

> It is an indispensable problem of speculative philosophy to show that its illusion respecting the contradiction rests on this, that we think of man in a different sense and relation when we call him free, and when we regard him as subject to the laws of nature.... It must therefore show that not only can both of these very well co-exist, but that both must be thought as necessarily united in the same subject....[14]

Notes

1 *Fundamental Principles of the Metaphysics of Morals*, 75-76.
2 ... The stipulation that the laws be deterministic is stronger than required by the reasoning, and will be relaxed.
3 The point depends on assuming that mental events may intelligibly be said to have a location; but it is an assumption that must be true if an identity theory is, and here I am not trying to prove the theory but to formulate it.
4 I am indebted to Lee Bowie for emphasizing this difficulty.

5   Charles Taylor, "Mind-Body Identity, a Side Issue?" *Philosophical Review* 76 (1967), 202.

6   J.J.C. Smart, "Sensations and Brain Processes," *Philosophical Review* 68 (1959), 141-56. The quoted passages are on pages 163-65 of the reprinted version in V.C. Chappell, ed., *The Philosophy of Mind* (Englewood Cliffs, NJ: Prentice Hall, 1962). For another example, see David K. Lewis, "An Argument for the Identity Theory," *Journal of Philosophy* 63 (1966), 17-25. Here the assumption is made explicit when Lewis takes events as universals (p. 17, footnotes 1 and 2). I do not suggest that Smart and Lewis are confused, only that their way of stating the identity theory tends to obscure the distinction between particular events and kinds of events on which the formulation of my theory depends.

7   Jaegwon Kim, "On the Psycho-Physical Identity Theory," *American Philosophical Quarterly* 3 (1966), 231.

8   Ibid., 227. S. Richard Brandt and Jaegwon Kim propose roughly the same criterion in "The Logic of the Identity Theory," *Journal of Philosophy* 64 (1967), 515-37. They remark that on their conception of event identity, the identity theory "makes a stronger claim than merely that there is a pervasive phenomenal-physical correlation," 518. I do not discuss the stronger claim.

9   Anomalous monism is more or less explicitly recognized as a possible position by Herbert Feigl, "The 'Mental' and the 'Physical,'" in H. Feigl, M. Scriven, and G. Maxwell, eds., *Minnesota Studies in the Philosophy of Science* 2 (Minneapolis: University of Minnesota Press, 1958), 370-497; Sydney Shoemaker, "Ziff's Other Minds," *Journal of Philosophy* 62 (1965), 587-89; David Randall Luce, "Mind-Body Identity and Psycho-Physical Correlation," *Philosophical Studies* 17 (1966), 1-7; Taylor, op. cit., 207. Something like my position is tentatively accepted by Thomas Nagel, "Physicalism," *Philosophical Review* 74 (1965), 339-56, and endorsed by P.F. Strawson, "Contribution to a Symposium on 'Determinism,'" in D.F. Pears, ed., *Freedom and the Will* (London: St. Martin's Press, 1963), 63-67.

10 The point that substitutivity of identity fails in the context of explanation is made in connection with the present subject by Norman Malcolm, "Scientific Materialism and the Identity Theory," *Dialogue* 3 (1964-5), 123-24.

11 The theme is developed in Roderick Chisholm, *Perceiving* (Ithaca, NY: Cornell University Press, 1957), Ch. 2.

12 The view is accepted by Richard C. Jeffrey, "Goodman's Query," *Journal of Philosophy* 63 (1966), 281-88; John R. Wallace, "Goodman, Logic, Induction," *Journal of Philosophy* 62 (1966), 310-28; and John M. Vickers, "Characteristics of Projectible Predicates," *Journal of Philosophy* 64 (1967), 280-85. Goodman, in "Comments," *Journal of Philosophy* 63 (1966), 328-31, disputes the lawlikeness of statements like "All emerires are grue." I cannot see, however, that he meets the point of my "Emeroses by Other Names," in Davidson, *Essays on Actions and Events* (Oxford: Clarendon Press, 1980), 225-27.

13 The influence of W.V. Quine's doctrine of the indeterminacy of translation, as in Ch. 2 of *Word and Object* (Cambridge, MA: MIT Press, 1960) is, I hope, obvi-

ous. In sect. 45, Quine develops the connection between translation and the propositional attitudes, and remarks that "Brentano's thesis of the irreducibility of intentional idioms is of a piece with the thesis of indeterminacy of translation," 221.

14   Op. cit., 76.

6

ACTIONS, REASONS, AND HUMEAN CAUSES[*]

Peter H. Hess

In this paper I shall dispel an illusion. Numbered amongst the victims of this illusion are many of those who subscribe to the time-honoured view according to which the causes of an action include, among other things, the agent's beliefs together with his desires, wants, intentions, etc. The reason why they labour under an illusion is because they think that they can find support for their position in the writings of Donald Davidson. I shall show not only that Davidson's views, as expressed in two of his articles, do not corroborate their position, but that his remarks, once they are carefully analysed, turn out to be so jejune as to be acceptable even to those who think that the traditional thesis ought to be completely abandoned.

The first of the two Davidson articles that I wish to consider[1] consists of an attempt to argue in favour of the following two claims:

> C1:R is a primary reason why an agent performed the action A under description d only if R consists of a pro attitude[2] of the agent toward actions with a certain property, and a belief of the agent that A, under the description d, has that property.[3]
> C2:A primary reason for an action is its cause.[4]

Since I do not have any quarrel with C1, I straightaway turn to consider C2. In his attempt to set the scene for his defence of C2, Davidson offers the following considerations: Since people frequently perform actions which they have a reason to perform even though that reason is not why they acted in that way, we need a scheme that gives "an account of the 'mysterious connection' between reasons and actions" and which applies in those cases where an agent acts because of his reasons.[5] C2 alone provides us with such a scheme and allows us "to turn the first 'and' to 'because' in 'He exercised and he wanted to reduce and thought exercise would do it.'"[6] I shall show that C2, if properly interpreted, proves unable to carry the burden Davidson shoulders it with. It, consequently, cannot be the only scheme that explains the "mysterious connection" between reasons and actions.

---

[*] Peter Hess, "Actions, Reasons, and Humean Causes," *Analysis* 40 (1981), 77-81. Reprinted with kind permission of the author.

We discover how weak C2 really is when we turn to Davidson's discussion of the Humean notion of causation.[7] Davidson agrees with Hume's contention that every true causal claim entails a corresponding true causal law. Yet he also admits that there aren't laws connecting primary reasons with actions. In order to show that these views are not incompatible with C2, he argues that Hume's claim is ambiguous:

> It may be that "A caused B" entails some particular law involving the predicates used in the descriptions "A" and "B" or it might mean that, "A caused B" entails that there exists a causal law instantiated by some true descriptions of A and B.[8]

Davidson opts in favour of the second of these two interpretations. "Only the second version of Hume's doctrine," he says, "can be made to fit with most causal explanations; it suits rationalizations [i.e., explanations referring to primary reasons] equally well."[9] He illustrates the error involved in the assumption that "singular causal statements necessarily indicate, by the concepts they employ, the concepts that will occur in the entailed law"[10] with the following example:

> Suppose a hurricane, which is reported on page 5 of Tuesday's *Times*, causes a catastrophe, which is reported on page 13 of Wednesday's *Tribune*. Then the event reported on page 5 of Tuesday's *Times* caused the event reported on page 13 of Wednesday's *Tribune*.[11]

It would clearly be erroneous here to look for a law connecting events of this kind. Hence Davidson concludes that "The laws whose existence is required if reasons are causes of actions do not, we may be sure, deal in the concepts in which rationalizations must deal."[12] He suggests that these laws may even be formulated in terms of classifications that are neurological, chemical, or physical.[13]

Before we examine how the matters just discussed affect the meaning of C2, let us look in some more detail at Davidson's example. We can agree, I suppose, that the event reported in the *Times*, apart from having the property of having been reported in that newspaper, also had certain other features the presence of which enabled it to cause a catastrophe. I am sure we can also agree that the hurricane would have caused a catastrophe, even if it had not been reported in the *Times*. The reason for this is two-fold: First, there have been and will be lots of hurricanes like the one described in the *Times* which have caused and will cause catastrophes like the one reported in the *Tribune*, even though neither they nor their consequences have been or will be described in either paper. Thus not every pair of the properties of the events in question can be incorporated into a true generalization. Furthermore, even if this could be done, not all of the resulting true generalizations would be law-like, i.e., not all of them would support counterfactual and sub-junctive statements. In fact, the properties "being reported in the *Times*" and "being reported in the *Tribune*" seem to figure in no law-like generalization under which the two events (i.e., the hurricane and the catastrophe) can be subsumed. And this shows that the presence or absence of these properties in no way affects the causal efficacy of the events whose properties they are. If we keep this in mind we will not be misled by such claims as "The event reported in the *Times* causes a catastrophe." We will not assume that one can diminish the havoc-wreaking potential of a hurricane by keeping quiet about it.

What, then, does all of this tell us about C2? It tells us that we ought to deal with the claim "Primary reasons are the causes of actions" with as much per-spicuity as we previously employed in dealing with the claim "Subject matter of *Times* report causes catastrophe." Davidson clearly intends C2 to assert that actions have causes and that these causes include the presence of primary rea-sons. His remarks, furthermore, suggest that he considers C2 to be perfectly compatible with the claim that the causal efficacy of whatever causes an action is in no way affected by the presence or absence of primary reasons.

Advocates of what Davidson calls "the ancient—and common-sense—posi-tion that rationalization is a species of ordinary causal explanation"[14] should not derive any comfort from what he offers them in the form of C2. They will agree that actions have causes (but, pace Melden,[15] so does just about every-one else) and they will not object to the claim that these causes include the presence of primary reasons. But they certainly will not accept the view that the causal efficacy of what causes an action is in no way affected by the pres-ence or absence of primary reasons. In view of this they will not even be able to claim that C2 gives at least an acceptable account of the "mysterious con-nection" between reasons and actions, for C2 does not. It merely reduces pri-mary reasons to the status of epiphenomena. This being the case, it is time for the denouement of the illusion that Davidson speaks on behalf of the tra-ditional view.

Lest it be thought that this way of interpreting C2 depends too heavily on the use it made of one particular illustration, I shall now show that it is com-patible with what Davidson says in another article,[16] in which he also discuss-es the causal efficacy of mental events. I shall also try to explain more clearly what I meant when I argued in the above that in Davidson's scheme of things primary reasons are reduced to the status of epiphenomena. In that second article Davidson endeavours to show that the following three principles are not inconsistent with one another:

(1) The Principle of Causal Interaction, according to which "at least some mental events interact causally with physical events."[17]

(2) The Principle of the Nomological Character of Causality, according to which "events related as cause and effect fall under strict deterministic laws."[18]

(3) The Principle of the Anomalism of the Mental, according to which "there are no strict deterministic laws on the basis of which mental events can be predicted and explained."[19]

The reason why Davidson thinks that each one of these principles is true, and thus the reason *why* he does not think that their conjunction will lead to a contradiction, is that he advocates a version of the Psycho-Physical Identity Theory which he dubs "Anomalous Monism." This theory asserts (1) that every mental event is identical with some physical event and (2) that there are no correlating laws which relate the mental to the physical. The reason why, according to Davidson, there are no such laws is that even though there may be true general statements linking the mental with the physical, none of these statements will be law-like.

I will now show that by accepting anomalous monism one reduces primary reasons (or, more precisely the mental properties an event has by virtue of the fact that it involves the presence of a primary reason) to the status of epiphenomena.

I begin with the following account of what I mean by "epiphenomenal":

A property P is epiphenomenal with respect to the relationship between an event C and its effect E iff
   (i) P is a property of C;
   (ii) It is not the case that C would not have caused E had it not had property P.[20]

If the theory of anomalous monism is true, then every mental property is epiphenomenal with respect to every mental event and its physical consequences. If there were even one mental property that is not epiphenomenal in that sense, then there would be at least one psychophysical law. But, according to Davidson, there aren't any such laws. Thus it follows that mental events possess the same causal potency that newsworthy events (such as hurricanes that have been described in the press) possess. Just as the latter do not lead to catastrophes because they have been reported in the press, so the former do not cause physical events because they have mental properties. Neither, of course, do they cause physical events because they involve the presence of primary reasons. All of this may, in fact, be true. The arguments that Davidson marshals in support of the three principles that were previously mentioned strongly suggest that it is true. But it is hardly a state of affairs that will comfort those who subscribe to the traditional view, according to which mental events cause physical events. The traditional view, surely, includes the assumption that there are at least some mental properties which are not epiphenomenal with respect to some mental events and their physical consequences.

This completes my argument. Let me make the following, concluding remarks:

I have endeavoured to explain why advocates of the traditional view concerning the causal efficacy of reasons should not turn to Davidson for support. I leave it to others to decide how important it was to make that point. But there is another issue which my paper, at least implicitly, deals with and which is of more far-reaching significance. Davidson's theory of Anomalous Monism attempts to show that the traditional view concerning the causal efficacy of primary reasons is compatible with the thesis which states that there are no strict psychophysical laws. Davidson's arguments in favour of the claim that the mental is nomologically irreducible are, as I said, most impressive. If, in view of this, one still wants to claim that reasons are causes, one must alter the traditional view so as to allow for the epiphenomenal character of the mental. To do this, and this has been the thesis of my paper, is to abandon the traditional view.

Notes

1 Donald Davidson, "Actions, Reasons, and Causes," *The Journal of Philosophy* LX (1963), 685-700.

2 Pro attitudes, according to Davidson, include "desires, wantings, urges, promptings, and a great variety of moral views, aesthetic principles, economic prejudices, social conventions, and public and private goals and values in so far as these can be interpreted as attitudes of an agent towards actions of a certain kind." Ibid., 686.

3 Ibid., 687.

4 Ibid., 693.

5 Ibid.

6 Ibid.

7 Part of his reply to objection C; Ibid., 696-99.

8 Ibid., 698.

9 Ibid.

10 Ibid.

11 Ibid.

12 Ibid., 699.

13 Ibid.

14 Ibid., 685.

15 A.I. Melden, *Free Action* (New York: Routledge and Kegan Paul, 1961).

16 Donald Davidson, "Mental Events," in L. Forster & J.W. Swanson, eds., *Experience and Theory* (New Haven, CT: Duckworth, 1971), essay 5 in this volume.

17 Ibid., 80, this volume, 86.

18 Ibid., 81, this volume, 86.

19 Ibid.

20 It is important to distinguish between this condition and one which states that "It is not the case that E would not have happened, had P not been a property of C." To see the difference, consider an action E (e.g., "John turns on a light-switch") and an event C the occurrence of which was causally sufficient for the occurrence of E and which, furthermore, included the presence of a *belief* P (e.g., "John believed that he could illuminate the room by turning on the light-switch"). An anomalous monist could not remain true to his belief that there are no law-like connections between the mental and the physical and, at the same time, claim that if C had not included the belief in question, C would not have caused E. He may, however, still be able to assert that if the agent had not entertained the belief which he did entertain, he would not have acted as he did. After all, there may be subjunctive and counterfactual conditionals which are true and contingent (i.e., unlike "Had the number of John's children been even, he would not have had three children") and which, nevertheless, are not subject to a causal interpretation.

7

HESS ON REASONS AND CAUSES[*]

Peter Smith

One of the many insights of Davidson's classic paper "Actions, Reasons, and Causes" was this: a singular causal truth and the corresponding law which backs it need not trade in the same family of concepts. Thus, to borrow a well-worn example, suppose, that the event reported on page 5 of the *Times* (namely Monday's hurricane) caused the event reported on page 13 of the *Tribune* (namely Tuesday's bridge collapse). It would obviously be insane to suppose that the truth of the singular causal claim needs to be warranted by a back-up law couched in terms of "page 5 reports" and so on; the property of being reported on page 5 is evidently not causally salient. And, as Davidson remarks, it would be scarcely less ridiculous to suppose that there are supporting laws which speak of "hurricanes" and such things as "bridge-failures." Of course, the property of being a hurricane is causally salient in a way that the property of being reported is not, for an event counts as a hurricane in virtue of its other, law-engaging, physical properties: but still, it is these other properties (pressure gradients and the like) which will no doubt be mentioned in a causal law backing up a singular causal claim about a given hurricane— the concept of a hurricane itself is too coarse to feature in the grounding laws. So, to repeat, a singular causal truth and its supporting law need not engage the same set of concepts. Therefore—to get to the key point—the explanation of an action by reference to a man's beliefs and desires may yet be causal, even if there are no back-up laws framed in psychological terms. For the backing law for a psychological explanation may be couched in quite other terms, perhaps physicalistic ones.

All this is by now excessively familiar, and would hardly bear repetition were it not for the fact that these points have recently been badly misunderstood by Peter Hess in his paper "Actions, Reasons, and Humean Causes."[1] Hess wants to show Davidson's handling of his points in fact gives no aid or comfort to the defender of the traditional commonsensical view that reasons are causes. On the contrary (Hess argues), Davidson takes the ground from under the traditionalist's feet, leaving us with a position that no self-respecting defender of the old view could recognize as his own. Let me explain.

* Peter Smith, "Hess on Reasons and Causes," *Analysis* 41 (1981), 206-09. Reprinted with kind permission of the author.

Consider again the statement that the event reported on p. 5 of the *Times* caused the event reported on p. 13 of the *Tribune*. Hess regards this as Davidson's paradigm of a heteronomic singular claim (i.e. the sort of singular causal claim which is warranted, if at all, by a law couched in quite distinct terms). Now, one feature of this supposed paradigm is that it identifies the events it asserts to be causally related via properties which are quite independent of what gives the events their causal efficacy. Hess seizes on this feature, and takes it to be shared in Davidson's view by the singular claim that (the onset of) a given belief or desire caused a particular action. Here too we have a heteronomic claim which again identifies the events which it asserts to be causally related via properties which are quite independent of what gives the events their causal efficacy. In other words, Hess thinks that in Davidson's view the property of being (the onset of) a belief or desire is no more a causally salient property of events than the property of being reported on page 5. Or in Hess's phrase, Davidson's position "reduces primary reasons to the status of epiphenomena."

Obviously, if this were Davidson's position, then it would indeed be an illusion to suppose that he was reformulating anything like a commonsensical causal theory of action. For while no one assumes that the event mentioned on page 5 caused a bridge to collapse by virtue of being so mentioned, a traditional theory of action does suppose that the event of coming to desire a beer causes one to open a can by virtue of being that desire. As Hess puts it, advocates of the common-sense position "will certainly not accept the view that the causal efficacy of whatever causes an action is in no way affected by the presence or absence of primary reasons."

But Hess has misconstrued Davidson. A heteronomic singular claim may be couched in causally irrelevant terms (as in the overworked newspaper example), but there is no necessity about this. The claim that Monday's hurricane caused Tuesday's bridge failure is again heteronomic, as Davidson insists, yet it identifies what produced the failure in causally salient terms (and of course it makes some sense to say that the hurricane caused the collapse by virtue of being a hurricane). So Davidson's view, that a singular claim relating reason and action is a heteronomic causal statement, leaves wide open the option of holding that the notions of belief and desire are (as the traditionalist thought) causally salient. And this option is the one that Davidson embraces. In brief, the concepts of belief and desire are more like the concept of a hurricane than of a reported event—causally salient even if not fit for appearing in hard-edged laws.

Hess, therefore, has badly misread the position in "Actions, Reasons, and Causes." He treats the newspaper reports example as a general paradigm of heteronomic claims, ignoring Davidson's own examples of other such claims that lack the feature of employing causally irrelevant concepts (the feature on which Hess places such weight). The mistake here is compounded by a misreading of the position of "Mental Events," to which Hess appeals for further support of his own argument. This additional mistake is perhaps also worth exposing.

Hess offers the following definition of what he means by "epiphenomenal":

A property P is epiphenomenal with respect to the relationship between an event C and its effect E iff
(i) P is a property of C;
(ii) It is not the case that C would not have caused E had it not had property P.

He then adds:

If the theory of anomalous monism is true, then every mental property is epiphenomenal with respect to every mental event and its physical consequences. If there were even one mental property that is not epiphenomenal in that sense, then there would be at least one psychophysical law. But, according to Davidson, there aren't any such laws.

So once more it apparently follows that mental events are like newsworthy events in respect of their causal potency. Just as the event reported on page 5 does not cause the bridge failure by virtue of the epiphenomenal property of being so reported, so the event which is (the onset of) a belief or desire does not cause the ensuing action by virtue of being a belief or desire. Again we are landed with a quite untraditional view.

But is Hess right in thinking that the doctrine of anomalous monism renders all mental properties epiphenomenal in his sense? Remember that the doctrine is quite compatible with the claim that mental properties are supervenient on (law-engaging) physical properties, in the sense that there cannot be two events alike in all such physical respects but differing in some mental respect. Or at least, Davidson plausibly argues that his monism is consistent with the supervenience thesis,[2] and Hess offers us no rebuttal. Suppose therefore that we accept the supervenience thesis. And let C be, say, the physical event which is the onset of Jack's desire for a beer, E the consequent event of Jack's opening the can, and P the mental property of being the onset of a desire for beer. Then is property P epiphenomenal?

Well, by the supervenience assumption, C cannot lack property P while remaining the same in all law-engaging physical respects (contrast, the case of the event which stays physically the same whether or not it gets reported on page 5). So, an event which lacks P must be an event with some different basic physical characteristics from those actually possessed by C, and on a plausible view about event identity, this will necessarily be a distinct individual event. But if that is right, then it will be vacuously true that C would not have caused E had it not had property P (for it would not then have existed, and so couldn't cause anything!). Thus, by the definition, the supervenient property P is not epiphenomenal, and Hess's argument does not go through.

If this counter-argument is resisted on the basis of an alternative view about event-identity, and I grant the issue is a disputable one, it will still be to no avail. For we can retreat to a simpler argument by dilemma. Either the supervenient mental property P is or is not epiphenomenal. If it isn't, then Hess's position collapses. If it is, then the property of being a hurricane, which equally supervenes on an event's basic law-engaging physical characteristics, will by parity of reasoning also be epiphenomenal. But any theory which can place mental states and hurricanes on a par as causal factors (even if they are dubbed "epiphenomena") will satisfy the most ardent traditionalist, and so again Hess fails to drive a wedge between Davidson and the traditional theorist.

Davidson's monistic causal theory of action allows beliefs and desires to be both causally salient and supervenient on the physical. It is only by overlooking these two familiar points that Hess can propound his jejune arguments.

Notes

1 Peter Hess, "Actions, Reasons, and Humean Causes," *Analysis* 40 (1981), 77-81, essay 6 in this volume.

2 See p. 214 of the reprint of "Mental Events" in *Essays on Actions and Events*, in this volume, 90-91.

8

THE ARGUMENT FOR ANOMALOUS MONISM[*]

Ted Honderich

Donald Davidson's Anomalous Monism, his engrossing Identity Theory of the mind,[1] emerges from reflection on what seems to be a contradiction. The seeming contradiction is a matter of three claims, the first of which is that there are causal connections between physical and mental events. The second is The Principle of the Nomological Character of Causality. Wherever there are causal connections between events, the events are connected by law. The third claim is that there are no psychophysical lawlike connections. We escape the seeming contradiction and get to Anomalous Monism by way of a certain understanding of the second claim.

While *causal* connection holds between events however described, "laws are linguistic; and so events can instantiate laws, and hence be explained or predicted in the light of laws, only as those events are described in one way or another.... the principle of the nomological character of causality must be read carefully: it says that when events are related as cause and effect, they have descriptions that instantiate a law. It does not say that every true singular statement of causality instantiates a law."[2] When E_1 and E_2 are cause and effect, it does not follow that they are in lawlike connection as E_1 and E_2, or under the descriptions "E_1" and "E_2." The two events may be so connected but need not be.

If a mental event causes a physical event, they can therefore be in lawlike connection under other descriptions. Given the third claim, that there are no psychophysical lawlike connections, any such mental event *must* be in lawlike connection under some other description. It must be so as a physical event. We therefore have an identity. However, the third claim comes into operation a second time at this point, and so what we have is a lawless identity. It is not a matter of law that the mental event is what it is, identical with a physical event. As the idea of Anomalous Monism is also expressed, on the assumption that types bring in law, we have token-identity but not type-identity.

Davidson has elaborated his conception of an event as an irreducible entity, not something to be removed from our ontology. An event, further, has an indefinite number of properties, features or aspects. When I speak of Dora's

* Ted Honderich, "The Argument for Anomalous Monism," *Analysis* 42 (1982), 59-64. Reprinted with kind permission of the author.

fall, I do not in those words fully describe all of that event. It was a fall from the top of the table, during her birthday speech, and so on.[3] This conception of events is not necessary to the proposition that causal connection as ordinarily conceived need not entail a lawlike connection in the same terms, but it will be simplest to proceed by way of the given ontology. Certain it *is* true that when I put some pears on the scale, something green and French did cause the pointer to move to the two-pound mark, but there in fact is no entailed law connecting greenness and Frenchness with the pointer's so moving. There is in fact no law at all connecting the event in virtue of its being of something green and French with the pointer's moving to the two-pound mark. There is no lawlike connection connecting the first event in virtue of greenness and Frenchness with the second event in virtue of its being the pointer's moving to the two-pound mark.

It is to be noticed that we have given clear sense to talk of something's being such and such *as something or other*, or *under a description*. To talk this way is to speak of certain properties of a thing rather than others. To say two things are not in lawlike connection under certain descriptions is to say that certain of their properties are not in lawlike connection, or, perhaps, that the things are not in lawlike connection in virtue of certain of their properties. Perhaps everyone has always understood "under a description," and "as" when it is so used, in this way. So far as I can see, Davidson does not disagree.[4] Certainly that lawlike connection holds in virtue of certain properties is not in conflict with the line that "laws are linguistic," understood as it must be. Davidson's doctrine of the nature of laws[5] is not fully developed, but presumably it takes lawlike connection to be no more a matter of language than causal connection is made so by the line that "causal statements are linguistic."

To return to the event of the pears, there is no denying that it is only certain properties of the event which are relevant to its being the cause it is. Davidson asserts, certainly, as already noted, that the substitution of coextensive descriptions in causal statements does not affect truth value.[6] We must distinguish between a cause and the feature we hit upon for describing it.[7] All of that, however, is consistent with the truth that neither the greenness nor the Frenchness of the pears was relevant to the event of the pears' being put on the scale in so far as that event caused the pointer to move to the two-pound mark. So with effect-events. That the scale's pointer was made in Sheffield is irrelevant to the event of the pointer's moving to the two-pound mark being the effect in question. John Mackie sets out the fact of causally-relevant properties clearly.[8]

Is there a difficulty in the idea that it is in virtue of certain of its properties rather than others that an event is the cause it is? Well, the event of the pears' being put on the scale would not have been the event it was if the pears were not green and French. Thus there would be a barrier to saying that *that* event would have caused the pointer's moving to the two-pound mark if the pears had not been green or French. *That* event would not have occurred. Does that make the pears being green and French causally relevant to the given effect?

It seems to me clear that it does not. Certain conditional connections hold between the weight of the pears and the pointer's movement, and they do not hold between the greenness or Frenchness of the pears and the pointer's movement.[9] The greenness and Frenchness were necessary to the event's being the event it was, but not necessary to the event's being the cause it was. Certainly it may be said that the cause that there was would not have existed if the pears had not been green and French. That is consistent with the greenness and Frenchness being causally irrelevant to the effect. That we say, as we do, that the cause that there was would not have existed if the pears had not been green and French is owed to a fact of language—roughly the fact that we take the whole for the part—and not to any fact of causal necessity about all properties of the pears. There is no such fact.

To press on, it seems clear that it does follow from the fact that E_1 caused E_2 in virtue of a property f of E_1 and property g of E_2 that E_1 and E_2 are in lawlike connection partly or wholly in virtue of properties f and g. If the ground for saying that two events are in some lawlike connection is that they are cause and effect, and it is the case that all of their properties save some residue are irrelevant to their being cause and effect, then they are in the given lawlike connection solely in virtue of that residue of properties. It can be granted not merely that not every true singular statement of causality entails that the events are in lawlike connection under the same descriptions, but also that none does. "Something weighing two pounds being put on the scale caused the pointer to move to the two-pound mark" does not entail that the events are in lawlike connection under the same descriptions. However, it *does* follow from any statement that the event of the pears' being put on the scale caused the pointer to move to the two-pound mark, and the statement that it did so in virtue of only certain properties, that the events were in lawlike connection by way of those properties. We can call this the Principle of the Nomological Character of Causally-Relevant Properties. It is consistent with and indeed required by any tolerable account of causation and is integral to any account which takes causal relations precisely specified to *be* a species of lawlike relations.[10]

If a mental event causes a physical event, what is the causally-relevant property, or what are the causally-relevant properties, of the mental event? In the case of a physical event which is an action, the mental event for Davidson is, very roughly, a belief and an attitude. More generally, mental events are characterized in terms of what Brentano called intentionality, despite certain problems. Any mental event, however, is identical with a physical event. To speak of a mental event is to speak of an event which also has physical properties. To repeat, then, what is causally-relevant with respect to the mental event?

As noted at the beginning, Davidson remarks that causality is a relation between individual events no matter how described. He goes on to remark that his first claim, the principle of causal interaction between the mental and physical, "deals with events in extension and is therefore blind to the mental-physical dichotomy."[11] The first remark, I take it, expresses the truth that we can speak of causal relations between two events however we describe them. In fact we can do better, which is to say we can specify causal relations as holding between the relevant properties of the events. Is the second remark to be taken as denying the proposition that the mental event is a cause in virtue of certain of its properties? If taken in that way, it is surely false. It is not in general mistaken to distinguish causally-relevant properties, and there is no reason to think that mental events are any exception.

Davidson's account of an action as being caused by a reason, roughly a belief and an attitude, suggests that he takes the mental events in question to be causal as mental. Elsewhere he accepts what can be called the conviction of the efficacy of the mental, "the efficacy of thought and purpose in the material world."[12] Again, we have it that Anomalous Monism is not to be confused with "nothing-but" materialism: "Conceiving the *Art of the Fugue* was nothing but a complex neural event." One possible answer to our question, then, is that it is as a mental event that a mental event causes a physical event. It is not a mental event as physical that does the work. Such denials of "epiphenomenalism" are of course common.

If it is a mental event as mental that causes a physical event, we have an unhappy upshot as soon as we add the truism that a typical physical event said to be caused by a mental event is an effect as a physical event. If we accept the first two of the claims which issue in Anomalous Monism, along with the idea that the mental as mental causes the physical, and the Principle of the Nomological Character of Causally-Relevant Properties, we have the denial of the third claim, that there are no psychophysical lawlike connections. Hence we have a denial of Anomalous Monism. If, on the other hand, we wish to retain the third claim, and accept the idea and the principle just mentioned, we must give up the first claim as we are now understanding it, that there is causal interaction between the mental as mental and the physical.

However, there is also the other possible answer to the question of what is causally-relevant with respect to a mental event. It is the answer that the mental event as physical causes the action. To give this answer is of course to cast a new light on the first claim, that the mental interacts causally with the physical. It becomes the claim that the mental as physical interacts causally with the purely physical. What is important, however, is that the resulting picture seems not to account for a conviction that lies behind acceptance of his first claim when it is naturally understood, as the claim that the mental as mental causes the physical. This is the conviction of the efficacy of the mental, already mentioned. It is the conviction that an event as mental is an ineliminable part of any full explanation of an action. It is the very root of the common denial of various epiphenomenalist doctrines.

Can this picture of the mind somehow be made tolerable? It cannot be done by a means already noticed, one which depends on the idea that an event would not be the cause it is if it were not a mental as well as a physical event. That will not make the mental character of the event causally relevant with respect to the action, and hence safeguard the conviction of mental efficacy. Nor, evidently, can we gain the end by way of the simple fact that an event can be said to be a cause even when it is picked out by way of a description of its causally irrelevant properties.

The doctrine of supervenience,[13] so far unmentioned, will come to mind. The picture we then get is this: it is a mental event as physical which causes an action; lawlike connection holds between the mental event as physical and the action, but not between the mental event as mental and that same event as physical; however, since the event as mental supervenes on the event as physical, the event as mental is efficacious with respect to the action. The final claim turns on what supervenience comes to, and what it comes to cannot be lawlike connection between the mental and the physical, and is indeed to be understood as no more than the holding of certain universal material conditionals.[14] That is to say that the connection between the mental and the physical is accidental. There is no nomic necessity about the event as physical being the mental event it is. Here, it seems, we do not get the efficacy of the mental.

I have not looked into the question of the truth of the first and third claims out of which Anomalous Monism arises.[15] All I have tried to establish is that the three claims, together with the fact of causally-relevant properties, the principle about their nomological character, and the conviction of the efficacy of the mental, are bad news for Anomalous Monism.

Notes

1 "Mental Events," in Lawrence Foster and J.W. Swanson, eds., *Experience and Theory* (London: Duckworth, 1970), essay 5 in this volume. See also "Psychology as Philosophy," in S.C. Brown, ed., *Philosophy of Psychology* (London: Macmillan, 1974) and "The Material Mind," in P. Suppes, L. Henkin, G.C. Moisil, A. Joja, eds., *Philosophy of Science IV* (Amsterdam: North-Holland Pub. Co., 1973). The three papers are reprinted in Donald Davidson, *Actions and Events* (Oxford: Clarendon, 1980), from which I take page references to all of Davidson's papers mentioned. I am most grateful to Davidson for comments on an earlier draft of

this essay, which led me to enlarge it. He is not responsible for the upshot, and it does not have his agreement. My thanks too to Colin McGinn.

2   "Mental Events," *Actions and Events*, p. 215, in this volume, 91.

3   "The Logical Form of Action Sentences," in Nicholas Rescher, ed., *The Logic of Decision and Action* (Pittsburgh: Pittsburgh University Press, 1967); "Events as Particulars," *Nous* 5 (1971).

4   "Eternal vs. Ephemeral Events," *Nous* 5 (1981). *Actions and Events*, 194-95.

5   "Emeroses by Other Names," *Journal of Philosophy* LXIII (1966).

6   "Causal Relations," *Journal of Philosophy* LXIC (1967). *Actions and Events*, 152.

7   "Causal Relations," op. cit., 155-56; "Mental Events," op. cit., 215, this volume, 91.

8   *The Cement of the Universe* (Oxford: Clarendon, 1974), 260. See also Ch. 3.

9   An analysis of causation in terms of certain conditionals is given in my "Causes and *if p, even if x, still q*," *Philosophy* 57 (1982), 291-317, but the point in question does not depend on it.

10 For an account of the latter kind see my "Causes and *if p, even if x, still q*," op. cit.

11 "Mental Events," op. cit., p. 215, this volume, 91.

12 "Mental Events," op. cit., pp. 224-5, this volume, 99.

13 "Mental Events," op, cit., p. 214, this volume, 91. See also "The Material Mind," op. cit., 253.

14 Clarified by Davidson in discussion.

15 For arguments against the third claim in particular, see my "Psychophysical Law-like Connections and Their Problem" and "Nomological Dualism; Reply to Four Critics," *Inquiry* (1981), No. 3, No. 4.

9

BAD NEWS FOR ANOMALOUS MONISM?[*]

Peter Smith

In his paper "The Argument for Anomalous Monism,"[1] Ted Honderich argues that the Davidsonian position has grave difficulty in accommodating a central conviction which any acceptable philosophy of mind should surely underwrite, namely our conviction that the mental is causally efficacious.

Davidson's type of monism is intended to reconcile the following propositions which are prima facie inconsistent. (1) There are causal connections between mental events and physical events. (2) Wherever there is a causal connection, there is a covering law. And (3), there are no psycho-physical laws. As is now well known, Davidson aims to reconcile these three propositions by noting that we must interpret the second one in a weak sense—i.e. as asserting only that, where there is a causal connection between events, there must be some descriptions of these events in virtue of which they instantiate a law. A given singular causal claim need not identify the events in question by means of concepts which are fit to feature in the supporting general law. This opens up the possibility that it could be true that Jane's desire caused her action consistently with there being no psycho-physical laws, by virtue of the particular desire and the action falling under physical descriptions which do instantiate a law. This possibility presupposes the identity of the mental with the physical: and the monism here (if we are to avoid the reintroduction of psycho-physical laws) must be anomalous.

Honderich argues that this familiar complex of ideas is not able to secure the causal efficacy of the mental. For the point that a singular causal claim need not be couched in terms which recur in the backing law is just the point that we can identify a cause and effect by means of properties which are not relevant to their causal linkage. Davidson is thus committed to distinguishing, among the properties of a given event, those in virtue of which it causes a certain upshot—and these properties will be the ones governed by the relevant background causal law. In the light of this, let's ask which properties of Jane's desire are relevant to its causing her action. The immediately plausible reply is that it is in virtue of its mental properties that the desire causes the action: or in Honderich's phrase, it is "the mental as mental" which causes the phys-

---

* Peter Smith, "Bad News for Anomalous Monism?" *Analysis* 42 (1982), 220-24.
  Reprinted with kind permission of the author.

ical. But this reply implies that there are, after all, nomological ties between mental properties and physical ones, and we are back with the unwanted psycho-physical laws. So suppose instead that we say that it is "the mental as physical" which causes the physical: in other words, suppose we maintain that the properties of Jane's desire which are relevant to its causing the action in question are among its physical properties. Note, however, that if we are to continue to avoid the re-introduction of psychophysical laws, then the connection between the mental and physical properties of a given event must be deemed not to be nomological. And according to Honderich, "that is to say that the connection between the mental and the physical is accidental." So it follows that, in particular, the connection between an event's having the property of being a desire and its causally relevant physical properties is accidental. But this conclusion seems intolerable; as Honderich puts it, "Here, it seems, we do not get the efficacy of the mental."

All this, claims Honderich, is bad news for anomalous monism. But it is worth pointing out that, whatever the merits of the argument, it certainly is not news. For here is Fred Stoutland writing in 1976:

... On Davidson's theory, the causal powers of propositional attitudes have no determinate connection with the fact that they are propositional attitudes. It is, on the one hand, because they are propositional attitudes that they account for intentionality (or figure in the explanation of intentional action); it is, on the other hand, (only) because they are identical with physical events that they cause behaviour. But that any particular event should be both a particular attitude and a particular physical event—that is, that the same event should have both a propositional attitude description and a physical description—is simply a brute fact for which there cannot, on Davidson's grounds, be an explanation.... [To avoid re-introducing psycho-physical laws] it must be a brute fact, without explanation, that an attitude causes the behaviour it does.[2]

The argument here is evidently the same as Honderich's; and Stoutland too, reasonably enough, finds its conclusion unacceptable. But does Davidson's anomalous monism really commit him to this conclusion? I think not.

The crucial move in the Stoutland/Honderich argument is their inference from the lack of any nomological connection between the mental and the physical to the claim that it is an "accident" or "brute fact" that a given event has the particular combination of mental and physical properties it displays. And this move should be resisted.

Let's begin by asking the anomalous monist how we are to pick out the physical event (or state) which is identical with a given mental event (or state). In other words, given a mental specification of an event, how are we to determine which physical event satisfies the specification? Of course, we cannot demand from the identity theorist a recipe which can in practice be applied in order to identify empirically the physical realization of a given mental state. The demand is the weaker one that we are provided with some nonarbitrary and well-motivated completion for such a schema as "The physical state which is X's belief that p at time t is that physical state such that ...," where the filling does in principle pick out a unique state.[3]

It seems clear enough how the monist must proceed here. He can hardly offer to identify X's belief with some physical state which lacks the right sort of causal connections with the behaviour we interpret as done because of that belief; for this would ratify what are, by ordinary standards, quite the wrong claims of the form "X did A because he believed that p." So, putting it crudely, we must identify X's mental states with physical states which are causally appropriate. Refining this rough idea, we arrive at the following suggestion: the physical state which is X's belief that p (for example) is that state which is (a) causally dependent on those antecedents which folk psychology recognizes as explaining X's belief (such as perceptual input), and such that (b) it is causally involved in the production of such behaviour as folk psychology interprets as actions done because X believes that p.

Now it is very easily seen that, if the anomalous monist does identify the physical state which is X's belief in this sort of way, then he is not vulnerable to the Stoutland/Honderich argument. Suppose that X flipped the switch because he believed it would turn on the light. Then the physical state which is X's belief is that state (whatever it is) which has the right causal relations to the antecedents and consequences of X's belief: and so in particular, X's belief is that physical state which (among other things) is causally involved in the production of the behaviour which we interpreted as X's flipping the switch because he believed it would turn on the light. So—very trivially—the physical state which is X's belief caused X's action. It is not an "accident" or "brute fact" that the belief (in virtue of its physical properties) caused the action; for the physical state which is the belief is partially *identified* as the state which has the right physical properties to cause the action! And note that none of this reinstates unacceptable psycho-physical laws. There is no route, from the thought that if X on a given occasion believes that p then he is in that particular physical state which has the antecedents and consequences of his belief, to the conclusion that there must be some general law-like correlation between X's believing p and a type of physical state directly identified in purely physical terms.

In short then, it can both be the case that there are no nomological links between the mental and the physical and yet also the case that it is no accident that X's belief (in virtue of its physical properties) causes the action it rationally explains. So the Stoutland/Honderich argument entirely collapses.

Against all this, it might be protested that the anomalous monist's method of identifying the physical state which is, for example, X's belief that p is in the present context something of a cheat. For the operative clauses (a) and (b) above help themselves to the "because" of folk-psychological explanation, and it was worries about the role of causality here that started off the whole argument in the first place. It is important to see how this implied accusation of circularity can be rebutted.

The accusation is presumably grounded in something like the following thought. We have tried to rescue the anomalous monist from the Stoutland/Honderich argument by suggesting that the physical state which is X's belief (and hence the causally relevant physical properties of his belief) is fixed in part by the requirement that it causes actions done because of that belief. But fixing which actions are done because of a given belief presupposes that we can establish some causal claims about beliefs: and—in the hypothesized absence of psycho-physical laws—this means bringing to bear some purely physical laws. However, these physical laws can only be applied if we have *already* set up an identification of a given belief with a specific physical state. So, on pain of circularity, this identification cannot in turn presuppose that we have already fixed which actions are done because of a given belief.

The obvious first reply to this line of thought is that it just isn't generally true that establishing causal claims requires "bringing laws to bear." I can know that on this occasion dropping the plate caused it to smash, without benefit of access to the relevant laws concerning e.g. the effect of stress on crystalline structures. Some general rules of thumb, falling well short of hard-edged laws, suffice to bolster my everyday bits of causal knowledge.[4] Likewise, folk-psychology provides rough generalizations which are not themselves law-like but which (it could again be argued) suffice to provide grounds for particular causal claims about beliefs and desires. This enables us to break into the supposed circle.

This first line of reply is sufficient as it stands. However, it is perhaps worth noting in conclusion the possibility of a more ambitious attack on the accusation of circularity. Let's consider more carefully the sense in which folk-psychology makes causal claims. Two views need to be distinguished here. The stronger one is that a claim such as "X flipped the switch because he believed it would turn on the light" provides a causal *explanation* of X's action. The more modest view is that such a claim mentions causes but is not itself a causal explanation. More generally, while beliefs are indeed states which cause actions, they do not rationally explain the action in virtue of being such states: rather it is the other way about—i.e. the belief is that physical state which causes the actions it rationalizes in virtue of being physically identified in precisely such a way as to fit that function. If the anomalous monist adopts this second view, then all appearance of circularity in his position evaporates.

This is not the place to rehearse in detail the virtues of the more modest view, or to discuss its relations to Davidson's position. Sceptics about the coherence of such a view might, however, reflect on the related case of teleological explanations in the light of Jonathan Bennett's fine discussion in his *Linguistic Behaviour.* There Bennett argues that a claim such as "The missile swerved to the left because it registered that its target had swerved" could provide a genuine explanation of the missile's trajectory, and there is a good sense in which this explanation is of a different type from causal mechanistic explanation. But, of course, the event which is the missile's registering of its target's change of course is doubtless a physical event. Suppose, then, we ask "which physical event?" The evident answer is: the one which is responsible for, among other things, making the missile swerve. So, the registering causes the swerve. In short then, teleological explanations are not causal explanations although they mention causes. The anomalous monist might well commend this as a model for our understanding of folk-psychological explanations, thus preserving the causal efficacy of the mental while side-stepping Honderich's attack.

Notes

1 Ted Honderich, "The Argument for Anomalous Monism." *Analysis* 42 (1982), 59-64, essay 8 in this volume.

2 Frederick Stoutland, "The Causation of Behaviour," in J. Hintikka, ed., *Essays on Wittgenstein in Honour of G.H. von Wright, Acta Philosophica Fennica* 28 (Amsterdam: North-Holland Pub. Co., 1976), 307-08. Stoutland expounded the argument in a paper read in Oxford and elsewhere in 1975, a descendant of which appears as "Oblique Causation and Reasons for Action," *Synthese* 43 (1980).

3 For more on the legitimacy of this demand, see my paper "On Identifying the Mental and the Physical," *Canadian Journal of Philosophy* 13 (1983), 227-38.

4 See Davidson in *Essays on Actions and Events*, e.g., 224, this volume, 98-99.

Anomalous Monism: Reply to Smith*

Ted Honderich

My paper "The Argument for Anomalous Monism"[1] advanced the argument that Donald Davidson needs to choose whether it is a mental event as mental or that same event as physical that is causal with respect to an ensuing action, and that either choice is fatal to Anomalous Monism. If it is the mental event as mental that is causal, we have psychophysical lawlike connection, which Anomalous Monism denies. If it is the mental event as physical, we have the inefficacy of the mental, which is intolerable and which Davidson appears to deny.

Peter Smith[2] claims the same argument was advanced earlier by Frederick Stoutland, and in that he is more or less right. Stoutland's version, of which I was unaware, is in ways inexplicit and involves certain different assumptions with which I disagree, but it is indeed a version of the same argument. My concern here is not to claim sole ownership of the goods but to see whether Smith is right in suggesting they are not worth owning.

He assumes, perhaps too quickly, that Davidson must allow that it is the mental event as physical which is a cause of the action. (It may be, rather, that attempts can be made to resist the argument not by supposing that it is the event as mental which is causal, but by relying in a certain way on the identity-proposition or by denying the propositions that produce the dilemma, notably the proposition about causally-relevant properties or characters.) Having assumed that it is the mental event as physical which is causal, Smith notes correctly that on Davidson's view it is not a matter of lawlike connection that the event as physical is the event as mental. That is all that I meant by saying that it is a matter of accident that the physical event is the mental event, and presumably what Stoutland meant by saying the identity is merely a "brute fact." The proposition that it is a matter of accident is not, as Smith supposes, an independent proposition got by inference from the proposition denying lawlike connection. To say the same thing again, it is nomologically inessential, to the event's being the physical event it was, that it was the men-

---

* Ted Honderich, "Anomalous Monism: Reply to Smith," *Analysis* 43 (1983), 147-49. Reprinted with kind permission of the author.

tal event it was. Hence, it is inessential to the relevant effect, the action, that the event was the mental event it was. Here we have epiphenomenalism, the inefficacy of the mental.

Smith's hope of securing the efficacy of the mental rests entirely on one thought. It is that the Anomalous Monist, when asked *which* physical event is to be taken as identical with the mental event, will answer that it is the physical event that has certain causal connections. It stands in causal connection with what ordinary belief ("folk psychology") takes as the explanatory or causal antecedents of the mental event, and the effects of the mental event, notably the relevant action.

Smith's hope is vain, and the answer he supplies to the given question on behalf of the Anomalous Monist does not come near to showing that the argument against Anomalous Monism "entirely collapses." The Anomalous Monist, having identified in Smith's way the physical event he has in mind, will presumably persist in the denial of lawlike connection noted above. It therefore remains as inessential as ever to a certain physical event's being as it is, and having the causal connections it does, that it is a mental event to which ordinary belief—but not the Anomalous Monist—assigns the same causal connections. *That* is the objection. It is an objection which does not collapse but rather is quite untouched by the thought as to the identification of the mental event.

To repeat, Smith writes "it is not an 'accident' or 'brute fact' that the belief (in virtue of its physical properties) caused the action; for the physical state which is the belief is partially *identified* as the state which has the right physical properties to cause the action!"[3] That is a non-sequitur. From the propositions that a state has physical properties which cause an action and which stand in certain other causal relations, and that the state is identical with one commonly believed in virtue of its mental properties to stand in those same relations, and that it is not a matter of lawlike connection that the state as physical is the state as mental, it does not follow that the mental properties of the state are essential to the action.

In the remainder of his paper, Smith considers and attempts to meet other rejoinders to his rescue attempt. I shall not consider this, except to remark that it certainly is mistaken to infer, from the fact that we can establish particular causal claims without knowing laws, that the items might be in causal connection without being in lawlike connection. Indeed, Davidson makes that point.[4] Smith's reflections require the inference. Nor shall I consider further and more fundamental difficulties which Anomalous Monism shares with any Identity Theory of the mind.[5]

Given Stoutland's paper, what I announced about Anomalous Monism was not news. If it had been news, it would have been bad news.

Notes

1   Ted Honderich, "The Argument for Anomalous Monism." *Analysis* 42 (1982), 59-64, essay 8 in this volume.
2   Peter Smith, "Bad News for Anomalous Monism?" *Analysis* 42 (1982), 220-24, essay 9 in this volume.
3   Ibid., 222, in this volume, 120.
4   Donald Davidson, *Essays on Actions and Events* (Clarendon Press, Oxford: 1980), 16-17, in this volume, 92-93.
5   For some of them see my "Psychophysical Lawlike Connections and Their Problem," *Inquiry* 24 (1981), and "Nomological Dualism: Reply to Four Critics," *Inquiry* 24 (1981).

Anomalous Monism and Epiphenomenalism: A Reply to Honderich[*]

Peter Smith

The fate of Davidson's version of the identity theory is an important enough issue for it to be worth commenting on Ted Honderich's brisk note "Anomalous Monism: Reply to Smith."[1]

The key argument of Honderich's original paper, as I read it, started from the premise (A) that the anomalous monist is committed to saying that it is, in a phrase, "the mental as physical" which causes a given behavioural upshot. In other words, it is in virtue of the event's physical properties that a mental event causes a given action. So, since our monist maintains that (B) there are no nomological links between a thing's mental and physical characteristics, it follows that (C) there are no nomological links between a mental event's mental properties and its causal physical properties in virtue of which it produces a certain upshot. So, on the monist's view, it seems to follow that (D) it is a mere accident that an event which has the mental characteristic of being a desire, for example, should have the causal power to bring about the action which commonsense psychology would say the desire produced. And this conclusion, I would agree, is intolerable, and runs counter to our ordinary presumptions about the efficacy of the mental.

In my reply, I accepted (A) and (B) for the sake of argument, and attempted to block this reductio of the Davidsonian position after stage (C). That is, I argued that our monist can insist that there is a good sense in which it is not an *accident* that a particular mental event, identified as such, has the physical causal powers it does have, without being committed to reinstating the unwanted psycho-physical laws. Honderich, however, finds my labours to be beside the point:

> Having assumed that it is the mental event as physical which is causal, Smith notes correctly that on Davidson's view it is not a matter of law-like connection that the event as physical is the event as mental. That is all that I meant by saying that it is a matter of accident that the physical

---

[*] Peter Smith, "Anomalous Monism and Epiphenomenalism: A Reply to Honderich," *Analysis* 41 (1984), 83-86. Reprinted with kind permission of the author.

event is the mental event ... The proposition that it is a matter of accident is not, as Smith supposes, an independent proposition got by inference from the proposition denying lawlike connection. To say the same thing again, it is nomologically inessential, to the event's being the physical event it was, that it was the mental event it was. Hence, it is inessential to the relevant effect, the action, that the event was the mental event it was. Here we have epiphenomenalism, the inefficacy of the mental.

But this is not entirely perspicuous. Let's start by considering the accusation of epiphenomenalism. Traditionally understood, this is the doctrine (E) that mental events do not cause physical events at all. And we should immediately note that this is *incompatible* with (C) and (D). For of course, it is one thing to assert that the causal powers of mental events are not nomologically related to (or are only accidentally related to) the mental properties of those events: it is quite another thing to deny that mental events have any causal powers at all. So which does Honderich now want to say that the anomalist monist is committed to: (C/D) or (E)?

It would seem that the Davidsonian monist who identifies each mental event with some physical event must be thoroughly wedded to the assertion that mental events (at least in virtue of their physical properties) *can* and *do* cause physical events. So it is extremely difficult to see how an accusation of epiphenomenalism against the Davidsonian could possibly arise. Certainly, Honderich's argument quoted above does not sustain such an accusation. For it obviously cannot follow from the thought that "it is inessential" to a given physical effect that its physical cause "was the mental event it was" that the mental event in question lacks all causal powers—for by hypothesis the mental event is identical to a physical event with such powers. Any suggestion of epiphenomenalism here would seem to be simply confused.

It might be replied to all this that I am just being horribly pedantic and, even if "epiphenomenalism" is traditionally used for the doctrine expressed by (E), Honderich is using the term in a permissibly stretched sense to cover the distinct but related doctrines (C) or (D); it is the suggestion that the anomalous monist is committed to one or both of these which is at the heart of his argument. But consider the following remark which Honderich makes in the course of discussing my attempt to block the argument I sketched at the outset. He argues that the monist, even if he adopts the manoeuvre I offered him,

will presumably persist in the denial of lawlike connection noted above. It therefore remains as inessential as ever to a certain physical event's being as it is, and having the causal connections it does, that it is a mental event to which ordinary belief—but not the Anomalous Monist—assigns the same causal connections. *That* is the objection.

Here, the interpolated remark implies that the monist does *not* assign causal connections to the mental event which ordinary belief sees as causing a certain upshot. So, the monist apparently *is* being taken to be an epiphenomenalist in the straightforward traditional sense. But, to repeat, this is extraordinary: the anomalous monist *of course* assigns the same causal connections to a mental event and the physical event which it is identical with: to do otherwise would be to abandon the token identity theory which is distinctively his.

Suppose, however, we ignore that troublesome interpolated remark and take it that Honderich's real complaint against the monist is *not* that he is an epiphenomenalist (in the traditional sense): what we are left with is the objection that "it is inessential" to a given physical event's causing a particular action that "it is the mental event to which ordinary belief ... assigns the same causal connections." And, as we saw from the first quotation above, Honderich now insists quite explicitly that all he means to signify by "inessential" here is that there is a lack of strict nomological connections. So, to make things absolutely clear, Honderich's complaint is that anomalous monism entails (C) there are no strict nomological connections between the causal physical properties of a particular mental event (in virtue of which it causes a certain action) and its mental properties (in virtue of which it is the desire, or whatever, which ordinary belief takes as the cause of the action). Well, let us grant that the Davidsonian position does indeed entail (C): *why is that supposed to be an objection?* For (C) just isn't the sort of proposition with respect to which we have clear pretheoretic intuitions: in other words, we can't say *a priori* that (C) is obviously absurd and that any theory of the mind which entails it is thereby ruled out. For while we certainly do want there to be some kind of connection between an event's mental properties and its causal powers, the technical issue whether the connection in question is a strict *nomological* one is just not one that can be decided in advance of our philosophical theorizing. Compare: we certainly want there to be some kind of connection between an event's being a hurricane and its having the physical properties in virtue of which it destroys buildings—but is it clear that this connection must be nomological?[2]

Of course, if we could infer from (C) that it is a mere accident—in the ordinary, humdrum sense—that an event's mental properties are co-instantiated with its causal powers, that would settle the issue. In other words, if we could show that anomalous monism does entail (D), that would indeed be damaging. But it was precisely the point of my earlier reply to argue that we can block this move from (C) to (D). Honderich does not show that my blocking manoeuvre fails, but only insists that it is unnecessary because the damage is already done once the argument gets to stage (C). I can only reiterate that, once (C) is distinguished from (D), there is nothing particularly counterintuitive in (C) as it stands, and the mere fact that a theory entails it is not an impressive objection.

In summary: anomalous monism does entail (C), as Honderich insists, but that is no obstacle to accepting the position. In the light of my previous paper, I claim that monism does *not* entail the much more damaging (D). And it most certainly does not entail the epiphenomenalist's (E). I leave it to others to judge how far Honderich's reasonings depend on confusing these three things.

Notes

1 Ted Honderich, "Anomalous Monism: Reply to Smith," *Analysis* 43 (1983), 147-49, essay 10 in this volume; for the preceding debate see Ted Honderich, "The Argument for Anomalous Monism," *Analysis* 42 (1982), 59-64, essay 8 in this volume, and Peter Smith, "Bad News for Anomalous Monism?" *Analysis* 42 (1982), 220-24, essay 9 in this volume.

2 Cf. my "Hess on Reasons and Causes," *Analysis* 41 (1981), essay 6 in this volume, the main point of which is in fact untouched by Denise Meyerson Taylor's discussion "Actions, Reasons and Causal Explanation," *Analysis* 42 (1982).

12

SMITH AND THE CHAMPION OF MAUVE[*]

Ted Honderich

As we go through the household of the Champion of Mauve, we notice many things painted mauve. Here a light-switch, there a bottle of gin, here his bedroom slippers. Take the slippers. The Champion of Mauve notes they are splendid slippers—they have the effect of keeping his feet really warm. This is the effect, he more particularly allows, of just the Hibernian fleece with which they are lined. He also allows that their being painted mauve isn't nomically necessary to their Hibernian fleece, their causal property whose effect is the keeping of his feet really warm. But, he adds, it would be a wonderful confusion to move on from that truth to any underrating of Mauve in connection with his warm feet. The slippers with Hibernian fleece *are identical with* the mauve slippers. So too the light-switch with its effective circuit-breaker *is* the mauve light-switch. The bottle with the gin in it *is* the mauve bottle of gin. Let us, he adds, have no confusion about efficacy in these matters either.

Enter Smith—Peter Smith—speaking of the mind and brain. More particularly, he speaks of a man's noticing of a kipper, his wondering if it is too old, and his intending to eat it. Take the last, says Smith. In this connection, there was a neural event which was a cause of the man's then eating the kipper. More particularly, there was an event with a neural property, which property was a cause of the action. Of properties of the event, only the neural property was a cause of the action. The event did also have a mental property, that of being our man's intention to eat the kipper. That property, Smith says, was not nomically necessary to the event's having the neural property. But, says Smith, do not fall into the wonderful confusion of underrating the man's intention to eat the kipper. That intention was a property of an event that was *identical with* the event that had the neural property. Noticing and wondering about the kipper involve like facts. Do not confusedly suppose, says Smith, that what I have said offends against any conviction that we actually have about the efficacy of the mental, any conviction we actually have of the falsehood of epiphenomenalism.

[*] Ted Honderich, "Smith and the Champion of Mauve," *Analysis* 44 (1984), 86-89. Reprinted with kind permission of the author.

My dispute with Smith, at bottom, is over whether he can distinguish himself in a relevant way from the Champion of Mauve. His "Anomalous Monism and Epiphenomenalism: A Reply to Honderich"[1] does not come near to persuading me that he can. He is committed, for all he has said, to an epiphenomenalism or denial of the efficacy of the mental which is quite as impossible to accept as the mauvism of the Champion of Mauve.

He offers two speculations as to what I take epiphenomenalism to be. The first is that it is that "mental events do not cause physical events at all." This he understands in a way prefigured above, as follows: there are no events with mental properties, which events somehow cause physical events. But, he says, I have already accepted in setting out the argument under consideration that there are such events. His second speculation is that I take epiphenomenalism to be no more than a central proposition of Anomalous Monism as set out, that an event's mental property is not in nomological connection with its physical, causal property. This too, as he might have said, was accepted by me in setting out the argument. What he does say is that this proposition does not by itself offend against any conviction we actually have.

Speculation is all right, but reading is better. In the original piece to which Smith is objecting I wrote:

> ... there is also the other possible answer to the question of what is causally-relevant with respect to a mental event. It is the answer that the mental event as physical causes the action. To give this answer is of course to cast a new light on the first claim [of Davidson's Anomalous Monism], that the mental interacts causally with the physical. It becomes the claim that the mental as physical interacts causally with the purely physical. What is important, however, is that the resulting picture seems not to account for a conviction that lies behind acceptance of his first claim when it is naturally understood, as the claim that the mental as mental causes the physical. That is the conviction of the efficacy of the mental, already mentioned. It is the conviction that an event as mental is an ineliminable part of any full explanation of an action. It is the very root of the common denial of epiphenomenalist doctrines.[2]

My plain statement of what I take the conviction of the efficacy of the mental to be, and hence my understanding of the opposed doctrines, epiphenomenalisms, is repeated and considered in another article.[3]

Smith does alight on a remark of mine in that rejoinder about "a mental event to which ordinary belief—but not the Anomalous Monist—assigns ... causal connections." He concludes from "but not the Anomalous Monist" that the epiphenomenalism I find in Anomalous Monism is as he first speculates, the proposition that mental events do not cause physical events at all.

My words were a bit careless, but he concludes wrongly, against clear evidence the other way, above all the passage quoted above.

To repeat, Smith rightly says that in setting out a view of the mind I took on board the proposition that there are events with mental properties, which events somehow cause physical events. What I went on to do was to claim that the given view of the mind was epiphenomenalist: it did not make the mental as mental an ineliminable part of the explanation of actions. Was I there contradicting what I had earlier assumed? Obviously not. Rather, I was concluding, as I still do, that the proposition as understood that there are events with mental properties, which events somehow cause physical events, does not suffice to give us the efficacy of the mental as defined. It does not give us the mental itself as explanatory.

To look at Smith's other speculation, I do indeed suppose that there is a proposition that offends against a conviction we actually have, and that Smith's view of the mind contains that proposition. It is that mental events as mental are *not* ineliminable parts of explanations of actions. I do not suppose that we are offended by the proposition in itself that an event's mental property is not in nomological connection with its physical, causal property. We do require, of course, that something be added to that proposition to give us the efficacy of the mental.

That brings us back to the main issue. What is to be added to the given proposition to give us what we want, that the mental as mental is essential to the explanation of actions? Smith's policy here, in which he persists, is to go on saying that an event which has a mental property is an event which also has a physical property that is causal with respect to an action. It won't do, and no amount of repetition and emphasis will help. There are many more problems and possibilities in this neighbourhood than have surfaced in this controversy, but it is plain that the so-called identity proposition is of no more use to Smith than is the like proposition to the Champion of Mauve. The Anomalous Monist can be as wedded as he wants to the proposition that *of course* a mental event in his sense causes a physical event. By way of that truth he is no nearer getting mental efficacy than the Champion of Mauve is to getting mauvish efficacy by going on saying that it *is* the mauve slippers that keep him really warm.

Smith has another problem, which has the same source. He approaches the matter we have been considering by asking how the Anomalist Monist in general picks out the neural events with which, in his way, he then identifies mental events.[4] Take intendings like those of the kipper-man imagined above—intendings to eat a kipper. What class of neural events does the Anomalous Monist look to? The answer given is that he looks to neural events that on his view do in virtue of their physicality actually have the causal antecedents and effects that common sense somehow assigns to the intendings, events as mental.

It is important to see what is going on here. The Anomalous Monist starts with a class of mental properties, certain intendings. He then specifies a class of physical properties, partly by their behavioural effects. Then, it is said, he "identifies" these two classes. But of course they do not become "identical" by fiat. More precisely, the Anomalous Monist cannot *decide* that in each instance there is one thing which has a certain mental property and a certain physical property. That is so at any rate, to be very brief, if the identity is not a mere matter of classification, as when I say the book is 328 things—the binding, some glue, and 326 pages.

Let us suppose that there really is what there must be if the view is to have a hope, some non-classificatory fact of identity or identity so-called with respect to the class of mental properties and the class of physical properties. So with noticings of kippers, wonderings about them, and so on. (The obscurity of the fact of identity is no doubt one source of the present controversy.) Why do the intendings not sometimes turn up with the kind of neural item which previously has gone with the noticings or the wonderings, or, of course, feeling melancholy about Aunt Alberta, or thinking happily of bell-jars, or feeling or thinking anything else? *What explains the non-classificatory fact of identity?* Until more is said there is a clear answer: *nothing*. This Anomalous Monism, having denied psychophysical nomic connection, is so far indistinguishable from what we all hoped had been put to rest, which is to say mere psychophysical parallelism. Will this be followed by a revival of Pre-Established Harmony? This Anomalous Monist's plight is illustrated by the fact that that would be *better*. It would offer *some* explanation of the fact in question.

I take it that Smith's defence of Anomalous Monism against my objection has not been anticipated by anyone else, as he pointed out my objection was anticipated by Frederick Stoutland. If this is so, his defence is bad news for Anomalous Monism.

Notes

1 *Analysis* 44 (1984), 83-86, essay 11 in this volume.
2 "The Argument for Anomalous Monism," *Analysis* 42 (1982), 63-64, this volume, 115-16.
3 "Nomological Dualism: Reply to Four Critics," *Inquiry* 24 (1981), 422, cited in my first rejoinder to Smith: "Anomalous Monism: Reply to Smith," *Analysis* 42 (1983), 149, this volume, 125.
4 "Bad News for Anomalous Monism?" *Analysis* 42 (1982), 220-24, essay 9 in this volume.

13

THINKING CAUSES*

Donald Davidson

In 1970 I proposed a theory about the relation between the mental and the physical that I called Anomalous Monism (*AM*).[1] *AM* holds that mental entities (particular time-and space-bound objects and events) are physical entities, but that mental concepts are not reducible by definition or natural law to physical concepts. The position is, in a general way, familiar: it endorses ontological reduction, but eschews conceptual reduction. What was new was the argument, which purported to derive *AM* from three premises, namely, (1) that mental events are causally related to physical events, (2) that singular causal relations are backed by strict laws, and (3) that there are no strict psycho-physical laws.[2] The first premise seemed to me obvious, the second true though contested (I did not present arguments for it), and the third true and worth arguing for. Many readers have found my arguments against the existence of strict psycho-physical laws obscure; others have decided the three premises are mutually inconsistent. But the complaints have most often been summed up by saying that *AM* makes the mental causally inert. The criticisms are connected: if *AM* makes the mental causally inert, then *AM* apparently implies the falsity of the first premise and hence the inconsistency of the three premises. The third premise seems to many critics the relevant offender, so they urge that it should be dropped.

In this paper I attempt three things: first, to defend *AM* against misunderstandings and misrepresentations. This will involve some clarification, and perhaps modification, of the original thesis. Second, I want to maintain that the three premises from which I argue to *AM* are consistent when taken together, and so *AM* is a tenable thesis (it is weaker than the premises). Third, I shall say why I do not think *AM* makes the mental causally powerless. I do not plan here to argue for the truth of *AM* or the premises on which it rests.

In "Mental Events"[3] I endorsed the idea that mental concepts[4] are supervenient, in a sense I explained, on physical concepts. I thought this would make it clear that, contrary to first impressions, *AM* and its entailing pre-

---

* Donald Davidson, "Thinking Causes" in J. Heil and A. Mele, eds., *Mental Causation* (Oxford: Clarendon Press, 1993). Reprinted with kind permission of the author.

misses were after all consistent. So what I am defending in this paper is in effect not only *AM* itself, but *AM* in conjunction with the three premises and the doctrine of supervenience. (In what follows, I shall abbreviate the expression "anomalous monism conjoined with premises (1)-(2)" by "*AM+P*"; "*AM+P+S*" will mean supervenience in addition to *AM+P*.)

When I wrote "Mental Events" I thought I knew that G.E. Moore had used the word "supervenience" to describe the relation between evaluative terms like "good" and descriptive terms like "sharp" or "inexpensive" or "pleasure-producing." Moore's idea seemed clear enough: something is good only because it has properties that can be specified in descriptive terms, but goodness can't be reduced to a descriptive property. In fact, Moore apparently never used the word "supervenient." I had probably found the word in R.M. Hare's *The Language of Morals*,[5] and applied it, as he had, to Moore. (Hare has since complained that I got the concept wrong: for him supervenience implies a form of what I call nomological reduction.[6]) In any case, the idea I had in mind is, I think, most economically expressed as follows: a predicate *p* is supervenient on a set of predicates *S* if and only if *p* does not distinguish any entities that cannot be distinguished by *S*.[7] Supervenience so understood obviously applies in an uninteresting sense to cases where *p* belongs to *S*, to cases where *p* is explicitly definable by means of the predicates in *S*, and to cases where there is a law to the effect that the extension of *p* is identical with the extension of a predicate definable in terms of the predicates in *S*. The interesting cases are those where *p* resists any of these forms of reduction. I gave as a non-controversial example of an interesting case the supervenience of semantic predicates on syntactical predicates: a truth predicate for a language cannot distinguish any sentences not distinguishable in purely syntactical terms, but for most languages truth is not definable in such terms. The example gives one possible meaning to the idea that truths expressible by the subvenient predicates "determine" the extension of the supervenient predicate, or that the extension of the supervenient predicate "depends" on the extensions of the subvenient predicates.

How can the possibility of a supervenient relation between the mental and the physical help to show that *AM* (or *AM+P*) is consistent, since supervenience says nothing about causality? The answer is simple: supervenience in any form implies monism; but it does not imply either definitional or nomological reduction. So if non-reductive supervenience is consistent (as the syntax-semantics example proves it is), so is *AM*. But supervenience is also consistent with premises (1) and (2), which are not implied by *AM*, since (1) and (2) concern causality, and supervenience says nothing about causality.

It is difficult, then, to see how *AM+P* together with supervenience can imply a contradiction. So it surprised me to read in a recent article by Jaegwon Kim that not only are the premises of *AM* inconsistent with one another, but "the notion of supervenience Davidson favours" is also inconsistent with the first premiss of AM.[8]

Let us look at these supposed inconsistencies. According to Kim,

> The fact is that under Davidson's anomalous monism, mentality does no causal work. Remember: on anomalous monism, events are causes only as they instantiate physical laws, and this means that an event's mental properties make no causal difference. And to suppose that altering an event's mental properties would also alter its physical properties and thereby affect its causal relations is to suppose that psycho-physical anomalism, a cardinal tenet of anomalous monism, is false.

Of course, if "mentality does no causal work" means that mental events do not enter into causal relations, the first premiss of *AM* is false, for it says mental events cause, and are caused by, physical events. This is not enough to prove *AM* itself inconsistent, but it certainly would show the three premisses of *AM* inconsistent with one another. And if Kim's last sentence quoted above is correct, then *AM* is inconsistent with any form of supervenience.

Why does Kim think *AM+P+S* is inconsistent? At least part of the answer is contained in the sentence in which Kim asks us to "remember" what he thinks is a feature of *AM+P*, and here I believe Kim speaks for many of the critics of my position. What Kim asks us to "remember" is that "on anomalous monism, events are causes only as they instantiate laws." This is not anything I have claimed. I could not have claimed it, since given my concept of events and of causality, it makes no sense to speak of an event being a cause "as" anything at all. *AM+P+S* is formulated on the assumption that events are non-abstract particulars, and that causal relations are extensional relations between such events. In his article, Kim does not dispute these two theses. But there is then no room for a concept of "cause as" which would make causality a relation among three or four entities rather than between two. On the view of events and causality assumed here,[9] it makes no more sense to say event *c* caused event *e* as instantiating law *l* than it makes to say *a* weighs less than *b* as belonging to sort *s*. If causality is a relation between events, it holds between them no matter how they are described. So there can be descriptions of two events (physical descriptions) which allow us to deduce from a law that if the first event occurred the second would occur, and other descriptions (mental descriptions) of the same events which invite no such inference. We can say, if we please (though I do not think this is a happy way of putting the point), that events instantiate a law only as described in one way rather than another, but we cannot say that an event caused another only as described. Redescribing an event cannot change what it causes, or change the event's causal efficacy. Events, unlike agents, do not care how what they cause is described: an agent may kill a bird because she wanted to perform an action that could be described as "my killing of that bird." But her killing of the bird might have been identical with her killing of the goose that laid the golden egg though "My killing of the goose that laid the golden egg" may have been the last description she wanted to have describe an action of hers.

Kim thinks that $AM+P$ cannot remain consistently anomalous if it holds that altering an event's mental properties would also alter its physical properties. This seems to be a mistake. $AM+P+S$ (which includes supervenience) does hold that altering an event's mental properties would also alter its physical properties. But supervenience does not imply the existence of psychophysical laws. To see this, it is only necessary to recognize that although supervenience entails that any change in a mental property p of a particular event e will be accompanied by a change in the physical properties of e, it does not entail that a change in p in other events will be accompanied by an identical change in the physical properties of those other events. Only the latter entailment would conflict with $AM+P$.

The definition of supervenience implies that a change in mental properties is always accompanied by a change in physical properties, but it does not imply that the same physical properties change with the same mental properties. Supervenience implies the first, because if a change in a mental property were not accompanied by a change in physical properties, there would be two events distinguished by their mental properties that were not distinguished by their physical properties, and supervenience, as I defined it, rules this out. Kim says supervenience "is best regarded as independent" of the thesis of $AM+P$. This is true in the sense that neither supervenience nor $AM+P$ entails the other. But it is not true that the consistency of supervenience is irrelevant to the consistency of $AM+P$ since, as I just argued, supervenience helps in showing not only that $AM+P$ is consistent, but also that there is a version of $AM+P$ that gives a plausible picture of the relation between the mental and the physical. Kim may have made this remark because he mistakenly thinks that my "weak" version of supervenience entails that "the removal of all mental properties from events of this world would have no consequence whatever on how physical properties are distributed over them."[10] In fact supervenience entails the reverse. For consider two events with the same physical properties, but one with some mental property and the other with that property removed. These cannot be the same event, since one has a property the other lacks. But then contrary to the definition of supervenience, mental properties would distinguish two events not distinguished by their physical properties.

But the point seems clear enough whatever one wants to say about supervenience: if causal relations and causal powers inhere in particular events and objects, then the way those events and objects are described, and the properties we happen to employ to pick them out or characterize them, cannot affect what they cause. Naming the American invasion of Panama "Operation Just Cause" does not alter the consequences of the event.

So far I have said little about laws because laws are not mentioned in the definition of supervenience, and the logical possibility of supervenience is important in establishing the consistency of *AM+P*. But of course the thesis that there are no strict psychophysical laws is one of the premises on the basis of which I argued for *AM*. So even if *AM* is consistent, there is a question whether the denial of such laws somehow undermines the claim that mental events are causally efficacious. I say "somehow" since it would seem that the efficacy of an event cannot depend on how the event is described, while whether an event can be called mental, or can be said to fall under a law, depends entirely on how the event can be described.

Let me digress briefly. The second assumption from which I argued to *AM* was that if two events are related as cause and effect, there must be a law that covers the case. In "Mental Events" I explained in some detail what I meant by a law in this context, and what I meant by "covering." A law (formulated in some language) covers a case if the law, conjoined with a sentence that says the event (described appropriately) occurred, entails a sentence that asserts the existence of the effect (appropriately described). I made clear that what I was calling a law in this context was something that one could at best hope to find in a developed physics: a generalization that was not only "law-like" and true, but was as deterministic as nature can be found to be, was free from caveats and *ceteris paribus* clauses; that could, therefore, be viewed as treating the universe as a closed system. I stressed that it was only laws of this kind (which I called "strict" laws) that I was arguing could not cover events when those events were described in the mental vocabulary. I allowed that there are not, and perhaps could not be expected to be, laws of this sort in the special sciences. Most, if not all, of the practical knowledge that we (or engineers, chemists, geneticists, geologists) have that allows us to explain and predict ordinary happenings does not involve strict laws. The best descriptions we are able to give of most events are not descriptions that fall under, or will ever fall under, strict laws.[11]

There are two reasons for reminding those interested in *AM* (or *AM+P* or *AM+P+S*) of these facts. The first is simply that much of the criticism of *AM+P* has ignored the distinction I painfully spelled out in "Mental Events" between the "strict" laws I think exist covering singular causal relations and the less than strict laws that can be couched in mental terms. Thus Kim, in the article I mentioned, begins by saying correctly that *AM+P* denies that there are precise or strict laws about mental events, but goes on to criticize *AM+P* for maintaining that "the mental is anomalous not only in that there are no laws relating mental events to other mental events but none relating them to physical events either."[12] In fact I have repeatedly said that if you want to call certain undeniably important regularities laws—the familiar regularities that link the mental with the mental (as formulated, for example in decision theory) or the mental with the physical—I have no objection; I merely say these are not, and cannot be reduced to, *strict* laws.

Because he ignores the distinction between strict laws and other sorts of regularities, it is by no means clear that Kim really holds views at odds with *AM+P*. Kim maintains, plausibly it seems to me, that any satisfactory account of the relation between the mental and the physical must permit appeal to "local correlations and dependencies between specific mental and physical properties." But then he adds, "The trouble is that once we begin talking about correlations and dependencies between specific psychological and physical properties, we are in effect talking about psycho-physical laws, and these laws raise the spectre of unwanted physical reductionism. Where there are psycho-physical laws, there is always the threat, or promise, of psycho-physical reduction."[13] But if the laws are not strict, the threat is averted, and the promise false. Kim offers no reason to think the laws can be strict; I have given arguments (which he does not mention or discuss in this article[14]) why I think they cannot. It is not clear that Kim has come to grips with *AM+P*.

Kim is by no means the only critic of *AM+P* to fail to notice the crucial importance of the distinction between strict and non-strict laws. Thus J.A. Fodor writes that he is going to defend the view that intentional (mental) properties are "causally responsible" and that there are "intentional causal laws ... contrary to the doctrine called 'anomalous monism.'" His defence is that in common sense and in many (all?) of the "special" sciences, there are plenty of laws that are far from strict. He cites as an example of a law in geology that mountains are apt to have snow on them; it is *because* Mt. Everest is a mountain that it has snow on it.[15] But as I have just pointed out, this defence of the causal efficacy of the mental is consistent with *AM+P*.

It is a question whether others who have attacked *AM+P* have taken the distinction between types of regularity fully into account. Fred Dretske, who has also maintained that *AM+P* makes the mental causally inert, has never claimed that there are strict psychophysical laws.[16] There is thus no clear reason to believe that the sort of account he wants to offer of how the mental causes the physical is itself inconsistent with *AM+P*. I don't think his account succeeds; but that is another matter. Dagfinn Føllesdal has also thought there must be psycho-physical laws; but he gives as an example of such a "law," "Any severely dehydrated person who drinks water will improve."[17] *AM+P* does not rule out such laws, for such a law is obviously far from strict, and it is not likely that it can be made truly exceptionless.

The second reason for paying attention to the distinction between the laws of an ideal physics and other generalizations (whether or not we call them laws) has to do with the logic of the argument that leads from the premisses to *AM*. The argument does not depend on the claim that there are no psycho-physical laws: the argument demands only that there are no laws that (i) contain psychological terms that cannot be eliminated from the laws nor reduced to the vocabulary of physics and (ii) that have the features of lacking *ceteris paribus* clauses and of belonging to a closed system like the laws of a finished physics. In other words, I argued from the assumptions that mental events are causally related to physical events, and that all causally related events instantiate the laws of physics, to the conclusion that mental events are identical with physical events: thus monism. The extent to which mental concepts fall short of being reducible to physical concepts measures the degree of anomaly. As far as I can see, the positions of both Kim and Fodor on the relation between the physical and the mental are consistent with *AM* and *AM+P*, and it seems to me possible that the same is true of Dretske and Føllesdal.

There remains an issue, however, that separates my views from Kim's and perhaps also from Fodor's. Fodor holds that mental (or intentional) concepts can't be reduced to the concepts of a finished physics, so in this respect his position is that of *AM+P*. Kim, on the other hand, believes in reduction. But he may simply have different standards for reduction than I do; if this is so, our difference on this point may be mainly verbal. But behind what may be merely a verbal point there lies a substantive issue: both Fodor and Kim seem to think that unless there are psycho-physical laws of some sort, the mental would have been shown to be powerless. I think the reasoning that leads them (and others) to this conclusion is confused.

Let's be clear about what is at stake. At this point I am not concerned with the question whether or not there are psychophysical laws. In the sense in which Kim and Fodor think there are laws linking mental and physical concepts, I also think there are laws; what I have claimed is that such laws are not strict, and that mental concepts are not reducible by definition or by strict "bridging" laws to physical concepts. But unlike my critics, I do not think it would prove that the mental is causally inert even if there were no psychophysical laws of any kind.

Suppose I create a table in which all the entries are definite descriptions of one sort or another of events. I refer to the events by giving the column and the row where the description is to be found: column 179 row 1044 for example is the event of my writing this sentence. Let us call the events listed in the table "table-events." The vocabulary needed to describe (needed to provide a definite description of) each event is just the vocabulary needed to pick out the column and row. These events have their causes and effects: for example event 179-1044 caused a certain rearrangement of electric flows in the random access memory of my computer. There are, I imagine, no interesting tablo-physical laws whatever, that is, laws linking events described in the table language and events described in the vocabulary of physics. Yet this fact does not show that table-events are not causally efficacious.

It will be retorted that it is simply irrelevant to the causal efficacy of table-events that they are table-events—that they are described in the table vocabulary. This is true. But it is also irrelevant to the causal efficacy of physical events that they can be described in the physical vocabulary. It is *events* that have the power to change things, not our various ways of describing them. Since the fact that an event is a mental event, i.e. that it can be described in a psychological vocabulary, can make no difference to the causes and effects of that event, it makes no sense to suppose that describing it in the psychological vocabulary might deprive the event of its potency. An event, mental or physical, by any other name smells just as strong.

The point seems so simple and so clear that it is hard to see how it can be doubted. Suppose Magellan notices that there are rocks ahead, an event that, through the intervening events such as his uttering orders to the helmsman, causes the ship to alter course. Magellan's noticing is a mental event, and it is causally efficacious. That event is also a physical event, a change in Magellan's body, and describable in the vocabulary of physics. As long as the predicates used to describe the mental event are not strictly reducible to the predicates of physics, all this is in accord with *AM+P.*

Yet according to Kim and others, *AM+P* implies that the mental is causally inert: Kim asks "What role does mentality play on Davidson's anomalous monism?," and he answers, "None whatever." Why does he think this? We get a hint when he says "on anomalous monism, events are causes or effects only as they instantiate physical laws." The same idea is expressed by the phrase "in virtue of": mentality is causally effective only if events are causes in *virtue of their mental properties.*[18] "Because of" has been recruited to express the same idea. Kim has even implied that it is my explicit view that "it is only under its physical description that a mental event can be seen to enter into a causal relation with a physical event (or any other event) by being subsumed under a causal law."[19] Those who are familiar with the literature will recognize other ways of putting the point: on *AM+P* (so one reads) the mental does not cause anything *qua* mental; the mental is not efficacious *as such.* This is the vein in which Ernest Sosa writes that "The key to [Davidson's] proposed solution ... is the idea that mental events enter into causal relations *not* as mental but only as physical."[20] Sosa does at least recognize that this is not my way of putting things, but he does not realize that I couldn't put things this way. For me, it is events that have causes and effects. Given this extensionalist view of causal relations, it makes no literal sense, as I remarked above, to speak of an event causing something as mental, or by virtue of its mental properties, or as described in one way or another.

But might it not happen that the mental properties of an event make no difference to its causal relations? Something like this is what critics have in mind when they say that according to *AM+P* the mental is inert. Of course, the idea that mental properties make no causal difference is consistent with the view that there are no psycho-physical laws (strict or not) and with the supposition that every singular causal relation between two events is backed by a strict (physical) law; it is also consistent with the thesis that mental events (i.e. events picked out by mental properties) are causally related to physical events. So *AM+P* is *consistent* with the (epiphenomenalist) view that the mental properties of events make no difference to causal relations. But this is not enough to discredit *AM+P*, for it does not follow that *AM implies* the causal inertness of the mental. What critics must show is that *AM* (or *AM+P*) implies the impotence of mental properties, and this I see no way of establishing.

Another way of putting the point is this: we have the makings of a refutation of *AM+P* provided it can be shown that *AM+P* is inconsistent with the supervenience of mental properties on physical properties. The refutation would consist, not in showing *AM+P* inconsistent, but in showing it inconsistent with supervenience, and so with the supposition that the mental properties of an event make a difference to its causal relations. For supervenience as I have defined it does, as we have seen, imply that if two events differ in their psychological properties, they differ in their physical properties (which we assume to be causally efficacious). If supervenience holds, psychological properties make a difference to the causal relations of an event, for they matter to the physical properties, and the physical properties matter to causal relations. It does nothing to undermine this argument to say "But the mental properties make a difference not *as* mental but only because they make a difference to the physical properties." Either they make a difference or they don't; if supervenience is true, they do.

How might one try to show that *AM+P* is inconsistent with supervenience? Kim, as we noted, thinks my version of supervenience implies that all mental properties could be withdrawn from the world and this would make no difference to causal relations; but this supposition turned out to be incompatible with my understanding of supervenience. He subsequently argues that there is no plausible way to understand my brand of supervenience because there is no plausible way to reconcile the demands that the mental be irreducible to the physical and yet be "dependent" on it.[21] But clearly supervenience gives a sense to the notion of dependence here, enough sense anyway to show that mental properties make a causal difference; so unless it can be shown that even weak supervenience is inconsistent with *AM+P*, it has not been shown that *AM+P* makes the mental causally inert.

Kim does have a point. Supervenience as I define it is consistent with the conjunction of *AM+P* and the assumption that there are no psycho-physical laws whatever, strict or not. It is not even slightly plausible that there are no important general causal connections between the mental and physical properties of events. I have always held that there are such connections; indeed much of my writing on action is devoted to spelling out the sort of general causal connections that are essential to our ways of understanding, describing, explaining, and predicting actions, what causes them, and what they cause. But why should the importance and ubiquity of such connections suggest that psychological concepts must be reducible to physical concepts—*strictly* reducible? Yet the failure of strict reducibility is all that is required to establish *AM*.

Why have there been so many confusions and bad arguments in the discussion of *AM, AM+P*, and supervenience? The main source of confusion, I think, is the fact that when it comes to events people find it hard to keep in mind the distinction between types and particulars. This in turn makes it easy to conflate singular causal connections with causal laws, and invites neglect of the difference between explaining an event and simply stating that a causal relation holds.

Of course those who have commented on *AM+P* cannot have failed to notice that the argument hangs on the distinction between particular events and types of events. But the distinction has nevertheless proved easy to overlook. Kim, for example, asks whether the identity of mental events with physical events solves the problem of the causal efficacy of the mental. It does not, he says, because what is at issue is "the causal efficacy of *mental properties* of events *vis-à-vis* their physical properties. Thus the items that need to be identified are properties—that is, we would need to identify mental properties with physical properties."[22] But properties are causally efficacious if they make a difference to what *individual* events cause, and supervenience ensures that mental properties do make a difference to what mental events cause. So why is the identity of *properties* required to make mental properties causally efficacious? It isn't; but one might think so if one were confusing individual events with classes of events, i.e. all those that share some property.

I sense a similar slippage in the argument when Kim introduces what he calls "the problem of causal-explanatory exclusion." This is the problem, he says, that "seems to arise from the fact that a cause, or causal explanation, of an event, when it is regarded as a full, sufficient cause or explanation, appears to *exclude* other *independent* purported causes or causal explanations of it."[23] The idea is that if physics does provide such "full, sufficient" explanations, there is no room for mental explanations unless these can be (fully, strictly?) reduced to physical explanations. What can this strange principle mean? If we consider an *event* that is a "full, sufficient" cause of another event, it must, as Mill pointed out long ago, include everything in the universe preceding the effect that has a causal bearing on it, some cross-section of the entire preceding light-cone; and even then, if we take "sufficient" seriously, we must assume perfect determinism. How can the existence of such an event "exclude" other causes? It can't, since by definition it includes everything that could be a cause. Given supervenience, such an event would include, as proper parts, all relevant mental events. What has all this to do with explanation? Well, if we ever had the laws of physics right, and we had the appropriate physical description of an event *and* of some cross-section of the preceding light-cone, we might be able to give a full and sufficient explanation of the second event. How could this exclude any other sort of explanation? It might *preclude* less complete physical explanations, in the sense that we would lose interest in them. But if mental concepts are not reducible to physical concepts, there is no reason to suppose we would lose interest in explanations in mental terms just because we had a complete physical explanation. What is true, of course, is that psychological explanations are never full and sufficient; like most explanations, they are interest-sensitive, and simply assume that a vast number of (unspecified and unspecifiable) factors that might have intervened between cause and effect did not. This does not mean they are not causal explanations, nor that physical explanations exclude them. It is only if we confuse causal relations, which hold only between particulars, with causal explanations, which, so far as they are "sufficient" must deal with laws, and so with types of events, that we would be tempted to accept the principle of "causal-explanatory exclusion."[24]

Let me give one more example of what I take to be error brought on by not taking seriously the distinction between particular events and their types. I draw the example from an article by Ernest Sosa; but similar examples can easily be found in the writings of Kim, Dretske,[25] Føllesdal, Honderich,[26] Achenstein,[27] Stoutland,[28] and Mark Johnston[29] (for additional references, see LePore and Loewer[30]). Suppose, Sosa argues, that someone is killed by a loud shot; then the loudness of the shot is irrelevant to its causing the death. "Had the gun been equipped with a silencer, the shot would have killed the victim just the same."[31] In the same way, Sosa thinks, *AM+P* entails that mental properties are irrelevant to what the events that have the properties cause. Such examples, whether about mental causation or physical, do not establish the conclusion. The crucial counterfactual is fatally (sorry) ambiguous. Had the gun been equipped with a silencer, a quiet shot, if aimed as the fatal shot was, and otherwise relevantly similar, would no doubt have resulted in *a* death. But it would not have been the *same* shot as the fatal shot, nor could the death it caused have been the same death. The ambiguity lies in the definite description "the shot": if "the shot" refers to the shot that would have been fired silently, then it is true that that shot might well have killed the victim. But if "the shot" is supposed to refer to the original loud shot, the argument misfires, for the same shot cannot be both loud and silent. Loudness, like a mental property, is supervenient on basic physical properties, and so makes a difference to what an event that has it causes.[32] Of course, both loud and silent (single) shots can cause a death; but not the same death.

Notes

1   "Mental Events," in Lawrence Foster and J.W. Swanson, eds., *Experience and Theory* (London: Duckworth, 1970), essay 5 in this volume.

2   This summary simplifies the original thesis and argument. Those not familiar with "Mental Events," should consult it for caveats and additional assumptions.

3   "Mental Events," in L. Foster and J.W. Swanson, eds., *Experience and Theory* (London: Duckworth, 1970), essay 5 in this volume.

4   In the present paper I do not distinguish concepts from properties or predicates, except to the extent that I allow that physics may well come to require predicates not now available.

5   R.M. Hare, *The Language of Morals* (Oxford: Clarendon Press, 1952).

6   R.M. Hare, "Supervenience," *Aristotelian Society Supplementary Volume* 58 (1984), 3, says, "supervenience brings with it the claim that there is some 'law' which binds what supervenes to what it supervenes upon ... what supervenience requires is that what supervenes is seen as an instance of some universal proposition linking it with what it supervenes upon." But so far as I can see, Hare's characterization of supervenience, on the page before the one from which the above quotation is taken, does not imply the existence of laws or law-like generalizations linking what supervenes to what it supervenes on. Hare compares his version of supervenience with Kim's "weak" supervenience, but Kim himself (correctly, I think) finds my version of supervenience very close to his "weak" supervenience, and as not entailing connecting laws.

7   In "Mental Events" I said the supervenience of the mental on the physical "might be taken to mean that there cannot be two events alike in all physical respects but differing in some mental respect." I intended this to be equivalent to the present formulation, but apparently it is easily misunderstood. In answer to a question about "Mental Events," I gave an unambiguous definition of supervenience which is clearly equivalent to the present one: a predicate p is supervenient on a set of predicates S if for every pair of objects such that p is true of one and not of the other there is a predicate in S that is true of one and not of the other. I suggested that it is a common fallacy in philosophy (of which the naturalistic fallacy is an example) to switch the order of the quantifiers in this formula. See Davidson, "Replies to Essays X-XII," in B. Vermazen and M. Hintikka, eds., *Essays on Davidson: Actions and Events* (Oxford: Clarendon Press, 1985), 242.

8   Jagewon Kim, "The Myth of Nonreductive Materialism," *Proceedings of the American Philosophical Association* 63 (1989), 6.

9   This view is spelled out in detail in the articles in the second part of Davidson, *Essays on Actions and Events* (Oxford: Clarendon Press, 1980).

10   Kim, op. cit., 35, n. 8.

11   Davidson, "Mental Events," op. cit., 216-23, this volume, . There I said, "I suppose most of our practical lore (and science) is heteronomic [i.e. not in the form of strict laws, and not reducible to such]. This is because a law can hope to be precise, explicit, and as exceptionless as possible only if it draws its concepts from a comprehensive closed theory," 219. Also see Vermazen and Hintikka, eds., *Essays on Davidson: Actions and Events* (Oxford: Clarendon Press, 1985), 242-52, and P. Pettit, R. Sylvan, and J. Norman, eds., *Metaphysics and Morality* (Oxford: Basil Blackwell, 1987), 41-48.

12   Kim, op. cit., 33.

13   Ibid., 42.

14   Ibid.

15   See J.A. Fodor, "Making Mind Matter More," *Philosophical Topics* 17 (1989), 59-80. The argument Fodor gives there is, though he does not realize it, a defence of *AM*, since he argues that although there may be no strict laws in geology, this does not show that such properties as being a mountain are not causally efficacious. As he says, to suppose that the lack of such strict laws makes geological properties epiphenomenal is absurd: "there are likely to be parallel arguments that all properties are inert excepting only those expressed by the vocabulary of physics." I think this is exactly right if one adds, "expressible in the vocabulary of physics or in a vocabulary definitionally or nomologically reducible to the vocabulary of physics." The same point is made in Fodor, *Psychosemantics* (Cambridge, MA: MIT Press, 1987), 5-6. There the example is "A meandering river erodes its outer banks unless, for example, the weather changes and the river dries up."

16   See Fred Dretske, "Reasons and Causes," *Philosophical Perspectives* 3 (1989), 1-15.

17   Daginn Føllesdal, "Causation and Explanation: A Problem in Davidson's View on Action and Mind," in E. Lepore and B. McLaughlin, eds., *Actions and Events: Perspectives on the Philosophy of Donald Davidson* (Oxford: Basil Blackwell, 1985), 311-23.

18   Kim, op. cit., 43.

19   Jaegwon Kim, "Epiphenomenal and Supervenient Causation," *Midwest Studies in Philosophy* 9 (1984), 267, this volume, 251.

20   Ernest Sosa, "Mind-Body Interaction and Supervenient Causation," *Midwest Studies in Philosophy* 9 (1984), 277, this volume, 262.

21   Jaegwon Kim, "The Myth of Nonreductive Materialism," *Proceedings of the American Philosophical Association* 63 (1989), 39-41.

22   Ibid., 45.

23   Ibid., 44.

24   Kim says a full, sufficient cause or explanation excludes other independent causes or explanations; in my discussion, I may seem to have neglected the condition of independence. I have, because dependence means entirely different things in the cases of events and of explanation. Events "depend" on one another causally, and the failure of psycho-physical laws has no bearing on the question of whether mental and physical events are causally related. Explanation, on the other hand, is an intentional concept; in explanation, dependence is geared to the ways in which things are described. There is no reason why logically independent explanations cannot be given of the same event (as Socrates points out in Plato's *Phaedo* 98 ff.).

25   Dretske, "Reasons and Causes," op. cit.

26   Ted Honderich, "The Argument for Anomalous Monism," *Analysis* 42 (1982), 59-64, essay 8 in this volume.

27   P. Achinstein, "The Causal Relation," *Midwest Studies in Philosophy* 4 (1979), 369-86.

28   Mark Johnston, "Why Having a Mind Matters," in E. Lepore and B. McLaughlin, eds., *Actions and Events: Perspectives on the Philosophy of Donald Davidson* (Oxford: Basil Blackwell, 1985), 408-26.

29   Frederick Stoutland, "The Causation of Behavior," in *Essays on Wittgenstein in Honor of G.H. Von Wright, Acta Philosophica Finnica* 28 (1976), 286-325.

30   E. Lepore and B. McLaughlin, eds., *Actions and Events: Perspectives on the Philosophy of Donald Davidson* (Oxford: Basil Blackwell, 1985).

31   Sosa, op. cit., 278.

32   It is sometimes suggested that if we cannot make sense of the idea of an event losing its psychological properties while remaining the same event, we are stuck with the idea that all of an event's properties are "essential." I have no theory about which properties of an event, if any, are essential, but it seems clear that to serve the purposes of my argument, mental properties need supervene on only those physical properties that are required for a complete causal account of the universe (i.e. that suffice for the formulation of a closed system of "strict" laws).

14

CAN SUPERVENIENCE AND "NON-STRICT LAWS" SAVE ANOMALOUS MONISM?*

Jaegwon Kim

In "Thinking Causes," Donald Davidson proposes to defend his doctrine of "anomalous monism" (*AM*) against "misunderstandings and misrepresentations" of his critics, myself included, who have called attention to its epiphenomenalist tendencies.[1] Although part of what I am going to say will be in direct reply to Davidson's specific points, I believe that several points of more general interest will emerge.

1. HAVE THE CRITICS OF *AM* (OR *AM+P*) CHARGED IT WITH INCONSISTENCY?

AM is the claim that, although mental properties are irreducible to physical ones, mental events are in fact physical events; and *P* is the conjunction of "the three premisses," as Davidson calls them, of *AM*: (1) mental events cause, and are caused by, physical events; (2) causally related events instantiate "strict" laws; and (3) there are no "strict" psycho-physical laws. Davidson quotes me as having said that "under Davidson's anomalous monism, mentality does no causal work,"[2] and he apparently takes this remark to contradict (1) and hence *AM+P*. What he says is this:

> If "mentality does no causal work" means that mental events do not enter into causal relations, the first premiss of *AM* is false, for it says mental events cause, and are caused by, physical events. This is not enough to prove *AM* itself inconsistent, but it certainly would show the three premisses of *AM* inconsistent with one another.[3]

I don't dispute any of this. What is curious, though, is that Davidson does not defend, or even explicitly affirm, the reading of "mentality does no causal work" suggested in the first sentence of the quotation. Thus it is puzzling why he is so certain that I have characterized *AM+P* as inconsistent; the paragraph in which the offending sentence occurs makes it abundantly clear, I dare say,

* Jaegwon Kim, "Can Supervenience and 'Non-Strict Laws' Save Anomalous Monism?" in J. Heil and A. Mele, eds., *Mental Causation* (Oxford: Clarendon, 1993), 19-26. Reprinted with kind permission of the author.

that by "mentality" I was referring to mental properties, not individual mental events.[4] In the context of *AM+P*, the claim "Mental events cause physical events" only comes to the assertion, which is not disputed by his commentators, that events with some mental property or other are causes of events with some physical property or other. The difficulty that has been voiced by the many critics whose names Davidson cites, and with an impressive if unsurprising unanimity, is precisely that the truth of this assertion does not ensure the causal efficacy of mental properties (compare: "The orange pills will relieve your headache").

2. HAVE THE CRITICS OF *AM* MADE AN ERROR IN CLAIMING THAT *AM+P* IS A FORM OF EPIPHENOMENALISM?

It must be admitted that Davidson's commentators have not always been careful to distinguish between the following two claims: (1) *AM+P* entails the causal inertness of mental properties, and (2) *AM+P* fails to provide mental properties with a causal role. According to Davidson, (1) is false; and in this he is arguably right.[5] However, this does not necessarily absolve *AM+P* of the charge of epiphenomenalism; for if something that purports to be a theory of mental causation assigns no causal role to mental properties—it has nothing to say about the causal powers of mental properties while saying plenty about those of physical properties—the theory can, it seems to me, reasonably be said to be epiphenomenalistic with regard to mental properties. Plainly (2) is true, and has never been seriously disputed; and the defenders of *AM* have focused, by and large, on extending *AM* by adding a positive account of the causal efficacy of mental properties.[6] In fact, that is Davidson's own approach in "Thinking Causes": he wants to supplement *AM+P* with supervenience (*S*), and perhaps also with "non-strict laws," to restore causal efficacy to mental properties, tacitly acknowledging that within the framework of *AM+P* mental properties have no causal role to play.

3. HAVE THE CRITICS TRIED TO TURN THE CAUSAL RELATION INTO A MULTI-TERMED, DESCRIPTION-DEPENDENT, INTENSIONAL RELATION?

Throughout "Thinking Causes," Davidson complains that his critics have tried to turn the binary relation of causation, "*c* causes *e*," into a multi-termed (that is, more than binary), possibly non-extensional, relation by employing such expressions as "*c* qua *P* causes *e* qua *M*," "*c* under description *D* causes *e* under description *D**," etc.[7] He is anxious to defend causation as an extensional binary relation whose relata are concrete events ("no matter how described"). But none of this has much to do with the main issue on hand, and getting rid of these admittedly inelegant locutions will not make it go away. The issue has always been *the causal efficacy of properties of events—no mat-*

ter how they, the events or the properties, are described. What the critics have argued is perfectly consistent with causation itself being a two-termed extensional relation over concrete events; their point is that such a relation isn't enough: we also need a way of talking about the causal role of properties, the role of properties of events in generating, or grounding, these two-termed causal relations between concrete events.

To talk about the role of properties in causation we don't need to introduce the "*qua*" locution or any other multi-termed causal relation, although I see nothing in principle objectionable about them; all that is necessary is the recognition that it makes sense to ask questions of the form "What is it about events *c* and *e* that makes it the case that *c* is a cause of *e*?" and be able to answer them, intelligibly and informatively, by saying something like "Because *c* is an event of kind *F* and *e* is one of kind *G* (and, you may add if you favour a nomic conception of causality, there is a law of an appropriate form connecting *F*-events with *G*-events)." This is only to acknowledge that the causal relation obtains between a pair of events because they are events of certain kinds, or have certain properties. How could anyone refuse to acknowledge this—unless, that is, he believed that causal relations were brute facts about events, having nothing to do with the kinds of events that they are? In fact, Davidson himself acknowledges in the end that it makes sense to discuss the causal relevance of properties; for, after all, he offers an account of it, based on supervenience and non-strict laws.

4. CAN YOU HAVE PSYCHO-PHYSICAL SUPERVENIENCE WITHOUT PSYCHO-PHYSICAL LAWS?

Well, that depends on what sort of supervenience you have in mind.[8] Davidson says that I made an error about the logic of supervenience in closely associating supervenience with laws; according to him, "supervenience does not imply the existence of psycho-physical laws," because "although supervenience entails that any change in a mental property *p* of a particular event *e* will be accompanied by a change in the physical properties of *e*, it does not entail that a change in *p* in other events will be accompanied by an identical change in the physical properties of those other events."[9] So far so good. But he goes on to add, "only the latter entailment would conflict with *AM+P*." Here, Davidson is plainly looking for the wrong kind of law; when the question of law is discussed in connection with supervenience, it almost always concerns laws *from* the base (or subvenient) properties *to* the supervenient properties (thus, physical-to-mental laws), not laws going in the opposite direction (mental-to-physical laws). Thus, assume that two systems are in the same total physical state (at the same or different times); psycho-physical supervenience implies this: *if the systems change in some identical physical respect Q, they must change in an identical psychological respect M.* In fact, mind-body supervenience (and supervenience in general) can be explained in terms of the existence of generalizations from the subvenient to the supervenient, thus: whenever anything has mental property M there is some physical property Q such that it has Q and everything that has Q has M. On certain plausible assumptions concerning property compositions, this formulation is demonstrably equivalent to the usual definition of supervenience in terms of indiscernibility in respect of supervenient and base properties.[10] There is of course a question as to whether the kind of supervenience Davidson says he has in mind, which appears to be equivalent to what I have called "weak supervenience," can impart to these generalizations an appropriate nomic force; but that isn't a question Davidson raises, and there is in any case a doubt as to whether weak supervenience can provide the kind of dependency relation that most philosophers want to associate with Supervenience.[11]

5. DOES $AM+P+S$ (THAT IS, DAVIDSONIAN SUPERVENIENCE) PROVIDE A SATISFACTORY ACCOUNT OF THE CAUSAL RELEVANCE OF MENTAL PROPERTIES?

On this question, Ernest Sosa[12] makes a number of cogent points in his reply, "Davidson's Thinking Causes," with which I am by and large in agreement. So I will make just one point.[13] "Causal relevance" may be one thing; "causal efficacy" another. An epiphenomenalist may argue, mimicking Davidson, that on his view mental properties are indeed causally relevant, since, according to his doctrine, what mental properties an event has makes a difference to what physical properties it has, and physical properties are causally efficacious. But that doesn't mean that he contradicts himself in refusing to allow causal efficacy to mental properties. If this is right, supervenience can at best show that mental properties are causally relevant, not that they are causally efficacious. And it would seem that to sustain the kind of position he has argued for in "Actions, Reasons, and Causes,"[14] Davidson may very well need causal efficacy, not just causal relevance, for mental properties. Mere causal relevance seems too weak to support the causal-explanatory "because" in rationalizing explanations. And it seems to me that most philosophers who believe in mental causation would want efficacy, not just relevance.

6. WHAT THEN OF $AM+P+NS$ (THE EXISTENCE OF "NON-STRICT" PSYCHO-PHYSICAL LAWS)?

From the text of "Thinking Causes," I am not certain that Davidson wants to embrace non-strict psycho-physical laws to account for the causal efficacy of mental properties, although that is the impression one gets. In any case, I think there are some serious difficulties with this approach for anyone who accepts $AM+P$. Whether NS can comfortably fit in with $AM+P$ is a question that has to wait until we are in possession of a clearer account of just what the "non-strictness" of non-strict laws consists in, or just what the much-bandied phrase "*ceteris paribus*" means when it qualifies a law. Davidson says that his position is consistent with Fodor's defence of mental causal efficacy based on non-strict laws hedged by "*ceteris paribus*" clauses. But it would be ill-advised for the anomalous monist to buy into Fodor's notion of "*ceteris paribus* law." For, according to Fodor, such a law has something like this form, "There exist conditions C_1, ... , C_m such that when they are satisfied, F-events cause G-events"; and when the C_i's have been identified, that will give us a strict law of the form "Under C_1^*, ... , C_m^*, F-events cause G-events," where each C_i^* is some value of the variable C_i that satisfies the open inner sentence.[15] Thus, on this account, a non-strict law is simply a strict law with some of its antecedent conditions existentially quantified. But that means that *where there is a non-strict psycho-physical law, there must be a strict psycho-physical law waiting to be discovered.* I think it obvious that the anomalous monist must reject this notion of non-strict law.

Moreover, it seems to me that, however the non-strictness of non-strict laws is explained, non-strict laws *are* laws and must carry an appropriate nomological force; given this, it isn't obvious that Davidson's fundamental argument against psycho-physical laws can allow even non-strict laws between the mental and the physical. As I understand it,[16] the gist of the argument is something like this: the mental domain and the physical domain are each governed by their own special synthetic a priori constitutive constraints (principles of rationality, in the case of the mental), and the existence of psycho-physical laws with their strong nomic force would ultimately bring these two sets of constitutive principles into conflict or at least jurisdictional disputes. Hence, if each domain is to retain its own integrity, there cannot be laws connecting them. It isn't clear why this argument, if it succeeds in banning strict psycho-physical laws, doesn't banish non-strict ones as well; at least, an explanation is called for. I have always thought that the power of the Davidsonian argument for mental anomalism is seen in the fact that, if it works at all, it should work against laws of all kinds—for example, statistical laws as well as deterministic ones (after all, the only strict laws we have may be statistical). Remember: non-strict laws, whatever they are, are supposed to be laws!

7. ARE THERE OTHER REASONS FOR BEING WARY OF *NS* ("NON-STRICT LAWS") IF YOU ARE AN ANOMALOUS MONIST?

Yes, there are. First, if you accept non-strict laws as nomological grounds of causal relations, you will need a convincing rationale for retaining Davidson's strict law requirement on causation. It can be seen, in fact, that having laws of both kinds ground causal relations opens up a serious new problem, "the problem of exclusion."[17] Suppose a mental event, *m*, causes an event *e* (which can be either mental or physical); *m*, as a mental event, must have some mental property, *M*, and let's assume that *M*, in virtue of a non-strict psycho-physical law relating it to some physical property of *e*, is causally efficacious in *m*'s causation of *e*. But, given the strict law requirement, *m* must also have a certain basic physical property *P* which is connected, by a strict law, to some property (presumably, another basic physical property) of *e*, and this fact grounds the causal relation between *m* and *e*. Thus, *m* turns out to have two properties each of which is causally efficacious in *m*'s causation of *e*, and, on *AM*, *M* and *P* are irreducibly distinct. We now face this question: given that the causal relation from *m* to *e* is grounded in the basic physical properties of *m* and *e* and a strict law relating them, what causal work is there for *M* to do?[18] *M*'s precise causal role in this picture—exactly what contribution *M* makes in the causation of *e*—is in need of an explanation. There are various moves one can make at this point, but the problem is there, especially for the adherents of *AM*.

The exclusion problem is a general problem with mental causation, something most of us have to contend with. There is, however, a further specific problem with *NS* that Davidson and friends of *AM* seem not to have recognized. It is this: *NS* may put anti-reductionism in serious jeopardy. One can still hold on to Davidson's claim that psychology is not reducible, by strict law, to some underlying physical theory. But why insist on reduction by strict laws only? *What's wrong with non-strict psycho-physical laws as "bridge" laws?* This is not an idle question; nor is it merely a verbal issue. For there seems to be a general consensus, among those who speak of the "strictness" of laws, that there are no strict laws outside basic physics, and Davidson seems to agree.[19] If this is correct, *there isn't going to be, and there has never been, any reduction anywhere in science—that is, if you insist on reduction via strict laws.* You are going to find strict laws only in basic physics, and you aren't going to reduce basic physics to basic physics! (At least, you are not going to find reductions outside basic physics.) This surely cannot be a sense of reduction that holds serious philosophical interest for us. If psychology is reducible by the same standards that apply to the best cases of theory reduction in the sciences (pick your favourite examples), why isn't that reduction enough? There has been a tendency, among some current anti-reductionists, to base their arguments on an unrealistically stringent and idealized model of reduction, thereby weakening their conclusions.

I think "non-strict laws" are bad news for anomalous monists. In embracing them they may end up losing anomalism from anomalous monism.

Notes

1   Donald Davidson, "Thinking Causes," in J. Heil and A. Mele, eds., *Mental Causation* (Oxford: Clarendon Press, 1993), 3-17, essay 13 in this volume.

2   Jaegwon Kim, "The Myth of Nonreductive Materialism," *Proceedings of the American Philosophical Association* 63 (1989), 35.

3   Davidson, op. cit., 6, this volume, 136.

4   The sentence that immediately precedes the one in question reads as follows: "For anomalous monism entails this: the very same network of causal relations would obtain in Davidson's world if you were to redistribute mental properties over its events any way you like; you would not disturb a single causal relation if you randomly and arbitrarily reassigned mental properties to events, or even removed mentality entirely from the world" (Kim, "The Myth of Nonreductive Materialism," op. cit., 34-35).

5   I believe Brian McLaughlin was the first to argue this point; see his "Type Epiphenomenalism, Type Dualism, and the Causal Priority of the Physical," *Philosophical Perspectives* 3 (1989), 109-35.

6   E.g. McLaughlin, op. cit.; E. Lepore and B. Loewer, "Mind Matters," *Journal of Philosophy* 84 (1987), 630-42. See also Terence Horgan, "Mental Quausation," *Philosophical Perspectives* 3 (1989), 47-76, essay 25 in this volume; C. MacDonald and G. MacDonald, "Mental Causes and Explanation of Action," *Philosophical Quarterly* 36 (1986), 145-58. The strategies that have been tried include the use of non-strict laws and certain causal counterfactuals.

7   Davidson includes me among those who have used such expressions, on the basis of my writing "on anomalous monism, events are causes only as they instantiate laws." The culprit in Davidson's light is the word "as"; I used it in the sense of "because" or "since," but Davidson apparently takes it in the sense of "qua" or "in the role of," which is a bit curious, given that "as" in my sentence functions as a grammatical conjunction, not a preposition.

8   See Jaegwon Kim, "Concepts of Supervenience," *Philosophy and Phenomenological Research* 65 (1984), 153-76, essay 22 in this volume, and "Supervenience as a Philosophical Concept," *Metaphilosophy* 21 (1990), 1-27.

9   Davidson, "Thinking Causes," op. cit., 6, this volume, 137.

10   Kim, "Concepts of Supervenience," op. cit., essay 22 in this volume, and "'Strong' and 'Global' Supervenience Revisited," *Philosophy and Phenomenological Research* 48 (1987), 315-26.

11   See Kim, "Concepts of Supervenience," op. cit., essay 22 in this volume.

12   Ernest Sosa, "Davidson's Thinking Causes," in J. Heil and A. Mele, eds., *Mental Causation* (Oxford: Clarendon, 1993), 41-50.

13   I have myself given an account of mental causation on the basis of supervenience; see e.g. Kim, "Causality, Identity, and Supervenience in the Mind-Body Problem," *Midwest Studies in Philosophy* 4 (1979), 31-49, and "Epiphenomenal

and Supervenient Causation," *Midwest Studies in Philosophy* 9 (1984), 257-70, essay 23 in this volume. My account is based on a supervenience relation stronger than Davidson's. I am inclined to think, however, that even this stronger supervenience relation may not be strong enough for a fully adequate account of mental causation.

14 Donald Davidson, "Actions, Reasons, and Causes," *Journal of Philosophy* 60 (1963), 685-700.

15 Jerry Fodor, "Making Mind Matter More," *Philosophical Topics* 17 (1989), 75-76

16 Jaegwon Kim, "Psychophysical Laws," in E. Lepore and B. McLaughlin eds., *Actions and Events: Perspectives on the Philosophy of Donald Davidson* (Oxford: Basil Blackwell, 1985), 369-86.

17 Jaegwon Kim, "Mechanism, Purpose and Explanatory Exclusion," *Philosophical Perspectives* 3 (1989), 77-108.

18 E. Lepore and B. Loewer, "More on Making Mind Matter," *Philosophical Topics* 17 (1989), 175-91, raise a similar difficulty with respect to Fodor's account of mental causation in terms of *ceteris paribus* psychological laws. There is a brief discussion of this issue in "Thinking Causes."

19 Davidson says, "I made clear that what I was calling a law in this context was something that one could at best hope to find in a developed physics" ("Thinking Causes," op. cit., 8, this volume, 138.). Others who hold a similar view include Fodor, and Lepore and Loewer. I am not sure I understand what Davidson means by "developed physics"; whatever it is, it follows that Davidson isn't going to find any reductions outside "developed physics."

PART III
Qualia

15

EPIPHENOMENAL QUALIA*

Frank Jackson

It is undeniable that the physical, chemical and biological sciences have provided a great deal of information about the world we live in and about ourselves. I will use the label "physical information" for this kind of information, and also for information that automatically comes along with it. For example, if a medical scientist tells me enough about the processes that go on in my nervous system, and about how they relate to happenings in the world around me, to what has happened in the past and is likely to happen in the future, to what happens to other similar and dissimilar organisms, and the like, he or she tells me—if I am clever enough to fit it together appropriately—about what is often called the functional role of those states in me (and in organisms in general in similar cases). This information, and its kin, I also label "physical."

I do not mean these sketchy remarks to constitute a definition of "physical information," and of the correlative notions of physical property, process, and so on, but to indicate what I have in mind here. It is well known that there are problems with giving a precise definition of these notions, and so of the thesis of Physicalism that all (correct) information is physical information.[1] But—unlike some—I take the question of definition to cut across the central problems I want to discuss in this paper.

I am what is sometimes known as a "qualia freak." I think that there are certain features of the bodily sensations especially, but also of certain perceptual experiences, which no amount of purely physical information includes. Tell me everything physical there is to tell about what is going on in a living brain, the kind of states, their functional role, their relation to what goes on at other times and in other brains, and so on and so forth, and be I as clever as can be in fitting it all together, you won't have told me about the hurtfulness of pains, the itchiness of itches, pangs of jealousy, or about the characteristic experience of tasting a lemon, smelling a rose, hearing a loud noise or seeing the sky.

* Frank Jackson, "Epiphenomenal Qualia," *Philosophical Quarterly* 32 (1982), 127-36. Reprinted with kind permission of the publisher.

There are many qualia freaks, and some of them say that their rejection of Physicalism is an unargued intuition.[2] I think that they are being unfair to themselves. They have the following argument. Nothing you could tell of a physical sort captures the smell of a rose, for instance. Therefore, Physicalism is false. By our lights this is a perfectly good argument. It is obviously not to the point to question its validity, and the premise is intuitively obviously true both to them and to me.

I must, however, admit that it is weak from a polemical point of view. There are, unfortunately for us, many who do not find the premise intuitively obvious. The task then is to present an argument whose premises are obvious to all, or at least to as many as possible. This I try to do in §I with what I will call "the Knowledge argument." In §II I contrast the Knowledge argument with the Modal argument and in §III with the "What is it like to be" argument. In §IV I tackle the question of the causal role of qualia. The major factor in stopping people from admitting qualia is the belief that they would have to be given a causal role with respect to the physical world and especially the brain;[3] and it is hard to do this without sounding like someone who believes in fairies. I seek in §IV to turn this objection by arguing that the view that qualia are epiphenomenal is a perfectly possible one.

I. THE KNOWLEDGE ARGUMENT FOR QUALIA

People vary considerably in their ability to discriminate colours. Suppose that in an experiment to catalogue this variation Fred is discovered. Fred has better colour vision than anyone else on record; he makes every discrimination that anyone has ever made, and moreover he makes one that we cannot even begin to make. Show him a batch of ripe tomatoes and he sorts them into two roughly equal groups and does so with complete consistency. That is, if you blindfold him, shuffle the tomatoes up, and then remove the blindfold and ask him to sort them out again, he sorts them into exactly the same two groups.

We ask Fred how he does it. He explains that all ripe tomatoes do not look the same colour to him, and in fact that this is true of a great many objects that we classify together as red. He sees two colours where we see one, and he has in consequence developed for his own use two words "red_1" and "red_2" to mark the difference. Perhaps he tells us that he has often tried to teach the difference between red_1 and red_2 to his friends but has got nowhere and has concluded that the rest of the world is red_1-red_2 colour-blind—or perhaps he has had partial success with his children, it doesn't matter. In any case he explains to us that it would be quite wrong to think that because "red" appears in both "red_1" and "red_2" that the two colours are shades of the one colour. He only uses the common term "red" to fit more easily into our restricted usage. To him red_1 and red_2 are as different from each other and all the other colours as yellow is from blue. And his discriminatory behaviour bears this out: he sorts red_1 from red_2 tomatoes with the greatest of ease in a wide variety of viewing circumstances. Moreover, an investigation of the physiological basis of Fred's exceptional ability reveals that Fred's optical system is able to separate out two groups of wave-lengths in the red spectrum as sharply as we are able to sort out yellow from blue.[4]

I think that we should admit that Fred can see, really see, at least one more colour than we can; red_1 is a different colour from red_2. We are to Fred as a totally red-green colour-blind person is to us. H.G. Wells' story "The Country of the Blind" is about a sighted person in a totally blind community.[5] This person never manages to convince them that he can see, that he has an extra sense. They ridicule this sense as quite inconceivable, and treat his capacity to avoid falling into ditches, to win fights and so on as precisely that capacity and nothing more. We would be making their mistake if we refused to allow that Fred can see one more colour than we can.

What kind of experience does Fred have when he sees red_1 and red_2? What is the new colour or colours like? We would dearly like to know but do not; and it seems that no amount of physical information about Fred's brain and optical system tells us. We find out perhaps that Fred's cones respond deferentially to certain light waves in the red section of the spectrum that make no difference to ours (or perhaps he has an extra cone) and that this leads in Fred to a wider range of those brain states responsible for visual discriminatory behaviour. But none of this tells us what we really want to know about his colour experience. There is something about it we don't know. But we know, we may suppose, everything about Fred's body, his behaviour and dispositions to behaviour and about his internal physiology, and everything about his history and relation to others that can be given in physical accounts of persons. We have all the physical information. Therefore, knowing all this is *not* knowing everything about Fred. It follows that Physicalism leaves something out.

To reinforce this conclusion, imagine that as a result of our investigations into the internal workings of Fred we find out how to make everyone's physiology like Fred's in the relevant respects; or perhaps Fred donates his body to science and on his death we are able to transplant his optical system into someone else—again the fine detail doesn't matter. The important point is that such a happening would create enormous interest. People would say, "At last we will know what it is like to see the extra colour, at last we will know how Fred has differed from us in the way he has struggled to tell us about for so long." Then it cannot be that we knew all along all about Fred. But *ex hypothesi* we did know all along everything about Fred that features in the physicalist scheme; hence the physicalist scheme leaves something out.

Put it this way. After the operation, we will know more about Fred and especially about his colour experiences. But beforehand we had all the physical information we could desire about his body and brain, and indeed everything that has ever featured in physicalist accounts of mind and consciousness. Hence there is more to know than all that. Hence Physicalism is incomplete.

Fred and the new colour(s) are of course essentially rhetorical devices. The same point can be made with normal people and familiar colours. Mary is a brilliant scientist who is, for whatever reason, forced to investigate the world from a black and white room *via* a black and white television monitor. She specialises in the neurophysiology of vision and acquires, let us suppose, all the physical information there is to obtain about what goes on when we see ripe tomatoes, or the sky, and use terms like "red," "blue," and so on. She discovers, for example, just which wavelength combinations from the sky stimulate the retina, and exactly how this produces *via* the central nervous system the contraction of the vocal chords and expulsion of air from the lungs that results in the uttering of the sentence "The sky is blue." (It can hardly be denied that it is in principle possible to obtain all this physical information from black and white television, otherwise the Open University would of *necessity* need to use colour television.)

What will happen when Mary is released from her black and white room or is given a colour television monitor? Will she *learn* anything or not? It seems just obvious that she will learn something about the world and our visual experience of it. But then it is inescapable that her previous knowledge was incomplete. But she had *all* the physical information. Ergo there is more to have than that, and Physicalism is false.

Clearly the same style of Knowledge argument could be deployed for taste, hearing, the bodily sensations and generally speaking for the various mental states which are said to have (as it is variously put) raw feels, phenomenal features or qualia. The conclusion in each case is that the qualia are left out of the physicalist story. And the polemical strength of the Knowledge argument is that it is so hard to deny the central claim that one can have all the physical information without having all the information there is to have.

II. THE MODAL ARGUMENT

By the Modal Argument I mean an argument of the following style.[6] Sceptics about other minds are not making a mistake in deductive logic, whatever else may be wrong with their position. No amount of physical information about another *logically entails* that he or she is conscious or feels anything at all. Consequently there is a possible world with organisms exactly like us in every physical respect (and remember that includes functional states, physical history, *et al.*) but which differ from us profoundly in that they have no conscious mental life at all. But then what is it that we have and they lack? Not anything physical *ex hypothesi*. In all physical regards we and they are exactly alike. Consequently there is more to us than the purely physical. Thus Physicalism is false.[7]

It is sometimes objected that the Modal argument misconceives Physicalism on the ground that that doctrine is advanced as a *contingent* truth.[8] But to say this is only to say that physicalists restrict their claim to *some* possible worlds, including especially ours; and the Modal argument is only directed against this lesser claim. If we in our world, let alone beings in any others, have features additional to those of our physical replicas in other possible worlds, then we have non-physical features or qualia.

The trouble rather with the Modal argument is that it rests on a disputable modal intuition. Disputable because it is disputed. Some sincerely deny that there can be physical replicas of us in other possible worlds which nevertheless lack consciousness. Moreover, at least one person who once had the intuition now has doubts.[9]

Head-counting may seem a poor approach to a discussion of the Modal argument. But frequently we can do no better when modal intuitions are in question, and remember our initial goal was to find the argument with the greatest polemical utility.

Of course, *qua* protagonists of the Knowledge argument we may well accept the modal intuition in question; but this will be a *consequence* of our already having an argument to the conclusion that qualia are left out of the physicalist story, not our ground for that conclusion. Moreover, the matter is complicated by the possibility that the connection between matters physical and qualia is like that sometimes held to obtain between aesthetic qualities and natural ones. Two possible worlds which agree in all "natural" respects (including the experiences of sentient creatures) must agree in all aesthetic qualities also, but it is plausibly held that the aesthetic qualities cannot be reduced to the natural.

III. THE "WHAT IS IT LIKE TO BE" ARGUMENT

In "What is it like to be a bat?" Thomas Nagel argues that no amount of physical information can tell us what it is like to be a bat, and indeed that we, human beings, cannot imagine what it is like to be a bat.[10] His reason is that what this is like can only be understood from a bat's point of view, which is not our point of view and is not something capturable in physical terms which are essentially terms understandable equally from many points of view.

It is important to distinguish this argument from the Knowledge argument. When I complained that all the physical knowledge about Fred was not enough to tell us what his special colour experience was like, I was not complaining that we weren't finding out what it is like to *be* Fred. I was complaining that there is something *about* his experience, a property of it, of which we were left ignorant. And if and when we come to know what this property is we still will not know what it is like to *be* Fred, but we will know more *about* him. No amount of knowledge about Fred, be it physical or not, amounts to knowledge "from the inside" concerning Fred. We are not Fred. There is thus a whole set of items of knowledge expressed by forms of words like "that it is *I myself* who is ..." which Fred has and we simply cannot have because we are not him.[11]

When Fred sees the colour he alone can see, one thing he knows is the way his experience of it differs from his experience of seeing red and so on, *another* is that he himself is seeing it. Physicalist and qualia freaks alike should acknowledge that no amount of information of whatever kind that *others* have *about* Fred amounts to knowledge of the second. My complaint though concerned the first and was that the special quality of his experience is certainly a fact about it, and one which Physicalism leaves out because no amount of physical information told us what it is.

Nagel speaks as if the problem he is raising is one of extrapolating from knowledge of one experience to another, of imagining what an unfamiliar experience would be like on the basis of familiar ones. In terms of Hume's example, from knowledge of some shades of blue we can work out what it would be like to see other shades of blue. Nagel argues that the trouble with bats *et al.* is that they are too unlike us. It is hard to see an objection to Physicalism here. Physicalism makes no special claims about the imaginative or extrapolative powers of human beings, and it is hard to see why it need do so.[12]

Anyway, our Knowledge argument makes no assumptions on this point. If Physicalism were true, enough physical information about Fred would obviate any need to extrapolate or to perform special feats of imagination or understanding in order to know all about his special colour experience. *The information would already be in our possession.* But it clearly isn't. That was the nub of the argument.

IV. THE BOGEY OF EPIPHENOMENALISM

Is there any really *good* reason for refusing to countenance the idea that qualia are causally impotent with respect to the physical world? I will argue for the answer no, but in doing this I will say nothing about two views associated with the classical epiphenomenalist position. The first is that mental *states* are inefficacious with respect to the physical world. All I will be concerned to defend is that it is possible to hold that certain *properties* of certain mental states, namely those I've called qualia, are such that their possession or absence makes no difference to the physical world. The second is that the mental is *totally* causally inefficacious. For all I will say it may be that you have to hold that the instantiation of *qualia* makes a difference to *other mental states* though not to anything physical. Indeed general considerations to do with how you could come to be aware of the instantiation of qualia suggest such a position.[13]

Three reasons are standardly given for holding that a quale like the hurtfulness of a pain must be causally efficacious in the physical world, and so, for instance, that its instantiation must sometimes make a difference to what happens in the brain. None, I will argue, has any real force. (I am much indebted to Alec Hyslop and John Lucas for convincing me of this.)

(i) It is supposed to be just obvious that the hurtfulness of pain is partly responsible for the subject seeking to avoid pain, saying "It hurts" and so on. But, to reverse Hume, anything can fail to cause anything. No matter how often *B* follows *A*, and no matter how initially obvious the causality of the connection seems, the hypothesis that *A* causes *B* can be overturned by an overarching theory which shows the two as distinct effects of a common underlying causal process.

To the untutored the image on the screen of Lee Marvin's fist moving from left to right immediately followed by the image of John Wayne's head moving in the same general direction looks as causal as anything.[14] And of course throughout countless Westerns images similar to the first are followed by images similar to the second. All this counts for precisely nothing when we know the over-arching theory concerning how the relevant images are both effects of an underlying causal process involving the projector and the film. The epiphenomenalist can say exactly the same about the connection between, for example, hurtfulness and behaviour. It is simply a consequence of the fact that certain happenings in the brain cause both.

(ii) The second objection relates to Darwin's Theory of Evolution. According to natural selection the traits that evolve over time are those conducive to physical survival. We may assume that qualia evolved over time—we have them, the earliest forms of life do not—and so we should expect qualia to be conducive to survival. The objection is that they could hardly help us to survive if they do nothing to the physical world.

The appeal of this argument is undeniable, but there is a good reply to it. Polar bears have particularly thick, warm coats. The Theory of Evolution explains this (we suppose) by pointing out that having a thick, warm coat is conducive to survival in the Arctic. But having a thick coat goes along with having a heavy coat, and having a heavy coat is *not* conducive to survival. It slows the animal down.

Does this mean that we have refuted Darwin because we have found an evolved trait—having a heavy coat—which is not conducive to survival? Clearly not. Having a heavy coat is an unavoidable concomitant of having a warm coat (in the context, modern insulation was not available), and the advantages for survival of having a warm coat outweighed the disadvantages of having a heavy one. The point is that all we can extract from Darwin's theory is that we should expect any evolved characteristic to be *either* conducive to survival *or* a by-product of one that is so conducive. The epiphenomenalist holds that qualia fall into the latter category. They are a by-product of certain brain processes that are highly conducive to survival.

(iii) The third objection is based on a point about how we come to know about other minds. We know about other minds by knowing about other behaviour, at least in part. The nature of the inference is a matter of some controversy, but it is not a matter of controversy that it proceeds from behaviour. That is why we think that stones do not feel and dogs do feel. But, runs the objection, how can a person's behaviour provide any reason for believing he has qualia like mine, or indeed any qualia at all, unless this behaviour can be regarded as the *outcome* of the qualia. Man Friday's footprint was evidence of Man Friday because footprints are causal outcomes of feet attached to people. And an epiphenomenalist cannot regard behaviour or indeed anything physical, as an outcome of qualia.

But consider my reading in *The Times* that Spurs won. This provides excellent evidence that *The Telegraph* has also reported that Spurs won, despite the fact that (I trust) *The Telegraph* does not get the results from *The Times*. They each send their own reporters to the game. *The Telegraph*'s report is in no sense an outcome of *The Times*'s, but the latter provides good evidence for the former nevertheless.

The reasoning involved can be reconstructed thus. I read in *The Times* that Spurs won. This gives me reason to think that Spurs won because I know that Spurs's winning is the most likely candidate to be what caused the report in *The Times*. But I also know that Spurs's winning would have had many effects, including almost certainly a report in *The Telegraph*.

I am arguing from one effect back to its cause and out again to another effect. The fact that neither effect causes the other is irrelevant. Now the epiphenomenalist allows that qualia are effects of what goes on in the brain. Qualia cause nothing physical but are caused by something physical. Hence the epiphenomenalist can argue from the behaviour of others to the qualia of others by arguing from the behaviour of others back to its causes in the brains of others and out again to their qualia.

You may well feel for one reason or another that this is a more dubious chain of reasoning than its model in the case of newspaper reports. You are right. The problem of other minds is a major philosophical problem, the problem of other newspaper reports is not. But there is no special problem of Epiphenomenalism as opposed to, say, Interactionism here.

There is a very understandable response to the three replies I have just made. "All right, there is no knockdown refutation of the existence of epiphenomenal qualia. But the fact remains that they are an excrescence. They do nothing, they *explain* nothing, they serve merely to soothe the intuitions of dualists, and it is left a total mystery how they fit into the world view of science. In short we do not and cannot understand the how and why of them."

This is perfectly true; but is no objection to qualia, for it rests on an overly optimistic view of the human animal, and its powers. We are the products of Evolution. We understand and sense what we need to understand and sense in order to survive. Epiphenomenal qualia are totally irrelevant to survival. At no stage of our evolution did natural selection favour those who could make sense of how they are caused and the laws governing them, or in fact why they exist at all. And that is why we can't.

It is not sufficiently appreciated that Physicalism is an extremely optimistic view of our powers. If it is true, we have, in very broad outline admittedly, a grasp of our place in the scheme of things. Certain matters of sheer complexity defeat us—there are an awful lot of neurons—but in principle we have it all. But consider the antecedent probability that everything in the Universe be of a kind that is relevant in some way or other to the survival of *homo sapiens*. It is very low surely. But then one must admit that it is very likely that there is a part of the whole scheme of things, maybe a big part, which no amount of evolution will ever bring us near to knowledge about or understanding. For the simple reason that such knowledge and understanding is irrelevant to survival.

Physicalists typically emphasise that we are a part of nature on their view, which is fair enough. But if we are a part of nature, we are as nature has left us after however many years of evolution it is, and each step in that evolutionary progression has been a matter of chance constrained just by the need to preserve or increase survival value. The wonder is that we understand as much as we do, and there is no wonder that there should be matters which fall quite outside our comprehension. Perhaps exactly how epiphenomenal qualia fit into the scheme of things is one such.

This may seem an unduly pessimistic view of our capacity to articulate a truly comprehensive picture of our world and our place in it. But suppose we discovered living on the bottom of the deepest oceans a sort of sea slug which manifested intelligence. Perhaps survival in the conditions required rational powers. Despite their intelligence, these sea slugs have only a very restricted conception of the world by comparison with ours, the explanation for this being the nature of their immediate environment. Nevertheless they have developed sciences which work surprisingly well in these restricted terms. They also have philosophers, called slugists. Some call themselves tough-minded slugists, others confess to being soft-minded slugists.

The tough-minded slugists hold that the restricted terms (or ones pretty like them which may be introduced as their sciences progress) suffice in principle to describe everything without remainder. These tough-minded slugists admit in moments of weakness to a feeling that their theory leaves something out. They resist this feeling and their opponents, the soft-minded slugists, by pointing out—absolutely correctly—that no slugist has ever succeeded in spelling out how this mysterious residue fits into the highly successful view that their sciences have and are developing of how their world works.

Our sea slugs don't exist, but they might. And there might also exist super beings which stand to us as we stand to the sea slugs. We cannot adopt the perspective of these super beings, because we are not them, but the possibility of such a perspective is, I think, an antidote to excessive optimism.

Notes

1 See, e.g., D.H. Mellor, "Materialism and Phenomenal Qualities," *Aristotelian Society Supp. Vol.* 47 (1973), 107-19; and J.W. Cornman, *Materialism and Sensations* (New Haven, CT: Yale University Press, 1971).

2 Particularly in discussion, but see, e.g., Keith Campbell, *Metaphysics* (Encino, CA: Dickenson Pub. Co., 1976), 67.

3 See, e.g., D.C. Dennett, "Current Issues in the Philosophy of Mind," *American Philosophical Quarterly* 15 (1978), 249-61.

4 Put this, and similar simplifications below, in terms of Land's theory if you prefer. See, e.g., Edwin H. Land, "Experiments in Color Vision," *Scientific American* 200 (1959), 84-99.

5 H.G. Wells, *The Country of the Blind and Other Stories* (London, n.d.).

6 See, e.g., Keith Campbell, *Body and Mind* (London: Macmillan, 1970); and Robert Kirk, "Sentience and Behaviour," *Mind* 83 (1974), 43-60.

7 I have presented the argument in an inter-world rather than the more usual intraworld fashion to avoid inessential complications to do with supervenience, causal anomalies and the like.

8 See, e.g., W.G. Lycan, "A New Lilliputian Argument Against Machine Functionalism," *Philosophical Studies* 35 (1979), 279-87, 280; and Don Locke, "Zombies, Schizophrenics and Purely Physical Objects," *Mind* 85 (1976), 97-99.

9 See R. Kirk, "From Physical Explicability to Full-Blooded Materialism," *The Philosophical Quarterly* 29 (1979), 229-37. See also the arguments against the modal intuition in, e.g., Sydney Shoemaker, "Functionalism and Qualia," *Philosophical Studies* 27 (1975), 291-315.

10 *The Philosophical Review* 83 (1974), 435-50. Two things need to be said about this article. One is that, despite my dissociations to come, I am much indebted to it. The other is that the emphasis changes through the article, and by the end Nagel is objecting not so much to Physicalism as to all extant theories of mind for ignoring points of view, including those that admit (irreducible) qualia.

11 Knowledge *de se* in the terms of David Lewis, "Attitudes De Dicto and De Se," *The Philosophical Review* 88 (1979), 513-43.

12 See Laurence Nemirow's comments on "What is it ..." in his review of T. Nagel, *Mortal Questions*, in *The Philosophical Review* 89 (1980), 473-77. I am indebted here in particular to a discussion with David Lewis.

13 See my review of K. Campbell, *Body and Mind*, in *Australasian Journal of Philosophy* 50 (1972), 77-80.

14 Cf. Jean Piaget, "The Child's Conception of Physical Causality," reprinted in *The Essential Piaget* (London: Routlege and Kegan, 1977).

16

JACKSON ON PHYSICAL INFORMATION AND QUALIA*

Terence Horgan

In a provocative recent paper, Frank Jackson argues against Physicalism by appeal to the qualitative or phenomenal features of our mental life.[1] He maintains that Physicalism is refuted by the fact that no amount of physical information could ever enable us to know what it is like to undergo a pain, have an itch, taste a lemon, smell a rose, hear a loud noise, or see the sky. He concludes that qualia are epiphenomenal, i.e., "their presence or absence makes no difference to the physical world."[2] In the present paper I shall argue that his attack on Physicalism is fallacious, being an equivocation on two different senses of the phrase "physical information."

I. THE KNOWLEDGE ARGUMENT

Jackson construes Physicalism as the thesis that "all (correct) information is physical information."[3] He considers it an open philosophical question how exactly to define "physical information," but he indicates that he employs this expression broadly enough to include whatever information the physical, chemical, and biological sciences provide about the world—including what is often called the functional role of various physicochemical and biological states of humans and other organisms. I myself think that Physicalism should instead be formulated as the conjunction of a general supervenience thesis and a general thesis about the physical nature of all substantival individuals,[4] but I shall accept Jackson's characterization for purposes of the present discussion. I also shall follow his practice of speaking of information, and of items of information, as though these are entities of some sort, distinct from sentences. I doubt that there are such entities, but avoiding apparent ontological commitment to them is not my present concern.

He does not say which kinds of currently popular mind-body theories count as Physicalistic in his sense—i.e., which kinds entail that all informa-

* Terence Horgan, "Jackson on Physical Information and Qualia," *Philosophical Quarterly* 34 (1984), 147-52. Reprinted with kind permission of the publisher.

tion about mentality is physical information. But I take it that he means to include type-type psychophysical identity theories, functionalist theories which embrace type-type identity claims, and functionalist theories which repudiate type-type identity claims.[5] It is less plausible to regard token-token identity theories as Physicalistic by themselves, however, since they tell us nothing about identity conditions for mental state-*types*, or mental properties.

He construes *qualia*, and so shall I, as properties of certain mental states: properties like the hurtfulness of pain, the itchiness of itches, and the qualitative character of one's experience when one is smelling a rose. The question, then, is whether Physicalism can accommodate these qualitative, or phenomenal, properties.

He uses the following line of reasoning, which he dubs the *knowledge argument*, in an effort to convince us that *qualia* are left out of any Physicalist story. Suppose that Fred can discriminate two groups of wavelengths in the red spectrum as consistently as we are able to sort out yellow from blue; and suppose he reports that the two kinds of red he can discriminate, which he calls red_1 and red_2, look as different to him as yellow and blue. Then Fred can see at least one more colour than we can; we are to Fred as a totally red-green colour-blind person is to us. Jackson writes:

> What kind of experience does Fred have when he sees red_1 and red_2? What is the new colour or colours like? We would dearly like to know but do not; and it seems that no amount of physical information about Fred's brain and optical system tells us ... There is something about [Fred's colour experiences] we don't know. But we know, we may suppose, everything about Fred's body, his behaviour and dispositions to behaviour and about his internal physiology, and everything about his history and relation to others that can be given in physical accounts of persons. We have all the physical information. Therefore, knowing all this is *not* knowing everything about Fred. It follows that Physicalism leaves something out.[6]

In short, what no amount of physical information can tell us is *what the new colour or colours are like*. Physicalism leaves out *qualia*.

This conclusion is reinforced, says Jackson, by supposing that one's own visual physiology is going to be surgically altered to match Fred's. After the operation one will know something about Fred's red_1 and red_2 experiences one did not know before, viz., what they are like. And this new information cannot be physical information, because *ex hypothesi* we had all the relevant physical information beforehand. So Physicalism must be false.

He goes on to note that Fred and the new colour(s) are inessential to the basic line of reasoning, which instead he formulated this way:

Mary is a brilliant scientist who is, for whatever reason, forced to investigate the world from a black and white room *via* a black and white television monitor. She specialises in the neurophysiology of vision and acquires, let us suppose, all the physical information there is to obtain about what goes on when we see ripe tomatoes, or the sky, and use terms like "red," "blue," and so on....

What will happen when Mary is released from her black and white room or is given a colour television monitor? Will she *learn* anything or not? It seems just obvious that she will learn something about the world and our visual experience of it. But then it is inescapable that her previous knowledge was incomplete. But she had *all* the physical information. *Ergo* there is more to have than that, and Physicalism is false.[7]

In short, what Mary learns are non-physical items of information: what it is like to see ripe tomatoes, what it is like to see the sky, and so on. She learns about qualia, which thus are non-physical properties.

II. CRITIQUE OF THE KNOWLEDGE ARGUMENT

Elsewhere I myself have argued, to the contrary, that *qualia* are physical properties,[8] yet I am quite prepared to concede that we do not know what Fred's red_1 and red_2 experiences are like, no matter how adequate a physical account we have of Fred's visual processes; and that Mary does not know what seeing ripe tomatoes and seeing the sky are like, prior to her first colour-experiences, despite having a fully adequate physical account of human visual processes. What I want to question is Jackson's supposition that a completely adequate physical account of a creature's visual processes gives us complete physical information about those processes. In one sense of "physical information," this supposition is virtually a tautology: for, physical information is just the formation that would be provided by a theoretically adequate physical account. But in another sense— the sense really required by the knowledge argument—the supposition is one that Physicalists can and should reject.

In order to develop this point, we need to characterize the two relevant senses of "physical information." Let S be a sentence that expresses information about processes of a certain specific kind, such as human perceptual processes. We shall say that S expresses *explicitly physical information* just in case S belongs to, or follows from, a theoretically adequate physical account of those processes. And we shall say that S expresses *ontologically physical information* just in case (i) all the entities referred to or quantified over in S are physical entities, and (ii) all the properties and relations expressed by the predicates in S are physical properties and relations. Thus, explicitly physical information is expressed in overtly physicalistic language, whereas ontologically physical information can be expressed by other sorts of language—for instance, mentalistic language.

One might think that information per se is independent of the language in which it is expressed, and thus that any sentence which expresses ontologically physical information has the same informational content as some sentence which expresses explicitly physical information. But in fact, the notion of information which Jackson employs in his knowledge argument is heavily intensional. He clearly holds that if one lacks an item of knowledge then one lacks the corresponding item of information: witness his inference from the claim that we don't *know* what Fred's red_1 and red_2 experiences are like to the conclusion that we lack *information* about those experiences, and the parallel inference from the claim that Mary doesn't know what colour-experiences are like to the conclusion that she lacks information about them. This close link between knowledge and information means that information inherits the intensionality of knowledge. Thus, since Lois Lane knows that Superman can fly but does not know that Clark Kent can fly, (1) and (2) must express different information even though they each attribute the same property to the same individual:

(1) Superman can fly.
(2) Clark Kent can fly.

So it is entirely likely that there are sentences which express ontologically physical information but not explicitly physical information.

Physicalism, construed as the doctrine that all information is physical information, is a claim about ontologically physical information. For, the Physicalist obviously does not mean to claim that the only genuine information-conveying language is the language of physical theories. Rather, he means to claim that whenever a genuine piece of information is conveyed in *any* kind of language (mentalistic language, for instance), the relevant entities, properties, and relations are all physical.

Let us now return to the knowledge argument. We shall focus on the case of Mary, but the following remarks will also apply, *mutatis mutandis*, to the case of Fred. Consider Mary at the moment when she finally has her first colour-experience—say, the experience of seeing ripe tomatoes. Jackson maintains, and I agree, that Mary obtains new knowledge at this moment, and thus new information: she finds out what it is like to see ripe tomatoes. How might she formulate this new knowledge? Not with a sentence like

(3) Seeing ripe tomatoes is like seeing bright sunsets,

because she presumably already has the knowledge expressed by (3) by virtue of having heard the reports of many human subjects in the course of her extensive visual-perception studies. And the same holds for any other similarity judgments that are commonly made about colour experiences. Rather, it seems she should express her new knowledge by means of an indexical term, as in (4):

(4) Seeing ripe tomatoes has *this* property,

where "this property" is used to designate the colour-*quale* that is instantiated in her present experience.[9] (We shall call this property *phenomenal redness*. It should not be confused, of course, with the redness-property instantiated in the tomatoes themselves.)

Now, (4) as used by Mary certainly doesn't express explicitly physical information; for it expresses new information, and she had all the relevant explicitly physical information beforehand. (The phrase "this property" is topic-neutral, rather than explicitly physical.) But (4) may very well express *ontologically* physical information. Phenomenal redness, the referent of "this property," may very well be a physical property. This possibility is not ruled out by the fact that Mary learns something new from her experience.

Sentence (4) expresses new information because Mary has a new perspective on phenomenal redness: viz., the first-person ostensive perspective. Her new information is about the phenomenal colour-property *as experienced*. Thus she could not have had this information prior to undergoing the relevant sort of experience herself. But these facts are compatible with Physicalism; there is no need to suppose that when she acquires experiential awareness of phenomenal redness, she thereby comes into contact with a property distinct from those already countenanced in her prior physical account of human perception. The perspective is new, and so is the accompanying capacity to designate the relevant property indexically in a first-person ostensive manner. But the property itself need not be new.

Of course if Physicalism is correct, then a fully adequate account of human perception and cognition would have to explain the human capacity to discriminate, and then ostensively designate, those physical properties of our own neural activity which are qualia. But nothing in the knowledge argument provides any reason to think that such an explanation could not be given.

We may conclude, therefore, that the knowledge argument is fallacious; it rests upon a subtle equivocation between two senses of "physical information." Although Mary, prior to her first colour experience, does have a complete stock of *explicitly* physical information about human visual processes, it is illegitimate to infer from this that she has a complete stock of *ontologically* physical information. Physicalists can and should claim that the new information she acquires, the information she expresses by using (4), is ontologically physical information. The information is new not because the *quale* she experiences is a non-physical property, but because she is now acquainted with this property from the experiential perspective.

Perhaps it will be replied that the phrase "this property" in (4) cannot designate a physical property, because if it did then (4) would express a piece of information which Mary had already: viz., the information that ripe-tomato perceptions possess the given physical property. But this reply ignores the all-important intensionality of the notion of information. Even though Superman is Clark Kent, nevertheless we must distinguish between the information that Superman can fly and the information that Clark Kent can fly. Similarly, even if phenomenal redness is a physical property, nevertheless we must distinguish between (i) the information that the given property, as physicalistically described, is possessed by ripe-tomato experiences, and (ii) the information which Mary expresses by (4).

Finally, if Physicalism is true then *qualia* presumably have all the effects which common sense attributes to them. The hurtfulness of pain is indeed partly causally responsible for the subject's seeking to avoid pain, for his saying "It hurts," and so on; and the phenomenal redness of ripe-tomato perceptions is indeed partly causally responsible for the subject's purchasing ripe tomatoes rather than unripe ones, for his calling ripe tomatoes red, and so on. If *qualia* are physical properties, then there is no need to defy common sense by claiming, with Jackson, that they are epiphenomenal properties, causally impotent with respect to the physical world.[10]

Notes

1   Frank Jackson, "Epiphenomenal Qualia," *The Philosophical Quarterly* 32 (1982), 127-36, essay 15 in this volume.

2   Ibid., 133, this volume, 164.

3   Ibid., 127, this volume, 159.

4   See Terence Horgan, "Token Physicalism, Supervenience, and the Generality of Physics," *Synthese* 49 (1981), 395-413; and "Supervenience and Microphysics," *Pacific Philosophical Quarterly* 63 (1982), 29-43. A number of other philosophers also have argued that physicalism should be understood in terms of supervenience. See Jaegwon Kim, "Supervenience and Nomological Incommensurables," *American Philosophical Quarterly* 15 (1978), 149-56; John Haugeland, "Weak Supervenience," *American Philosophical Quarterly* 19 (1982), 93-103; and David Lewis, "New Work for a Theory of Universals," *Australasian Journal of Philosophy* 61 (1983), 343-77.

5   Functionalists often argue against type-type identity theory on the grounds that creatures who are radically different from humans in their physico-chemical makeup (e.g., Martians) could instantiate the same psychological state-types as humans. Cf. Hilary Putnam, "Psychological Predicates," in W.H. Capitan and

D.D. Merrill, eds., *Art, Mind, and Religion* (Pittsburgh: University of Pittsburgh Press, 1967). But D.M. Armstrong and David Lewis are functionalists who embrace type-type identity theory by treating mental state-type names as population-relative non-rigid designators; thus, under the Armstrong-Lewis view, "pain" designates one physico-chemical state-type relative to humans, and a different one relative to Martians. See D.M. Armstrong, *A Materialist Theory of Mind* (London: Routledge and Kegan Paul, 1968); David Lewis, "An Argument for the Identity Theory," *The Journal of Philosophy* 63 (1966), 17-25; and especially David Lewis, "Mad Pain and Martian Pain," in Ned Block, ed., *Readings in Philosophy of Psychology*, Vol. 1 (Cambridge, MA: Harvard University Press, 1980).

Jackson, I take it, wants to count as physical not only physico-chemical state-types or properties, but also the more abstract kinds of state-types involved in Putnam's style of functionalism.

6   Jackson, op. cit., 129, in this volume, 161.

7   Ibid., 130, in this volume, 162.

8   Terence Horgan, "Functionalism, Qualia, and the Inverted Spectrum," *Philosophy and Phenomenological Research* 44 (1984), 453-70. There I also contend, however, that no form of functionalism can accommodate *qualia.* I argue, contrary to most functionalists, that *qualia*-names denote specific physico-chemical properties, rather than abstract functional properties. And I argue, contrary to Armstrong and Lewis (op. cit.), that *qualia*-names are rigid designators, rather than functionally-definable non-rigid designators.

9   Does (4) by itself convey the information which Mary expresses by using (4)? I think not. Rather, since (4) employs an indexical term essentially, it seems that in order to obtain the information which Mary expresses by (4), a member of Mary's audience would have to experience phenomenal redness himself, and would have to know that Mary is using "this property" to designate the same property that he experiences. Knowledge about what *qualia* are like cannot be obtained by descriptive means alone, but requires the experiencing of those qualia.

10   Indeed, even if *qualia* are non-physical they may not be epiphenomenal. As long as they are supervenient upon physical properties, I think it can plausibly be argued that they inherit the causal efficacy of the properties upon which they supervene. Cf. Jaegwon Kim, "Causality, Identity, and Supervenience in the Mind-Body Problem," *Midwest Studies in Philosophy* 4 (1979), 31-49.

17

Physicalism and the Cognitive Role of Acquaintance[*]

Lawrence Nemirow

I. SOME THEORIES OF THE COGNITIVE ROLE OF ACQUAINTANCE

In a classical essay on the mind-body problem, Herbert Feigl briefly raises a perplexing problem for physicalism in the philosophy of mind, the view that a physical theory of nature can fully describe mental activity.[1] The problem is to fit the epistemology of experience into a physicalist frame of reference, and to capture, within the framework of physical science, the cognitive role of direct acquaintance with experience.

The physicalist framework, according to Feigl, is essentially objective, in that creatures with diverse sensory systems can formulate and test a physical hypothesis. In theory, no particular sensory organs are crucial to the capacity to advance physical science. Even a congenitally deaf-blind person "could in principle construct and confirm a complete system of the natural sciences."[2] Feigl pictures the method of science as the "triangulation of entities in logical space" grounded on types of sensory input none of which is, by itself, indispensable to the formulation and testing of the hypothesis.[3]

By contrast, the most remarkable information about a sensory experience appears to be *subjective*—accessible only to those who can employ a sensory organ of the same type as the one that produces the experience. As Feigl observes, the "philosophically intriguing problems" regarding direct acquaintance with experience "are best expressed by asking, e.g., 'What is it that the blind man cannot know concerning colour qualities?'"[4] The problem for physicalism is to account for the salient knowledge of visual experience that a scientist without eyes could not infer.

Feigl attacks the problem by denying the premise that there is such knowledge. According to him, a blind person must lack only acquaintance with the experience of sight and knowledge by acquaintance of it. Although acquaintance is not knowledge (because "mere having or living through is not knowledge in any sense"), knowledge by acquaintance "is propositional, and does

---

[*] Laurence Nemirow, "Physicalism and the Cognitive Role of Acquaintance," in W. Lycan ed., *Mind and Cognition: A Reader* (Oxford: Blackwell Press, 1990). Reprinted with kind permission of the publisher.

make truth claims."[5] Someone might know by acquaintance that he is seeing a bright colour, for example. But that knowledge, Feigl observes, could be inferred by a blind psychologist, incapable of experiencing colour, who examines the behaviour and anatomy of the subject of experience.

Feigl underestimates the difficulty. Even if we grant that a congenitally blind psychologist might triangulate the experience of sight, thus confirming that it occurs and discerning all of its physiological aspects, he would not thereby learn what the experience of seeing is *like*. Knowledge of what seeing is like cannot be inferred from nonvisual sensory input.

Nor could Feigl plausibly assert that "knowledge of what an experience is like" amounts to mere acquaintance and thus fails to stand for genuine knowledge. Such an assertion would fail to account for our use of the vocabulary of knowledge in talking about what an experience is like. We speak of "knowing" what an experience is like, as well as "realizing," "discovering," "learning," "remembering" and "forgetting" what an experience is like, and in so doing we describe a common yet elusive kind of knowledge. Mainly, there is knowledge of what it's like to see that can be learned, remembered and forgotten, but it eludes those who are uninitiated to the experience of sight.

Knowledge of what an experience is like signifies genuine knowledge that does not yield to the method of triangulation. Some opponents of physicalism rely on this fact to show that physical science can never completely explain experience.

In what I shall call the "subjective qualities hypothesis," Thomas Nagel analyzes knowing what an experience is like as an act of appreciating its subjective qualities— qualities, that is, the attributions of which express subjective information, as defined above.[6] According to him, information about subjective qualities may be understood only from the "point of view of the experiencer." For Nagel, this means that a person must imagine an experience in order to understand its subjective quality.[7] Such understanding, he contends, evades creatures whose sensory apparatus is so unlike that of the experiencer that they cannot imagine from his point of view. Nagel thus concludes that physicalism is false, for he agrees with Feigl that physical science presupposes no particular sensory capacities.[8]

Frank Jackson engages a less burdened account of the argument against physicalism, which is referred to below as the "knowledge argument."[9] Declining to demarcate the class of physical properties (hence dispensing with the notion of objectivity), and making no attempt to explain what is peculiarly nonphysical about the mental (thus avoiding the concept of subjectivity), he merely observes that no amount of physical theorizing will convey to the uninitiated what it's like to see in colour. Hypothetical neurophysiologists who could make observations only in black and white would learn less about the world than if they could learn what seeing in colour is like. Yet no physical understanding would elude them by reason of their optical disability. So it must follow that physical science cannot describe the way things are mentally.

Nagel and Jackson are right to disagree with Feigl, but their own accounts of the cognitive role of acquaintance are nevertheless flawed. Contrary to Feigl, what the blind cannot know about seeing escapes scientific triangulation. But Nagel and Jackson too quickly conclude that what the blind cannot know is physically indescribable goings-on. That conclusion, I shall argue, is based on three familiar philosophical errors. The first mistake is to confound distinct types of knowledge by treating an ability as propositional knowledge. A second mistake is to confuse grammar and logic by assuming that a grammatical singular term must function as a referring term. The third mistake—and, arguably, the philosophically deep mistake—is to mischaracterize imagining, by equating the act of imagining the experience of a quality with the act of intellectually apprehending the quality itself.

II. THE ABILITY EQUATION

The knowledge argument rests on a shaky inference. From the premise that knowing what it's like escapes physical theorizing, the inference is made that there is information about what it's like that escapes physical science. In short, it is assumed that knowledge of what it's like must be knowledge of the way things are. But that assumption ignores the fact that the vocabulary of knowledge also applies to abilities.[10]

As Nagel's own theory provides, however, knowing what it's like essentially correlates with knowing how to imagine. Ask Harry if he knows what seeing chartreuse is like. If he takes you seriously, he may make an effort to imagine the sight of chartreuse. If he believes that he can imagine seeing chartreuse, he will affirm that he knows what seeing chartreuse is like; otherwise, he will deny that he knows it. It would be nonsense for Harry to insist that he can easily visualize chartreuse, but does not know what seeing it is like, or to maintain that he knows just what it's like, but cannot visualize it. (Throughout this paper, I use the expressions "visualizing a colour" and "imagining the sight of a colour" interchangeably. Visualizing is not identical to imagining, but visualizing is the special type of imagining that one must be able to perform in order to know what seeing a colour is like.)

The correlation stated above suggests an equation: Knowing what it's like may be identified with knowing how to imagine.

The more seriously we take this ability equation, the easier it becomes to resist the knowledge argument. The latter assumes that science cannot convey what it's like to see red. The premise is uncontentious, for science does not seek to instill imaginative abilities. But the knowledge argument concludes that physical science cannot describe certain information about seeing red. The inference is invalid because it presumes that knowing what it's like is propositional knowledge rather than an ability.

The ability equation is confirmed by its explanatory power. It accounts for several facts that, considered together, threaten to undermine physicalism. First, the equation explains why it is appropriate to use the vocabulary of knowledge in discussing what an experience is like. It may be appropriate to speak of "discovering," "knowing," "remembering," "forgetting" what an experience is like because such expressions are used to speak about abilities.

Moreover, the ability equation obviates the need to attribute subjectivity to experience on the ground that knowing what it's like belongs only to those who are able to imagine having the experience (only to those who, as Nagel puts it, can "adopt the experiencer's point of view"). The ability equation avoids having to explain the correlation by transforming it into an equation, and thus circumvents the subjective qualities hypothesis.

The ability equation further explains the linguistic inexpressibility of knowing what it's like. It is a perennial philosophical puzzle that the congenitally blind cannot be told what seeing red is like. Opponents of physicalism may explain the puzzle by referring to inexpressible qualities of experience. But a more elegant explanation is that knowing what it's like is a linguistically inexpressible ability, like the ability to wiggle your ears or the ability to ride a bicycle.

But more must be said. After all, many kinds of knowing how can be expressed verbally. A complete resolution of the puzzle, then, will require a description of the conditions of inexpressibility, together with a demonstration that knowing what it's like satisfies the conditions.

How are abilities communicated? As R.M. Hare tells us, "knowing how to do something is normally communicated, *where it can be communicated at all,* by means of imperative sentences, as can be seen by looking at a cookery book."[11] Putting it schematically, we tell someone how to do A by telling him to do B, where the expression "B" is within the student's repertoire. A description of an action may be said to fall within a person's repertoire provided (i) the person has the ability to perform the action as described, and (ii) the person understands the description: that is, he understands that he can act so as to satisfy it.

Specifically, the ability to imagine a colour (that is, knowing what the colour is like) may be communicated to someone who has within his repertoire a description of an action by which visualizing can be accomplished. Normally, the ability to visualize a colour can be exercised only by the performance of one of three mental actions:

(1) Directly visualizing the colour itself.
(2) Remembering a visual experience of the colour.
(3) Visualizing or remembering similar colours and interpolating. (This third way of visualizing is, of course, Hume's way.)

It is only contingently true that this list is exhaustive. Someone with an abnormal imaginative capacity might provide a counterexample: Perhaps he could visualize green by banging his head against a wall, or by remembering a humiliating experience. But for most of us, the only activities that amount to visualizing a given colour are the activities on the list. Consequently, we may tell those who are able to visualize or remember similar colours that they can imagine by visualizing or remembering and interpolating; and we may instruct others to refresh their recollection by remembering previous experiences of the colour. As for those who are unable to follow any of these instructions, imagining is expressible only as such. These uninitiated, therefore, cannot be told what it's like to see green.

This account generalizes to all cases of knowing what it's like. It is generally, albeit contingently, true that imagining an experience may be accomplished only by (1) imagining the experience itself, (2) remembering previous experiences, or (3) imagining or remembering similar experiences and interpolating. So the ability to imagine an experience is describable only as imagining for those who cannot do (2) or (3). Those people might be able to imagine, and imagining might be expressible to them as such. But they cannot be told how if they do not already know. Accordingly, the uninitiated cannot be told what it's like.

In sum, the advantages of the ability equation are these: Forgoing nonphysical aspects of experience,[12] it renders the knowledge argument invalid. It also explains the pertinence of the vocabulary of knowledge, the essential connection between knowing what it's like and imaginative capacities, and the inexpressibility of knowing what it's like.

III. THE ABILITY ANALYSIS

The ability equation prompts an ability analysis. The expression "x knows how to visualize red" either should replace or can be used to paraphrase "x knows what the experience of seeing red is like." This analysis demystifies the subexpression "what the experience of seeing red is like." On a naive reading, the subexpression is a name for a quality of experience. The latter must be subjective (in Nagel's terms) because only those who are able to visualize red can understand what seeing red is like. Under the analysis, however, the subexpression is a "pseudo-singular term"—an expression that has the grammatical form of a singular term, but, on analysis, does not even purport to refer. Like some other pseudo-singular terms (such as the term "sake" in the sentence, "she did it for her country's sake") the term "what it's like" is syncategoramatic; in other words, it is not separately analyzed.

Although the ability analysis palpably parses the meaning of the phrase "knowing what it's like," those who generally doubt the meaningfulness of synonymy may view the analysis as a possible linguistic reform that would preserve the explanatory power of the phrase while eliminating the use of a mis-leading singular term. In any event, the analysis should forestall the tempta-tion to treat the expression "what it's like" as a referring expression in virtue of its grammatical form.[13]

IV. THE COGNITIVE ROLE OF IMAGINING:
SOME METAPHYSICAL APPREHENSIONS

A polemically successful answer to the subjective qualities hypothesis and the knowledge argument must explain the intuitive appeal of the contention that what it's like is irreducibly nonphysical information about experience. The following points together may help accomplish that task:

(i) Knowing what an experience is like is the same as knowing how to imagine having the experience.

(ii) It is intuitively appealing, albeit incorrect, to analyze the act of imag-ining an experience of an instance of a certain universal as the intellectu-al apprehension of the universal itself.

Sentence (i), of course, repeats the ability equation, elaborated in the earlier parts of this paper. Sentence (ii) expresses a familiar point that underlies sev-eral classical discussions of universals.[14]

Sentence (ii) incorporates the thesis of Berkeley and Hume that the imagination represents particulars rather than apprehends universals. To visualize red, for example, is to apprehend neither the quality of being red nor the quality of seeing red; it is only to represent particular perceptions of a particular shade of red. Similarly, to imagine pain is not intellectually to apprehend the quality of being in pain; it is to represent a particular painful experience. "For myself, I find indeed I have a faculty of imagin-ing, or representing to myself, the idea of those *particular* things I have perceived ..."[15]

Berkeley and Hume dispelled the philosophical clouds surrounding imag-inative representation.[16] Quite obviously, however, an intuitive fog persists. Imagining pain just seems to reveal its painful nature.

The persistent illusion that imagination grants direct access to universals may be explained by what gives imagining its functional utility. We can begin to understand imagination functionally by considering its role in our reason-ing, both propositional and practical. Berkeley illuminated that role when he wrote: "[A]n idea which, considered in itself, is particular, becomes general by being made to represent or stand for all other particular ideas of the same sort."[17]

Successfully visualizing a colour, for example, engenders the ability to com-pare the colour to other colours. So visualizing a colour permits us to draw conclusions (or reason propositionally) about other colours as if we were see-ing the imagined colour. (I might conclude that the colour I am imagining is a deeper shade of purple than the colour I am witnessing.) Imagining seeing a colour thus functionally represents seeing the colour in our propositional reasoning about colours.

So too, successfully imagining a pain of a certain intensity enables us to consider what we would accept as compensation for agreeing to undergo pain of the same degree of intensity. By imagining pain we are able to draw conclusions (or reason practically) about whether to avoid impending pain as if we were experiencing ongoing pain. (I might conclude that the pain that I imagine the dentist would inflict upon me is not worth the intended benefits of a trip to the dentist.) Imagining pain thus functionally represents actual pain in our reasoning about future pain. Part of the functional utility of imag-ining, then, is that it engenders abilities to reason about experiences, both propositionally and practically, as if we were having an experience of the sort imagined.

We can explain the role of imagining in reasoning by invoking a notion of triangulation, although one that differs from Feigl's concept of triangu-lation. A key difference is the direction of the inferences in each case. For Feigl, triangulation in physical science involves inferences from sensory experiences, no one of which is critical, to an hypothesis of physical events. Such patterns of inference account for the capacity of scientific inquiry to reach objective generalizations. In reasoning from what an experience is like, a person begins by imagining particular experiences, and draws spe-cific inferences about actual or future sensory experiences, none of which is itself critical to the function of the imagination. Such lines of inference in turn begin to account for the general utilities of imagining that cause imagining to appear to grant direct access to the essential qualities of experience.

Sentences (i) and (ii) together produce the conclusion that knowing what it's like to be in pain is an ability that is appealingly analyzed as the ability to apprehend a universal. If we were to treat what is appealing as fact, Nagel's theory of subjective qualities would follow. We would attribute a special understanding of what pain is only to those who know what it's *like*.

V. OBJECTIONS AND REPLIES

One objection to the ability equation is that knowing how to imagine is too sophisticated an ability to attribute to everyone (or thing) who may know what it's like. For such an ability is, for all we know, well beyond the capabili-ties of creatures to whom we may on occasion attribute knowledge of what an experience is like—creatures such as cats and infants. But anything that is true of mature persons by reason of knowing what an experience is like should also be true of cats and infants who know what it's like—a point that apparently refutes the ability equation.

Rather than providing counterexamples to the ability equation, however, these hard cases suggest only that there are auxiliary concepts of "what it's like" that are triggered by nonparadigmatic applications of the phrase, and which would often be inapposite to use when speaking of mature persons.

If we say of a cat that it knows what the smell of abalone is like, for example, we might mean merely that, exposed to the smell, it will come running to its dish. The proposition apparently does not imply that the cat knows how to imagine the smell.

To apply the mature concept of knowing what the smell of abalone is like to a person, however, is not to assume any such behavioural correlation. Such an attribution directly describes what a person knows how to do in the privacy of his own mind, not how he would behave when exposed to the smell.

Similarly, we might say of an infant that he knows what a certain taste is like, without intending to imply that the infant knows how to imagine the taste. We may mean only that he can recognize the taste. On the other hand, when we use the mature concept of knowing what a taste is like, we mean more than that. We additionally attribute the ability to imagine. Someone might appropriately claim, "I can recognize the taste of chestnuts, I feel sure, but I have forgotten just what the taste is like." Similarly, no one is surprised to forget how to imagine a certain melody (what it's like to hear the melody), while remembering how to recognize the melody; or to forget what someone's face is like (what it's like to see his face), without forgetting how to recognize the face.

Someone might question the recognition examples by asking what the ability to imagine amounts to over and above the ability to recognize. As explained in the previous section of this paper, the ability to imagine is, at least in part, an ability to reason propositionally and practically as if one were having an experience of the sort imagined. The recognition examples suggest also that the ability to imagine produces certain other practical abilities that do not ordinarily fall under the rubric of practical reasoning. For example, if Beth can recognize but not imagine a melody, then she cannot imagine variations on it either. But if Beth can imagine the melody, not only can she imagine variations on it (assuming she has some modest musical talent), she can also ascertain whether one note of the melody is higher or lower than the next. Further, she can tap its beat or hum the tune. And she might even try to imagine hearing the notes in reverse order. But Beth could perform none of these tasks if she could only recognize without imagining. Similarly, if Frank can vividly imagine what the burglar looks like, then he can describe his looks so that a police artist might render a likeness. But if he could only recognize without imagining, he would be unable to describe in any detail how the burglar looks.

In any event, as the examples of sophisticated attributions of knowing what it's like show, such attributions do ascribe imaginative abilities, while the auxiliary concepts of knowing what it's like, such as conditioned response or recognitional ability do not.[18]

A second objection to the ability equation relies on the concept of successful imagining. Successful imagining, so the objection goes, presupposes subjective qualities (or qualities the attribution of which may be understood only by those with the right sensory capacities) for this reason: the ability successfully to imagine is the ability to entertain a truly representative state; but representation is a relationship between imagined and imagining states based on the similarity of their subjective qualities.

The crucial point in this objection is unmotivated. Assume for argument's sake, both that imagining constitutes mental representation, and that the relationship of representation holds between imagined and imagining states just in case they are similar with respect to certain qualities. What argument demonstrates that those qualities are subjective? The case had better not be that knowledge of what those qualities are like depends on acquaintance. That would merely repeat the knowledge argument, which the ability equation renders invalid. To be sure, an understanding of imaginative representation might require acquaintance with it; but such understanding itself consists of imaginative abilities rather than knowledge that may be summarized propositionally.

VI. FINAL REMARKS

The principal importance of acquaintance in cognition is the production of sophisticated imaginative abilities that give rise to an elaborate network of other abilities, including abilities to reason, both propositionally and practically, and to behave as if the person doing the imagining were having an experience of the sort imagined. These imaginative abilities are of such importance cognitively that they may properly be characterized as constituting a deep understanding of experience. Thus it does justice to the cognitive significance of acquaintance to equate knowledge of what an experience is like with the ability to imagine.

Acknowledgment

I am deeply grateful to David Lewis for his support, and to Joanne Kadish for discussion and for detailed comments on earlier drafts.

Notes

1　Feigl, *The "Mental" and the "Physical"* (Minneapolis: University of Minnesota Press, 1967), especially 66-69.
2　Ibid., 66.
3　Ibid., 66-68.
4　Ibid., 68.
5　Ibid.
6　See "What is it like to be a bat?" *Philosophical Review* 84 (1974), 435-50; reprinted in Nagel, *Mortal Questions* (Cambridge: Cambridge University Press, 1979), 165-81. (All page references are to *Mortal Questions*.)
7　Nagel equates the act of taking up the experiencer's point of view with the act of imagining having the experience many times throughout "What is it like to be a bat?" See, for example, 178.
8　Ibid., 172.
9　Frank Jackson, "Epiphenomenal qualia," *Philosophical Quarterly* 32 (1982), 127-36, essay 15 in this volume. For a less sympathetic presentation of the argument against physicalism based on what the blind cannot know, see section IV of Paul E. Meehl, "The compleat autocerebroscopist," in Paul Feyerabend and Grover Maxwell, eds., *Mind, Matter and Method* (Minneapolis: University of Minnesota Press, 1966).
10　See Gilbert Ryle, *The Concept of Mind* (New York: Barnes & Noble, 1949), 27-32.
11　R.M. Hare, *Practical Inferences* (Berkeley: University of California Press, 1972), 3. (Emphasis added.)
12　It should be considered an advantage of an explanatory hypothesis if it facilitates physicalist reduction. Such a contribution is praiseworthy from the point of view of advancing systematization, which is an important criterion of theory selection. See Oppenheim and Kemeny, "On reduction," *Philosophical Studies* 7 (1956), 9-16.
13　Frank Jackson and David Lewis have observed that the ability analysis may be read either as countenancing, or as not countenancing, an inference from "Sam knows how to imagine seeing chartreuse" to "Sam knows that he knows how to imagine seeing chartreuse." The analysandum shares the same ambiguity, which is excellent confirmation of the analysis.
14　Berkeley, *A Treatise Concerning the Principles of Human Knowledge*, especially the Introduction; and Hume, *A Treatise of Human Nature*, part 1, section VII.
15　*A Treatise Concerning the Principles of Human Knowledge*, paragraph 10 of the Introduction. (Emphasis added.)
16　I find the Berkeley-Hume argument, so construed, to be compelling, but I do not believe that there is a knockdown refutation of the view that the imagination apprehends universals. My own prejudice is based on a preference for explanatory simplicity. See note 12.

17   *A Treatise Concerning the Principles of Human Knowledge*, paragraph 12 of the Introduction.

18   A phrase of the form "knowing what it's like to be a—" expresses the sophisticated concept of knowing what it's like because it entails complex imaginative capabilities rather than any characteristic recognitional or conditioned responses. Assuming that cats do not know how to imagine (which is consistent with, but not necessarily entailed by, auxiliary attributions to cats of knowing what it's like), it would follow that a cat does not know what it's like to be a cat. Or, more to the point, there is no knowledge of what it's like to be a cat.

18

REDUCTION, QUALIA, AND
THE DIRECT INTROSPECTION OF BRAIN STATES*

Paul M. Churchland

Do the phenomenological or qualitative features of our sensations constitute a permanent barrier to the reductive aspirations of any materialistic neuroscience? I here argue that they do not. Specifically, I wish to address the recent anti-reductionist arguments posed by Thomas Nagel,[1] Frank Jackson,[2] and Howard Robinson.[3] And I wish to explore the possibility of human subjective consciousness within a conceptual environment constituted by a matured and successful neuroscience....

IV. JACKSON'S KNOWLEDGE ARGUMENT

Imagine a brilliant neuroscientist named Mary, who has lived her entire life in a room that is rigorously controlled to display only various shades of black, white, and grey. She learns about the outside world by means of a black/white television monitor, and, being brilliant, she manages to transcend these obstacles. She becomes the world's greatest neuroscientist, all from within this room. In particular, she comes to know everything there is to know about the physical structure and activity of the brain and its visual system, of its actual and possible states.

But there would still be something she did *not* know, and could not even imagine, about the actual experiences of all the other people who live outside her black/white room, and about her possible experiences were she finally to leave her room: the nature of the experience of seeing a ripe tomato, what it is like to see red or have a sensation-of-red. Therefore, complete knowledge of the physical facts of visual perception and its related brain activity *still leaves something out*. Therefore, materialism cannot give an adequate reductionist account of all mental phenomena.

To give a conveniently tightened version of this argument:

---

* Paul Churchland, "Reduction, Qualia, and the Direct Introspection of Brain States," *Journal of Philosophy* 82 (1985), 8-28. Reprinted with kind permission of the author and the publisher.

(1) Mary knows everything there is to know about brain states and their properties.

(2) It is not the case that Mary knows everything there is to know about sensations and their properties.

Therefore, by Leibniz's law,

(3) Sensations and their properties ≠ brain states and their properties.

It is tempting to insist that we here confront just another instance of the intensional fallacy ... but Jackson's defenders[4] insist that 'knows *about*' is a perfectly transparent, entirely extensional context. Let us suppose that it is. We can, I think, find at least two other shortcomings in this sort of argument.

The First Shortcoming: This defect is simplicity itself. 'Knows about' may be transparent in both premises, but it is not *univocal* in both premises. (David Lewis[5] and Laurence Nemirow[6] have both raised this same objection, though their analysis of the ambiguity at issue differs from mine.) Jackson's argument is valid only if 'knows about' is univocal in both premises. But the kind of knowledge addressed in premise 1 seems pretty clearly to be different from the kind of knowledge addressed in (2). Knowledge in (1) seems to be a matter of having mastered a set of sentences or propositions, the kind one finds written in neuroscience texts, whereas knowledge in (2) seems to be a matter of having a representation of redness in some prelinguistic or sublinguistic medium of representation for sensory variables, or to be a matter of being able to *make* certain sensory discriminations, or something along these lines.

Lewis and Nemirow plump for the "ability" analysis of the relevant sense of 'knows about', but they need not be so narrowly committed, and the complaint of equivocation need not be so narrowly based. As my alternative gloss illustrates, other analyses of 'knowledge by acquaintance' are possible, and the charge of equivocation will be sustained so long as the type of knowledge invoked in premise 1 is distinct from the type invoked in premise 2. Importantly, they do seem very different, even in advance of a settled analysis of the latter.

In short, the difference between a person who knows all about the visual cortex but has never enjoyed a sensation of red, and a person who knows no neuroscience but knows well the sensation of red, may reside not in *what* is respectively known by each (brain states by the former, qualia by the latter), but rather in the different *type* of knowledge each has *of exactly the same thing*. The difference is in the manner of the knowing, not in the nature of the thing(s) known. If one replaces the ambiguous occurrences of 'knows about' in Jackson's argument with the two different expansions suggested above, the resulting argument is a clear non sequitur.

(a) Mary has mastered the complete set of true propositions about people's brain states.

(b) Mary does *not* have a representation of redness in her prelinguistic medium of representation for sensory variables.

Therefore, by Leibniz's law,

(c) The redness sensation ≠ any brain state.

Premises a and b are compossible, even on a materialist view. But they do not entail (c).

In sum, there are pretty clearly more ways of "having knowledge" than having mastered a set of sentences. And nothing in materialism precludes this. The materialist can freely admit that one has "knowledge" of one's sensations in a way that is independent of the scientific theories one has learned. This does not mean that sensations are beyond the reach of physical science. *It just means that the brain uses more modes and media of representation than the simple storage of sentences.* And this proposition is pretty obviously true: almost certainly the brain uses a considerable variety of modes and media of representation, perhaps hundreds of them. Jackson's argument, and Nagel's, exploit this variety illegitimately: both arguments equivocate on 'knows about'.

This criticism is supported by the observation that, if Jackson's form of argument were sound, it would prove far too much. Suppose that Jackson were arguing, not against materialism, but against dualism: against the view that there exists a nonmaterial substance—call it "ectoplasm"—whose hidden constitution and nomic intricacies ground all mental phenomena. Let our cloistered Mary be an "ectoplasmologist" this time, and let her know$_1$ everything there is to know about the ectoplasmic processes underlying vision. There would still be something she did not know$_2$: what it is like to see red. Dualism is therefore inadequate to account for all mental phenomena!

This argument is as plausible as Jackson's, and for the same reason: it exploits the same equivocation. But the truth is, such arguments show nothing, one way or the other, about how mental phenomena might be accounted for.

The Second Shortcoming: There is a further shortcoming with Jackson's argument, one of profound importance for understanding one of the most exciting consequences to be expected from a successful neuroscientific account of mind. I draw your attention to the assumption that even a utopian knowledge of neuroscience *must* leave Mary hopelessly in the dark about the subjective qualitative nature of sensations not-yet-enjoyed. It is true, of course, that no sentence of the form "x is a sensation-of-red" will be deducible from premises restricted to the language of neuroscience. But this is no point against the reducibility of phenomenological properties.... Direct deducibility is an intolerably strong demand on reduction, and if this is all the objection comes to, then there is no objection worth addressing. What the defender of emergent qualia must have in mind here, I think, is the claim that Mary could not even *imagine* what the relevant experience would be like, despite her exhaustive neuroscientific knowledge, and hence must still be missing certain crucial information.

This claim, however, is simply false. Given the truth of premise 1, premise 2 seems plausible to Jackson, Nagel, and Robinson only because none of these philosophers has adequately considered how much one might know if, as premise 1 asserts, one knew *everything* there is to know about the physical brain and nervous system. In particular, none of these philosophers has even begun to consider the changes in our introspective apprehension of our internal states that could follow upon a wholesale revision in our conceptual framework for our internal states.

The fact is, we can indeed imagine how neuroscientific information would give Mary detailed information about the qualia of various sensations.... In particular, suppose that Mary has learned to conceptualize her inner life, even in introspection, in terms of the completed neuroscience we are to imagine. So she does not identify her visual sensations crudely as "a sensation-of-black", "a sensation-of-grey", or "a sensation-of-white"; rather she identifies them more revealingly as various spiking frequencies in the nth layer of the occipital cortex (or whatever). If Mary has the relevant neuroscientific concepts for the sensational states at issue (viz., sensations-of-*red*), but has never yet been *in* those states, she may well be able to imagine being in the relevant cortical state, and imagine it with substantial success, even in advance of receiving external stimuli that would actually produce it.

One test of her ability in this regard would be to give her a stimulus that would (finally) produce in her the relevant state (viz., a spiking frequency of 90 hz in the gamma network: a "sensation-of-red" to us), and see whether she can identify it correctly *on introspective grounds alone*, as "a spiking frequency of 90 hz: the kind a tomato would cause." It does not seem to me to be impossible that she should succeed in this, and do so regularly on similar tests for other states, conceptualized clearly by her, but not previously enjoyed.

This may seem to some an outlandish suggestion, but the following will show that it is not. Musical chords are auditory phenomena that the young and unpracticed ear hears as undivided wholes, discriminable one from another, but without elements or internal structure. A musical education changes this, and one comes to hear chords as groups of discriminable notes. If one is sufficiently practiced to have absolute pitch, one can even name the notes of an apprehended chord. And the reverse is also true: if a set of notes is specified verbally, a trained pianist or guitarist can identify the chord and recall its sound in auditory imagination. Moreover, a really skilled individual can construct, in auditory imagination, the sound of a chord he may never have heard before, and certainly does not remember. Specify for him a relatively unusual one—an F#9th*add*13th for example—and let him brood for a bit. Then play for him three or four chords, one of which is the target, and see whether he can pick it out as the sound that meets the description. Skilled musicians can do this. Why is a similar skill beyond all possibility for Mary?

"Ah," it is tempting to reply, "musicians can do this only because chords are audibly structured sets of elements. Sensations of colour are not."

But neither did chords seem, initially, to be structured sets of elements. They also seemed to be undifferentiated wholes. Why should it be unthinkable that sensations of colour possess a comparable internal structure, unnoticed so far, but awaiting our determined and informed inspection? Jackson's argument, to be successful, must rule this possibility out, and it is difficult to see how he can do this a priori. Especially since there has recently emerged excellent empirical evidence to suggest that *our sensations of colour are indeed structured sets of elements.*

The retinex theory of colour vision recently proposed by Edwin Land[7] represents any colour apprehendable by the human visual system as being uniquely specified by its joint position along three vertices—its reflectance efficiencies at three critical wavelengths, those wavelengths to which the retina's triune cone system is selectively responsive. Since colours are apprehended by us, it is a good hypothesis that those three parameters are represented in our visual systems and that our sensations of colour are in some direct way determined by them. Sensations of colour may turn out literally to be three-element chords in some neural medium! In the face of all this, I do not see why it is even briefly plausible to insist that it is utterly impossible for a conceptually sophisticated Mary accurately to imagine, and subsequently to pick out, colour sensations she has not previously enjoyed. We can already foresee how it might actually be done.

The preceding argument does not collapse the distinction (between knowledge-by-description and knowledge-by-acquaintance) urged earlier in the discussion of equivocation. But it does show that the "taxonomies" that reside in our prelinguistic media of representation can be profoundly shaped by the taxonomies that reside in the lingustic medium, especially if one has had long practice at the observational discrimination of items that answer to those linguistically embodied categories. This is just a further illustration of the plasticity of human perception.

I do not mean to suggest, of course, that there will be no limits to what Mary can imagine. Her brain is finite, and its specific anatomy will have specific limitations. For example, if a bat's brain includes computational machinery that the human brain simply lacks (which seems likely), then the subjective character of some of the bat's internal states may well be beyond human imagination. Clearly, however, the elusiveness of the bat's inner life here stems not from the metaphysical "emergence" of its internal qualia, but only from the finite capacities of our idiosyncratically human brains. Within those sheerly structural limitations, our imaginations may soar far beyond what Jackson, Nagel, and Robinson suspect, if we possess a neuroscientific conceptual framework that is at last adequate to the intricate phenomena at issue.

I suggest then, that those of us who prize the flux and content of our subjective phenomenological experience need not view the advance of materialistic neuroscience with fear and foreboding. Quite the contrary. The genuine arrival of a materialist kinematics and dynamics for psychological states and cognitive processes will constitute not a gloom in which our inner life is suppressed or eclipsed, but rather a dawning, in which its marvelous intricacies are finally *revealed*—most notably, if we apply ourselves, in direct self-conscious introspection.

Notes

1   "What is it Like to be a Bat?" *Philosophical Review* 83 (1974), 435-50; page references to Nagel are to this paper.

2   "Epiphenomenal Qualia," *Philosophical Quarterly* 32 (1982), 127-36, essay 15 in this volume.

3   *Matter and Sense* (New York: Cambridge, 1982), 4.

4   See, for example, Keith Campbell, "Abstract Particulars and the Philosophy of Mind," *Australasian Journal of Philosophy* 61 (1983), 129-41.

5   "Postscript to 'Mad Pain and Martian Pain,'" *Philosophical Papers*, vol. I (New York: Oxford, 1983).

6   "Review of Thomas Nagel, *Mortal Questions*," *Philosophical Review* 89 (1980), 473-77.

7   "The Retinex Theory of Colour Vision," *Scientific American* (December 1977), 108-28.

19

PHYSICALISM AND PHENOMENAL PROPERTIES*

Earl Conee

I

Frank Jackson has offered a plausible epistemic argument against physicalism —"the knowledge argument."[1] Here is a paraphrase:

> Suppose that Mary has spent her whole life in a grey room. Through a black-and-white TV in the room Mary has learned all that science could ever convey about colour-perception. Mary "acquires all the physical information there is to obtain about what goes on when we see a ripe tomato, or the sky, and use terms like 'red', 'blue', and so on."[2] Now suppose that Mary leaves the room for the first time and sees a clear blue sky. It seems obvious that Mary could learn something new by seeing something blue for the first time. She could learn how blue looks. But if so, then this is not physical information, since she already knew all the physical facts about colour-perception when she was in the grey room. The existence of this additional information refutes physicalism—the thesis that all correct information is physical information.

Physicalists can object to Jackson's argument by denying that what Mary could learn from seeing the sky is a matter of acquiring new information, or by denying that what would count as "new information" has to be non-physical information. Both sorts of objection have already been made. David Lewis and Laurence Nemirow, in effect contend that what Mary could acquire is not new information, but rather new abilities,[3,4] Terence Horgan contends that, for all Jackson has shown, it is left open that Mary's "new information" is physical information.[5]

The aims of the present paper are to refute these objections to Jackson's argument, and to present what I take to be a correct objection. The con-

* Earl Conee, "Physicalism and Phenomenal Qualities," *Philosophical Quarterly* 35 (1985), 296-302. Reprinted with kind permission of the publisher. For a revised version of Conee's reply to the knowledge argument, see his "Phenomenal Knowledge," *Australasian Journal of Philosophy* 72 (1994), 136-50.

siderations underlying this objection also serve to render physicalism more attractive, especially to those who feel the force of Jackson's knowledge argument.

II

As Lewis and Nemirow's work applies to my paraphrase of the knowledge argument, they object to the tacit inference at the end from the assumption that Mary could learn something which is not physical information, to the conclusion that there is some non-physical information that Mary could learn. Before we evaluate their objection, there is a terminological matter to get out of the way. Lewis and Nemirow discuss the issue largely in terms of the phrase "knowing what it's like." As this usage has it, what Mary could learn by seeing the sky would result in her "knowing what it's like" to see something blue.[6] Lewis discusses the case of learning the taste of the spice Vegemite:

> [K]nowing what it's like is not the possession of information at all. It isn't the elimination of any hitherto open possibilities. Rather, knowing what it's like is the possession of abilities: abilities to recognize, abilities to imagine, abilities to predict one's behaviour by means of imaginative experiments. (Someone who knows what it's like to taste Vegemite can easily and reliably predict whether he would eat a second helping of Vegemite ice cream.) Lessons cannot impart these abilities—who would have thought they could? There is a state of knowing what it's like, sure enough. And Vegemite has a special power to produce that state. But phenomenal information and its special subject matter do not exist.[7]

This account does not identify particular abilities as necessary or sufficient for "knowing what it's like" in any given case.[8] Nemirow's view is more specific:

> As for understanding an experience, we may construe that as an ability to place oneself, at will, in a state representative of the experience. I understand the experience of seeing red if I can at will visualize red.[9]

There are objections to any view that purports to explain "knowing what it's like" solely in terms of abilities. It is quite probable that by seeing the sky Mary would acquire abilities such as those Lewis and Nemirow mention. And it is equally probable that were Mary to acquire a suitable cluster of abilities—the ones that intuitively go with learning what the sky looks like—then she would learn what she learns by seeing the sky. But there is a further fact. There is a fact about what actually gives her these abilities. It is because she knows how the sky looks that she knows how to recognize things as being the same colour as the sky, and how to visualize the sky. Since this knowledge helps to explain how she manages to have the abilities, it cannot simply reduce to her having them.

Notice that such knowledge is not the only possible way to acquire the relevant abilities. Suppose that Mary is colour-blind in the blue region of the spectrum. Still, by a fluke of brain connections she might get a certain queasy feeling in her stomach that reliably inclines her to judge that what she is looking at is the same colour as the sky. An exotic brain operation might impart to her the ability to visualize the sky while she is unaware of how the sky looks, never having exercised this ability. Notice too that Mary might learn how the sky looks without getting any of these abilities.[10] She might have no ability to form mental images at will, and no ability to recall the look of the sky when she turns her attention to anything else. Yet still, she could know how the sky looks while she sees it. Such considerations show that Mary's learning is not identical to acquiring any abilities.

III

Horgan's objection to Jackson's argument is intended to show that what Mary learns may be "physical information" in the crucial sense. He relies on the following distinction:

> [Where S expresses information about perceptual processes, w]e shall say that S expresses *explicitly physical information* just in case S belongs to, or follows from, a theoretically adequate account of those processes. And we shall say S expresses *ontologically physical information* just in case (i) all entities referred to or quantified over in S are physical entities and (ii) all properties and relations expressed by the predicates in S are physical properties and relations.[11]

Horgan considers how Mary might formulate the new information that she acquires by seeing things outside the grey room. He supplies the following sentence as an example of an appropriate formulation:

> (4) Seeing red ripe tomatoes has *this* property: where 'this property' is used to designate the colour-*quale* that is instantiated in her present experience.

Horgan grants that (4) expresses new information, and that (4) does not express explicitly physical information. But according to him the right formulation of physicalism is that all correct information is ontologically physical information. And he holds that (4) may express only ontologically physical information:

> The referent of 'this property' may very well be a physical property. This is not ruled out by the fact that Mary learns something new from her experience.[12]

Horgan is enabled to say this by his view of what constitutes new information in this context. He indicates that some differences in formulation are sufficient:

> Sentence (4) expresses new information because Mary has a new perspective on phenomenal redness: viz. the first-person ostensive perspective. Her new information is about the phenomenal colour-property *as experienced*. Thus she could not have had this information prior to undergoing the relevant sort of experience herself. But these facts are compatible with Physicalism; there is no need to suppose that when she acquires experiential awareness of phenomenal redness, she thereby comes into contact with a property distinct from those already countenanced in her prior physical account of human perception. The perspective is new, and so is the accompanying capacity to designate the relevant property indexically in a first-person ostensive manner. But the property itself need not be new.[13]

Thus, Horgan thinks that (4) formulates "new information" because of the new way in which Mary is able to make reference to phenomenal redness, not because any entity or property is new to her. In Horgan's view Mary's black-and-white instruction may have already informed her, concerning what is in fact phenomenal redness, that it is a property involved in seeing red ripe tomatoes. But only by actually seeing red ripe tomatoes could Mary be in a position to express that fact by the use of (4).

Horgan offers support for his proposal that this sort of difference suffices for the relevant sense of "new information" to apply. But whether or not he is right about that, there is a problem for his position.

Assume that Mary has already learned about phenomenal redness during her black-and-white study of the complete science of colour-perception. There is some predicate in the language of advanced electrochemistry, R, that in fact expresses phenomenal redness. Mary must have understood R, since she learned all of the relevant scientific information. In thinking of what R expresses, there was some way of representing its content that she was aware of. It seems quite likely that this would be a complicated representation, some logical construction out of sophisticated electrical and chemical notions. This representation is what Mary was immediately aware of in thinking of phenomenal redness.

Now consider what happens when Mary first sees something red. She becomes aware of a simple visual presentation—the look of something red. It can be maintained that she is then aware of the physical property which is phenomenal redness, something that she was already acquainted with when she learned the physical facts of colour-perception. But it seems beyond doubt that something new is also involved in her experience. Things do not seem the same to Mary as they did when she was aware of phenomenal redness by means of the representation consisting in electrochemical notions. Only some new element can account for this difference in how things appear. If it is insisted that seeing something red really is a matter of being aware of the physical property of phenomenal redness, then to include the new conscious element we must add that phenomenal redness now manifests itself to Mary in a new way, or add that Mary now has a new way of apprehending phenomenal redness, or add other words to that effect. What is ineluctable is that there is something new, whether or not it is a "manifestation" or a "way of apprehending" something previously encountered.

The new element is involved in facts that are new to Mary. The word 'thusly' functions in English as a contextually defined adverb. Mary can use 'thusly' to express what is new in her experience and formulate a new fact by saying:

(4′) Seeing something red is experienced thusly.

(4′) seems undeniably to express something that Mary learns, something not contained in her complete knowledge of the black-and-white physical information about colour-vision. We can avoid the issue of whether what she learns is properly called "new information." We can say in neutral language that she becomes acquainted with something new and learns a new fact involving it. Again we have arrived at an anti-physicalist conclusion—there is this non-physical element in experience and there are non-physical facts involving it.

Horgan's work provides no objection to this way of construing the case against physicalism. He acknowledges that Mary gains a new perspective on a physical fact. But he seeks to reduce what is conveyed by this perspective to a new linguistic capacity, a certain capacity to reformulate the same physical fact. Yet the truth seems to be that Mary also becomes aware of something new and learns a new fact involving it. It would have been natural to call the new element itself "phenomenal redness." But we can reserve that term for a property expressed in the physical science that Mary already knew, so long as we find some way, such as (4), to put into words a fact that Mary discovers by becoming acquainted with the look of red tomatoes. Mary's new perspective yields acquaintance with a new fact about how things appear from that perspective.

So far, some version of the anti-physicalist argument seems destined to prevail.

IV

In seeing something red for the first time Mary becomes immediately aware of a phenomenal colour-quality. It is extremely plausible that her black-and-white education in colour-perception did not acquaint her with this quality. But it is also extremely plausible that the quality is physical. It seems to result from, and to cause, plainly physical events. For example, the quality certainly seems to be partly responsible for the sounds that Mary would produce in describing it. There seem to be no grounds for counting this sort of causal sequence as involving an intervention of something from outside nature, or for supposing that a physical explanation of Mary's utterances must remain incomplete or incorrect.

Jackson recognizes the implausibility of accepting non-physical causes of these physical changes—he likens it to believing in fairies. He denies that phenomenal qualities are physical, but declares them to be epiphenomenal. He argues convincingly that we have no *conclusive* ground for attributing effects to phenomenal qualities—possibly both the qualities and their apparent effects are effects of a common physical cause.

We have seen no reason to *deny* that phenomenal qualities have their apparent physical effects, though, except for Jackson's argument for the non-physical nature of the qualities, together with the difficulties concerning non-physical interventions. So let us look at his argument once again. We can observe that there is a consistent way to affirm both of these extremely plausible claims—that Mary becomes newly aware of a colour-quality, and that the quality is physical. These claims can be easily reconciled if it is impossible for anyone to learn absolutely all of the correct physical information in black and white. In particular, Mary could not know the physical facts that essentially involve the phenomenal qualities of colour-perception until she is acquainted with these qualities by experience. This requires us to deny Jackson's premise that Mary could know all the physical facts while in the grey room.[14]

Why might we have reasonably thought that exhaustive black-and-white physical knowledge is possible? The reason seems to be that the predicates of all imaginable developed forms of chemistry, physics and physiology seem understandable without actually using colour-vision. And it seems quite likely on empirical grounds that events within these domains are sufficient causes of all the caused events that are expressible by use of such predicates.

Yet it is consistent with all this that there are other physical qualities which are not expressed by such predicates, qualities with instances having causal roles within these domains. To see this, let 'C' be a straightforwardly physical predicate, and let 'E' be another, where the instantiation of C is causally sufficient for that of E. Suppose further that there is no other event express-ible in what we can call "the black-and-white-learnable physical vocabulary" that is caused by C and affects E. Finally suppose that E happens just after C.

These assumptions leave it open that there is another physical event—call it 'Q' for the instantiation of a phenomenal quality—that is caused by C and causes E, and begins to occur not before C begins and not after E begins. C is by hypothesis causally sufficient for E. But a fuller explanation could be that this is so because C is causally sufficient for Q, and Q is causally sufficient for E. If the causal facts are like that, then explanation of E by an event like C within the expressive power of the black-and-white-learnable physical vocabulary would not seem to require appeal to other events for a complete explanation. The explanation of E by C would give no reason to suppose there was any intermediate event in the causal chain.

The crucial further fact, though, is that this sort of causal history would not entail the absence of intermediate links. Our consideration of the role of phenomenal qualities has given us reason to think that they constitute such additional links. If we hold on to what seems plausible—Mary's discovery of the phenomenal quality, the causal role of such qualities, and the physical character of whatever has such a role—then it is worthwhile to exploit this possibility by supposing that phenomenal qualities are physical, properties that have the causal traits of Q. It is consistent with this supposition to main-tain both that some physical facts can be learned only through experiencing the phenomenal qualities essentially involved in those facts, and that black-and-white physical science can forgo such facts with no apparent incom-pleteness.

Notes

1   Frank Jackson, "Epiphenomenal Qualia," *Philosophical Quarterly* 32 (1982), 127-36, essay 15 in this volume.

2   Ibid., 130, in this volume, 162.

3   David Lewis, "Postscript to 'Mad Pain and Martian Pain,'" in *Philosophical Papers* vol. 1 (New York: Oxford Press, 1983), 130-32.

4   Laurence Nemirow, "Review of Thomas Nagel's Mortal Question," *Philosophical Review* 89 (1980), 473-77.

5   Terence Horgan, "Jackson on Physical Information and Qualia," *Philosophical Quartely* 34 (1984), 147-53, essay 16 in this volume.

6   This phrase is not well suited to convey the right idea. The word 'like' should not be there. Literally interpreted, "knowing what it is like" e.g. to see the sky, is identical to knowing the thing or things to which seeing the sky is similar. This is comparative knowledge of the form: seeing the sky is like such-and-such. A person could have this knowledge without knowing the look of the sky itself.

But the latter—knowing how the sky looks—is what it is plausible to suppose must be new to Mary.

7   Lewis, op. cit., 131.

8   I surmise that in a fuller discussion Lewis would say about this mental state what he says about others for which there are terms in common sense psychological discourse. If so, then he would say that the knowing-what-it's-like state among human beings is equal by definition to the state that in human beings typically occupies the functional role that the knowing-what-it's-like state is assigned by common sense psychology. (See Lewis, op. cit., 122-30.) On this sort of view, no ability would be necessary or sufficient. Rather, some—the common sense ones—would be by definition typical in humans.

9   Nemirow, op. cit., 475.

10 This point that the abilities are neither necessary nor sufficient for the learning does not refute the definition attributed to Lewis in note 8 above. But an extension of this sort of point does work. Notice that it might have been typical for humans to know how the sky looks without having any of the abilities that in actuality normally come from this knowledge. And it might have been typical to get the abilities in a way other than by knowing the look of the sky. Such (admittedly extraordinary) possible circumstances show the independence of the knowledge from the defining conditions indicated in note 8.

11 Horgan, op. cit., 150, this volume, 171.

12 Ibid., 151, in this volume, 173.

13 Ibid.

14 Strictly speaking this is not quite right. Merely always having been in a room without colour is not a necessarily insuperable barrier to having the experiences of colour vision. Various direct brain stimulations could bring about such experiences. It even seems possible that black-and-white scientific instruction itself might somehow bring about hallucinations in colour. But such cases would also be a matter of learning by experience, rather than learning from the content of the science. In a more rigorous formulation of Jackson's argument, the relevant premise would say that it is possible for someone without colour experiences to learn all of the actual physical information about colour perception. Strictly speaking, it is this premise that is to be denied.

20

What Mary Didn't Know*[1]

Frank Jackson

Mary is confined to a black-and-white room, is educated through black-and-white books and through lectures relayed on black-and-white television. In this way she learns everything there is to know about the physical nature of the world. She knows all the physical facts about us and our environment, in a wide sense of "physical" which includes everything in *completed* physics, chemistry, and neurophysiology, and all there is to know about the causal and relational facts consequent upon all this, including of course functional roles. If physicalism is true, she knows all there is to know. For to suppose otherwise is to suppose that there is more to know than every physical fact, and that is just what physicalism denies.

Physicalism is not the noncontroversial thesis that the actual world is largely physical, but the challenging thesis that it is entirely physical. This is why physicalists must hold that complete physical knowledge is complete knowledge simpliciter. For suppose it is not complete: then our world must differ from a world, *W(P)*, for which it is complete, and the difference must be in nonphysical facts; for our world and *W(P)* agree in all matters physical, Hence, physicalism would be false at our world [though contingently so, for it would be true at *W(P)*].[2]

It seems, however, that Mary does not know all there is to know. For when she is let out of the black-and-white room or given a colour television, she will learn what it is like to see something red, say. This is rightly described as *learning*—she will not say "ho, hum." Hence, physicalism is false. This is the knowledge argument against physicalism in one of its manifestations.[3] This note is in reply to three objections to it mounted by Paul M. Churchland.[4]

I. THREE CLARIFICATIONS

The knowledge argument does not rest on the dubious claim that logically you cannot imagine what sensing red is like unless you have sensed red. Powers of imagination are not to the point. The contention about Mary is not

---

* Frank Jackson, "What Mary Didn't Know," *Journal of Philosophy* 83 (1986), 127-36.
  Reprinted with kind permission of the author and the publisher.

that, despite her fantastic grasp of neurophysiology and everything else physical, she *could not imagine* what it is like to sense red; it is that, as a matter of fact, she *would not know*. But if physicalism is true, she would know; and no great powers of imagination would be called for. Imagination is a faculty that those who *lack* knowledge need to fall back on.

Secondly, the intensionality of knowledge is not to the point. The argument does not rest on assuming falsely that, if S knows that a is F and if $a = b$, then S knows that b is F. It is concerned with the nature of Mary's total body of knowledge before she is released: is it complete, or do some facts escape it? What is to the point is that S may know that a is F and *know* that $a = b$, yet arguably not know that b is F, by virtue of not being sufficiently logically alert to follow the consequences through. If Mary's lack of knowledge were at all like this, there would be no threat to physicalism in it. But it is very hard to believe that her lack of knowledge could be remedied merely by her explicitly following through enough logical consequences of her vast physical knowledge. Endowing her with great logical acumen and persistence is not in itself enough to fill in the gaps in her knowledge. On being let out, she will not say "I could have worked all this out before by making some more purely logical inferences."

Thirdly, the knowledge Mary lacked which is of particular point for the knowledge argument against physicalism is *knowledge about the experiences of others*, not about her own. When she is let out, she has new experiences, colour experiences she has never had before. It is not, therefore, an objection to physicalism that she learns *something* on being let out. Before she was let out, she could not have known facts about her experience of red, for there were no such facts to know. That physicalist and nonphysicalist alike can agree on. After she is let out, things change; and physicalism can happily admit that she learns this; after all, some physical things will change, for instance, her brain states and their functional roles. The trouble for physicalism is that, after Mary sees her first ripe tomato, she will realize how impoverished her conception of the mental life of *others* has been *all along*. She will realize that there was, all the time she was carrying out her laborious investigations into the neurophysiologies of others and into the functional roles of their internal states, something about these people she was quite unaware of. All along their experiences (or many of them, those got from tomatoes, the sky,...) had a feature conspicuous to them, but until now hidden from her (in fact, not in logic). But she knew all the physical facts about them all along; hence, what she did not know until her release is not a physical fact about their experiences. But it is a fact about them. That is the trouble for physicalism.

II. CHURCHLAND'S THREE OBJECTIONS

(i) Churchland's first objection is that the knowledge argument contains a defect that "is simplicity itself."[5] The argument equivocates on the sense of "knows about." How so? Churchland suggests that the following is "a conveniently tightened version" of the knowledge argument:

(1) Mary knows everything there is to know about brain states and their properties.
(2) It is not the case that Mary knows everything there is to know about sensations and their properties.

Therefore, by Leibniz's law,

(3) Sensations and their properties ≠ brain states and their properties.[6]

Churchland observes, plausibly enough, that the type or kind of knowledge involved in premise 1 is distinct from the kind of knowledge involved in premise 2. We might follow his lead and tag the first "knowledge by description," and the second "knowledge by acquaintance"; but, whatever the tags, he is right that the displayed argument involves a highly dubious use of Leibniz's law.

My reply is that the displayed argument may be convenient, but it is not accurate. It is not the knowledge argument. Take, for instance, premise 1. The whole thrust of the knowledge argument is that Mary (before her release) does *not* know everything there is to know about brain states and their properties, because she does not know about certain qualia associated with them. What is complete, according to the argument, is her knowledge of matters physical. A convenient and accurate way of displaying the argument is:

(1)′ Mary (before her release) knows everything physical there is to know about other people.
(2)′ Mary (before her release) does not know everything there is to know about other people (because she *learns* something about them on her release).

Therefore,

(3)′ There are truths about other people (and herself) which escape the physicalist story.[7]

What is immediately to the point is not the kind, manner, or type of knowledge Mary has, but what she knows. What she knows beforehand is ex hypothesi everything physical there is to know, but is it everything there is to know? That is the crucial question.

There is, though, a relevant challenge involving questions about kinds of knowledge. It concerns the *support* for premise 2′ . The case for premise 2′ is that Mary learns something on her release, she acquires knowledge, and that entails that her knowledge beforehand (*what* she knew, never mind whether by description, acquaintance, or whatever) was incomplete. The challenge, mounted by David Lewis and Laurence Nemirow, is that on her release Mary does *not* learn something or acquire knowledge in the relevant sense. What Mary acquires when she is released is a certain representational or imaginative ability; it is knowledge how rather than knowledge that. Hence, a physicalist can admit that Mary acquires something very significant of a knowledge kind—which can hardly be denied—without admitting that this shows that her earlier factual knowledge is defective. She knew all *that* there was to know about the experiences of others beforehand, but lacked an ability until after her release.[8]

Now it is certainly true that Mary will acquire abilities of various kinds after her release. She will, for instance, be able to imagine what seeing red is like, be able to remember what it is like, and be able to understand why her friends regarded her as so deprived (something which, until her release, had always mystified her). But is it plausible that that is all she will acquire? Suppose she received a lecture on skepticism about other minds while she was incarcerated. On her release she sees a ripe tomato in normal conditions, and so has a sensation of red. Her first reaction is to say that she now knows more about the kind of experiences others have when looking at ripe tomatoes. She then remembers the lecture and starts to worry. Does she really know more about what their experiences are like, or is she indulging in a wild generalization from one case? In the end she decides she does know, and that skepticism is mistaken (even if, like so many of us, she is not sure how to demonstrate its errors). What was she to-ing and fro-ing about—her abilities? Surely not; her representational abilities were a known constant throughout. What else then was she agonizing about than whether or not she had gained factual knowledge of others? There would be nothing to agonize about if ability was *all* she acquired on her release.

I grant that I have no *proof* that Mary acquires on her release, as well as abilities, factual knowledge about the experiences of others—and not just because I have no disproof of skepticism. My claim is that the knowledge argument is a valid argument from highly plausible, though admittedly not demonstrable, premises to the conclusion that physicalism is false. And that, after all, is about as good an objection as one could expect in this area of philosophy.

(ii) Churchland's second objection is that there must be something wrong with the argument, for it proves too much.[9] Suppose Mary received a special series of lectures over her black-and-white television from a full-blown dualist, explaining the "laws" governing the behaviour of "ectoplasm" and telling her about qualia. This would not affect the plausibility of the claim that on her release she learns something. So if the argument works against physicalism, it works against dualism too.

My reply is that lectures about qualia over black-and-white television do not tell Mary all there is to know about qualia. They may tell her some things about qualia, for instance, that they do not appear in the physicalist's story, and that the quale we use 'yellow' for is nearly as different from the one we use 'blue' for as is white from black. But why should it be supposed that they tell her everything about qualia? On the other hand, it is plausible that lectures over black-and-white television might in principle tell Mary everything in the physicalist's story. You do not need colour television to learn physics or functionalist psychology. To obtain a good argument against dualism (attribute dualism; ectoplasm is a bit of fun), the premise in the knowledge argument that Mary has the full story according to physicalism before her release has to be replaced by a premise that she has the full story according to dualism. The former is plausible; the latter is not. Hence, there is no "parity of reasons" trouble for dualists who use the knowledge argument.

(iii) Churchland's third objection is that the knowledge argument claims "that Mary could not even *imagine* what the relevant experience would be like, despite her exhaustive neuroscientific knowledge, and hence must still be missing certain crucial information,"[10] a claim he goes on to argue against.

But, as we emphasized earlier, the knowledge argument claims that Mary would not know what the relevant experience is like. What she could imagine is another matter. If her knowledge is defective, despite being all there is to know according to physicalism, then physicalism is false, whatever her powers of imagination.

Notes

1 I am much indebted to discussions with David Lewis and with Robert Pargetter.

2 The claim here is not that, if physicalism is true, only what is expressed in explicitly physical language is an item of knowledge. It is that, if physicalism is true, then if you know everything expressed or expressible in explicitly physical language, you know everything. *Pace* Terence Horgan, "Jackson on Physical Information and Qualia," *Philosophical Quarterly* 36 (1984), 147-52, essay 16 in this volume.

3 Namely, that in my "Epiphenomenal Qualia," *Philosophical Quarterly* 32 (1982), 127-36, essay 15 in this volume. See also Thomas Nagel, "What Is It Like to Be a Bat?" *Philosophical Review* 83 (1974), 435-50, and Howard Robinson, *Matter and Sense* (New York: Cambridge, 1982).

4 Paul Churchland, "Reduction, Qualia, and the Direct Introspection of Brain States," *Journal of Philosophy* 82 (1985), 8-28, essay 18 in this volume.

5 Ibid., 23, this volume, 187-88.

6   Ibid.

7   See Laurence Nemirow, review of Thomas Nagel, *Mortal Questions, Philosophical Review* 89 (1980), 473-77, and David Lewis, "Postscript to 'Mad Pain and Martian Pain,'" *Philosophical Papers*, vol. I (New York: Oxford, 1983). Churchland mentions both Nemirow and Lewis, and it may be that he intended his objection to be essentially the one I have just given. However, he says quite explicitly (bottom of p. 23) that his objection does not need an "ability" analysis of the relevant knowledge.

8   Churchland, op. cit., 24-25, this volume, 188.

9   Ibid., 25, this volume, 189-90.

10 Ibid., 25, this volume, 189-90.

"Epiphenomenal" Qualia?*

Daniel Dennett

There is another philosophical thought experiment about our experience of colour that has proven irresistible: Frank Jackson's[1] much-discussed case of Mary, the colour scientist who has never seen colours. Like a good thought experiment, its point is immediately evident to even the uninitiated. In fact it is a bad thought experiment, an intuition pump that actually encourages us to misunderstand its premises!

> Mary is a brilliant scientist who is, for whatever reason, forced to investigate the world from a black-and-white room *via* a black-and-white television monitor. She specializes in the neurophysiology of vision and acquires, let us suppose, all the physical information there is to obtain about what goes on when we see ripe tomatoes, or the sky, and use terms like *red, blue,* and so on. She discovers, for example, just which wavelength combinations from the sky stimulate the retina, and exactly how this produces *via* the central nervous system the contraction of the vocal chords and expulsion of air from the lungs that results in the uttering of the sentence "The sky is blue." ... What will happen when Mary is released from her black-and-white room or is given a colour television monitor? Will she *learn* anything or not? It seems just obvious that she will learn something about the world and our visual experience of it. But then it is inescapable that her previous knowledge was incomplete. But she had *all* the physical information. *Ergo* there is more to have than that, and Physicalism is false....[2]

The point could hardly be clearer. Mary has had no experience of colour at all (there are no mirrors to look at her face in, she's obliged to wear black gloves, etc., etc.), and so, at that special moment when her captors finally let her come out into the coloured world which she knows only by description (and black-and-white diagrams), "it seems just obvious," as Jackson says, that she will learn something. Indeed, we can all vividly imagine her, seeing a red

---

* From *Consciousness Explained* by Daniel Dennett. Copyright © 1991 by Daniel C. Dennett. Reprinted by permission of Little, Brown and Company, (Inc.).

rose for the first time and exclaiming, "So *that's* what red looks like!" And it may also occur to us that if the first coloured things she is shown are, say, unlabeled wooden blocks, and she is told only that one of them is red and the other blue, she won't have the faintest idea which is which until she somehow learns which colour words go with her newfound experiences.

That is how almost everyone imagines this thought experiment—not just the uninitiated, but the shrewdest, most battle-hardened philosophers.[3] Only Paul Churchland[4] has offered any serious resistance to the *image*, so vividly conjured up by the thought experiment, of Mary's dramatic discovery. The image is wrong; if that is the way you imagine the case, you are simply not following directions! The reason no one follows directions is because what they ask you to imagine is so preposterously immense, you can't even try. The crucial premise is that "She has *all* the physical information." That is not readily imaginable, so no one bothers. They just imagine that she knows lots and lots—perhaps they imagine that she knows everything that anyone knows *today* about the neurophysiology of colour vision. But that's just a drop in the bucket, and it's not surprising that Mary would learn something if *that* were all she knew.

To bring out the illusion of imagination here, let me continue the story in a surprising—but legitimate—way:

And so, one day, Mary's captors decided it was time for her to see colours. As a trick, they prepared a bright blue banana to present as her first colour experience ever. Mary took one look at it and said "Hey! You tried to trick me! Bananas are yellow, but this one is blue!" Her captors were dumfounded. How did she do it? "Simple," she replied. "You have to remember that I know everything—absolutely everything—that could ever be known about the physical causes and effects of colour vision. So of course before you brought the banana in, I had already written down, in exquisite detail, exactly what physical impression a yellow object or a blue object (or a green object, etc.) would make on my nervous system. So I already knew exactly what thoughts I would have (because, after all, the 'mere disposition' to think about this or that is not one of your famous qualia, is it?). I was not in the slightest surprised by my experience of blue (what surprised me was that you would try such a second-rate trick on me). I realize it is hard for you to imagine that I could know so much about my reactive dispositions that the way blue affected me came as no surprise. Of course it's hard for you to imagine. It's hard for anyone to imagine the consequences of someone knowing absolutely everything physical about anything!"

Surely I've cheated, you think. I must be hiding some impossibility behind the veil of Mary's remarks. Can you prove it? My point is not that my way of telling the rest of the story proves that Mary doesn't learn anything, but that the usual way of imagining the story doesn't prove that she does. It doesn't prove anything; it simply pumps the intuition that she does ("it seems just obvious") by lulling you into imagining something other than what the premises require.

It is of course true that in any realistic, readily imaginable version of the story, Mary would come to learn something, but in any realistic, readily imaginable version she might know a lot, but she would not know everything physical. Simply imagining that Mary knows a lot, and leaving it at that, is not a good way to figure out the implications of her having "all the physical information"—any more than imagining she is filthy rich would be a good way to figure out the implications of the hypothesis that she owned everything. It may help us imagine the extent of the powers her knowledge gives her if we begin by enumerating a few of the things she obviously knows in advance. She knows black and white and shades of grey, and she knows the difference between the colour of any object and such surface properties as glossiness versus matte, and she knows all about the difference between luminance boundaries and colour boundaries (luminance boundaries are those that show up on black-and-white television, to put it roughly). And she knows precisely which effects—described in neurophysiological terms—each particular colour will have on her nervous system. So the only task that remains is for her to figure out a way of identifying those neurophysiological effects "from the inside." You may find you can readily imagine her making a little progress on this—for instance, figuring out tricky ways in which she would be able to tell that some colour, whatever it is, is not yellow, or not red. How? By noting some salient and specific reaction that her brain would have only for yellow or only for red. But if you allow her even a little entry into her colour space in this way, you should conclude that she can leverage her way to complete advance knowledge, because she doesn't just know the salient reactions, she knows them all.

Recall Julius and Ethel Rosenberg's Jell-O box, which they turned into an M-detector. Now imagine their surprise if an impostor were to show up with a "matching" piece that was not the original. "Impossible!" they cry. "Not impossible," says the impostor, "just difficult. I had all the information required to reconstruct an M-detector, and to make another thing with shape-property M." Mary had enough information (in the original case, if correctly imagined) to figure out just what her red-detectors and blue-detectors were, and hence to identify them in advance. Not the usual way of coming to learn about colours, but Mary is not your usual person.

I know that this will not satisfy many of Mary's philosophical fans, and that there is a lot more to be said, but—and this is my main point—the actual proving must go on in an arena far removed from Jackson's example, which is a classic provoker of Philosophers' Syndrome: mistaking a failure of imagination for an insight into necessity. Some of the philosophers who have dealt with the case of Mary may not care that they have imagined it wrong, since they have simply used it as a springboard into discussions that shed light on various independently interesting and important issues. I will not pursue those issues here, since I am interested in directly considering the conclusion that Jackson himself draws from his example: visual experiences have qualia that are "epiphenomenal."

The term "epiphenomena" is in common use today by both philosophers and psychologists (and other cognitive scientists). It is used with the presumption that its meaning is familiar and agreed upon, when in fact, philosophers and cognitive scientists use the term with *entirely* different meanings— a strange fact made even stranger to me by the fact that although I have pointed this out time and again, no one seems to care. Since "epiphenomenalism" often seems to be the last remaining safe haven for qualia, and since this appearance of safety is due entirely to the confusion between these two meanings, I must become a scold, and put those who use the term on the defensive.

According to the *Shorter Oxford English Dictionary*, the term "epiphenomenon" first appears in 1706 as a term in pathology, "a secondary appearance or symptom." The evolutionary biologist Thomas Huxley[5] was probably the writer who extended the term to its current use in psychology, where it means a nonfunctional property or by-product. Huxley used the term in his discussion of the evolution of consciousness and his claim that epiphenomenal properties (like the "whistle of the steam engine") could not be explained by natural selection.

Here is a clear instance of this use of the word:

Why do people who are thinking hard bite their lips and tap their feet? Are these actions just epiphenomena that accompany the core processes of feeling and thinking or might they themselves be integral parts of these processes?[6]

Notice that the authors mean to assert that these actions, while perfectly detectable, play no enabling role, no designed role, in the processes of feeling and thinking; they are nonfunctional. In the same spirit, the hum of the computer is epiphenomenal, as is your shadow when you make yourself a cup of tea. Epiphenomena are mere by-products, but as such they are products with lots of effects in the world: tapping your feet makes a recordable noise, and your shadow has its effects on photographic film, not to mention the slight cooling of the surfaces it spreads itself over.

The standard philosophical meaning is different: "*x* is epiphenomenal" means "*x* is an effect but itself has no effects in the physical world whatever."[7] Are these meanings really so different? Yes, as different as the meanings of *murder* and *death.* The philosophical meaning is stronger: Anything that has no effects whatever in the physical world surely has no effects on the function of anything, but the converse doesn't follow, as the example from Zajonc and Markus makes obvious.

In fact, the philosophical meaning is too strong; it yields a concept of no utility whatsoever.[8] Since *x* has no physical effects (according to this definition), no instrument can detect the presence of *x* directly or indirectly; the way the world goes is not modulated in the slightest by the presence or absence of *x*. How then, could there ever be any empirical reason to assert the presence of *x*? Suppose, for instance, that Otto insists that he (for one) has epiphenomenal qualia. Why does he say this? Not because they have some effect on him, somehow guiding him or alerting him as he makes his avowals. By the very definition of epiphenomena (in the philosophical sense), Otto's heartfelt avowals that he has epiphenomena *could not* be evidence for himself or anyone else that he does have them, since he would be saying exactly the same thing even if he didn't have them. But perhaps Otto has some "internal" evidence?

Here there's a loophole, but not an attractive one. Epiphenomena, remember, are defined as having no effect in the physical world. If Otto wants to embrace out-and-out dualism, he can claim that his epiphenomenal qualia have no effects in the physical world, but do have effects in his (nonphysical) mental world.[9] For instance, they *cause some of his (nonphysical) beliefs,* such as his belief that he has epiphenomenal qualia. But this is just a temporary escape from embarrassment. For now on pain of contradiction, his beliefs, in turn, can have no effect in the physical world. If he suddenly lost his epiphenomenal qualia, he would no longer believe he had them, but he'd still go right on *saying* he did. He just wouldn't believe what he was saying! (Nor could he tell you that he didn't believe what he was saying, or do anything at all that revealed that he no longer believed what he was saying.) So the only way Otto could "justify" his belief in epiphenomena would be by retreating into a solipsistic world where there is only himself, his beliefs and his qualia, cut off from all effects in the world. Far from being a "safe" way of being a materialist and having your qualia too, this is at best a way of endorsing the most radical solipsism, by cutting off your mind—your beliefs and your experiences—from any commerce with the material world.

If qualia are epiphenomenal in the standard philosophical sense, their occurrence can't explain the way things happen (in the material world) since, by definition, things would happen exactly the same without them. There could not be an empirical reason, then, for believing in epiphenomena. Could there be another sort of reason for asserting their existence? What sort of reason? An *a priori* reason, presumably. But what? No one has ever offered one—good, bad, or indifferent—that I have seen. If someone wants to object that I am being a "verificationist" about these epiphenomena, I reply: Isn't everyone a verificationist about *this* sort of assertion? Consider, for instance, the hypothesis that there are fourteen epiphenomenal gremlins in each cylinder of an internal combustion engine. These gremlins have no mass, no energy, no physical properties; they do not make the engine run smoother or rougher, faster or slower. There is *and could be* no empirical evidence of their presence, and no empirical way in principle of distinguishing this hypothesis from its rivals: there are twelve or thirteen or fifteen . . . gremlins. By what principle does one defend one's wholesale dismissal of such nonsense? A verificationist principle, or just plain common sense?

Ah, but there's a difference! [says Otto.] There is no independent motivation for taking the hypothesis of these gremlins seriously. You just made them up on the spur of the moment. Qualia, in contrast, have been around for a long time, playing a major role in our conceptual scheme!

And what if some benighted people have been thinking for generations that gremlins made their cars go, and by now have been pushed back by the march of science into the forlorn claim that the gremlins are there, all right, but are epiphenomenal? Is it a mistake for us to dismiss their "hypothesis" out of hand? Whatever the principle is that we rely on when we give the back of our hand to such nonsense, it suffices to dismiss the doctrine that qualia are epiphenomenal in this philosophical sense. These are not views that deserve to be discussed with a straight face.

It's hard to believe that the philosophers who have recently described their views as epiphenomenalism can be making such a woebegone mistake. Are they, perhaps, just asserting that qualia are epiphenomenal in Huxley's sense? Qualia, on this reading, *are* physical effects and *have* physical effects; they just aren't functional. Any materialist should be happy to admit that this hypothesis is true—if we identify qualia with reactive dispositions, for instance. As we noted in the discussion of enjoyment, even though some bulges or biases in our quality spaces are functional—or used to be functional—others are just brute happenstance. Why don't I like broccoli? Probably for no reason at all; my negative reactive disposition is purely epiphenomenal, a by-product of my wiring with no significance. It has no function, but has plenty of effects. In any designed system, some properties are crucial while others are more or less revisable *ad lib.* Everything has to be some way or another, but often the ways don't matter. The gearshift lever on a car may have to be a certain length and a certain strength, but whether it is round or square or oval in cross section is an epiphenomenal property, in Huxley's sense....

If we think of all the properties of our nervous systems that enable us to see, hear, smell, taste, and touch things, we can divide them, roughly, into the properties that play truly crucial roles in mediating the information processing, and the epiphenomenal properties that are more or less revisable *ad lib*... When a philosopher surmises that qualia are epiphenomenal properties of brain states, this might mean that qualia could turn out to be local variations in the heat generated by neuronal metabolism. That cannot be what epiphenomenalists have in mind, can it? If it is, then qualia as epiphenomena are no challenge to materialism.

The time has come to put the burden of proof squarely on those who persist in using the term. The philosophical sense of the term is simply ridiculous; Huxley's sense is relatively clear and unproblematic—and irrelevant to the philosophical arguments. No other sense of the term has any currency. So if anyone claims to uphold a variety of epiphenomenalism, try to be polite, but ask: What *are* you talking about? ...

Notes

1   Frank Jackson, "Epiphenomenal Qualia," *Philosophical Quarterly* 32 (1982), 127-36, essay 15 in this volume.
2   Ibid., 128, this volume, 162.
3   Michael Tye, "The Subjective Qualities of Experience," *Mind* 95 (1986), 1-17; David Lewis, "What Experience Teaches," in W. Lycan, ed., *Mind and Cognition: A Reader* (Oxford: Blackwell, 1988); Brian Loar, "Phenomenal Properties," in J.E. Tomberlin, ed., *Philosophical Perspectives, 4: Action Theory and the Philosophy of Mind* (Atascadero, CA: Ridgeview, 1990), 81-108; William Lycan, "What Is the Subjectivity of the Mental?" in Tomberlin, op. cit., 109-30; Laurence Nemirow, "Physicalism and the Cognitive Role of Acquaintance," in Lycan, op. cit., 490-99, essay 17 in this volume; Gilbert Harman, "The Intrinsic Quality of Experience," in Tomberlin, op. cit., 31-52; Ned Block, "Inverted Earth," in Tomberlin, op. cit., 53-79; Robert van Gulick, "Understanding the Phenomenal Mind: Are We All Just Armadillos?" presented at the conference "The Phenomenal Mind— How Is It Possible and Why Is It Necessary?" Zentrum für Interdisziplinäre Forschung, Bielefeld, Germany, May 14-17, 1990.
4   Paul Churchland, "Reduction, Qualia, and the Direct Introspection of Brain States," *Journal of Philosophy* 82 (1985), 8-28, essay 18 in this volume; "Knowing Qualia: A Reply to Jackson," in Churchland, *A Neurocomputational Perspective: The Nature of Mind and the Structure of Science* (Cambridge, MA: MIT Press, 1990), 67-76.
5   T.H. Huxley, "On the Hypothesis that Animals Are Automata, and its History," in Leonard Huxley, ed., *Methods and Results: Essays* (London: MacMillan, 1902), essay 3 in this volume.
6   R. Zajonic and H. Markus, "Affect and Cognition: The Hard Interface," in C. Izard, J. Kagan, and R. Zajonic, eds., *Emotion, Cognition and Behavior* (Cambridge: Cambridge University Press, 1984), 74.
7   See C.D. Broad, *Mind and its Place in Nature* (London: Routledge and Kegan Paul, 1925), 118, for the definition that inaugurates, or at any rate establishes, the philosophical usage.

8   Harman, op. cit.; I. Fox, "On the Nature and Cognitive Function of Phenomenal Content—Part One," *Philosophical Topics* 17 (1989), 81-117.

9   Broad, op. cit., closed this loophole by definition, but it's free for the asking.

PART IV

Supervenience

Concepts of Supervenience*[1]

Jaegwon Kim

I. INTRODUCTION

We think of the world around us not as a mere assemblage of unrelated objects, events, and facts, but as constituting a system, something that shows *structure*, and whose constituents are connected with one another in significant ways. This view of the world seems fundamental to our scheme of things; it is reflected in the commonplace assumption that things that happen in one place can make a difference to things that happen in another in a way that enables us to make sense of one thing in terms of another, infer information about one thing from information about another, or affect one thing by affecting another. Central to this idea of interconnectedness of things is a notion of *dependence* (or, its converse, *determination*): things are connected with one another in that whether something exists, or what properties it has, is *dependent on*, or *determined by*, what other things exist and what kinds of things they are. It is in virtue of these dependency or determinative relationships that the world can be made intelligible; and by exploiting them we are able to intervene in the course of events and alter it to suit our wishes. Activities like explanation, prediction, and control would make little sense for a world devoid of such connections. The idea that "real connections" exist and the idea that the world is intelligible and controllable are arguably equivalent ideas.

Causation is a pre-eminent example of what I am calling determinative or dependency relations; apart from those that are logically based, such as entailment, it is the only explicitly recognized and widely discussed relation of this kind. Causes determine their effects, and effects are dependent, for their existence and properties, on their causes. It is not for nothing that Hume called causation "the cement of the universe";[2] causation is the cosmic glue that binds discrete objects and events together, making them mutually significant—even in Hume's atomistic world—and thereby helping to provide a necessary basis for the prediction and control of natural phenomena. It is congenial to the broadly realist view of the world that most of us accept

* Jaegwon Kim, "Concepts of Supervenience," *Philosophy and Phenomenological Research* 45 (1984), 153-76. Reprinted with kind permission of the publisher.

to think of the network of causal relations in the world as underlying, and supporting, the network of explanatory and other epistemic relations represented in our knowledge of it.

The part-whole relation is also important; however, its importance seems to derive largely from the belief that many crucial aspects of a whole including its existence and nature are dependent on those of its parts. That is, mereological relations[3] are significant because mereological determination, or "mereological supervenience,"[4] is, or is thought to be, a pervasive fact.

There has lately been an increasing interest in the concept of *supervenience*, especially for its possible applications to the mind-body problem, microreduction, and physicalism. It is useful to think of supervenience as belonging in that class of relations, including causation, that have philosophical importance because they represent ways in which objects, properties, facts, events, and the like enter into dependency relationships with one another, creating a system of interconnections that give structure to the world and our experience of it. Modes of dependency or determination may differ from one another in various ways; if supervenience is thought of as such a mode, questions arise as to exactly how it differs from others, whether it is a single homogeneous relation or represents in reality two or more distinguishable relationships, and whether supervenient determination presents a philosophically significant alternative to other determinative relations.

The idea of supervenience seems to have originated in moral philosophy. In the following well-known passage G.E. Moore describes a certain dependency relationship between moral and nonmoral properties that has later come to be called "supervenience":

... if a given thing possesses any kind of intrinsic value in a certain degree, then not only must that same thing possess it, under all circumstances, in the same degree, but also anything *exactly like it*, must, under all circumstances, possess it in exactly the same degree.[5]

Moore himself, however, seems not to have used the term "supervenience"; it was R.M. Hare, I believe, who, writing many years later, gave it the philosophical currency it now enjoys. The following passage from Hare is now generally recognized as a classic source that helped to shape the initial contours of the concept:

First, let us take that characteristic of "good" which has been called its supervenience. Suppose that we say "St. Francis was a good man." It is logically impossible to say this and to maintain at the same time that there might have been another man placed exactly in the same circumstances as St. Francis, and who behaved in exactly the same way, but who differed from St. Francis in this respect only, that he was not a good man.[6]

Here, Hare speaks of supervenience as a "characteristic" of the term "good." However, it is clear that it is more usefully construed as a relation, a relation between "good" and terms that denote such things as patterns of behavior and traits of character. What Hare is saying is that it is "logically impossible" for there to be two persons who are exactly alike in these latter respects and yet differ in respect of being a good man. It is also clear that supervenience is better thought of as a relation not between properties or terms taken singly but between sets or families of them. Thus, we can say that all valuational properties (that is, the set of all valuational properties) are supervenient upon the set of all natural or descriptive properties. We shall in this paper discuss supervenience chiefly for properties rather than predicates; the choice here is indifferent to an extent, but, as we shall see, not wholly so. One could also speak of supervenience for sentences, facts, events, propositions, and languages; I shall argue below that fact supervenience can be understood in terms of property supervenience. It will become plausible, I believe, that property supervenience is fundamental, and that supervenience for most other entities can be explained in terms of it.

It is this evident generalizability beyond the sphere of ethics that makes supervenience an attractive and promising concept worthy of closer attention. Perhaps because of this, one now sees an increasing use of the term "supervenience" in a variety of areas, indicating the presence of substantial shared intuitive content. Thus, the aesthetic properties of a work of art have been claimed to be supervenient on its physical properties.[7] Some philosophers have found in psychophysical supervenience an attractive alternative to reductionist physicalism; it is thought that the supervenience thesis acknowledges the primacy of the physical without committing us to the stronger claims of physical reductionism.[8] The idea that valuational terms in general supervene on nonvaluational ones has been extended to epistemic terms, terms used for making epistemic appraisals, such as "evident," "certain," and "justified." The view that criteria of epistemic justification must be stated in nonepistemic terms can be thought of as an expression of the thesis that epistemic properties are supervenient on nonepistemic characteristics and relationships (e.g., causal properties and logical relations).[9] Leibniz's obscure doctrine of the dispensability of relational judgments is perhaps interpretable as the thesis that relations are supervenient on properties.[10] Quine's thesis of translational indeterminacy is usefully construed as the denial of the claim that meaning supervenes on the totality of physical fact.[11] Mereological supervenience has already been mentioned. There are other interesting questions we might formulate in terms of supervenience: Are causal relations supervenient on particular matters of noncausal fact? Are laws supervenient on their instances? Do theories supervene on data? Often the belief that there is a supervenience relation in a given domain, for example in the domain of the mental vis-à-vis the physical, forms an implicit premise of great importance that motivates and shapes the specific theories concerning that domain. Acceptance or rejection of the supervenience of the mental on the physical leads to the most basic division between theories of the mind-body relation: theories that accept psychophysical supervenience are fundamentally materialist, and those that reject it are fundamentally anti-materialist. This difference seems philosophically more basic and more significant than the usual classification of mind-body theories as "monist" or "dualist."[12]

This paper is intended as a general discussion of supervenience as a relation of dependency or determination. I shall be claiming that there are two separable concepts of supervenience, one stronger than the other, and that often what is offered in a philosophical discussion is the weaker of the two whereas what is needed is the stronger one. I shall also argue that the stronger relation is equivalent to "global supervenience,"[13] an alternative conception favoured by some writers. One issue that will receive attention is what supervenience between two domains entails about the existence of kind-to-kind connections between them, and what this means for such relations as definability and reducibility between the two domains.

II. WEAK SUPERVENIENCE

The passage quoted above from Hare suggests this initial conception of the supervenience relation: the moral is supervenient on the natural in the sense that if two objects (persons, acts, states of affairs, and the like) are alike in all natural respects they must of necessity be alike in all moral respects. That is to say, things cannot differ with respect to some moral characteristic unless there is some natural property with respect to which they differ. Much the same idea is present in Donald Davidson's formulation of psychophysical supervenience:

> Although the position I describe denies there are psychophysical laws, it is consistent with the view that mental characteristics are in some sense dependent, or supervenient, on physical characteristics. Such supervenience might be taken to mean that there cannot be two events alike in all physical respects but differing in some mental respects, or that an object cannot alter in some mental respects without altering in some physical respects.[14]

Here Davidson gives two explanations of supervenience, the first stated for events and the second for objects. I am not focusing on the fact that one is for events and the other for objects; I am only interested in the general forms of the two explanations, and want to point to the fact that the first conforms to the pattern indicated in Hare's statement: mental characteristics supervene on physical ones in that no two things (objects, events, and the like) could differ with respect to some mental characteristic unless they differed also in some physical characteristic—that is, coincidence in the physical entails coincidence in the mental. If we were to create an exact physical replica of you, it and you would be psychologically indistinguishable. (Davidson's second explanation, as I shall suggest later, indicates a stronger relation of supervenience.)

A general analysis of supervenience that captures these ideas is straight-forwardly developed. Let A and B be two nonempty families of properties (for simplicity we exclude relations) closed under the usual Boolean property-forming operations, complementation, conjunction, and disjunction (and perhaps others such as infinite conjunction and disjunction). This then is a definition of "weak supervenience" (the reason for calling it "weak" will be made clear below):

A *weakly supervenes* on B if and only if necessarily for any x and y if x and y share all properties in B then x and y share all properties in A—that is, indiscernibility with respect to B entails indiscernibility with respect to A.

We shall call A the *supervenient family* and B the *supervenience base* (family); properties in A are *supervenient properties*, and those in B are the *base properties*.

As an example: consider the set, A, containing the property of being a good man (G) and having the Boolean closure property; and let B be the set containing the property of being courageous (C), that of being benevolent (V), and that of being honest (H), and closed under the Boolean operations. A contains only two properties, G and –G, besides the tautological one (G v –G) and the impossible one (G & –G). Suppose A weakly supervenes on B. This means that if two men share the same properties in B, say, both are honest and benevolent but lack courage (this will insure they share all other properties in B), then they must both be good men or neither is (they of course cannot differ in regard to the tautological or impossible property). Or, what is the same, if one is a good man but the other is not, there must be some property in B with respect to which they differ (say, the first is courageous but the second is not). Any differences in A must be accounted for by some difference in B.

To fix this further in mind consider what we may call B-maximal properties: these are the strongest consistent properties constructible in B, and for our present example there are eight of these: C & V & H, C & V & –H, C & –V & H,..., –C & –V & –H. These properties are mutually exclusive, and every object must have just one of these. Clearly, two objects are indiscernible in B just in case they have the same B-maximal property. Weak supervenience of A on B therefore comes to this: any two objects with the same B-maximal property must have the same properties in A—they are both G, or both –G. Or, using the terminology of "possible world," we may say: there is no possible world in which two objects have the same B-maximal property and yet differ in respect of G.

Given weak supervenience of A and B, therefore, within each possible world generalizations of the following form will hold:

(1) $(\forall x)[B_i(x) \rightarrow G^*(x)]$,

where, for each i, B_i is a B-maximal property and G^* is either G or $-G$. Whether G or $-G$ is to be associated with a given B-maximal property is a feature of the specific possible world; but within each world these exceptionless universal conditionals between the property of being a good man on the one hand and the virtues of courage, benevolence, and honesty on the other must hold. Within each world, in fact, the following biconditionals hold:

(2) $(\forall x)[B^*(x) \leftrightarrow G(x)]$
    $(\forall x)[B\#(x) \leftrightarrow -G(x)]$

where B^* and $B\#$ are each a disjunction of B-maximal properties.

All of these points remain valid for weak supervenience generally, when B is finite; if B is not finite, these results will depend on the formability of B-maximal properties, which requires infinite conjunction, and their infinite disjunctions. I shall argue later that these operations are acceptable for properties (as distinguished from predicates), and they will be assumed in some of the formal arguments below (it will be clear exactly where they are used).

I dwell on these details in order to make the point that, although the definition of "weak supervenience" follows very closely the bench-mark explanations of supervenience in the literature, as witness the quotations from Hare and Davidson, the relation it defines is considerably weaker than one might have expected—indeed, too weak for some of its typical intended applications. The key to seeing this is that in a generalization of the form (1) above, which associates a supervenient property for each maximal property in the base family, whether G^* is G or $-G$ depends on the particular world under consideration, and is not a feature invariant across possible worlds. This means that weak supervenience of A and B (returning to our example) permits the following:

(a) In this world anyone who is courageous, benevolent, and honest is a good man, but in another possible world no such man is good; in fact, every such man is evil in this other world.
(b) Again, in this world anyone who has courage, benevolence, and honesty is good; in another world exactly like this one in respect of the distribution of these virtues, no man is good.
(c) In another possible world just like this one in respect of who has, or lacks, these traits of character, every man is good.

It is plain that weak supervenience permits these possibilities, for it only requires that *within* any possible world there not be two things agreeing in B but diverging in A, and this condition is met in each of these cases. It does not require that if in another world an object has the same B-properties that it has in this world, it must also have the same A-properties it has in this one. The particular associations between A-properties and B-properties in a given world cannot be counted on to carry over into other worlds.

Thus, weak supervenience falls short of the following condition: fixing the base properties of an object fixes its supervenient properties. This condition expresses a presumptive desideratum on the explication of supervenience: base properties must *determine* supervenient properties in the sense that once the former are fixed for an object, there is no freedom to vary the latter for that object. Weak supervenience goes some way toward this idea of determination: if you fix the base properties of two objects in the same way in a given world then you must fix their supervenient properties in the same way in that world. But under weak supervenience that is as far as the base properties constrain the attribution of the supervenient properties. That this is less than what we might expect of a relation of determination or dependence can be seen in various ways. Determination or dependence is naturally thought of as carrying a certain modal force: if being a good man is dependent on, or is determined by, certain traits of character, then having these traits must *insure* or *guarantee* being a good man (or lacking certain of these traits must insure that one not be a good man). The connection between these traits and being a good man must be more than a *de facto* coincidence that varies from world to world. We should be able to say: although Charles is not a good man, he would be one if only he *had* some benevolence in his nature as well as being honest and courageous. We should also be able to say: anyone who has these three virtues *would* be a good man although it is unfortunate that no one has them all. Claims like these seem integral to what we mean when we speak of "good-making characteristics": any "X-making characteristic" must be such that if anything had it, it must of necessity have X (at least, it must necessarily be of positive relevance to its having X). Weak supervenience of moral upon nonmoral properties does not entail that there are nonmoral "conditions" or "criteria" for moral properties.

Another idea that is often associated with the idea of supervenience is this: if the moral supervenes on the nonmoral, any two worlds exactly alike in all nonmoral respects must be alike in all moral respects (in fact, they must be one and the same world). But this does not obtain under weak supervenience, as we have already seen. Similar points can be made about psychophysical supervenience: weak psychophysical supervenience is consistent with the existence of a world that is just like the actual one in every physical detail but in which no mentality, no consciousness, is manifested, and also a world that is just like ours except that a low-grade pain permeates every object everywhere. Thus, if we were to look, with Davidson, to supervenience for a relation of dependency for the mental vis-à-vis the physical, we would likely not find it in weak supervenience.

I find the following remarks by Moore instructive as well as surprising:

> I should never have thought of suggesting that goodness was "non-natural," unless I had supposed that it was "derivative" in the sense that, whenever a thing is good (in the sense in question) its goodness (in Mr. Broad's words) "depends on the presence of certain non-ethical characteristics" possessed by the thing in question: I have always supposed that it did so "depend" in the sense that, if a thing is good (in my sense), then that it is so *follows* from the fact that it possesses certain natural intrinsic properties, which are such that from the fact that it is good it does *not* follow conversely that it has those properties.[15]

We need not know exactly what Moore meant here by the term "follow" or "depend" to know that its force exceeds weak supervenience. For weak supervenience, as we have seen, only requires that any two things having the same natural properties must be either both good or both not good. This surely is not enough for saying that a thing's being good "follows" from its having the natural properties it has; weak supervenience, therefore, cannot explicate the notion of "dependence" Moore had in mind.

Does weak supervenience then have any useful philosophical applications? Although it is evidently not strong enough to serve as an analysis of a full relation of dependence or determination, I believe it marks an interesting and significant relation of partial dependence or determination. Consider the case of moral supervenience again: perhaps all Hare wanted was weak supervenience.[16] Under weak supervenience there would be an inconsistency in one's commending an object (saying that it is good) but failing to commend another that is, or is believed to be, exactly like it in all descriptive details; however, there is nothing inconsistent, or incoherent, in failing to commend either while acknowledging the same descriptive properties of the two objects. This, in essence, is the prescription "Treat like cases alike" in ethical contexts. Weak supervenience, therefore, gives us the much discussed *Principle of Universalizability* of ethical judgments understood as a *consistency requirement*.[17] There is, however, a stronger sense in which the universalizability of ethical judgments has been understood: every singular ethical judgment must be supportable by a fully *general covering principle*. This stronger requirement goes beyond weak supervenience, corresponding rather to the notion of "strong supervenience" to be explained in the following section. That these two versions of the Universalizability Principle turn out to correspond nicely with the two concepts of supervenience distinguished in this paper speaks well for the naturalness as well as philosophical interest of the two concepts. These remarks about two Principles of Universalizability obviously apply to other cases involving valuational judgments (e.g., in aesthetics and epistemology).

Davidson has likened the relationship between the semantic notion of truth and syntactical concepts to psychophysical supervenience: in spite of the fact that truth is not definable or reducible in terms of syntax there is a sense in which the truth of a sentence depends on its syntactic properties.[18] This can, I think, be taken as something like weak supervenience: any two sentences that are syntactically indiscernible are in fact the same sentence and must therefore have the same truth value. But obviously the truth value of a sentence cannot in general be relied on to be stable from world to world. Davidson's use of this example to explain supervenience points to the possibility that weak supervenience is also what he had in mind in speaking of psychophysical supervenience. This interpretation fits in neatly with Davidson's doctrine of psychophysical anomalism to the effect that there are no lawlike connections between mental and physical kinds. Lawlike connections must be stable over possible worlds (at least relative to some accessibility condition), and such connections between the mental and the physical are exactly what weak psychophysical supervenience does not require. On the other hand, this interpretation has a weakness: any robust materialist position should affirm, I think, that what is material determines all that there is in the world,[19] and this weak supervenience cannot give us. Although I am not sure whether Davidson would accept a full materialist position in my sense it seems that he wants more than weak supervenience.

Although it falls short of full-fledged materialism, weak psychophysical supervenience may be a possible thesis worth pondering: one might argue, for example, that although no physical fact about an organism, whether its behaviour or its physiology, compels us to attribute to it some particular mental state, or any mental state at all, consistency requires that if two organisms manifest the same behaviour and physiology, the same mental state must be attributed to each, and that this is the only constraint on the ascription of mental states. I think some such view may be held by those who take the attribution of mental states as just another case of positing theoretical explanatory states (relative to, say, behaviour), and who take the possibility of the "inverted spectrum" seriously.

Another related case is this: even if, as many philosophers believe, theories are "underdetermined" by all possible data, they may be weakly supervenient on data in the following sense: although no set of data compels the choice of a particular explanatory theory, "relevantly similar data" must be explained by "relevantly similar theories." Weak supervenience as applied here thus yields a consistency requirement on theory construction in the same way that weak moral supervenience yields a consistency requirement on ethical judgments, clarifying one precise way in which data constrain theory. There may be other interesting applications of weak supervenience; I hope, though, that what we have seen is enough to persuade us of its potential interest as a philosophical concept.

III. STRONG SUPERVENIENCE

A clue to an appropriate way of strengthening weak supervenience to obtain a stronger relation is seen when we consider the following equivalent formulation of weak supervenience:

> A *weakly supervenes* on B if and only if necessarily for any property F in A, if an object x has F, then there exists a property G in B such that x has G, and if any y has G it has F.

Let us first see that the two definitions are equivalent. First, we show weak supervenience given by the earlier definition entails that newly defined. Assume that for some F in A, x has F. We need to show, for some G in B, that x has G, and that anything y with G has F. Let G be the B-maximal property of x (in any given world under consideration). Then trivially x has G. To show that anything y with G has B: suppose some y has G. Since both x and y have G and G is a B-maximal property, x and y share all properties in B. So by weak supervenience as first defined, x and y must share all properties in A. But F is in A and x has F. So y, too, must have F.

Second, to show that the second definition entails the first: assume x and y share all properties in B, and suppose they do not share all properties in A—that is, for some F in A, x has F but y does not. Since x has F, weak supervenience as defined in the second definition entails that for some G in B, x has G, and anything with G has F. By assumption, x and y share all properties in B; so y, too, has G, whence y has F, yielding a contradiction.

The key aspect of the second definition is its last clause, the requirement that any object having G also has F. The force of this clause is that within each world this G-F generalization must hold; it does not require that the G-F connection be stable across worlds. This suggests that in order to get a stronger supervenience relation that will insure the stability of connections between supervenient properties and their base properties, we should try prefixing this clause with a suitable modal operator. It turns out that this yields what we want.[20]

This approach is also suggested by the second explanation of supervenience offered by Davidson in the passage quoted earlier; as will be recalled, the explanation was this: "an object cannot alter in some mental respect without altering in some physical respect." The modal force of "cannot" and reference to mental and physical "respects" strongly suggest that a proper way to understand what Davidson has in mind here is in terms of a connection between mental and physical characteristics that is constant over possible worlds. The last quoted passage from Moore on the "dependence" of goodness on natural properties, too, suggests a similar approach.

So let A and B be families of properties closed under Boolean operations as before:

> A *strongly supervenes* on B just in case, necessarily, for each x and each property F in A, if x has F, then there is a property G in B such that x has G, and necessarily if any y has G, it has F.

To illustrate this, let us return to the example of being a good man and the three character traits of courage, benevolence, and honesty. The idea of strong supervenience comes to this: if St. Francis is a good man, there must be some combination of these virtues (say, honesty and benevolence) such that St. Francis has it, and anyone who has it *must* be a good man. This particular combination of the traits, however, need not be the only one in the base family that can "ground" being a good man; Socrates, too, is a good man, but the virtues that he has are courage and honesty rather than honesty and benevolence. Socrates is a good man in virtue of being courageous and honest while St. Francis is a good man in virtue of being honest and benevolent. Generally speaking, a supervenient property will have *alternative supervenience bases*—base properties that are each sufficient for the supervening property. If A strongly supervenes on B, the B-maximal property of an object is a supervenience base for every A-property the object has. But a B-maximal property will often be stronger than is needed to serve as a base for a given A-property, and what is of interest would be a *minimal base* in the sense that any property weaker than it is not a supervenience base. (In contrast, B-maximal properties can be called "maximal bases.") If being a good man strongly supervenes on natural properties, any good man's maximal natural property (perhaps, a long conjunction of all his natural properties) would be a supervenience base for being a good man; however, this is obviously more than what we need (it would include the person's height, weight, date of birth, etc.) and would be less than perspicuous. On the other hand, the conjunctive property of being honest and benevolent may constitute a minimal base—a substantially more informative and more useful notion that justifies us in saying that this man is good *in virtue of* his honesty and benevolence, that his being good *consists in* his having these traits of character, or that he is good *because* he is honest and benevolent.[21]

The modal term "necessarily" occurs twice in the definition of strong supervenience. It is neither possible nor desirable to specify in advance how necessity is to be understood here; an appropriate specification must depend on the particular supervenience thesis under consideration, and different readings of "necessarily" will yield different supervenience theses to consider. For example, if one is interested in the supervenience of moral upon natural characteristics, both occurrences of the term are perhaps best taken to signal logical or metaphysical necessity. For psychophysical supervenience it is possible to interpret the first occurrence as metaphysical necessity and the second as nomological necessity; it is also possible to interpret both as metaphysical, or both as nomological. In the case of mereological supervenience the most plausible construal may be that the first occurrence signifies metaphysical necessity and the second nomological or physical necessity. The main point is that different readings of the modal terms will generate different supervenience theses, and that this flexibility is a desirable feature of the definition as stated. We should, therefore, leave an exact interpretation of "necessarily" as a parameter to be fixed for particular cases of application.

The following relationship between the two concepts of supervenience is obvious:

> (3) Strong supervenience entails weak supervenience; weak supervenience does not entail strong supervenience.

The following is also obvious:

> (4) Both supervenience relations are transitive, reflexive, and neither symmetric nor asymmetric.

In most cases of interest supervenience seems in fact asymmetric; for example, although many have claimed the supervenience of valuational on nonvaluational properties, it is apparent that the converse does not hold. Similarly, although psychophysical supervenience is an arguable view, it would be manifestly implausible to hold that the physical supervenes on the psychological. This asymmetry of supervenience may well be the core of the idea of asymmetric dependence we associate with the supervenience relation. For when we look at the relationship as specified in the definition between a strongly supervenient property and its base property, all that we have is that the base property entails the supervenient property. This alone does not warrant us to say that the supervening property is *dependent on*, or *determined by*, the base, or that an object has the supervening property *in virtue of* having the base property. These latter relations strongly hint at an asymmetric relation. We have learned from work on causation and causal modal logic the hard lesson that the idea of causal dependence or determination is not so easily or directly obtained from straightforward modal notions alone; the same in all likelihood is true of the idea of supervenient determination and dependence. Ideas of dependence and determination, whether causal, supervenient, or of other sorts, stubbornly resist capture in simpler and more transparent terms. The only possibly helpful suggestion I have is this: the asymmetric dependence of a supervenient property upon its base property may well derive from the asymmetric dependence of a comprehensive and integrated system of properties, of which it is an element, upon a similarly comprehensive and systematic family of base properties. Thus, the supposed dependence of, say, pain as a mental occurrence on some electrochemical processes of the nervous system may well be due to the asymmetric supervenient dependence of the whole family of mental phenomena on physical processes. This latter asymmetry, according to the present account, is simply the fact (if it is a fact) that the mental strongly supervenes, in the sense defined here, on the physical but not conversely. So what I am suggesting is a kind of holism: individual dependencies are grounded in the dependency between systems, not the other way around.

IV. GLOBAL SUPERVENIENCE AND KIND-TO-KIND CONNECTIONS

We now turn to another approach to analyzing supervenience, an approach favored by some writers on psychophysical supervenience and materialism.[22] This alternative approach speaks globally of "worlds" and "languages" and yields what may be called a concept of "global" or "world supervenience."[23] Thus, psychophysical supervenience has been explained by saying that worlds that are physically indiscernible are psychologically indiscernible (in fact, such worlds are one and the same). The supervenience of the moral on the nonmoral too could be explained in a similar way: there could not be two worlds that are indistinguishable in every nonmoral detail and yet differ in some moral respect. As will be recalled, we used such formulations in our discussion of the weakness of weak supervenience. Some might prefer this global approach to our own with the thought that by making explicit references to property-to-property connections between the supervenient family and its base (as in our second definition of weak supervenience and that of strong supervenience), our definitions beg an important question against those who invoke supervenience precisely because of its promise as a dependency relation free of commitment to property-to-property connections that smacks of discredited reductionism of various sorts.

Now, whether two worlds are discernible or indiscernible psychologically (or physically, etc.) is essentially a matter of how psychological properties are distributed over the individuals of the two worlds. If the worlds differ in respect of some general psychological fact, this must be reflected in some difference in the singular psychological facts they contain. Thus, to say that two worlds are psychologically discernible is tantamount to saying that for some psychological property P and an individual x, x has P in one but not in the other; to say that two worlds are psychologically indiscernible is to say that for every psychological property P and every individual x, x has P in one just in case x has P in the other.

Let A and B be sets of properties as before, and consider:

A *globally supervenes* on B just in case worlds that are indiscernible with respect to B ("B-indiscernible," for short) are also A-indiscernible.

Discussion in Section II has already shown that global supervenience is stronger than weak supervenience. Here is an argument to show that global supervenience is equivalent to strong supervenience. To show strong supervenience entails global supervenience: assume w_1 and w_2 are B-indiscernible but A-discernible. Then for some F in A and some x, F(x) in w_1 but $-F(x)$ in

w_2. Let B* be the B-maximal property of x in w_1; then, by the strong super-venience of A on B, necessarily $(\forall y)[B*(y) \rightarrow F(y)]$. Since w_2 is B-indis-cernible from w_1, B*(x) in w_2. Hence, F(x) in w_2, yielding a contradiction. Next, to show the converse: suppose strong supervenience fails. Then, for some object x and property F in A such that F(x), if any G is in B and x has G, G fails to entail F. ("G entails F" is short for "Necessarily anything having G has F.") This is equivalent to saying that for this x and F, the B-maximal property of x does not entail F. Let w* be the actual world: in w* we have F(x) and B*(x). Consider another world w# that is just like w* in the distribution of B-properties over individuals; in particular, B*(x) in w#. However, since B* does not entail F, we can consistently suppose that –F(x) in w#. Thus, w* and w# are B-indiscernible but A-discernible; that is, A does not globally super-vene on B. This completes the argument.

Global supervenience, therefore, is nothing but strong supervenience. The equivalence of these two concepts has a mutually reinforcing effect: the fact that two independently conceived notions turn out to be equivalent tes-tifies to their naturalness and intuitive philosophical content. Moreover, it shows that in terms of commitment to kind-to-kind correlations there is no difference at all between global and strong supervenience; the thought that global supervenience is free from such commitments is a mistake.

What if we defined global supervenience for "facts"? We might have some-thing like this: "Facts of kind P supervene on facts of kind Q just in case worlds that are identical in regard to facts of kind Q are identical in regard to facts of kind P." This formulation does not explicitly mention properties of individuals in either the analysandum or the analysans; however, it seems essentially equivalent to our formulation above in terms of properties. For what is it for two worlds to be "identical in regard to facts of kind P"? Think of worlds as certain maximal classes of facts; then for two worlds to be identi-cal in regard to facts of kind P is for them to contain the same facts of kind P. The maximality condition on worlds as classes of facts would presumably entail that two worlds contain the same facts of kind P if and only if they con-tain the same *singular facts* of kind P. A singular fact, I take it, is something of the form *a is F*, where a is an individual and *F* a property; and to say that the fact that a is *F* is a fact of kind P (say, a psychological fact) amounts, arguably, to saying that *F* is a property of kind P (say, a psychological property). It fol-lows then that for two worlds to be identical in regard to facts of kind P is for the following to hold: for any property *F* of kind P and any x, x has *F* in one world if and only if x has *F* in the other. Thus, the notion of identity of worlds in regard to facts of kind P comes to the notion earlier explained of indis-cernibility of worlds with respect to a set of properties of kind P. Moreover, it is by now evident that on the present construal of "facts" and of what it is for a fact to be "of kind P," talk of "properties of kind P" can in general replace talk of "facts of kind P" in discussions of supervenience, and, in particular, that supervenience of facts is reducible to supervenience of properties.[24]

What does the supervenience of A and B imply about the existence of correlations between the properties in the two families? Part of the answer is already clear from the definitions of weak and strong supervenience:

(4) If A weakly supervenes on B, then for every F in A there is a property G in B such that $(\forall x)[G(x) \rightarrow F(x)]$.

(5) If A strongly supervenes on B, then for every F in A there is a property G in B such that *necessarily* $(\forall x)[G(x) \rightarrow F(x)]$.

Our earlier discussion showed that if infinite conjunction and disjunction are assumed, (4) can be strengthened to:

(4a) If A weakly supervenes on B, then for each property F in A there is a property G in B such that $(\forall x)[G(x) \leftrightarrow F(x)]$, that is, each A-property has a coextension in B.

Under the same assumption, a companion result can be shown for (5) as well:

(5a) If A strongly supervenes on B, then for each property F in A there is a property G in B such that necessarily $(\forall x)[G(x) \leftrightarrow F(x)]$, that is, every A-property has a *necessary coextension* in B.

The following proves (5a): Let F be a property in A. We may assume F to be contingent; i.e., some x has F in some possible world w. ((5a) is trivially true for noncontingent F.) By the definition of strong supervenience there is a property G in B such that x has G (in w) and necessarily $(\forall y)[G(y) \rightarrow F(y)]$. Let $B_{x,w}$ be the B-maximal property x has in w. We have then:

Necessarily $(\forall y)[B_{x,w}(y) \rightarrow G(y)]$,

whence:

Necessarily $(\forall y)[B_{x,w}(y) \rightarrow F(y)]$.

And for each v that has F in a world u, we will have:

Necessarily $(\forall y)[B_{v,u}(y) \rightarrow F(y)]$.

Let B* be the infinite disjunction of these B-maximal properties; then

Necessarily $(\forall y)[B^*(y) \rightarrow F(y)]$.

It is easy to see we also have the converse:

Necessarily $(\forall y)[F(y) \rightarrow B^*(y)]$.

For suppose not; then in some world w#, there is an object x such that $F(x)$, but not $B^*(x)$. But by strong supervenience there is some property K in B such that $K(x)$ in w# and necessarily $(\forall y)[K(y) \rightarrow F(y)]$. Let B# be the B-maximal property of x in w#. Then, as before, necessarily $(\forall y)[B\#(y) \rightarrow F(y)]$, and it follows that B# is one of the disjuncts in B^*. Hence, x must have B^*, yielding a contradiction. We thus have:

Necessarily $(\forall y)[B^*(y) \leftrightarrow F(y)]$.

Note that the force of "necessarily" in this biconditional is that of the inner modal term (that is, the second occurrence of "necessarily") in the definition of strong supervenience. Depending on whether in a given case of supervenience we have logical, metaphysical, or nomological necessity for this term, we have in that sense of necessity a necessarily coextensive property in the base family for every supervenient property. In the case of nomological necessity, some might question this; we will take up this issue in the following section.

V. SOME PHILOSOPHICAL CONSIDERATIONS

The principal conclusions of the preceding section are, first, that strong supervenience is committed to the existence of a necessary coextension in the base family for each supervenient property; and, second, that this commitment cannot be avoided by embracing global supervenience. For the two supervenience relations are in fact one. This should be found prima facie disturbing by some philosophers who have used supervenience to formulate certain philosophical claims. As we saw earlier, a full sense of dependency cannot be captured by weak supervenience; strong or global supervenience is needed. But to have this degree of dependency is *ipso facto* to be committed to the existence of a pervasive system of necessary property-to-property entailments, as is evident from the very definition of strong supervenience. And (5a) strengthens this: each supervenient property has a necessarily *coextensive* property in the base family. This may be more than what some philosophers thought they had bargained for.

We have already noted a possible dilemma in which Davidson may find himself: weak psychophysical supervenience appears too weak to yield materialism, but strong supervenience seems too strong in entailing the existence of a pervasive system of psychophysical equivalences. But Davidson's prime motive for advocating psychophysical supervenience is precisely to acknowledge the dependence of the mental on the physical but at the same time deny that there are laws connecting psychological and physical properties. What our results seem to show is this: if you want psychophysical dependence, you had better be prepared for psychophysical laws—or, at any rate, necessary psychophysical entailments. Some might dispute this line of thought on the ground that "nomological properties," i.e., those that are admissible in laws, are not closed under Boolean operations—that is, these operations, when applied to such properties, do not always yield properties fit to appear in laws.[25] B-maximal properties, their infinite disjunctions, and the like are "too complex," "too artificial and unnatural," and "too heterogeneous," it is argued, to be "natural kinds."

This raises various complex issues about the ontology and epistemology of laws, reduction, definition, and the like. I can, however, only indicate here the general approach I think we ought to take. First, we need to be sensitive to the distinction between *predicates* and *properties*, and beware that complexity or artificiality attaching to predicates (or linguistic constructions in general) need not attach to the properties they express. A long Boolean combination of predicates would normally be complex *qua* predicate; on the other hand, the property it expresses need not inherit that complexity (the Boolean expression may be equivalent to a short and simple one). The definitions in this paper have been framed for properties, not predicates; such operations as infinite conjunctions and infinite disjunctions would be highly questionable for predicates, but not necessarily for properties—any more than infinite unions and intersections are for classes. The property of being less than one meter long can be thought of as an infinite disjunction (e.g., of all properties of the form, being less than $n/n + 1$ meters long, for every natural number n). In fact, we could do with sets of properties, dispensing with infinite conjunctions and disjunctions. The main point is that there is no direct inference from the constructional details of properties to their complexity or artificiality, whatever these things may mean for properties.

When we speak of laws, we may have in mind either sentences or some nonlinguistic, nonconceptual, objective connections between properties. If laws are taken to be sentences, our results do not show that psychophysical supervenience entails the existence of biconditional laws. For we are given no guarantee that there are predicates, especially reasonably simple and perspicuous ones, to represent the constructed properties. Reformulating our basic definitions in terms of predicates rather than properties will not help; for that would make infinitary procedures highly dubious, perhaps unacceptable. Moreover, strong psychophysical supervenience stated for psychological and physical predicates seems considerably less plausible than when stated for properties: it asserts that for each psychological predicate there is a physical predicate that (logically or nomologically) entails it. What is the physical predicate that entails, say, "being bored"? It seems that we would at least need to appeal to "ideal physical languages" and the like to get started, and this might bring us right back to talk of properties.

If, on the other hand, laws are construed as objective connections between properties, which can be expressed by sentences or statements ("nomological" or "lawlike statements"), then (5a) must be accepted as stating that there are biconditional laws—if laws are "only" nomologically necessary, then equivalences that are at least as strong as laws—between supervenient and base properties. But what are the implications of this? Does it mean that the supervenient properties (or theories formulated in terms of them) are necessarily "reducible" to their bases? That moral properties are definable in naturalistic terms, that psychology is reducible to physical theory, and so on? It might seem that these biconditional laws, or necessary equivalences, supply the "bridge laws" required by the classical conception of intertheoretic reduction. But this conclusion would be premature. Reduction, explanation, and the like are epistemic activities, and the mere fact that such equivalences or biconditionals "exist" is no guarantee that they are, or will ever become, *available* for reductive or explanatory uses. "Availability" here is best understood, I think, in terms of representation in a well-confirmed explanatory theory, and this in turn will depend on, among other things, our own cognitive powers, and our proclivities and idiosyncrasies in matters of what we find comfortable and satisfying as explanations. So the existence of a necessary physical coextension for every psychological property would have no direct bearing on our ability to carry out a physical reduction of psychology.

What we could more reasonably expect is this: as science makes progress, it will succeed in identifying an increasing number of *local* physical coextensions for psychological properties, that is, physical coextensions *restricted to specific domains* (e.g., particular biological species); and a sufficiently broad system of such local coextensions can serve as a base for "local reductions" of psychological theories. As many have pointed out, any given mental state is likely to have "multiple physical realizations" over distinct physical structures or biological species; however, for any given species or kind of structure, there may well be a uniform base, and if a comprehensive array of such bases is identified for, say, human psychological states, then human psychology could be "locally reduced" to physical theory.[26] If Martian psychological states, because of the different Martian anatomy and physiology, have different physical bases, Martian psychology would have to receive a different local physical reduction, even if the Martians and humans instantiate the same psychology.

Moore held the view that goodness is a "simple nonnatural" property, where by "simple" he meant indefinability and by "nonnatural" inaccessibility through normal sensory experience. Given this, it is somewhat remarkable that he was entirely unperturbed by the supervenience of goodness on natural properties. In fact, in the passage last quoted he says that *unless* he had thought that the goodness of an object "followed" from its natural properties he would "never have thought of suggesting that goodness was 'non-natural'." If the goodness of a thing "follows" from its natural properties which, we may assume, are accessible through normal sense-experience, why then isn't goodness itself so accessible? Perhaps, it might be replied that accessibility in this sense isn't the issue; what is crucial is that goodness has no direct or immediate "presentation" in sensory experience. But if goodness does follow from natural properties, why isn't this enough as a basis for a naturalistic epistemology of goodness, and why doesn't this make the intuitionist moral epistemology at best otiose?

It is interesting to note Moore's observation that, although the goodness of a thing follows from certain of its natural properties, from the fact that it is good it does *not* follow that it has these natural properties. Would our (5a) have discomfited Moore? Probably not, for the term "follow" as used by Moore, and perhaps also in its general philosophical usage, appears to have an unmistakable epistemological dimension: if goodness "follows" from certain natural properties, we should be able to "see" or "infer" that a thing is good by seeing that it has these natural properties. The necessary naturalistic coextension of goodness, as far as the arguments of this paper go, has no such epistemological status: we know it must exist, if strong supervenience obtains, but may never know "what it is." Nor can such a coextension be expected to provide a definitional basis for the term "good"; in fact, its existence does not suffice even to show the "in principle" definability of "good" in naturalistic terms. For the notion of definition carries certain semantic and epistemological associations, and even if we could identify the underlying naturalistic coextension of goodness we cannot expect these associations to hold for it.

We seem to have reached the conclusion that supervenience relations by themselves imply nothing directly about such relationships as definability and reducibility, if the possibility involved in "definability" or "reducibility" is construed in a fairly strong and realistic sense. However, as I shall argue later, there is a critical tension between acceptance of a supervenience thesis with regard to a pair of domains and rejection of all significant epistemic or conceptual relationships between the domains. But let us first briefly turn to the issue of autonomy.

What does supervenience imply about the autonomy of what supervenes in relation to its base? Although a thorough discussion would require a more precise understanding of the relevant concept of autonomy, it seems that weak supervenience can be entirely consistent with autonomy; that, in fact, may be one of its chief attractions. However, the case is different with strong supervenience: under strong supervenience, the base wholly determines the supervening properties. If strong psychophysical supervenience holds, what happens in the realm of the mind is determined in every detail by what happens in the physical realm. This determinative relation is an objective matter; it does not depend on whether anyone knows anything about it, or what expressions are used to talk about mind and body. Unlike in the case of reduction and definition, epistemological considerations do not intrude here. That is perhaps why global supervenience is often used to state the doctrine of materialism. Likewise, strong supervenience of moral upon natural properties may signal a form of "moral naturalism"—not the definitional thesis of ethical naturalism, but a metaphysical thesis that recognizes the ontological primacy of the natural over the moral.[27]

Thinking about causal determination will, I believe, give us a useful point of analogy in thinking about supervenient determination. If causal determinism ("Every event has a cause") holds, every occurrence has a temporally earlier determinative condition. However, this says nothing about how successful we shall be in identifying causes and framing causal explanations; it is also silent on how successful we shall be in discovering causal laws. Explanation is an epistemological affair, and the claim that all events are causally explainable is an epistemological thesis, or a methodological doctrine, not entailed by the metaphysical thesis of universal causation alone (unless the former is expressly read so as to mean the latter). Similarly, the thesis that a given domain supervenes on another is a metaphysical thesis about an objectively existent dependency relation between the two domains; it says nothing about whether or how the details of the dependency relation will become known so as to enable us to formulate explanations, reductions, or definitions.

Having sundered the metaphysical thesis of causal determinism from its associated epistemological thesis about the possibility of causal explanation, we are now in a position to bring them together and appreciate their mutual relevance. There is, first, this much direct relationship: where there is no causal relation, there can be no correct causal explanation. When an event causes another, that constitutes the objective fact that makes a corresponding causal explanation "correct" or "true." More generally, we can think of the thesis of causal determinism as providing a metaphysical basis for the methodological strategy or principle enjoining us to search for explanations of natural events in terms of their causal antecedents, and also providing an explanation of why this strategy works as well as it does. Acceptance of causal determinism, therefore, can be viewed as an expression of a commitment to the method of causal explanation as an epistemological strategy. Conversely, it is our success, limited though it may be, in discovering causal connections and formulating causal explanations that forms an essential basis of our belief in causal determinism.

Similarly, the belief that a supervenience relation obtains for a pair of domains can motivate our search for specific property-to-property connections in terms of which illuminating reductions and edifying definitions might be formulated. Where strong supervenience obtains, (5a) gives us the assurance that such connections in the form of necessary equivalences are there to be discovered, without of course the further assurance that we shall succeed in discovering them or that they will be representable in an explanatory theory. A case in point is mereological supervenience, the doctrine that the macro-properties of material things are supervenient on their microproperties. It is this metaphysical doctrine of atomism that seems to underlie and support the enormously productive research strategy of micro-reduction in modern theoretical science. And, conversely, the success of this research strategy reinforces our belief in mereological supervenience. Perhaps, similar remarks apply to moral supervenience: the belief that the moral supervenes on the nonmoral may have shaped some of the major assumptions and tasks of moral philosophy, such as the search for naturalistic definitions of ethical terms, the belief that there must be nonmoral "criteria" for moral ascriptions, the belief that there are such things as "good-making" or "right-making char-acteristics," and the perennial attempts to state conditions for the rationality of acts or justness of institutions in naturalistic and descriptive terms.

I think these remarks explain the point of (5a): it helps us to see the con-nection between the thesis of supervenience concerning a pair of domains and a certain epistemological strategy we may adopt in regard to them. It explains how the belief in the supervenience thesis can lead to, and in turn be support-ed by, the expectation that one domain can be understood—reduced, defined, explained, etc.—in terms of the other through the discovery of necessary equiv-alences that (5a) assures us must exist. The tension I alluded to earlier, several paragraphs back, arises precisely because this connection is contravened in embracing supervenience but rejecting at the same time a significant concep-tual or epistemic relationship. That is to say, there is a sense, though a weak one, of possibility in which (5a) shows that strong supervenience entails the possibility of reduction or definition across the domains involved.[28]

Notes

1   An earlier version of this paper was presented at the Herbert Heidelberger Memorial Conference at University of Massachusetts and Smith College in April, 1983. I dedicate this paper to Herb's memory.

2   In An Abstract of *A Treatise of Human Nature*.

3   [Part-whole relations]

4   See Jaegwon Kim, "Supervenience and Nomological Incommensurables," *American Philosophical Quarterly* 15 (1978), 149-56.

5   *Philosophical Studies* (London: Routledge and Paul, 1922), 261.

6   *The Language of Morals* (Oxford: Clarendon, 1952), 145.

7   Frank Sibley, "Aesthetic Concepts," *Philosophical Review* 68 (1959), 421-50; Jer-rold Levinson, "Aesthetic Supervenience," *Southern Journal of Philosophy* 22, Sup-plement (1984), 93-110.

8   See note 12; also Kim, "Psychophysical Supervenience," *Philosophical Studies* 41 (1982), 51-70, and "Psychophysical Supervenience as a Mind-Body Theory," *Brain and Cognition Theory* 5 (1982); Stephen P. Stich, "Autonomous Psychology and the Belief-Desire Thesis," *The Monist* 61 (1978), 573-91; John Haugeland, "Weak Supervenience," *American Philosophical Quarterly* 19 (1982), 93-103.

9   See Ernest Sosa, "The Foundations of Foundationalism," *Nous* 14 (1980), 547-
    64, esp. 551. Also Alvin I. Goldman, "What is Justified Belief?" in G.S. Pappas,
    ed., *Justification and Knowledge* (Dordrecht, Holland: Reidel, 1979), in which
    Goldman says he is looking for nonepistemic conditions for justified belief.

10 See, e.g., Hide Ishiguro, *Leibniz's Philosophy of Logic and Language* (Ithaca, NY:
    Cornell University Press, 1972). It seems that Leibniz used the Latin word
    "supervenire" in stating his theory; see the quotation in footnote 3 on p. 71 of
    Ishiguro, op. cit.

11 This is especially clear in Quine's reply to Chomsky in D. Davidson and J. Hin-
    tikka, eds., *Words and Objections* (Dordrecht, Holland: Reidel, 1969), esp. 302 f.

12 For more details on this point, see Kim, "Psychophysical Supervenience as a
    Mind-Body Theory," op. cit.

13 This claim is controversial; see "'Strong' and 'Global' Supervenience Revisited,"
    Philosophy and Phenomenological Research 48 (1987), 315-26, and "Postscripts on
    Supervenience," in Kim, *Supervenience and Mind* (Cambridge: Cambridge Uni-
    versity Press, 1993).

14 "Mental Events" in *Experience* and *Theory*, ed. L. Foster and J.W. Swanson
    (Amherst, 1979), 88, in this volume, 90-91.

15 In Moore's "A Reply to My Critics" in P.A. Schilpp, ed., *The Philosophy of G.E.
    Moore* (Chicago and Evanston, IL, 1942), 588.

16 According to Haugeland's report of a conversation with Hare (in Haugeland,
    op. cit.), it seems likely that what Hare had in mind is only my weak superve-
    nience. This impression is confirmed by Professor Hare's inaugural address to
    the Aristotelian Society entitled "Supervenience," *Aristotelian Society*, Supplemen-
    tary Volume 58 (1984), 1-16. The notions of "supervenience" and "entailment"
    as Hare explains them in his address turn out to correspond, roughly, to my
    weak and strong supervenience, respectively.

17 The distinction between two versions of the universalizability requirement is
    borrowed from J. Howard Sobel's unpublished notes on "Dependent Proper-
    ties"; I also owe to Sobel the quotation from Moore's "Reply" (see note 15).
    Also useful in this connection are Monroe C. Beardsley, "On the Generality of
    Critical Reasons," *Journal of Philosophy* 59 (1962), 477-86; and Robert L. Holmes,
    "Descriptivism, Supervenience, and Universalizability," *Journal of Philosophy* 63
    (1966), 113-19.

18 "Mental Events," op. cit., 88, this volume, 90-91.

19 For formulations of materialism see Terence Horgan, "Supervenience and
    Microphysics," *Pacific Philosophical Quarterly* 63 (1982): 29-43; Horgan, "Superve-
    nience and Cosmic Hermeneutics," *Southern Journal of Philosophy* 22, Supplement
    (1984), 19-38. David Lewis, "New Work for a Theory of Universals," *Australasian
    Journal of Philosophy* 61 (1983), 343-77; for a related approach see Geoffrey Hell-
    man and Frank Thompson, "Physicalism: Ontology, Determination and Reduc-
    tion," *Journal of Philosophy* 72 (1975), 551-64, and "Physicalist Materialism," *Nous*
    11 (1977), 309-45.

20   In an earlier paper, "Supervenience and Nomological Incommensurables," op. cit., I said, incorrectly, that weak supervenience as defined by the first definition in this paper could be "equivalently defined" by a definition that in effect defines "strong supervenience" below. David Sanford's careful comments led me to see that this was a mistake, and that there in fact were two concepts of interest here. I was also helped by Barry Loewer who sent me his unpublished material on supervenience in which an essentially identical distinction is made. Others who have pointed out to me the failure of the claimed equivalence include Anthony Anderson and James Van Cleve (in his unpublished "Defining Supervenience"). I first made use of this distinction in "Psychophysical Supervenience as a Mind-Body Theory," op. cit.

21   Similar problems arise for the notion of a causal condition; often what is of interest is a minimal set of conditions sufficient for the effect, not just any sufficient set.

22   See the papers by Horgan, Haugeland, and Lewis cited in notes 8 and 19.

23   I borrow the term "global supervenience" from Paul Teller in his "Relational Holism and Quantum Mechanics," *British Journal for the Philosophy of Science* 37 (1986), 71-81.

24   Supervenience for states and events, too, is reducible to property supervenience if they are construed as property exemplifications; for such a conception of states and events see my "Events as Property Exemplifications," in M. Brand and D. Walton, eds., *Action Theory* (Dordrecht, Holland: Reidel, 1976), 159-77. If the alternative conception of events associated with Davidson (see, e.g., "The Individuation of Events" in Davidson, *Essays on Actions and Events* [Oxford: Clarendon Press, 1980]) is adopted, events could simply be treated as individuals, that is, as values of the variables "x," "y," etc., in the definitions of supervenience, again making a special notion of event supervenience unnecessary.

25   For interesting considerations along these lines see Paul Teller's "Comments on Kim's Paper," *Southern Journal of Philosophy* 22, Supplement (1984), 57-61. My remarks here, which include reactions to some of Teller's critical points, represent a modification and elaboration of the views I defended earlier, especially in "Supervenience and Nomological Incommensurables," op. cit.

26   On "local reductions" see Kim, "Psychophysical Supervenience as a Mind-Body Theory," op. cit.; also Robert C. Richardson, "Functionalism and Reductionism," *Philosophy of Science* 46 (1979), 533-58.

27   For a discussion of moral supervenience in relation to the problem of moral realism see S.W. Blackburn, "Moral Realism," in J. Casey, ed., *Morality and Moral Reasoning* (London: Methuen, 1971).

28   In addition to the persons whose help has already been cited, I am indebted to David Benfield, Earl Conee, Fred Feldman, John Heil, Terence Horgan, Arnold Koslow, Brian McLaughlin, Robert Richardson, Ernest Sosa, and Paul Teller.

23

EPIPHENOMENAL AND SUPERVENIENT CAUSATION*

Jaegwon Kim

1. EPIPHENOMENAL CAUSATION

Jonathan Edwards held the doctrine that ordinary material things do not persist through time but are at each moment created, and recreated, by God ex nihilo. He writes:

> If the existence of created *substance*, in each successive moment, be wholly the effect of God's immediate power, in *that* moment, without any dependence on prior existence, as much as the first creation out of *nothing*, then what exists at this moment, by this power, is a *new effect*, and simply and absolutely considered, not the same with any past existence, though it be like it, and follows it according to a certain established method.[1]

Thus, the present "time slice" of this table, although it is very much like the one preceding it, has no causal connection with it; for each slice is a wholly distinct creation by God. The temporal parts of this table are successive effects of an underlying persisting cause, God's creative activity. In arguing for this doctrine, Edwards offers the following striking analogy:

> The *images* of things in a glass, as we keep our eye upon them, seem to remain precisely the same, with a continuing, perfect identity. But it is known to be otherwise. Philosophers well know that these images are constantly *renewed*, by the impression and reflection of new rays of light; so that the image impressed by the former rays is constantly vanishing, and a *new* image impressed by *new* rays every moment, both on the glass and on the eye.... And the new images being put on *immediately* or *instantly*, do not make them the same, any more than if it were done with the intermission of an *hour* or a *day*. The image that exists at this moment is not at all *derived* from the image which existed at the last pre-

---

* Jaegwon Kim, "Epiphenonenal and Supervenient Causation," *Midwest Studies in Philosophy* 9 (1984), 257-70. Reprinted with kind permission of the publisher.

ceding moment. As may be seen, because if the succession of new *rays* be intercepted, by something interposed between the object and the glass, the image immediately ceases; the *past existence* of the image has no influence to uphold it, so much as for a moment.[2]

Two successive mirror reflections of an object are not directly causally linked to each other; in particular, the earlier one is not a cause of the later one, even though the usual requirements of "Humean causation," including that of spatiotemporal contiguity, may be met. If all we ever observed were mirror images, like the shadows in Plato's cave, we might very well be misled into ascribing a cause-effect relation to the two images; but we know better, as Edwards says. The succession of images is only a reflection of the real causal process at the level of the objects reflected.

Edwards's example anticipates one that Wesley Salmon has recently used to illustrate the difference between "causal processes" and "pseudoprocesses":[3] consider a rotating spotlight, located at the centre of a circular room, casting a spot of light on the wall. According to Salmon, a light ray traveling from the spotlight to the wall is a causal process, whereas the motion of the spot of light on the wall is only a pseudoprocess. Each spot of light on the wall is caused by a light ray traveling from the spotlight; however, it is not the cause of the spot of light appearing on the wall an instant later. Two successive spots of light on the wall are related to each other as two successive mirror images are related. Both pairs mimic causal processes and are apt to be mistaken for such. Neither, however, is a process involving a real causal chain.

By "epiphenomenal causation" I have in mind roughly the sort of apparent causal relation in the examples of Edwards and Salmon. I say "roughly" because, as will become clear later, they are somewhat less central cases of epiphenomenal causation, as this notion will be used in this paper; these examples are helpful, however, in the initial fixing of the concept that I have in mind. In any event, Edwards's contention was that all causal relations holding for material bodies, events, and processes are cases of epiphenomenal causation, the only true causation being limited to God's own creative actions. The world is constantly created anew by God; we may think that fire causes smoke, but it is only that God creates fire at one instant and then smoke an instant later. There is no direct causal connection between the fire and the smoke. The relation between them is one of epiphenomenal causation.

Another case of epiphenomenal causation, familiar in daily life, is the succession of symptoms associated with a disease: the symptoms are not mutually related in the cause-effect relationship, although to the medically naive they may appear to be so related. The appearance of a causal connection here merely points to the real causal process underlying the symptoms.

It should be clear that by saying that two events are related in an epiphenomenal causal relation I do not mean to suggest that the events themselves are "epiphenomena." The standard current use of this term comes from discussions of epiphenomenalism as a theory of the mind-body relation, and to call an event an "epiphenomenon" in this context is taken to mean that though it is a causal effect of other events, it has no causal potency of its own: it can be the cause of no other event, being the absolute terminal link of a causal chain. It is dubious that this notion of an epiphenomenon makes sense—for example, it is doubtful how such events could be known to exist.[4] In this paper I use the modifier "epiphenomenal" in "epiphenomenal causation" to qualify the causal relation, not the events standing in that relation.

One might object at this point that these examples of the so-called epiphenomenal causation are not cases of causation at all and that it is misleading to label them as such, because "epiphenomenal causation" sounds as though it is a *kind* of causal relation. In reply, I shall say two things: first, even though it is true that an earlier mirror image is not a cause of a later one, it is also true that there *is* a causal relation between the two—the two are successive effects of the same underlying causal process. To leave the matter where we have simply denied that the first is the cause of the second would be to ignore an important causal fact about the relation between the two events. Second, I shall argue that the central cases of epiphenomenal causation that will interest us will be seen to involve "real" causal relations and that epiphenomenal causal relations of this kind are pervasively present all around us.

What is common to these cases and the earlier examples, such as Edwards's mirror images, which do not seem to involve real causal relations, is just this: they all involve at least *apparent* causal relations that are *grounded* in some underlying causal processes. These causal relations, whether only apparent or real, *are reducible to more fundamental causal relations.* If one takes the view that reducibility entails eliminability, there perhaps is no significant difference between the two types of cases. But then there also is the apparently opposed view: to be reduced is to be legitimized. I believe in any case that my use of the term "epiphenomenon" is entirely consistent with the standard dictionary definition of "epiphenomenon" as "secondary symptom," "secondary phenomenon," or "something that happens in addition"; the idea that an epiphenomenon is causally inert is best taken as a philosophical doctrine of epiphenomenalism as a theory about the nature of the mental, not as something that merely arises out of the meaning of the term "epiphenomenon."

The principal claims that I want to defend in this paper are the following: that macrocausation should be viewed as a kind of epiphenomenal causation in the broad sense sketched above; that macrocausation as epiphenomenal causation should be explained as "supervenient causation" in the sense to be explained below; and that psychological causation, that is, causation involving psychological events, is plausibly assimilated to macrocausation—that is, it is to be construed as supervenient epiphenomenal causation.

2. MACROCAUSATION AS SUPERVENIENT CAUSATION

By "macrocausation" I have in mind causal relations involving macroevents and states, where a macroevent or state is understood as the exemplification of a macroproperty by an object at a time (this characterization can be generalized to macrorelations in obvious ways). The micro-macro distinction is of course relative: temperature is macro relative to molecular motion; properties of molecules are macro relative to properties and relationships characterizing atoms and more basic particles, and so on. For our present discussion, however, the paradigmatic examples of macroobjects and properties are medium-sized material bodies around us and their observable properties. Thus, fire causing smoke would be a case of macrocausation; so is the rising temperature causing a metallic object to expand. All observable phenomena are macrophenomena in relation to the familiar theoretical objects of physics; hence, our first claim entails that all causal relations involving observable phenomena—all causal relations familiar from daily experience—are cases of epiphenomenal causation.

My defence of this claim is two-pronged. The first prong consists in a general argument to the effect that a certain familiar and plausible reductionist perspective requires us to view macrocausation as epiphenomenal causation. The second prong consists in the observation that modern theoretical science treats macrocausation as reducible epiphenomenal causation and that this has proved to be an extremely successful explanatory and predictive research strategy.

First, the general argument: philosophers have observed, in connection with the mind-body problem, that a thoroughgoing physicalism can no more readily tolerate the existence of irreducible psychological features or properties than irreducible psychological objects (e.g., Cartesian souls, visual images).[5] The thought behind this may be something like this: if F is an irreducible psychical feature, then its existence implies that something is F. (If F is never exemplified, being a mere "concept" of something psychical, the physicalist has nothing to worry about.) This means that there would be a physically irreducible event or state of this thing's being F, or a physically irreducible fact, namely the fact that the thing is F. So the world remains bifurcated: the physical domain and a distinct, irreducible psychical domain; and physical theory fails as a complete and comprehensive theory of the world. Moreover, we might want to inquire into the *cause* of something's being F. This gives rise to three possibilities, none of them palatable to the physicalist: first, the cause of the psychical event is a mystery not accessible to scientific inquiry; second, an autonomous psychical science emerges; third, physical theory provides a causal account of the psychical phenomena. The last possibility may be the worst, from the physicalist point of view: given the irreducibility of the psychical phenomena, this could only mean that physical theory would lose its *closed* character, by countenancing within its domain irreducibly nonphysical events and properties.

Parallel considerations should motivate the rejection of macrocausation as an irreducible feature of the world. It seems to be a fundamental methodological precept of theoretical physical science that we ought to formulate microstructural theories of objects and their properties—that is, to try to understand the behaviour and properties of objects and processes in terms of the properties and relationships characterizing their microconstituents. The philosophical supposition that grounds this research strategy seems to be the belief that macroproperties are determined by, or supervenient upon, microproperties. This Democritean doctrine of mereological supervenience, or microdeterminism, forms the metaphysical backbone of the method of microreduction,[6] somewhat in the same way that the principle of causal determinism constitutes the objective basis of the method of causal explanation. (I shall return to these themes below.)

In this global microdeterministic picture there is no place for irreducible macrocausal relations. We expect any causal relation between two macroevents (x's being F and y's being G, where F and G are macroproperties) to be microreductively explainable in terms of more fundamental causal processes, like any other facts involving macroproperties and events. If the causal relation is backed up by a law relating F and G, we would expect this macrolaw to be microreducible. A standard example: the rising temperature of a gas confined within a rigid chamber causes its pressure to rise. This macrocausal relation is subsumed under a macrolaw (the gas law), which in turn is microreduced by the kinetic theory of gases. This explains, and reduces, the macrocausal relation. If the causal relation is at bottom just some sort of counterfactual dependency, then the macrocounterfactual "If x had not been F, y would not have been G" should be grounded in some lawlike connection involving microproperties associated with x and y in relation to F and G; or else, there should be some more basic counterfactual dependencies involving microconstituents of x and y that can explain the counterfactual dependency between F and G. It would be difficult to believe that this macrocounterfactual is a fundamental and irreducible fact about the world. At least, that should be our attitude if we accept the universal thesis of mereological supervenience and the validity of microreductive research strategy.

What is the general form of the reduction of a macrocausal relation to a microcausal process? The following model is attractively simple: if the macrocausal relation to be reduced is one from an instance of property F to an instance of property G, we need to correlate F with some microproperty $m(F)$, and also G with $m(G)$, and then show that $m(F)$ and $m(G)$ are appropriately causally connected. Showing the latter may take the form of exhibiting a precise law that connects the two microproperties, or a causal mechanism whereby an instance of F leads to an instance of G. How is the correlation between F and m(F) to be understood? The strongest claim defended by some philosophers is that F and m(F) are one and the same property.[7] The thought is that such property identities are necessary for the required microreduction to go through. Taking this identity approach, however, would force a reconstrual of the notions of microproperty and macroproperty; how could one and the same property be both a microproperty and a macroproperty? But a more serious problem is this: in the given instance under consideration, the macroproperty may be "realized" or "grounded" in m(F), but in another instance F may be realized or grounded in a different microproperty m*(F), and there may be many other microproperties that can realize F, in that if anything has one of them, then necessarily it also exhibits F as a result. And it may well be that from the explanatory-causal point of view, the possibly infinite disjunction of these underlying microproperties could hardly be considered as a unitary property suitable as a reductive base.

The foregoing is a point often made in connection with the mind-body problem and used sometimes to support the "functionalist" view of the mental.[8] The multiple realizability of a state relative to a more basic level of analysis, or a richer descriptive vocabulary, appears to hold, with equal plausibility, for macrophysical characteristics in relation to microphysical properties and processes; perhaps this is a pervasive feature of mereological reduction. For these reasons, among others, I suggest the use of the concept of *supervenience*, which allows for the possibility of *alternative supervenience bases* for a given supervenient property, as particularly well suited for the purposes on hand. The core idea of supervenience as a relation between two families of properties is that the supervenient properties are in some sense *determined by*, or *dependent on*, the properties on which they supervene. More formally, *the supervenience of a family A of properties on another family B* can be explained as follows: necessarily, for any property F in A, if any object x has F, then there exists a property G in B such that x has G, and necessarily anything having G has F.[9] When properties F and G are related as specified in the definition, we may say that F is *supervenient* on G, and that G is a *supervenience base* of F. On this account, it is clear that a property in the supervenient family can have multiple supervenience bases: an object x has F, and for x the supervenience base of F is G; however, another object y that also has F does not have G, but rather has G*, as its supervenience base for F; and so on. Thus, if we think of macroproperties as supervenient on microproperties, the account allows for a given macroproperty F to be supervenient on a number of distinct microproperties; that is, an object has a certain macroproperty (e.g., fragility) in virtue of having a certain microproperty (e.g., a certain crystalline structure) on which the macroproperty supervenes; another object has the same macroproperty in virtue of having a different microproperty (another kind of crystalline structure); and so on.

The notion of *event supervenience* is easily explained on the basis of property supervenience: an event, x's having F, supervenes on the event, x's having G, just in case x has G and G is a supervenience base of F.

So the general schema for reducing a macrocausal relation between two events, x's having F and y's having G, where F and G are macroproperties, is this: x's having F supervenes on x's having m(F), y's having G supervenes on y's having m(G), where m(F) and m(G) are microproperties relative to F and G, and there is an appropriate causal connection between x's having m(F) and y's having m(G).

Any causal relation conforming to the pattern set forth above will be called a "supervenient causal relation." For the pattern can be taken to show the causal relation itself to be supervenient upon an underlying causal process through the supervenience of its relata upon the events involved in the underlying process.

I have left the causal relation between the two microevents unspecified; for it is not part of my present aim to advocate a particular analysis of causation. Generally, however, we would expect it to be mediated by laws, whether deterministic or statistical, and in favourable cases we may even have an account in terms of a mechanism by which one microstate evolves into another. But the kind of position I want to advocate here concerning macrocausation is largely independent of the particular views concerning the analysis of causation. Moreover, I do not wish to tie the fate of my general views about macrocausation too closely to the fate of my proposal regarding a proper construal of the relation between macroproperties and the microproperties on which they "depend." Although the use of mereological supervenience is an integral part of the total account being sketched here, the main points of the general picture of macrocausation I am advancing are independent of the question of what particular account is to be accepted for the macro-micro relation. What are these points? There are two: (1) macrocausal relations should be viewed as in general reducible to microcausal relations, and (2) the mechanism of the reduction involves identifying the microstates on which the macrostates in question depend, or with which they are correlated, and showing that a proper causal relation obtains for these microstates. Thus, to affirm (1) is to accept the view that macrocausation is to be viewed as epiphenomenal causation. To affirm that macrocausation is supervenient causation is to accept a particular account of the mechanism of reduction referred to in (2).

The sort of account I have given should be found attractive by those philosophers who believe that precise laws are rare—perhaps nonexistent—for macroproperties and states, at least those that are routinely referred to in ordinary causal talk, and that they must be "redescribed" at a more basic level before precise laws could be brought to bear on them.[10] My account in essence adds two things to this view: first, that *whether or not* there are macrolawlike connections, macrocausal relations ought to be viewed as reducible to microcausal relations, and second, that what sanctions a given microre-description of a macrostate can be taken as a supervenience relation—that is to say, the relation between a macrodescription and a corresponding microre-description can be understood in terms of supervenience.

The broad metaphysical conviction that underlies these proposals is the belief that ultimately the world—at least, the physical world—is the way it is because the microworld is the way it is—because there are so many of just these sorts of microentities (elementary particles, atoms, or what not), and they behave in accordance with just these laws. As Terence Horgan has put it, worlds that are microphysically identical are one and the same world.[11] Even those who would reject this universal thesis of microdeterminism might find the following more restricted thesis plausible: worlds that are microphysical-ly identical are one world from the physical point of view. This doctrine urges us to see macrocausal relations as emerging out of properties and relations holding for microentities, and this naturally leads to a search of microreduc-tive accounts of macrocausal relations as well as other macroproperties, states, and facts. In fact, causal relations pervade our very conceptions of physical properties, states, and events (consider, for example, "heat," "mag-netic," "gene"), and the reduction of causal relations, which often takes the form of exhibiting the micromechanisms underlying macrocausal relations, is probably the most important part of microreductive research. Causal rela-tions that resist microreduction must be considered "causal danglers," which, like the notorious "nomological danglers," are an acute embarrassment to the physicalist view of the world.

There is ample evidence that the method of microreduction has been extremely successful in modern science, and it seems evident that much of the reduction that has been accomplished involves the reduction of macro-causal laws and relations.[12] The reduction of gas laws within the kinetic the-ory of gases is of course a case in point; such examples are legion. Given our interest in identifying and understanding causal connections, it is not sur-prising that a predominant part of the reductive efforts in scientific research is directed toward the microreduction of macrocausal laws and relations. These last few remarks constitute the promised second prong of my defense of the claim that macrocausation ought to be viewed as epiphenomenal cau-sation—and, more specifically, as supervenient causation.

3. MEREOLOGICAL SUPERVENIENCE AND MICRODETERMINISM

The foregoing discussion moved fairly freely among such doctrines and con-cepts as microreduction, microexplanation, mereological supervenience, and microdeterminism, and I think it may be helpful to set forth their rela-tionships more precisely. First of all, I am taking mereological supervenience and microdeterminism as a thesis concerning the objective features of the world—a metaphysical doctrine—roughly, as I said, to the effect that the macroworld is the way it is because the microworld is the way it is. The two doctrines can of course be sharpened and separated from each other. Mereological supervenience is usefully taken to be a general thesis affirming the supervenience of the characteristics of wholes on the properties and relationships characterizing their proper parts. Here, "characteristics" is understood to include relations, such as causal relations, among wholes. Mereological supervenience (in the sense of supervenience explained in the preceding section) requires that each macrocharacteristic be grounded in some specific microcharacteristics, and in this way it goes beyond the less specific thesis, earlier mentioned, that worlds that are microphysically identical are one and the same (physical) world. It may be convenient to reserve the term "microdeterminism" for this less specific thesis. It is plausible to think that under some reasonable assumptions, mereological supervenience as applied to the physical world entails microdeterminism; I am inclined to believe that, again under some reasonable assumptions, the converse entailment also holds.

In any event, it is useful to think of mereological supervenience and microdeterminism as constituting the metaphysical basis of the method of microreduction and microexplanation. By this I mean that the metaphysical doctrine rationalizes our microreductive proclivities by legitimatizing microreduction as a paradigm of scientific understanding and helping to explain why the microreductive method works as well as it does. Underlying this remark is the view that explanatory or reductive connections, as essentially epistemological connections, must themselves be grounded in the objective determinative connections holding for the events in the world. The root idea of causal determinism is the belief that the existence and properties of an event are determined by its temporally antecedent conditions. The metaphysical thesis of causal determinism can be thought of as the objective basis of the method of causal explanation—the method of seeking "laws of succession" and formulating explanations of events in terms of their antecedent conditions. Mereological supervenience views the world as determined along the part-whole dimension, whereas the causal determinism views it as determined along the temporal dimension; they respectively provide a metaphysical basis for the method of microreduction and that of causal explanation.

These are rather speculative and bald remarks; they are intended only to give a rough picture of the metaphysical terrain within which my more specific remarks concerning macrocausal relations can be located.

4. MENTAL CAUSATION AS SUPERVENIENT CAUSATION

To say that the causal relation between two macroevents is a case of epiphenomenal causation is not to be understood to mean that the relation is illusory or unreal. In this respect, Jonathan Edwards's case of mirror images, Salmon's moving spot of light, and the case of successive symptoms of a disease differ from our central cases of macrocausal relations. For in those cases, the causal relations are indeed only apparent: although the events are causally *related* in a broad sense, there is no direct causal relation *from* one event *to* the other—that is to say, one event is not the cause of the other. On the other hand, the causal relation between rising temperatures and increasing pressures of gases is no less "real" for being microreducible. To take microreducibility as impunging the reality of what is being reduced would make all of our observable world unreal. However, one reason for bundling the two types of cases together under "epiphenomenal causation" is the existence of another sense of "real" in which reduction does make what is reduced "less real," a sense in which modern physics is sometimes thought to have shown the unreality of ordinary material objects or a sense in which secondary qualities are sometimes thought to be "less real" than primary qualities. As I mentioned earlier, reducibility is often taken to imply eliminability; but this is a complex and unfruitful question to pursue here. There is, however, another more concrete reason for viewing these two kinds of cases under the same rubric; in both there is present an *apparent* causal relation that is explained, or explained away, at a more fundamental level. The difference between the two cases is this: macrocausal relations are *supervenient causal relations*—supervenient upon microcausal relations—whereas cases like Edwards's mirror images are not. This can be seen by reflecting on the fact that in a perfectly straightforward sense, mirror images, symptoms of a disease, and so on are causal effects of the underlying processes—they are not mereologically supervenient upon those processes. This is the theoretical difference between the two cases: some epiphenomenal causal relations are supervenient causal relations, and these are among the ones that are "real"; there are also cases of epiphenomenal causation that do not involve direct causal connections, and these include ones in which the events involved are successive causal effects of some underlying process.

What of causal relations involving mental events? Consider a typical case in which we would say a mental event causes a physical event: a sharp pain in my thumb causes a jerky withdrawal of my hand. It is hardly conceivable that the pain sensation qua mental event acts directly on the muscles of my arm, causing them to contract. I assume we have by now a fairly detailed story of what goes on at the physiological level when a limb movement takes place, and no amount of intuitive conviction or philosophical argument about the reality of psychophysical causation is going to pre-empt that story. If the pain is to play a causal role in the withdrawal of my hand, it must do so by somehow *making use of* the usual physiological causal path to this bodily event; it looks as though the causal path from the pain to the limb motion must *merge* with the physiological path at a certain point. There cannot be two independent, separate causal paths to the limb motion. But at what point does the mental causal path from the pain "merge" with the physiological path? If there is such a point, that must be where psychophysical causal action takes place. The trouble, of course, is that it is difficult to conceive the possibility of some nonphysical event causally influencing the course of physical processes.[13] Apart from the sheer impossibility of coherently imagining the details of what might have to be the case if some nonphysical agent is going to affect the course of purely physical events, there is a deeper problem that any such non-physical intervention in a physical system would jeopardize the closed character of physical theory. It would force us to accept a conception of the physical in which to give a causal account of, say, the motion of a physical particle, it is sometimes necessary to go outside the physical system and appeal to some nonphysical agency and invoke some irreducible psychophysical law. Many will find this just not credible.

The difficulty of accounting for the possibility of psychophysical causation is simply resolved if one is willing to accept psychophysical identity: the pain is in fact a certain neural state, and the problem of accounting for the psychophysical causal relation is nothing but that of accounting for the causal relation between two physical states. On the other hand, if for various reasons, one is averse to accepting a straightforward identity thesis, as many philosophers are, then the problem of accounting for psychophysical causation confronts us as a difficult problem, indeed.[14] The classical form of epiphenomenalism fails to provide a satisfactory solution, for it denies that mental-to-physical causal action ever takes place: mental phenomena are totally causally inert. And this is what many thinkers find so difficult to accept. If our reasons and desires have no causal efficacy at all in influencing our bodily actions, then perhaps no one has ever performed a single intentional action![15]

It seems to me that what is being advocated as "new" epiphenomenalism is not much help either. According to Keith Campbell, mental states are in fact brain states, but they have residual irreducible phenomenal properties as well; however, these phenomenal properties are causally impotent.[16] This position is akin to one of the two characterizations of epiphenomenalism offered by C.D. Broad some decades ago:

> Epiphenomenalism may be taken to assert one of two things. (a) That certain events which have physiological characteristics have *also* mental characteristics, and that no events which lack physiological characteristics have mental characteristics. That many events which have physiological characteristics are not known to have mental characteristics. And that an event which has mental characteristics never causes another event in virtue of its mental characteristics, but only in virtue of its physiological characteristics. Or (b) that no event has both mental and phys-

iological characteristics; but that the complete cause of any event which has mental characteristics is an event or set of events which has physiological characteristics. And that no event which has mental characteristics is a cause-factor in the causation of any other event whatever, whether mental or physiological.[17]

The only significant difference between Broad's (a) and Campbell's epiphenomenalism seems to be that Broad's epiphenomenalism is formulated for all *mental* characteristics, presumably including intentional states such as belief and desire as well as phenomenal states, whereas Campbell is happy to take a straight physicalist approach with regard to mental states not involving phenomenal qualia. It is interesting to note that some versions of the currently popular "token identity" thesis are also strikingly similar to Broad's epiphenomenalism. Consider, for example, the influential "anomalous monism" of Donald Davidson.[18] According to this account, there are no type-type correlations between the mental and the physical; however, each individual mental event is in fact a physical event in the following sense: any event that has a mental description has also a physical description. Further, it is only under its physical description that a mental event can be seen to enter into a causal relation with a physical event (or any other event) by being subsumed under a causal law. If we read "mental characteristic" for "mental description" and "physiological characteristic" for "physical description" then something very much like Broad's (a) above emerges from Davidson's anomalous monism.

Broad's epiphenomenalism, however, did not satisfy philosophers who looked for a place for our commonsense conviction in the reality of psychophysical causation. Thus, William Kneale refers to "the great paradox of epiphenomenalism," which arises from "the suggestion that we are necessarily mistaken in all our ordinary thought about human action."[19] It seems to me that, for similar reasons, Davidson's anomalous monism fails to do full justice to psychophysical causation—that is, it fails to provide an account of psychophysical causation in which the mental *qua mental* has any real causal role to play. Consider Davidson's account: whether or not a given event has a mental description (optional reading: whether it has a mental characteristic) seems entirely irrelevant to what causal relations it enters into. Its causal powers are wholly determined by the physical description or characteristic that holds for it; for it is under its physical description that it may be subsumed under a causal law. And Davidson explicitly denies any possibility of a nomological connection between an event's mental description and its physical description that could bring the mental into the causal picture.[20]

The delicate task is to find an account that will give the mental a substantial enough causal role to let us avoid "the great paradox of epiphenomenalism" without infringing upon the closedness of physical causal systems. I suggest that we view psychophysical causal relations—in fact, all causal relations involving psychological events—as epiphenomenal supervenient causal relations. More specifically, when a mental event M causes a physical event P, this is so because M is supervenient upon a physical event, P*, and P* causes P. This latter may itself be a supervenient causal relation, but that is no matter: what is important is that, at some point, purely physical causal processes take over. Similarly, when mental event M causes another mental event M*, this is so because M supervenes on a physical state P, and similarly M* on P*, and P causes P*.

Thus, if a pain causes the sensation of fear an instant later, this account tells the following story: the pain is supervenient on a brain state, this brain state causes another appropriate brain state, and given this second brain state, the fear sensation must occur, for it is supervenient upon that brain state. I think this is a plausible picture that, among other things, nicely accounts for the temporal gaps and discontinuities in the series of causally related mental events. Returning to the case of a pain causing a hand to withdraw, we should note that, on the present account, no causal path from the pain "merges" with the physiological causal chain at any point. For there is no separate path from the pain to the limb withdrawal; there is only one causal path in this situation, namely the one from the neural state upon which the pain supervenes to the movement of the hand.

Does this proposal satisfy the desiderata we set for an adequate account of psychophysical causation? It would be foolish to pretend that the proposed account accords to the mental the full causal potency we accord to fundamental physical processes. On the other hand, it does not treat mental phenomena as causally inert epiphenomena; nor does it reduce mental causation to the status of a mere chimera. Mental causation does take place; it is only that it is epiphenomenal causation, that is, a causal relation that is reducible to, or explainable by, the causal processes taking place at a more basic physical level. And this, according to the present account, is also precisely what happens with macrophysical causation relations. *Epiphenomenal causal relations involving psychological events, therefore, are no less real or substantial than those involving macrophysical events. They are both supervenient causal relations.* It seems to me that this is sufficient to redeem the causal powers we ordinarily attribute to mental events. Does the account meet the other desideratum of respecting the closed character of physical theory? It evidently does; for supervenient epiphenomenal causation does not place the supervenient events at the level of the underlying causal processes to which it is reduced. Mental events do not become part of the fundamental physical causal chains any more than macrophysical events become part of the microphysical causal chains that underlie them.

One remaining question is whether psychological events do supervene on physical events and processes. If psychological states are conceived as some sort of inner theoretical states posited to explain the observable behavior of organisms, there is little doubt that they will be supervenient on physical states.[21] However, there are serious questions as to whether that is a satisfactory conception of the mental; and I believe these questions lead to a serious doubt as to whether *intentional* mental states, namely those with propositional content such as beliefs and desires, are determined wholly by the physical details of the organism or even by the total physical environment that includes the organism. However, this need not be taken as casting doubt on the account of psychological causation offered here; I think we may more appropriately take it as an occasion for reconsidering whether, and in what way, intentional psychological states enter into causal relations—especially with physical events. I think that the two questions, whether intentional psychological states are supervenient on the physical and whether they enter into *law-based* causal relations with physical processes, are arguably equivalent questions. Psychophysical supervenience is a good deal more plausible, I believe, with regard to phenomenal mental states, and I am prepared to let the account of psychological causation proposed here stand for all psychological events and states that are physically supervenient.

Notes

1 Jonathan Edwards, *Doctrine of Original Sin Defended* (1758), Part IV, Chap. II. The quotation is taken from *Jonathan Edwards*, edited by C.H. Faust and T.H. Johnson (New York, 1935), 335. I owe this interesting reference to Roderick M. Chisholm's discussion of Edwards's views in connection with the "Doctrine of Temporal Parts," in *Person and Object* (La Salle, IL, 1976). 138ff.

2 Faust and Johnson, *Jonathan Edwards*, 336.

3 Wesley C. Salmon, "An 'At-At' Theory of Causal Influence," *Philosophy of Science* 44 (1977), 215-24.

4 For a discussion of the issues see John Lachs, "Epiphenomenalism and the Notion of Cause," *Journal of Philosophy* 60 (1963), 141-45.

5 For example, see J.J.C. Smart, "Sensations and Brain Processes," *Philosophical Review* 68 (1958), 141-56.

6 The thesis of mereological supervenience [supervenience of the whole on its parts, ed.] itself need not carry a commitment to atomism.

7 There is a large literature on this and related issues concerning microreduction; see, e.g., Lawrence Sklar, "Types of Inter-Theoretic Reduction," *British Journal for the Philosophy of Science* 18 (1967), 109-24; Robert L. Causey, *Unity of Science* (Dordrecht, Holland: Reidel, 1977).

8 See, e.g., Hilary Putnam, "The Nature of Mental States," and Ned Block and J. A. Fodor, "What Psychological States Are Not," both in Ned Block, ed., *Readings in Philosophy of Psychology*, vol. 1 (Cambridge, MA: Harvard Universty Press, 1980).

9   This corresponds to "strong supervenience" as characterized in my "Concepts of Supervenience," [essay 22 in this volume] ... for a general discussion of supervenience see also my "Supervenience and Nomological Incommensurables," *American Philosophical Quarterly* 15 (1978), 149-56....

10 For an influential view of this kind see Donald Davidson, "Causal Relations," *Journal of Philosophy* 64 (1967), 691-703.

11 See Terence Horgan, "Supervenience and Microphysics," *Pacific Philosophical Quarterly* 63 (1982), 29-43; see also David Lewis, "New Work for a Theory of Universals," *Australasian Journal of Philosophy* 61 (1983), 343-77.

12 See the somewhat dated but still useful "Unity of Science as a Working Hypothesis," by Paul Oppenheim and Hilary Putnam, in Herbert Feigl et al., eds., *Minnesota Studies in the Philosophy of Science*, vol. 2 (Minneapolis: University of Minnesota Press, 1958).

13 For an effective description of the difficulty see Richard Taylor, *Metaphysics*, 3rd ed. (Englewood Cliffs, NJ: Prentice Hall, 1983), chap. 3.

14 For some arguments against the identity thesis see Putnam, "The Nature of Mental States"; Saul Kripke, *Naming and Necessity* (Cambridge, MA: Harvard University Press, 1980), 144-55. For discussions of the problem of psychophysical causation see, e.g., J.L. Mackie, "Mind, Brain, and Causation," *Midwest Studies in Philosophy* 4 (1979), 19-30; and my "Causality, Identity and Supervenience in the Mind-Body Problem," *Midwest Studies in Philosophy* 4 (1979), 31-49.

15 See, e.g., Norman Malcolm, "The Conceivability of Mechanism," *Philosophical Review* 77 (1968), 45-72.

16 *Body and Mind* (New York: Anchor Books, 1970), chap. 6.

17 *The Mind and Its Place in Nature* (London, 1925), 472.

18 In "Mental Events," reprinted in Davidson, *Essays on Actions and Events* (New York, 1980), essay 5 in this volume.

19 William Kneale, "Broad on Mental Events and Epiphenomenalism," in P.A. Schilpp, ed., *The Philosophy of C.D. Broad* (New York: Open Court, 1959), 453. See also Jerome A. Shaffer, *Philosophy of Mind* (Englewood Cliffs, NJ: Prentice Hall, 1968), 68-71; Taylor, *Metaphysics*, chap. 4.

20 See his "Mental Events" for an extended argument against psychophysical lawlike connections. I give an analysis, and a partial defense, of Davidson's arguments in "Psychophysical Laws," in E. LePore and B. McLaughlin, eds., *Actions and Events: Perspectives on the Philosophy of Donald Davidson* (Oxford: Basil Blackwell, 1985), 369-86.

21 For details see my "Psychophysical Supervenience," *Philosophical Studies* 41 (1982), 51-70.

24

Mind-Body Interaction and Supervenient Causation*

Ernest Sosa

The mind-body problem arises because of our status as double agents apparently en rapport both with the mental and with the physical. We think, desire, decide, plan, suffer passions, fall into moods, are subject to sensory experiences, ostensibly perceive, intend, reason, make believe, and so on. We also move, have a certain geographical position, a certain height and weight, and we are sometimes hit or cut or burned. In other words, human beings have both minds and bodies. What is the relation between these? Religion often tells us that we are really embodied souls released at death from our bodily prisons. Could this be right?

It is said that our supposed problem is nothing more than a pseudoquestion and a waste of time, that we should admit only what is verifiable by means of perceptual observation; and hence that any supposed thought, desire, or experience not reducible to bodily behavior is a meaningless delusion. But these sayings are unphilosophical. We will not be bullied into blocking out a whole dimension of intellectual experience for the sake of a neat fit between some preconceived physicalist theory and the data left in view. We are mental beings at least as surely as we are physical beings, and if our mental lives are not reducible to the physical, then so much the worse for any preconceived physicalism.

Whether or not the mental is reducible to the physical, or for that matter the other way around, one thing stands out for its plausibility on the relation between the two. The body is often a puppet of the mind and the stream of consciousness often moves in a physical bed. Desires, beliefs, and decisions appear for all the world to affect our physical movements, at least now and then: pains, tickles, and sensory experiences derive from cuts, feathers, and open eyes, at least on some occasions.

Concerning the difficulty "pointed out since the days of Descartes in see-

* Ernest Sosa, "Mind-Body Interaction and Supervenient Causation," *Midwest Studies in Philosophy*, 9 (1984), 271-81. Ed. Peter A. French, Theodore E. Uehling, Jr., Howard K. Wettstein (Minneapolis: University of Minnesota Press, 1984). Reprinted with kind permission of the publisher.

ing how two such diverse things as matter and mind could possible affect each other," J.B. Pratt once complained that "the *a priori* denial of the possibility of such causal relation is pure dogma."[1] Thirty-eight years later, C.J. Ducasse was to lodge a very similar complaint as follows:

> [Contrary] to what is sometimes alleged, causation of a physical by a psychical event, or of a psychical event by stimulation of a physical sense organ, is not in the least paradoxical. The causality relation ... does not presuppose at all that its cause-term and its effect-term both belong to the same ontological category, but only that both of them be *events*.... Moreover, the objection that we cannot understand how a psychical event could cause a physical one (or vice-versa) has no basis other than blindness to the fact that the "how" of causation is capable at all of being either mysterious or understood only in cases of *remote* causation, never in cases of *proximate* causation.[2]

What we have in view so far is hence entirely receptive to the religious conception of people as embodied souls quite possibly immortal despite the dissolution of their bodies. But other conceptions of people are equally compatible with the data in view. Thus people may simply be identical with their bodies. Bodies do move, and who says they cannot think? Is there any way to decide between these?

Four key notions figure prominently within the data in view: the notions of body, of mind or soul, of spatial location, and of causation. Now whatever else may be true of bodies, at least they are lodged in space and in time, for they have height and they move. As for minds or souls, at least they are subjects of consciousness and they are also in time, since for one thing their desires wax and wane. Now according to tradition a soul is substantially simple, since complexity would tend to show mortality through eventual dissolution into parts. But if a soul is simple and immortal then it cannot be lodged in space, for anything lodged in space must have distinct subparts: a left half and a right half, say, or a bottom half and a top half. So we reach the conclusion that whereas bodies endure through time while filling space, souls endure without such extension.

What of our third key notion, that of spatial location? It is not true that only three-dimensional bodies are located in space, since shadows, smiles, and surfaces are so located. It does seem true, however, or at least much more plausible, that nothing is *fundamentally* located in space unless it has three-dimensional volume. Thus a smile is located on a face, and a shadow on the surface upon which it is cast. As for surfaces, their location would seem to derive from the location of outermost shells of the objects whose surface they are (shells that preserve relations among parts unchanged from the way they in fact are at the time when a certain location is attributed to the surface).

In keeping with these reflections and in view of numerous pro examples and none counter, let us assume the following at least provisionally as a general principle concerning location in space.

TFLS That Three-Dimensionality is Fundamental for Location in Space: Anything, x, not three-dimensional but located in space must be located superveniently on the location in space of something y such that (a) y is three-dimensional and (b) (the existence of) x supervenes on (the existence of) y.

Thus nothing is fundamentally located in space unless it is three-dimensional and three dimensionally located in space. It accords with this that a smile is derivative from a smiling face, and that the location of a smile is derivative from the location of the smiling face from which it derives; also, that a surface is derivative from a surfaced solid, and that the location of a surface is derivative from the location of the surfaced solid from which it derives; and also, finally, that a shadow is derivative from a shadowed solid, and that the location of a shadow is derivative from the location of the shadowed solid from which it derives. And so on. (Our principle can be made more precise, and more can be done in support of it by appeal to further pro examples. But here I wish to argue only that it does deserve such attention, by showing how it serves crucially in an interesting argument for a philosophically important conclusion. So we assume it provisionally and continue our argument.)

What of our fourth key notion, finally, that of causation? Can we bring it into sharper focus, with greater definition of detail? To begin, consider an example. Someone takes a picture of you, a photograph. Your image is imprinted on a piece of film. The film is imprinted with an image of a face that looks a certain way *because* you have a certain physiognomy. But your physiognomy causes the image on the film only in virtue of the fact that certain conditions hold at a given time with respect to you and the piece of film. The film is in a camera aimed in your direction, and you and the camera are not too far apart, there are no obstacles obstructing the line of sight, you are facing the camera at the time, and there is enough light, and so on; and it is only in virtue of the fact that these conditions all hold that your facial appearance causes the image on the film.

It seems quite evident, moreover, that if any twin of yours is ever noncausally related to a twin of that piece of film in just the way you are now noncausally related to that piece of film, and in exactly similar noncausal conditions, then once again an image will appear on the film as a causal result of the physiognomy of the man.[3]

Take another example. A karate expert hits a board and splits it in two. The board splits in two *because* of the blow by the man. And if this is so it is presumably in virtue of certain noncausal conditions that hold at the time, including the board's thickness; its composition; the angle, speed, and force of the blow; etc. And it seems quite evident, moreover, that if anything non-causally a perfect twin of that board is hit by anyone noncausally a perfect twin of that man with a blow exactly like that blow in all noncausal respects, then that new board must also split just as did the old, because of the blow.

When causation ties together a pair of particular things like a piece of film and a human being, or a wood board and a karate chop, it is always in virtue of certain noncausal properties or relations holding of the members of the pair, so that any pair equally propertied and related would be equally tied together by causation. This principle is encapsulated in the saying that causal relations among particulars derive from causal relations among their properties and relations. Any other set of particulars with just the same (noncausal) properties and relations must also be linked by causal relations in just the same way.

Consider now someone in pain because his body is in contact with a flame. If distress is a mental state, then the one in distress is a simple, unextended, and immortal soul, or so we are told. So we have two things, the soul in distress and the body in the fire, and somehow the distress in the soul is caused by the flames on the body. But if that is so, then there must be certain non-causal properties of that particular soul, and certain noncausal properties of that particular body, and certain noncausal relations between the two, such that when any soul with such properties of that soul and any body with such properties of that body are related by such relations between that soul and that body, the new soul will be in just the same distress once again because of flames licking the new body. But just what properties or relations could these be?

There are many bodies and many souls, or so we are told. What makes the events in a given body causally relevant to a given soul, or the events in a given soul causally relevant to a given body?

Could it be a special relation of embodiment or of ownership, so that direct causal interactions take place between a soul and a body only if that soul is embodied in that body, or only if that soul owns that body in the sense that it is its body? But neither this embodiment nor this ownership is clear enough to be illuminating. A soul is not in its body the way a pilot is in his ship. Just how then is it embodied in that body? And if a soul does own its body in just the sense in which a pilot owns his ship, i.e., legally and even morally, that only moves the question to a deeper level. For if you own something legally or morally, there must be something about its relation to you other than your ownership of it that makes you its owner. Thus it may be that you inherited it, or that it is a fruit of your labors, or the like. If a given soul does own a certain body, then, what relation can there be between them that makes that soul the owner of that body? It won't do now to reply that it is just the moral or legal ownership of that body by that soul. But if it is not moral or legal ownership, then what kind of ownership is it that permits a soul to interact directly with a given body?

If embodiment and ownership are not to be explained by reference to the spatial inclusion of a pilot in his ship or to the moral or legal ownership of a ship by its pilot, perhaps they are explicable by reference to a notion of direct causal effects. Thus we might say that x has a direct causal effect on y iff an event in x has an effect on y without first having an effect on anything that is not a part of y. A soul then would have direct causal effects exclusively or for the most part only on a given body, and that body would then have direct causal effects exclusively or for the most part only on that soul, all of which would signify the embodiment of that soul in that body and the ownership of that body by that soul.

That seems indeed a promising analysis of embodiment or ownership until we reflect on our goal in introducing these notions. What we wanted from these notions, after all, was some way of specifying what relation it is that makes a given body subject to the direct causal action of a given soul, and what it is that makes a given soul subject to the direct causal action of a given body. From this point of view the notions of embodiment and of ownership turn out to be useless under analysis. For it is useless to be told that what makes something subject to direct causal interaction with something else is that it is indeed subject to direct causal interaction with it. And that is precisely what the answer by reference to ownership or embodiment resolves to under analysis.

Our picture begins to look bleak for immortal souls. What pairs physical objects as proper mates for causal interaction is in general their places in the all-encompassing spatial framework of physical reality. It is their spatial relations that pair the piece of film with the man photographed, and distinguishes him as the cause from the billions of other men in existence including his exact look-alikes.

We are told that each of the billions of men in existence has his own immortal soul. What framework serves to sustain the one-one pairing of souls and bodies in the way that the spatial framework sustains the pairing of photographic images of people and the people whose images they are? What non-causal relation between souls and bodies might possibly marry a particular soul to a particular body as its proper mate for a certain causal interaction at a certain time? We have found no plausible answer for this question.

Even if for that reason we reject the supposed causal interaction between body and soul, nevertheless, there remains the possibility of interaction between the mental and the physical, of interaction not between substances but only between events, between mental events and physical events. Two sorts of monism, both the neutral and the anomalous, offer to buttress the possibility of such interaction.

In introducing his anomalous monism, Donald Davidson introduces also a concept of supervenience into the recent literature on the mind-body problem:

> Although the position I describe denies there are psychophysical laws, it is consistent with the view that mental characteristics are in some sense dependent, or supervenient, on physical characteristics. Such supervenience might be taken to mean that there cannot be two events alike in all physical respects but differing in some mental respect, or that an object cannot alter in some mental respect without altering in some physical respect. Dependence or supervenience of this kind does not entail reducibility through law or definition....[4]

Supervenience has long been known in axiology and ethical theory, where values are said to supervene upon facts. And values do seem to supervene thus at least in Davidson's sense that it is not possible for two things to be exactly alike in all nonevaluative respects but unlike in some evaluative respect.

Such *supervenience* of evaluative properties is linked closely to the *universalizability* of value judgments and their special dependence on *reasons* and *principles*. If an apple is a good apple it must be so in virtue of certain reasons: perhaps because it is large, sweet, and juicy. There must be some such reasons that make the good apple good. If so, and if these are *all* the reasons in virtue of which that particular apple is a good apple, then (a) *all* apples that are large, sweet, and juicy are also equally good apples (universalizability to a principle governing the goodness of apples); and (b) the property of being a good apple exemplified by that apple *supervenes* on its properties of being large, sweet, and juicy (in that particular case: depends on, is derived from such properties).

Supervenience would seem to pertain in fact not only to evaluative properties but also, for example, to any "determinable," which would always supervene on one or another of its corresponding "determinates." For example, if our apple is chromatically colored (colored but not white, black, or grey), it surely will be so in virtue of some reason: perhaps because it is red, or because it is yellow. If so, and if what makes it chromatically colored is that it is red, then (a) *all* red apples are equally chromatically colored; and (b) the property of being chromatically colored exemplified by that apple *supervenes* on its property of being red (depends on, or is derived from that property).

Although the supervenience of main interest to us here is that of properties, there is a concept of ontological supervenience or derivation with much wider scope. As we have seen, smiles derive from smiling faces, shadows from shadowed surfaces, and surfaces in turn from the existence of outermost layers of the things whose surfaces they are. And so on.

Supervenience is moreover a key concept of ontology and metaphysics. From the Greeks on, our tradition perennially seeks an underlying reality on which all intellectual appearance may be seen to supervene. The underlying reality may be found in ethereal forms, in material atoms, in monads, or in spirits and their ideas. But in each case there is much else that derives from the fundamental by ontological supervenience.

Restricting ourselves once more to the supervenience of properties from other properties: How more exactly are we to conceive of such supervenience?

We have first Davidson's suggestion:

WS Weak Supervenience: A set of properties A supervenes on a set of properties B iff indiscernibility in respect of B necessitates (necessarily implies) indiscernibility in respect of A, and change in respect of A necessitates change in respect of B.

Compare such weak supervenience with the following stronger variety:

SS Strong Supervenience: A set of properties A supervenes on a set of properties B iff nothing can have any property in A without also having certain properties in B such that anything that ever had such properties in B, necessarily would also have the property in A.

Note that strong supervenience necessitates weak supervenience, but not conversely.[5]

James Cornman's "neutral monism" is rather similar to Davidson's anomalous monism.[6] And this similarity of doctrine brings with it also similarity of arguments.

In each case we are told that there are mental events in human beings that are both causes and effects. But mental properties (predicates) have no place in any network of psychophysical laws—on pain, so Cornman argues, of violating certain principles of conservation (such as the principle of the conservation of momentum). Only physical properties fit into laws of nature. All the same, if an event x causes an event y, there must be a law that relates x to y on the basis of their properties and relations (predicates). Therefore, any mental event that is cause or effect of any other event must have physical properties lawfully connected with some physical properties of its cause or effect.

Regarding principles of conservation, in the first place, those involve isolated systems. But to suppose that physical nature, as we know it, is an isolated system is to suppose that the known physical forces—for example, electricity and gravitation—are all the forces that ever act on anything physical. And it is doubtful that we have the right to feel sure of any such assumption. Too much remains unexplained: about people, for example, their actions and their thoughts. That being so, it would be a mere physicalist pretension to claim knowledge of all forces affecting human thought and action, and to suppose that full explanation awaits only the filling in of details.

Davidson develops his anomalous monism to show, like Kant, that though apparently incompatible, certain independently attractive principles are after all compatible.

> The first principle asserts that at least some mental events interact causally with physical events.... The second principle is that where there is causality, there must be a law: events related as cause and effect fall under strict deterministic laws.... The third principle is that there are no strict deterministic laws on the basis of which mental events can be predicted and explained....[7]

The key to his proposed solution for this three-pronged paradox is the idea that mental events enter into causal relations *not* as mental but only as physical. (I try to convey the main idea here very briefly in my words, though I doubt Davidson would himself accept these words; so far as I know, he does not recognize the terminology of an event causing something or being caused by something "*as* such-and-such.")

Does that key really unlock a resolution to Davidson's Paradox? I cannot believe that it does, as I can't see that it does justice to the full meaning of his first principle. Some examples may convey my doubt.

A gun goes off, a shot is fired, and it kills someone. The loud noise is the shot. Thus, if the victim is killed by the shot, it's the loud noise that kills the victim.

Compare this. I extend my hand because of a certain neurological event. That event is my sudden desire to quench my thirst. Thus, if my grasping is caused by that neurological event, it's my sudden desire that causes my grasping.

We have considered a case of causality directed from the mind to the body. Let us turn to one in reverse direction.

First an analogous case. The tenor misses a very high note as the entire roof caves in. His miss is the end of that concert. Thus, if his miss is caused by the slipping of his wig, it's the slipping of his wig that causes the end of the concert.

Compare this. A certain physical event (which is in fact my catching sight of some water) causes a certain neurological event (which is in fact my sudden desire to quench my thirst). Thus, if the neurological event is caused by the physical event, it's the physical event that causes my sudden desire.

Yes, in a certain sense the victim is killed by the loud noise; not by the loud noise as a loud noise, however, but only by the loud noise as a shot, or the like. Similarly, assuming the anomalism of the mental, though my extending my hand is, in a certain sense, caused by my sudden desire to quench my thirst, it is not caused by my desire qua desire but only by my desire qua *neurological* event of a certain sort. Besides, the loudness of the shot has no causal relevance to the death of the victim: had the gun been equipped with a silencer, the shot would have killed the victim just the same. Similarly, the being a desire of my desire has no causal relevance to my extending my hand (if the mental is indeed anomalous): if the event that is in fact my desire had not been my desire but had remained a neurological event of a certain sort, then it would have caused my extending my hand just the same.

In parallel fashion, it is true that the slipping of the tenor's wig causes the end of the concert, but it does not cause the end of the concert *to be* the end of the concert. That is caused by the cave-in of the roof. In the same way, if we accept the anomalism of the mental, then *although* it is true that my sudden desire to quench my thirst is caused by a certain physical event (which is in fact identical to my catching sight of water), *still* that physical event does not cause my sudden desire *to be* my sudden desire. That, apparently, for anomalous and for neutral monism, has *no* cause or causal explanation.

I conclude that neither neutral monism nor anomalous monism is really compatible with the full content of our deep and firm conviction that mind and body each acts causally on the other.

And what shall we say to the second principle, of the three that jointly yield the paradox? According to that principle, "... where there is causality, there must be a law: events related as cause and effect fall under strict deterministic laws." But why must there always be a law to cover any causal relation linking events x and y? What enables us to assume such a general truth?

Our plan has been: first, to reflect briefly and generally on our nature as persons; second, to formulate the principle of the supervenience of causality; and then, third, to draw certain consequences from that principle for two doctrines about our nature: (a) interactionism; and (b) neutral or anomalous monism.

One consequence for interactionism is that there can be no interaction between an immaterial soul and a material body. That of course has been the view of so many, since Gassendi to the present, that it is firmly settled as a platitude of introductory philosophy. What may perhaps be novel in our inference from the supervenience of causation is an *explanation* of why such interaction is impossible or at least implausible.

Though we reject substantial interaction, however, that leaves standing the possibility of interaction between the physical and the mental; not interaction between body and soul, of course, but only interaction between mental events and physical events. Both neutral and anomalous monism offer to buttress the possibility of such interaction, but we have found the offer empty. According to such monism, the various ways of being mental are all absurd and barren. Their presence is caused by nothing and causes nothing; it can never be explained and can explain nothing.

The supervenience of causation requires that we reject substantial interaction. But far from requiring also the rejection of interaction between mental and physical properties, it offers support for the hypothesis of such interaction.

When told that a burn causes a pain, we may understand and accept what we are told as the claim that the burn *as such* causes the pain *as such*: in other words, that the burn's *being* a burn causes the pain *to be* a pain. (Recall the similar claim that the cave-in of the roof causes the end of the concert. And note the contrast with the claim that the slipping of the tenor's wig causes the end of the concert. Even though the tenor's miss is indeed the end of the concert—the last note— the slipping of his wig causes his miss to be a miss but it does not cause his miss to be the end of the concert. That is caused by the cave-in of the roof.) But if we understand the statement that the burn causes the pain as the statement that the burn's being a burn causes the pain to be a pain, then that causal relation between events supervenes on certain properties of that burn and certain properties of that pain, and certain relations between the two, such that, if ever there be a pair of events like that pair in all such respects, the being a burn of one member of the pair would cause the being a pain of the other. And such supervenience of the causal relation may now be explained as something required by its very analysis, provided we can accept the following proposed analysis:

> The having of property P by event x, $<P, x>$, causes event y to have property Q, $<Q, y>$, iff there are properties of x, including P, and properties of y, and a relation R between x and y, such that it is nomologically necessary that whenever an event has such properties of x and bears relation R to some other event with such properties of y, then that other event also has Q.

If this analysis, or one like it, is right, we may easily understand why the causal relation between events x and y supervenes without fail on noncausal properties and relations of x and y. For the notion that x causes y may then be understood as the notion that x, qua possessor of some property P, causes y, qua possessor of some property Q. In other words, we understand

> Event x causes event y

as

> There are properties P and Q such that $<P, x>$ causes $<Q, y>$.

And this last, according to its very analysis, requires that there be properties of x, including P, and properties of y, as well as a relation R between x and y, such that by law of nature whenever an event turns out to have such properties of x and to be related by that relation R to have some event with such properties of y, then that other event also has Q.[8]

In this way we *explain* (a) the fact that where there is causality there must be a law, and also (b) the fact that the causal relation among particular things or events supervenes on noncausal properties and relations of such things or events. This double explanatory power of such an analysis seems a weighty reason in its favour—or at least in favour of the view that some such analysis is bound to be right.

Note finally that if that analysis or one like it is in fact correct, and if we believe that burns cause pains to be painful, it follows that the mental property of being painful cannot be causally unconnected with the physical. Accordingly, combining an analysis like ours with the belief that burns cause pains to be painful yields an interactionism of mental and physical properties.[9]

What shall we conclude about the person? If the mental life of a person interacts with his physical career, the person cannot be fundamentally immaterial. One must then be either one's body (or part of it) or something that supervenes on one's body (or a part of it).

A person passes away without the vanishing of his body, since it's his body we bury. It follows that the person is never identical to his body. There remains then only the other possibility: that the person supervenes on a live body with certain abilities and capacities. When a body loses life, it no longer constitutes a person. Thus the person is not identical with any body, but is constituted by some body when that body has the properties required for such constitution. Supervening as a person always does on his body (or a part), the person is superveniently located where his body (or a part) is located; it is this spatial relation with his body that enables the causal interaction between them.[10]

Notes

1   J.B. Pratt, *Matter and Spirit* (New York, 1922).

2   C.J. Ducasse, "In Defense of Dualism," in Sidney Hook, ed., *Dimensions of Mind* (New York: New York University Press, 1960), 85-90; 88.

3   A relation or condition is causal if and only if it includes the relation of causation—of X causing Y—as a logical constituent.

4   Donald Davidson, "Mental Events," in L. Foster and J.W. Swanson, eds., *Experience and Theory* (Amherst: University of Massachusetts Press, 1978), 88, this volume, 90-91.

5   Jaegwon Kim defines and compares such concepts in "Psychological Supervenience as a Mind-Body Theory," in *Cognition and Brain Theory* V (1982). He has moreover pointed out to me (in correspondence) that dropping the last clause in the definition of weak supervenience yields a concept of supervenience that is even weaker. And we agree also (in conversation) in recognizing stronger forms of supervenience that involve a kind of formal causation (a by-virtue-of relation) apparently not definable by the modal notions.

6   James Cornman, "A Nonreductive Identity Theory about Mind and Body," in Joel Feinberg, ed., *Reason and Responsibility* (Belmont, CA: Dickenson, 1981).

7   Davidson, "Mental Events," 80-81, this volume, 86. James Van Cleve showed me the need to look here at the wider context, which makes it clear that the first principle

involves causation in both directions, and that the third principle is based on an assumption that there are no psychophysical laws whatever, in either direction.

8   Davidson's suggestion in "Causal Relations," in E. Sosa, ed., *Causation and Conditionals* (Oxford: Oxford University Press, 1975), about the logical form of causal laws—according to which the causal relation between events is an inseparable constituent of such laws—seems incompatible on pain of circularity with our notion that the causal relation between events has an analysis on the basis of a proposition affirming the existence of a causal law that links properties and relations of these events. If that is so, it closes our avenue to an explanation for the principle that where there is causality, there must be a law. Closing that avenue incurs some obligation to try to open another, for such a principle stands in need of explanation.

9   So far we have raised doubts about a proposed resolution to Davidson's Paradox that focuses on the first of its three prongs. But closing an avenue to the resolution of a paradox leaves some obligation to try to open another. Our reflections so far imply focusing on the third rather than the first of the three prongs. They imply rejecting the principle that "there are no strict deterministic laws on the basis of which mental events can be predicted and explained." In fact, it seems to me that our assumptions can be weakened in such a way that all three principles may be retained. The main steps involved would include these: (i) introducing a strict and restrictive sense of "law" to serve in principle three; and (ii) revising our analysis of causation in such a way that $<P, x>$ may cause $<Q, y>$ even though there is no (strict) law connecting P and Q themselves but only properties P' and Q' related in some (to-be-specified) way to P and Q. (Thus for the cave-in of the concert hall to cause the death of fifteen people, it is not required that there be a strict law connecting the property of being the cave-in of the concert hall with the property of being the death of fifteen people. What is required, rather, is perhaps something closer to this: that there be a (very complex) property P' of a certain event on which the property of that event of being the cave-in of the concert hall supervenes, and a property Q' of another event on which the property of that event of being the death of fifteen people supervenes, such that $<P', x>$ does cause $<Q', y>$ according to our analysis of causation as it presently stands.) But there would also be a third important step: (iii) recognizing that the expression 'X causes Y' is context-dependent (in ways some of which have been much discussed).

10 Beside the problem of the supervenience of causation, at least two further problems challenge the soul as innermost seat of a person's psychology: (a) Since diversity and its deductive progeny (e.g., diversity-or-loving) cannot stand as the *sole* relations between two intrinsically indistinguishable entities, and since souls are not spatially related and presumably can be intrinsically indistinguishable entities, what relation can it be (or what relations can they be) that would accompany the diversity of souls? (b) Since capacities, skills, abilities, virtues, and vices are dispositional properties or potentialities, and since these require a ground in intrinsic properties of their bearers, what sorts of intrinsic properties could provide it in immaterial souls? What to say in answer seems in each case occult.

25

From Supervenience to Superdupervenience: Meeting the Demands of a Material World*

Terence Horgan

The term "supervenience" derives etymologically from the Latin "super", meaning *on, above,* or *additional;* and from the Latin verb "venire", meaning *to come.* In nonphilosophical contexts the word is used primarily in a temporal way—typically to mean "coming or occurring as something novel, additional, or unexpected". In philosophical contexts it is primarily used non-temporally, to signify a metaphysical and/or conceptual determination-relation; here the etymology appears to be spatially quasi-metaphorical, the idea being that something supervenient comes above—is "grounded by"—that on which it supervenes.

The term in its current philosophical usage evidently entered the analytic philosophy literature in a classic work of twentieth century metaethics, Hare:

> Let me illustrate one of the most characteristic features of value-words in terms of a particular example. It is a feature sometimes described by saying that "good" and other such words are names of "supervenient" or "consequential" properties. Suppose that a picture is hanging upon the wall and we are discussing whether it is a good picture; that is to say, we are debating whether to assent to, or dissent from, the judgment "*P* is a good picture."... Suppose that there is another picture next to *P* in the gallery (I will call it *Q*).... Now there is one thing that we cannot say; we cannot say "*P* is exactly like *Q* in all respects save this one, that *P* is a good picture and *Q* not."... There must be some *further* difference between them to make one good and the other not.[1]

Professor Hare has recently written, however, that this use of the term was already current in Oxford, and did not originate with him.[2] And the concept we currently express by "supervenience," although not the word itself, had already been invoked in moral philosophy by G.E. Moore,[3] who held that

---

* Terence Horgan, "From Supervenience to Superdupervenience: Meeting the Demands of a Material World," *Mind* 102 (1993), 555-86. Reprinted by permission of Oxford University Press.

intrinsic value is (as we would now say) supervenient on non-normative properties. Moore wrote:

> [I]f a given thing possesses any kind of intrinsic value in a certain degree, then not only must that same thing possess it, under all circumstances, in the same degree, but also anything *exactly like it*, must, under all circumstances, possess it in exactly the same degree. Or, to put it in the corresponding negative form: it is not *possible* that of two exactly similar things one should possess it and the other not, or that one should possess it in one degree, and the other in a different one.[4]

Supervenience, then, is a modal notion. As David Lewis puts it, "Supervenience means that there *could* be no difference of one sort without difference of the other sort."[5]

Although the concept of supervenience has been employed for a variety of purposes in recent philosophy, a rather dominant tendency since the early 1970's has been to invoke it in efforts to articulate a broadly materialistic, or physicalistic, position in philosophy of mind or in metaphysics generally. Often it has been invoked with the goal of articulating a materialistic metaphysical picture that eschews various strictures on inter-level connections that were sometimes built into earlier formulations of materialism—in particular, the requirement that psychological and other "higher-order" properties be *reducible* to physicochemical properties.

Lately, however, the wave of relative enthusiasm about supervenience theses has begun to subside. There now seems to be emerging[6] an attitude of sober reassessment, accompanied by a suspicion that supervenience theses per se do less work philosophically than some had hoped they would.

I think this change of mood was in many ways inevitable, given certain ironic facts about the history of the notion of supervenience in philosophical thought during the 20th century. There is much to be learned from this history about both the uses and the limitations of supervenience theses, especially with respect to materialism. So the first half of this paper, §§ 1-4, will be a historical overview, aimed at highlighting some key ironies and drawing some important lessons for materialist metaphysics. The principal moral will be that supervenience relations, in order to figure in a broadly materialistic worldview, must be explainable rather than *sui generis*.

I will next take up some issues that have figured prominently in recent philosophical discussions of supervenience:[7] how to formulate supervenience theses (§ 5); supervenience and the causal/explanatory efficacy of higher-order properties (§ 6); supervenience and inter-theoretic reduction (§ 7). Finally (§ 8) I will return to the issue whose importance is the central moral of §§ 1-4, but which has so far gone largely unnoticed in the philosophical literature: the explainability of supervenience relations.

Let me make several preliminary points. First, I take it that the question of what constitutes a broadly materialistic, or physicalistic, worldview is itself a philosophical question.[8] Although many philosophers, myself included, are disposed toward *some* sort of materialistic metaphysics, it is no simple matter to articulate such a view. Much of the philosophical interest of the notion of supervenience lies in its potential usefulness in this respect.

Second, for reasons of simplicity I will generally talk in terms of the basic physical level of description (the level of physics per se) vis-à-vis other levels of description—and often in terms of the physical vis-à-vis the mental. But much of what I will say presumably can be extended to inter-level supervenience relations more generally.

Third, for reasons of simplicity I will conduct the discussion in a way that presupposes an ontology of properties and facts. The language of properties and facts allows for perspicuous formulation of the central theses and issues I will be concerned with. But analogous theses and issues presumably would arise even under a more nominalistic ontology, although nominalists might seek to reformulate them or might deny that talk of facts and properties carries genuine ontological commitment to these putative entities.[9]

1. BRITISH EMERGENTISM

It will be instructive to begin by considering supervenience in relation to an account of the special sciences that has been dubbed "British emergentism" in a splendid and fascinating recent paper.[10] The British emergentist tradition began in the middle of the nineteenth century and flourished in the first quarter of this century. It began with John Stuart Mill's *System of Logic*,[11] then traced through Alexander Bain's *Logic*,[12] George Henry Lewes's *Problems of Life and Mind*,[13] Samuel Alexander's *Space, Time, and Deity*,[14] Lloyd Morgan's *Emergent Evolution*,[15] and finally C.D. Broad's *The Mind and Its Place In Nature*.[16] The latter was the last major work in this tradition, although the tradition continues even today in the work of a few authors, notably the neurophysiologist Roger Sperry.

The British emergentists were not substance-dualists; they held that all particulars are physical entities wholly constituted out of physical entities as their parts. But they were not full-fledged materialists either, because they denied that physics is a causally complete science. They maintained that at various junctures in the course of evolution, complex physical entities came into being that had certain non-physical, "emergent," properties. These properties, they claimed, are fundamental force-generating properties, over and above the force-generating properties of physics; when such a property is instantiated by an individual, the *total* causal forces operative within the individual are a combination of physical and non-physical forces, and the resulting behavior of the individual is different from what it would have been had the emergent force(s) not been operative alongside the lower-level forces.[17] Furthermore, there is no explanation for why emergent properties come into being, or why they generate the specific non-physical forces they do. These facts are metaphysically and scientifically basic, in much the same way that fundamental laws of physics are basic; they are unexplained explainers, which must be accepted (in Samuel Alexander's striking phrase) "with natural piety." Putative examples of emergent properties included (i) chemical-bonding properties of molecules, which were held to be emergent from physical properties of atoms or their constituents; (ii) self-maintenance and reproductive properties of living things, emergent from physical and chemical properties; and (iii) mental properties of creatures with consciousness, emergent from physical, chemical, and biological properties.[18]

There are two reasons I mention British emergentism in connection with supervenience. First, the term "supervenient" was employed by Morgan in contexts where synchronic inter-level relations among properties were under consideration. Here is a representative passage:

> I speak of events at any given level in the pyramid of emergent evolution as "involving" concurrent events at lower levels. Now what emerges at any given level affords an instance of what I speak of as a new kind of relatedness of which there are no instances at lower levels. The world has been successively enriched through the advent of vital and of conscious relations. This we must accept "with natural piety" as Mr. Alexander puts it. If it be found as somehow given, it is to be taken as we find it.
>
> But when some new kind of relatedness is supervenient (say at the level of life), the way in which the physical events which are involved run their course is different in virtue of its presence—different from what it would have been if life had been absent. [19]

The temporal or diachronic meaning of "supervenient" is certainly involved here; in part Morgan is saying, "… when some new kind of relatedness has been arrived upon in the course of evolution …". On the other hand, synchronic inter-level dependence is evidently involved too; he is talking about higher-level events vis-à-vis *concurrent* lower-level events. In effect, then, Morgan's usage of "supervenient" connotes (as does the term "emergence" itself) both diachronic novelty and synchronic dependence.[20]

A second reason I mention British emergentism is in order to pose two questions well worth asking about emergentism and synchronic inter-level dependence relations. (1) Could the British emergentists have held, consistently with their other principal doctrines, that emergent properties are *supervenient* (in the contemporary philosophical sense) on lower level properties— i.e., that individuals cannot differ in their emergent properties without also differing in their lower-order properties? (2) *Did* they hold this view?

As regards the second question, I think the textual evidence supports an affirmative answer, although not decisively. For instance, Broad wrote:

[N]o amount of knowledge about how the constituents of a living body behave in isolation or in other and non-living wholes might suffice to enable us to predict the characteristic behaviour of a living organism. This possibility is perfectly compatible with the view that the characteristic behaviour of a living body is completely determined by the nature and arrangement of the chemical compounds which compose it, in the sense that any whole which is composed of such compounds in such an arrangement will show vital behaviour and that nothing else will do so.[21]

Given the remarks in the wider context in which this passage occurs, it is fairly clear that Broad actually advocated the determination thesis here mentioned. Moreover, it is plausible that the sort of determination he had in mind is full-fledged supervenience, rather than a weaker kind of dependence in which the nature and arrangement of a body's constituent chemical compounds only figures as a *precondition* for the instantiation of a given emergent vital property, without *guaranteeing* its instantiation. But Broad and the other emergentists were not totally unambiguous about which of these two kinds of synchronic dependence they believed in.[22]

In any event, the first question is the more important one for our purposes here. The answer to this question, as far as I can see, is affirmative. Certain higher-level properties could be supervenient on lower-level ones (ultimately on physical ones) and also possess the two key features the emergentists stressed: (i) the supervenient higher-order properties could be fundamental causal properties, generating causal forces over and above physical causal forces; and (ii) the connections between lower-order and higher-order properties—supervenience connections—could be metaphysically fundamental, hence unexplainable.[23]

There are important lessons in the fact that the thesis of physical supervenience is consistent with the central doctrines of British emergentism, because those doctrines should surely be repudiated by anyone who advocates a broadly materialistic metaphysics. A materialist position should surely assert, contrary to emergentism, (i) that physics is causally complete (i.e., all fundamental causal forces are physical forces, and the laws of physics are never violated); and (ii) that any metaphysically basic facts or laws—any unexplained explainers, so to speak—are facts or laws within physics itself. So the two principal lessons of British emergentism are these:

(L1) All properties and facts could be supervenient on physical properties and facts even if physics is not causally complete; for, certain non-physical properties could be supervenient on physical properties and yet causally basic (in the sense that they generate fundamental causal forces over and above physical forces). Yet a materialistic metaphysical position should assert the causal completeness of physics.

(L2) All properties and facts could be supervenient on physical properties and facts even if certain supervenience facts are metaphysically *sui generis*, unexplainable in more fundamental terms. Yet a materialistic metaphysical position should assert that all supervenience facts are explainable—indeed, explainable in some materialistically acceptable way.

I take it that any supervenient properties whose supervenience is materialistically explainable would not be causally basic properties in the sense of (L1). On the other hand, a metaphysical position affirming that there are supervenient properties whose supervenience is not materialistically explainable would not deserve the label "materialism," not even if it did affirm the causal completeness of physics.

2. MOORE AND META-ETHICAL NON-NATURALISM

The classic articulation of meta-ethical non-naturalism in the 20th century was given by G.E. Moore.[24] Moore held that there are objective moral properties and facts, and that these are not *natural* properties and facts of the sort that are investigated in the sciences; rather, moral goodness and moral rightness are simple, unanalyzable, non-natural, properties. As already remarked, although Moore did not use the word "supervenience," he quite clearly held that moral properties are supervenient on natural properties—specifically, that certain propositions of the form "Anything that has natural property *P* also possesses the property of intrinsic goodness" are (*synthetic*) necessary truths. He also maintained that these propositions do not depend for their truth (or their necessity) upon anything else; the synthetic necessary connections they express are metaphysically rock bottom, and thus are not explainable by any other facts.

The thesis that all properties and facts are supervenient on physical properties and facts is consistent with a non-materialist metaphysical position; this is a general moral we have already extracted from British emergentism. The moral is strongly reinforced by the fact that Moore's non-naturalist metaphysical position is consistent with—and indeed, incorporated—the thesis that moral properties and facts are supervenient on natural properties and facts. Surely no materialist or naturalist metaphysical position could embrace Moore's meta-ethics. For one thing, Moore's putative non-natural moral properties are just intolerably queer, from a broadly naturalistic perspective. Moreover, the metaphysical queerness is only worsened by the contention that there are unexplainable, synthetic, necessary connections linking natural properties to moral ones. Both points were well stated by J.L. Mackie:

> If there were objective values, they would be entities or qualities or relations of a very strange sort, utterly different from anything else in the universe ... An objective good would .... [have] to-be-pursuedness built into it. Similarly, if there were objective principles of right and wrong, any wrong (possible) course of action would have not-to-be-doneness somehow built right into it. Or we should have something like Clarke's necessary relations of fitness between situations and actions, so that a situation would have a demand for such-and-such an action somehow built into it.[25]

> What is the connection between the natural fact that an action is a piece of deliberate cruelty—say, causing pain just for fun—and the moral fact that it is wrong? It cannot be an entailment, a logical or semantic necessity. Yet it is not merely that the two features occur together. The wrongness must somehow be "consequential" or "supervenient": it is wrong because it is a piece of deliberate cruelty. But just what *in the world* is signified by this "because"?[26]

The first of these passages nicely expresses why Moorean moral properties are so hard to stomach.[27] The second passage is plausibly construed as pointing out the metaphysical oddness, from a broadly naturalistic perspective, of non-analytic, inter-level, necessitation relations that are *sui generis* and unexplainable.[28]

3. HARE AND META-ETHICAL NON-COGNITIVISM

Although supervenience is typically regarded nowadays as an inter-level relation between properties or facts, it was not so regarded by the analytic philosopher who first used the term in print, Professor Hare. Hare was one of the principal advocates in this century of the meta-ethical position commonly called non-cognitivism; and on this view, there *are* no moral properties or moral facts. For Hare, supervenience in morals is a conceptual/semantic constraint on moral discourse and moral judgment; it is part of the "logic" of value-words (as was said in Oxford in the 1950's). Thus, if one uses moral language in a way that violates the supervenience constraint, one thereby abuses the very meaning of moral terms; and if one professes moral beliefs whose linguistic expression would violate the supervenience constraint, then either one misunderstands what one claims to believe, or else one's moral beliefs manifest a certain sort of inconsistency.

In the preceding two sections I have emphasized the need for supervenience relations to be explainable, rather than metaphysically *sui generis*. Let me now stress two points about the explanation of moral supervenience, in connection with Hare's views and those of other moral irrealists. First, explanations of moral supervenience appear relatively easy to give for a moral irrealist, and irrealists have in fact given them. For Hare, the primary function of evaluative terms, like "good," "ought," and "right," is not to ascribe properties to objects, but rather to commend (in the case of "good") and prescribe (in the case of "right"); the overarching purpose of value words is to *teach standards*. So the explanation for supervenience, as a consistency constraint on human moral judgments and moral discourse, will advert to this objective. Hare wrote:

> Now since it is the purpose of the word "good" and other value-words to be used for teaching standards, their logic is in accord with this purpose. We are therefore in a position at last to explain the feature of the word "good" which I pointed out at the beginning of this investigation [viz., supervenience]. The reason why I cannot apply the word "good" to one picture, if I refuse to apply it to another picture which I agree to be in all respects exactly similar, is that by doing this I should be defeating the purpose for which the word is designed.[29]

Second, it is substantially easier to explain supervenience as a conceptual/semantic constraint on moral discourse and moral judgment than to explain it as a putative relation between (i) non-moral properties and facts, and (ii) putatively objective, in-the-world, moral properties and facts. For, there are many mutually incompatible pairings of non-normative sentences and predicates with moral sentences and predicates, each of which fully respects supervenience qua conceptual/semantic constraint. Yet according to moral realism, only one of these pairings captures the *objective facts* about the specific natural/moral supervenience relations in the world.[30] So moral realists, insofar as they are not content to regard these supervenience relations as just *sui generis*, face a very demanding explanatory burden, over and above accounting for supervenience qua conceptual/semantic constraint: viz., they must also explain why certain specific claims about supervenience relations are the objectively *true* ones; thus why other such claims are (despite being compatible with the semantic constraint) objectively false. Or, at any rate, they must argue that such explanations are possible in principle, and must say something about the general form such explanations would take.[31]

So not all manifestations of supervenience need necessarily involve genuine higher-order properties or facts; and in general, explaining supervenience relations where there *are* such facts can be a substantially more demanding task than explaining supervenience as a mere constraint on discourse or judgment. For some kinds of discourse, it might turn out that only the less demanding kind of explanation is possible; for such cases, the proper *metaphysical* account of the discourse is likely to be an irrealist account. So here are two further morals concerning supervenience and metaphysics, in addition to those stated in § 1:

(L3) A metaphysical position, materialistic or otherwise, can combine supervenience as a doctrine about the terms and concepts in a given body of discourse with ontological irrealism about the discourse.

(L4) For some forms of discourse, it might turn out that although a materialistically acceptable explanation can be given for supervenience as a conceptual/semantic constraint on the discourse, no materialistically acceptable explanation can be given for putative in-the-world supervenience relations between lower-order properties and putative higher-order properties seemingly posited by the discourse.

Let us say that supervenience is *ontological* if it is an objective relation between lower-order properties and facts and genuine, objective, higher-order properties and facts.[32] Let us say that supervenience for a given mode of discourse is *robustly* explainable if it is explainable as ontological—i.e., explainable not merely as a conceptual/semantic constraint, but as an objective necessitation relation between lower-order and higher-order properties and facts. The general moral we obtain from lessons (Ll)-(L4), then, is this: any genuinely materialistic metaphysics should countenance inter-level supervenience connections only if they are explainable in a materialistically acceptable way, and should countenance *ontological* inter-level supervenience relations only if they are *robustly* explainable in a materialistically acceptable way.

4. DAVIDSON AND THE MATERIALIST APPROPRIATION OF SUPERVENIENCE

The notion of supervenience made its entrance into discussions of materialism in a seminal paper in the philosophy of mind.[33] Here Davidson articulated and defended his "anomalous monism," a position with these key contentions: (i) every concrete, spatio-temporally located, mental event is identical to a concrete physical event; (ii) mental properties (event-types) are not identical to physical properties, and are not reducible to them via definition or law. The claim that physics is causally complete figured explicitly as a premise in his overall argument for this position; so did the claim that there are no strict psycho-physical laws, for which he gave a well-known subsidiary argument appealing largely to the allegedly holistic nature of propositional-attitude attribution.

The invocation of supervenience entered, briefly, in the context of emphasizing his rejection of psychophysical type-type identity and reducibility, and also by way of saying something positive about relations between physical and mental characteristics. Here is the key passage, frequently quoted:

> Although the position I describe denies there are psychophysical laws, it is consistent with the view that mental characteristics are in some sense dependent, or supervenient, on physical characteristics. Such supervenience might be taken to mean that there cannot be two events exactly alike in all physical respects but differing in some mental respect, or that an object cannot alter in some mental respect without altering in some physical respect. Dependence or supervenience of this kind does not entail reducibility through law or definition....[34]

In another paper Davidson not only claimed that the supervenience of the mental on the physical is consistent with anomalous monism, but he went on to explicitly advocate such a dependence thesis. Concerning the theme of "the relation between psychological descriptions and characterizations of events, and physical (or biological or physiological) descriptions," he said:

> Although, as I am urging, psychological characteristics cannot be reduced to the others, nevertheless they may be (and I think are) strongly dependent on them. Indeed, there is a sense in which the physical characteristics of an event (or object or state) *determine* the psychological characteristics: in G.E. Moore's word, psychological concepts are *supervenient* on physical concepts. Moore's way of explaining this relation (which he maintained held between evaluative and descriptive characteristics) is this: it is impossible for two events (objects, states) to agree in all their physical characteristics (in Moore's case, their descriptive characteristics) and to differ in their psychological characteristics (evaluative).[35]

Although Davidson was mistaken in attributing the *word* "supervenient" to Moore, he was of course correct in attributing to him the concept. (Note too the *modal* characterization of supervenience in both passages, and the similarity to Moore's own formulation I quoted at the outset.)

Davidson's invocation of supervenience in connection with the mind/body problem resonated strongly among philosophers working in philosophy of mind and metaphysics; there commenced a rapid and fairly widespread appropriation of supervenience into these branches of philosophy.[36] Two features of the above-quoted remarks are especially striking, and both evidently contributed to the subsequent popularity of supervenience among materialistically-minded philosophers. First is Davidson's firm and explicit rejection of the *reducibility* of psychological characteristics to physical ones. In embracing a version of materialism that does not assert either the identity or the nomic equivalence of mental properties with physical properties, Davidson was evidently loosening the requirements for inter-level "fit" between different levels of description, in particular the physical and mental levels. Many philosophers were attracted by the thought that a broadly materialistic metaphysics can eschew reductionism, and supervenience seemed to hold out the promise of being a non-reductive inter-level relation that could figure centrally in a non-reductive materialism.

Second (and closely related), the passages implicitly suggest that psychophysical supervenience is an inter-level metaphysical determination-relation that renders mental properties *materialistically respectable*, as it were. The idea is that a reasonable materialism need only claim that physical facts and properties are the ontically *basic* ones, the ones that fix or determine all the facts. And supervenience of higher-order properties and facts on physical facts, it seemed, is just this sort of determination.

In light of the lessons we have drawn in earlier sections, however, it should be clear that mere supervenience of higher-order properties and facts on physical properties and facts cannot be enough to confer materialistic respectability. Moore in particular comes to mind—which is strikingly ironic, since Davidson actually cites Moore when he invokes supervenience. So it is not really surprising that doubts have now begun to emerge about whether supervenience, by itself, can carry as much weight in explicating a plausible materialism as some philosophers initially thought it could. Stephen Schiffer nicely expresses the reasons for scepticism, and the related irony:

Tough-minded physicalist types (including many Logical Positivists) agreed [with Moore] that moral properties could not be reduced to natural properties ... but had no sympathy at all with Moore's positive thesis, which postulated a realm of non-natural properties and facts. These properties, it was felt, could not be made sense of within a scientific world view: they were obscurantist and produced more problems than they solved. At the same time, philosophers who abhorred Moore's irreducibly non-natural properties knew he also held this thesis about them: that it was not possible for two things or events to be alike in all physical respects while differing in some moral property .... No one thought that Moore's positive theory of moral properties was in any way mitigated by this further supervenience thesis. How could being told that non-natural moral properties stood in the supervenience relation to physical properties make them any more palatable? On the contrary, invoking a special primitive metaphysical relation of supervenience to explain how non-natural moral properties were related to physical properties was just to add mystery to mystery, to cover one obscurantist move with another. I therefore find it more than a little ironic, and puzzling, that supervenience is nowadays being heralded as a way of making non-pleonastic, irreducibly nonnatural mental properties cohere with an acceptably naturalistic solution to the mind-body problem.[37]

These remarks reinforce and underscore the negative moral that already emerged in §§ 1-3. The moral is not that supervenience cannot be an important part of a broadly materialistic metaphysics, but rather this: putative supervenience relations that are themselves unexplainable and *sui generis* cannot play such a role. The corresponding positive moral is that the sort of inter-level relation needed by the materialist who is also a realist about a given mode of discourse (e.g., mental discourse) is not bare supervenience, but rather what I hereby dub *superdupervenience*: viz., ontological supervenience that is robustly explainable in a materialistically explainable way.[38] Superdupervenience would indeed constitute a kind of ontic determination which is itself materialistically kosher, and which thereby confers materialistic respectability on higher-order properties and facts.

I will return to superdupervenience in § 8 below, after addressing three issues that have received substantial recent discussion. For the most part, the points I will make about supervenience in §§ 5-7 will apply, mutatis mutandis, to superdupervenience as well.

5. VERSIONS OF SUPERVENIENCE:
WEAK, STRONG, GLOBAL, AND REGIONAL

As philosophers began to turn in the 1970's to the notion of supervenience in attempts to articulate broadly materialist positions in philosophy of mind and metaphysics, there began to emerge a bewildering panoply of alternative ways of articulating supervenience theses themselves.[39]

One parameter that can vary from one supervenience thesis to another is the class of possible worlds that fall within the scope of a given thesis. Some, e.g., Moore's thesis that intrinsic value is supervenient on natural properties, are plausibly construed as involving all possible worlds. Supervenience theses of interest to materialists, however, seem more plausibly construed as involving all *physically* possible worlds. The question of how best to characterize the notion of physical possibility, for this purpose, is somewhat delicate, especially if (i) one holds (as does Lewis,[40] for instance) that actual-world laws often get slightly violated in "nearby" possible worlds relevant to assessing the actual-world truth values of counterfactual conditionals, and (ii) one wants one's supervenience thesis to include those worlds.[41]

Another much-discussed distinction is between what Kim[42] calls "weak" and "strong" supervenience. Let A and B be two sets of properties, where we think of the A properties as supervenient on the B properties. Using the necessity operator "$\Box$" of modal logic, the two kinds of supervenience can be expressed as follows:

Weak Supervenience:
$\Box (\forall x)(\forall F_{\in A})$ {x has F $\to$ ($\exists G_{\in B}$) [x has G & ($\forall y$) (y has G $\to$ y has F)]}
(Necessarily, if anything has property *F* in *A*, there exists a property *G* in *B* such that the thing has *G*, and everything that has *G* has *F*.)

Strong Supervenience:
$\Box (\forall x)(\forall F_{\in A})$ {x has F $\to$ ($\exists G_{\in B}$) [x has G & $\Box$ ($\forall y$) (y has G $\to$ y has F)]}
(Necessarily, if anything has property *F* in *A*, there exists a property *G* in *B* such that the thing has *G*, and necessarily everything that has *G* has *F*.)

Weak supervenience pertains only to things that occupy the same possible world; it says that *within* any world, all things that are *B*-indiscernible are also *A*-indiscernible. Strong supervenience pertains across possible worlds; it says that for any worlds *w* and *w'* and any things *x* and *y* (in *w* and *w'* respectively), if *x* in *w* is *B*-indiscernible from *y* in *w'*, then *x* in *w* is *A*-indiscernible from *y* in *w'*. It is sometimes alleged that ordinary-language formulations of supervenience theses, like those of Moore, Hare, and Davidson I quoted earlier, only express weak supervenience; and it is often urged that strong supervenience better reflects the kind of inter-level dependence relation that supervenience theses are intended to capture.

Why should one think that familiar ordinary-language formulations really only express weak supervenience? Evidently the principal reason is an understandable tendency to try translating those formulations into the formalism of modal logic, and to do so in a manner reflecting their surface grammar. Since the ordinary-language formulations typically only exhibit one occurrence of a modal expression like "can" or "could," not two occurrences, one construes them as merely expressing weak supervenience.

But ordinary language is a subtle thing. If we attend carefully to the way modal expressions operate in discourse about supervenience, we find something happening that is not easily and directly expressible using the sentential modal operators of modal logic: viz., the *transworldly* comparison of individuals. This point is nicely illustrated in certain remarks about supervenience in Hare.[43] Although the passage I quoted initially, where Hare first introduces the notion, does not illustrate this phenomenon by concrete example (since the example involves two pictures situated side by side), the following passages clearly involve transworldly comparisons:

[T]ake ... that characteristic of "good" which has been called its supervenience. Suppose we say "St. Francis was a good man." It is logically impossible to say this and to maintain at the same time that there might have been another man placed in exactly the same circumstances as St.

Francis, and who behaved in exactly the same way, but who differed in this respect only, that he was not a good man.[44]

The actual action couldn't have been right and the hypothetical action not right, unless there had been some *other* difference between the actions, or their circumstances, or their motives, or something else. Actions cannot differ only as regards their rightness, any more than pictures or anything else can differ only as regards their goodness.[45]

Hare is comparing St. Francis as he is in the *actual* world with a hypothetical, non-actual man; and he is comparing an action that is right in the *actual* world with a hypothetical, non-actual, action. So the first sentence of the second passage, for instance, means this:

In no possible world w does the hypothetical action differ from the actual action in this respect only: the actual action in the actual world is right but the hypothetical action in w is not right.

And in context the sentence "Actions cannot differ only as regards their goodness" clearly generalizes this transworldly observation. Thus, even though the sentence only contains one occurrence of the modal word "can," it means this:

In no possible worlds w and w' are there actions x and x' that differ in this respect only: x in w is right but x' in w' is not right.

So it is a mistake to think that ordinary-language formulations of supervenience really only express weak supervenience—a mistake which largely rests on the mistaken assumption that the occurrences of ordinary-language modal words are translatable one-for-one into formal language by occurrences of the sentential necessity or possibility operators of modal logic. David Lewis puts the point nicely:

Supervenience means that there *could* be no difference of one sort without difference of the other sort .... What we want is modality, but not the sentential modal operator .... [T]he real effect of the "could" seems to be to *un*restrict quantifiers which would normally range over this-worldly things. Among all the worlds, or among all the things in all the worlds (or less than all, if there is some restriction), there is no difference of the one sort without differences of the other sort. Whether the things that differ are part of the same world is neither here nor there.[46]

These remarks clearly apply to the two passages lately quoted from Hare. Once this fact is appreciated, it should become apparent that they also apply to the passages I quoted earlier from Hare, Moore, and Davidson.[47] The upshot is that so-called weak supervenience, despite all the attention it has received in the recent literature, is essentially a philosophical red herring. Ordinary-language formulations like those of Moore and Hare really express strong supervenience, not weak supervenience.[48] The charge that these formulations need replacing by stronger ones is mistaken, because the necessitation relation they express is strong supervenience.[49]

Another issue in formulating supervenience theses arises from the fact that traditional formulations are what might be called *co-instantiation* theses: they are worded in a way that requires supervenient properties and subvenient properties to be instantiated by the *same individual.* This requirement creates at least two kinds of concern. For one thing, there seem to be numerous higher-order properties of individuals that depend for their instantiation not merely on the lower-order properties of the individual itself, but also on a wider range of lower-order properties and relations involving various other individuals too. For instance, the property *being a bank*, instantiated by the brick building on Main Street, is not supervenient on (intrinsic) physical properties of the bank itself; rather, the building's having this social-institutional property depends on a considerably broader range of physical facts and features, some of which are involved in subserving the social practice of banking.

In addition, some ontologies (arguably, even some broadly *materialist* ontologies) might posit not only supervenient properties, but also supervenient *individuals.* For instance, some philosophers maintain that a statue is distinct from the hunk of matter that composes it, on the grounds that the two entities have differing modal and counterfactual properties. Some philosophers take seriously the apparent ontological commitments of discourse about universities, corporations, and nations; and also deny that these entities are literally identical to mereological sums of persons, land-masses, etc. Yet supervenience theses as traditionally formulated typically presuppose that a *single* individual instantiates both the subvenient property and the supervenient property.

One suggestion for accommodating these kinds of considerations is to formulate supervenience theses in terms of entire possible worlds. Kim[50] calls this *global* supervenience, a phrase now widely used. Standardly the idea of global *physical* supervenience, for instance, is expressed in some such way as this:

Global Physical Supervenience
There are no two physically possible worlds which are exactly alike in all physical respects but different in some other respect.

As is often pointed out, however,[51] purely global supervenience seems too weak to fully capture the idea that the physical facts determine all the facts.

For, the global thesis does not exclude the possibility that there are two spatio-temporal regions, within either the same physically possible world or two different ones, that are exactly alike in all intrinsic physical respects but different in some intrinsic nonphysical respect—say, different in the respect that mental properties are instantiated by individuals in one region, but not by their physical duplicates in the other.

A natural strategy for accommodating this problem, proposed in Horgan,[52] is to strengthen global supervenience into what I will here dub *regional* supervenience. Several notions need introducing as a prelude. First, we must distinguish between *intrinsic* and *nonintrinsic* features, relative to a spatio-temporal region of a physically possible world. Roughly, a feature is intrinsic to a given region if its presence does not depend, in a broadly logical sense of "depend," upon what happens outside the region; otherwise it is nonintrinsic. Suppose, for instance, that Oscar suddenly wants a glass of water. Oscar's having this property is not an intrinsic feature of the spatio-temporal region directly occupied by Oscar's body during the time-stretch the token desire episode occurs; for, the property's instantiation depends on the fact that the larger spatio-temporal environment in which Oscar acquired the word "water" contains H_2O rather than XYZ.

Second, we must distinguish between *qualitative* and *non-qualitative* intrinsic features of spatio-temporal regions. Roughly, the latter are those which depend, in the broadly logical sense, on the existence of specific individuals within the specific region. Consider, for instance, the fact that Tommy Flanagan is a jazz pianist. Tommy's having this property is an intrinsic feature of the spatio-temporal region r occupied by our solar system within the past millennium. But suppose our universe contains another region r', a region remote from r and causally isolated from it, and yet indiscernible from it. Tommy's being a jazz pianist is *not* an intrinsic feature of r', because Tommy himself is not even an occupant of r'. Rather, r' has a distinct but qualitatively indistinguishable feature—viz., that Tommy's *doppelgänger*, who is qualitatively indistinguishable from Tommy himself, is a jazz pianist.

With these distinctions at hand, the thesis of regional physical supervenience can now be stated as follows, letting a *P-region* be a spatio-temporal region of a physically possible world:

Regional Physical Supervenience
There are no two *P*-regions that are exactly alike in all qualitative intrinsic physical features but different in some other qualitative intrinsic feature.

That is (putting it in the ordinary-language modal idiom), there could not be two spatiotemporal regions that are exactly alike in all qualitative intrinsic physical features but different in some other qualitative intrinsic feature. This is, of course, a thesis of strong supervenience: whether the regions being compared are in the same world or different worlds is neither here nor there. In addition, the thesis of global physical supervenience is just a special case of the regional thesis—the case where the P-regions are entire possible worlds.

Regional physical supervenience also avoids yet another problem about standard coinstantiation formulations, which can be formulated as a dilemma.[53] Consider the following thesis:

Physical Co-instantiation Supervenience
Necessarily, for any higher-order property F, if anything has F then there exists a physical property G such that the thing has G, and necessarily, everything with G has F.

(Here the term "necessarily" is to be understood as a sentential modal operator ranging over all physically possible worlds.) The dilemma is this: do we, or don't we, interpret this thesis as saying that property G is an *intrinsic* physical property of the object instantiating F? Suppose we do. Then the thesis is too strong to be credible, because certain higher-order properties of individuals (e.g., wide-content mental properties like *wanting a drink of water*) do not supervene on the individual's intrinsic physical properties. Suppose we don't. Then, without some restriction on what may count as a non-intrinsic physical property, the thesis turns out to be no stronger than mere *global* physical supervenience. This is because we could always let G be some physical property which, by its very construction, is guaranteed to have these features: (i) in some physically possible world, G and F are simultaneously coinstantiated by some single individual; (ii) for any world w, G is instantiated in w no more than once; and (iii) G is instantiated only in physically possible worlds with a particular total physical history h.[54] Assuming the truth of global physical supervenience (which says that physically possible worlds with the same total physical history are exactly alike, and hence are identical), a property G of this kind would be a *degenerate* supervenience base for property F, because G would never be instantiated in any physically possible world except for a single co-instantiation, in a single world, with F. Thus, if such a non-intrinsic physical property G can count as a supervenience base for F, then the thesis of physical co-instantiation supervenience does not rule out any putative possibilities that are not already ruled out by mere global supervenience. So the upshot of the dilemma is that the thesis is either too strong to be credible or too weak to express adequately the idea that the physical facts determine all the facts.

Regional physical supervenience avoids both horns of this dilemma. It meets the other goals that motivate turning away from standard co-instantiation formulations of supervenience, viz., allowing for higher-order properties with a "wide" supervenience base, and allowing for supervenient individuals.

And it overcomes the excessive weakness of mere global physical supervenience. So it has much to recommend it, as a general articulation of the idea that there could be no difference of a non-physical sort without difference of the physical sort.[55]

6. MENTAL QUAUSATION AND THE CAUSAL COMPLETENESS OF PHYSICS

The philosophical issue I call the problem of mental quausation[56] came into recent prominence in philosophy of mind in the wake of Davidson's non-reductive brand of materialism.[57] Since Davidson's anomalous monism asserts that every token mental event is identical to a token physical event, his view obviously allows token mental events to be part of the causal nexus. However, the question arises whether a token event's being *mental*, or its tokening the specific event *type* it does, can play any genuine role in causation or causal explanation, given Davidson's contention that mental properties are not reducible to physical properties. Although token mental events themselves are causally efficacious, are they efficacious qua mental? If not, then it seems we are left with a version of epiphenomenalism, a version hardly less objectionable than versions which deny that mental events are causes at all. The issue of mental quausation arises not only for Davidson's anomalism, but also for any metaphysical position that denies that mental properties are type-identical to physical properties. The question is whether mental properties are causally/explanatorily efficacious, and (if they are) what such efficacy might consist in.[58]

As I pointed out in § 1 (this being one lesson of British emergentism), any broadly materialistic metaphysical position needs to claim that physics is causally complete. This means that non-physical properties cannot be causally basic properties—ones that generate fundamental forces that combine with physical forces to yield net forces different from the net resultants of physical forces. So for a materialist who repudiates psycho-physical property identities, and yet also seeks to vindicate the causal/explanatory efficacy of mental properties, the burden is to develop some kind of *compatibilist* account of mental quausation. On such an account there must be multiple levels of genuine causal/explanatory efficacy; these levels must not be directly in competition, and thus the higher levels must not be "screened off" or "excluded" by more basic levels.

This is a large and active research area in current philosophy, and is intertwined in various ways with issues involving supervenience. For instance, Kim[59] has suggested that higher-order causal explanations involving non-physical properties can co-exist with physical explanations only if they cite higher-order properties that are supervenient on physical properties that figure directly in underlying physical explanations of the same phenomena. And a number of philosophers have claimed recently that mental properties, in order to be causal/explanatory, must at least be supervenient on physical properties that are *intrinsic* to the cognizer—must supervene, as the slogan goes, "on what's in the head."[60]

Neither of these suggestions is anything like self-evident, however, and I think both deserve to be regarded with suspicion. Consider first Kim's conception of "supervenient causation" (as he calls it). As I understand him, Kim maintains that a higher-order property F, in order to be causally/explanatorily efficacious (when instantiated by an individual i at a time t), must be supervenient on a specific physical property G which (1) *physically realizes F* (in i, at t), and (2) figures centrally in a physical causal explanation of the phenomenon that F itself purportedly explains. This demand may well be excessive, however. Here is a substantially weaker inter-level requirement, which still features supervenience prominently:

> A higher-order property F, in order to be causally/explanatorily efficacious, must be physically realized by a physical property G that (i) figures centrally in a physical causal explanation of the phenomenon that F itself purportedly explains, and (ii) is *part* of a (perhaps conjunctive) total physical property H which is itself a supervenience base for F.[61]

Prima facie, there are causally efficacious higher-order properties that meet this weaker condition but do not meet Kim's condition. Take, for example, the *syntactic* properties of those token physical states in a computer which are token symbol strings. These syntactic properties arguably have causal/explanatory efficacy: the state-transitions in the machine are systematically sensitive to syntactic properties, qua syntactic. But although syntactic properties are realized by certain patterns of electrical current, this is only by virtue of the role of those patterns in the whole physical system. Thus the supervenience base for a syntactic property is wider than the property's physical realization.

Consider next the contention that causally efficacious mental properties must be supervenient on what's in the head. This too is far from self-evident, especially since garden-variety mentalistic causal explanations frequently cite wide-content mental properties. Although it seems true enough that *physical* properties of a cognizer must supervene on what's in the cognizer's head in order to figure in causal explanations of behaviour, maybe this requirement does not transmit upward to the mental level. Notice that the necessary condition I proposed above, for higher-order causal/explanatory efficacy, can be satisfied by wide-content mental properties that do not supervene on a cognizer's intrinsic physical properties. And under at least *some* general accounts of higher-order causal/explanatory efficacy,[62] wide-content properties fare just fine despite not supervening on what's in the head.

So the general point I would like to urge, with respect to the matter of supervenience and mental quausation, is cautionary. Philosophers who claim that causally efficacious mental properties must supervene directly on the physical properties that realize them, or must anyway supervene on physical properties intrinsic to the cognizer, owe us powerful arguments for these contentions; for, under close scrutiny such claims are less credible than they might initially appear to be. Materialists who back away from type-type psychophysical identity claims, but who also seek to vindicate the causal/explanatory efficacy of mental properties, are already committed to some form of compatibilism on the issue of mental quausation. Since they are stuck with this compatibilist commitment anyway, they should take seriously the possibility that the right kind of compatibilism will vindicate the causal/explanatory efficacy of mental properties that do not supervene on the properties that physically realize them, and perhaps will also vindicate the causal/explanatory efficacy of mental properties that do not even supervene on what's in the head.

7. SUPERVENIENCE AND INTER-LEVEL REDUCTION

I remarked in § 4 that one reason why the notion of supervenience caught on, in attempts to formulate a broadly materialistic position in philosophy of mind and metaphysics, was the feeling among many philosophers that traditional formulations of materialism posited an unduly tight, reductive, connection between the facts and properties posited by physics and higher-order facts and properties. The thought was that inter-level supervenience connections can be looser, and thus that supervenience-based materialism could be a *non-reductive* materialism.

But even among those who have embraced supervenience in connection with materialist metaphysics, there has been an ongoing debate about whether a viable materialism can really be non-reductive. The most ardent defender of the negative position is the philosopher who has perhaps been most active and influential in exploring and advocating supervenience in metaphysics and philosophy of mind, Jaegwon Kim.

To begin with, it should be noted that the words "reduction" and "reductive" are subject to a range of uses, some more stringent than others. Under fairly liberal (but not necessarily inappropriate) standards of usage, a metaphysical position will count as reductive merely by virtue of asserting (i) the causal completeness of physics, and (ii) the thesis of regional physical supervenience. The debate just mentioned, however, involves a more stringent notion of reduction, a notion linked closely to certain paradigmatic inter-theoretic relations in science, like the relation between classical thermodynamics and molecular statistical mechanics. Parties on one side of this debate, who typically call themselves "non-reductive materialists," hold that a viable non-eliminative materialistic position need not assert that the special sciences generally, and mentalistic psychology in particular, are reducible to physics in the manner in which thermodynamics is reducible to molecular statistical mechanics.[63] Their opponents[64] deny this; they maintain that non-reductive materialism is not a viable metaphysical position, and thus that the serious contenders are reductive materialism and eliminative materialism.

This debate is quite complex, involving a variety of issues that are intertwined in various complicated ways.[65] One broad strand concerns the prerequisites for genuine inter-theoretic reduction itself. Must a genuine reduction involve outright *identities* between higher-order and lower-order theoretical properties (for instance, temperature and mean molecular kinetic energy), or is it enough for reductively related properties to be merely nomically equivalent? Can the reducing properties be disjunctive, even radically or infinitely disjunctive?

Another strand is the matter of quausation. Presumably any adequate account of inter-theoretic reduction must constrain inter-level relations strongly enough to vindicate the causal/explanatory efficacy of higher-order theoretical properties. But there are a variety of philosophical views about the requirements for quausation; and this complex issue thus becomes intertwined with discussions of reduction. For instance, if one is an incompatibilist about quausation, and one also accepts the causal completeness of physics, then one will hold that higher order theoretical properties can have causal/explanatory efficacy only if they are *identical* to certain physical properties; this will be a reason for claiming that genuine inter-theoretic reduction involves inter-level property-identities, rather than mere nomic coextensions.

Let me turn briefly to Kim's position, as I understand it. Kim rejects the contention that mental properties in particular, and special-science properties in general, are identical to physical properties; he maintains instead that in general, higher-order theoretical properties are supervenient on lower-level properties, and ultimately on physical properties. He affirms the causal/explanatory efficacy of mental properties, and of special-science properties in general; as already noted in § 6, he maintains that supervenience transmits causal/explanatory efficacy from physical properties to higher-order properties that supervene on them. (As we saw, this is a version of compatibilism about quausation, albeit a rather restrictive version.) As regards inter-theoretic reduction, he denies that genuine reductions must involve inter-level property-identities. He maintains instead that full-fledged reductions can be effected by inter-theoretic "bridge laws" expressing the nomic equivalence of lower-level and higher-level properties, provided that the laws of the higher-level theory are derivable from those of the lower-level theory plus the bridge laws. Finally, and with these other views as backdrop, he contends that a viable non-eliminativist position in philosophy of mind will inevitably end up committed to the reducibility of mentalistic psychology to natural science, and ultimately to physics.

Although I cannot here canvass the various arguments that Kim and others have employed in support of this contention, let me focus on one key argument. Concerning strong supervenience (as characterized in § 5 above) he writes:

> [I]t says that whenever a supervening property P is instantiated by an object, there is a subvenient property Q such that the instantiating object has it and the following conditional holds: necessarily if anything has Q, then it has P. So the picture we have is that for supervenient property P, there is a set of properties, Q_1, Q_2, ... in the subvenient set such that each Q_i is necessarily sufficient for P. Assume this list contains all the subvenient properties each of which is sufficient for P. Consider their disjunction .... This disjunction ... is necessarily coextensive with P .... So P and UQ_i are necessarily coextensive, and whether the modality here is metaphysical, logical, or nomological, it should be strong enough to give us a serviceable "bridge law" for reduction .... Some philosophers will resist this inference .... There are two questions, and only two as far as I can see, that can be raised here: (1) Is disjunction a proper way of forming properties out of properties? (2) Given that disjunction is a permissible property-forming operation, is it proper to form infinite disjunctions?[66]

He then takes up arguments that have been given supporting negative answers to questions (1) and (2), and explains why he does not find them compelling.

Let me enter the dialectic at this point, by posing a third question: Are radically disjunctive properties *causal/explanatory* properties? Arguably, in general they are not; rather, on any given occasion when a higher-order theoretical property P is instantiated, the underlying physical causal/explanatory property that is operative (on that occasion) will be whichever specific *disjunct* Q_i from the disjunctive property UQ_i, is instantiated (on that occasion)—and not the property UQ_i itself. Furthermore, a very plausible-looking condition on genuine reduction is that each higher-order causal/explanatory property be nomically coextensive not just with any old lower-order property, but with some lower-order *causal/explanatory* property. For, if this condition is not met, then the higher-order causal/explanatory properties will cross-classify the lower-order ones, and thus will figure in higher-order causal/explanatory generalizations that are not directly mirrored at the lower theoretical level. In paradigmatic inter-theoretic reductions, by contrast, higher-order theoretical properties are not multiply realizable in this way; rather, higher-order theoretical laws *are* directly mirrored by lower-level causal/explanatory generalizations. (The Boyle/Charles law of thermodynamics, which links a gas's temperature, pressure, and volume, is directly mirrored by the law of molecular statistical mechanics linking a gas's mean molecular kinetic energy, mean surface pressure, and volume). Arguably, this kind of inter-level mirroring is the very essence of genuine inter-theoretic reduction.

Considerations involving multiple realization, along the lines just sketched, are among the reasons why many materialistically-minded philosophers, myself included, deny that reductive materialism is the only viable alternative to eliminativism. But the reductionists remain unconvinced by multiple-realization arguments,[67] and meanwhile maintain an active dialectical siege against non-reductive materialism.

8. SUPERDUPERVENIENCE

Our conclusion at the end of § 4 was that the sort of inter-level relation that would confer materialistic "respectability" on higher-order properties and facts would be not bare ontological supervenience, but superdupervenience—ontological supervenience that is robustly explainable in a materialistically acceptable way. (Recall that *ontological* supervenience is an objective relation between lower-order properties and facts, and genuine, objective, higher-order properties and facts; it is not merely a conceptual/semantic constraint on higher-order discourse. And, to give a robust explanation of supervenience is to explain it qua ontological, rather than explaining it merely as a feature of the "logic" of the higher-order terms and concepts.) Hereafter, unless I indicate otherwise, when I speak of explaining supervenience I will mean robustly explaining ontological supervenience in a materialistically acceptable way.

Although the task of explaining supervenience has been little appreciated and little discussed in the philosophical literature, it is time for that to change. I will conclude this essay with some brief remarks on the matter, set forth in a fairly staccato fashion.

First, in considering how inter-level supervenience relations might be materialistically explained, three interrelated questions arise:

The Standpoint Question: What sorts of facts, over and above physical facts and physical laws, could combine with physical facts and laws to yield materialistically kosher explanations of inter-level supervenience relations, and why would it be kosher to cite such facts in these explanations?

The Target Question: What facts specifically need explaining in order to explain a given inter-level supervenience relation, and why would a materialistic explanation of *these* facts constitute an explanation of that supervenience relation?

The Resource Question: Do there exist adequate explanatory resources to provide such explanations?

In order to get explanation off the ground, it seems we need to know *something* about the higher-order properties whose supervenience on physical properties is the target of explanation. The standpoint question and the target question, which are largely complementary, both arise from this apparent need for information about higher-order properties. The standpoint question[68] arises because apparently we need *some* facts other than those of basic physics. It is hard to see how one could possibly explain an inter-level necessitation relation without employing, as part of one's explanans, *some* sorts of "connecting statements" in which purely physical properties and facts somehow get linked to higher-order properties. But which such facts are kosher, and why? The target question involves the explanandum: the to-be-explained facts. We need to know which facts are such that explaining *these* facts materialistically would constitute explaining why the higher-order properties supervene on the physical the way they do, and we need to know *why* these facts are the crucial ones. Philosophers need to get clearer about the standpoint and target questions. And they also need to ask, for any given domain of putative higher-order properties, whether there really exist adequate explanatory resources to yield materialistically kosher explanations of specific inter-level supervenience relations involving these properties; this is the resource question.

Second, the problem of explaining supervenience does not go away if the generalizations of a higher-level theory or explanatory framework happen to be derivable from physics plus some set of "bridge laws" expressing the nomic coextensiveness of higher-order properties with physical properties. For, there remains the need to explain why these bridge laws *themselves* are true in all physically possible worlds.[69] Bridge laws, after all, are not part of physics; they should not be scientifically and metaphysically rock-bottom, *sui generis* and unexplainable. Furthermore, even if the inter-theoretic bridge laws really express property identities (rather than the mere nomic coextensiveness of higher-order properties and physical ones), an analogous explanatory task arises anyway—although now the key questions are about inter-level linkages between terms and/or concepts. In virtue of what does such-and-such physical property, rather than various other candidate physical properties, count as the property expressed by a given higher-order theoretical predicate?

Third, for at least *some* kinds of properties we seem to have a fairly good idea about what would count as a materialistically acceptable explanation of why such a property is supervenient on a given configuration of physical properties. Consider, for instance, the property *liquidity*. We understand well enough the essential features, or defining conditions, of liquidity: if a quantity of stuff is liquid, then it will neither spontaneously dissipate into the atmosphere nor retain a rigid shape when unconstrained, but instead will tend to flow, and to assume the shape of a vessel that contains it. Thus, explaining why liquidity supervenes on certain microphysical properties is essentially a matter of explaining why any quantity of stuff with these microphysical properties will exhibit those macro-features. (As regards the target question, this suffices to explain the supervenience of liquidity because those macro-features are *definitive* of liquidity. As regards the standpoint problem, it seems explanatorily kosher to assume a "connecting principle" linking the macro-features to liquidity, precisely because those features *are* definitive; the connecting principle expresses a fact about what liquidity *is*.)

Fourth, a variety of recent so-called "naturalizing" projects, in philosophy of mind and elsewhere in philosophy, can be regarded as being, in effect, attempts to articulate the essential or definitive characteristics of certain higher-order properties (e.g., mental properties) in such a way that these properties, as so characterized, are susceptible to materialistic explanations of their supervenience. Functionalism in the philosophy of mind provides an example: if mental properties were identical with certain functional properties whose definitive causal roles involve typical-cause relations to sensory stimulation, bodily motion, and one another, then specific physical/mental supervenience relations presumably would be materialistically explainable in terms of causal/dispositional roles of categorial physical properties. Co-variance accounts of intentional content[70] provide another example: if the instantiating of a given intentional property, with content "that p," were essentially a matter of instantiating some physical property whose occurrence systematically co-varies with the circumstance that p, then the supervenience of the content-property could be explained by citing the fact that the realizing physical property P covaries with the circumstance that p.

Naturalizing projects are thus *reductive* in a certain sense, even though they are not committed to the kinds of type-type inter-level connections that make for inter-theoretic reduction in science. Their goal is to give a tractable specification in non-intentional and non-mental vocabulary (although not necessarily in the vocabulary of physics), of sufficient conditions (or sufficient and necessary conditions) for the instantiation of mental properties. To the extent that this could be done, it would pave the way for physicalistic explanations of supervenience connections.

But fifth, there are a variety of reasons for being sceptical about such naturalizing projects. For one thing, reductive accounts of this kind usually end up susceptible to counterexamples of one sort or another; inductive evidence, based on past failures both in this arena and in other philosophical arenas where attempts at reductive analyses have been pursued, suggests that there always will be counterexamples to such proposals. In addition, it seems likely that human concepts of mental states, and indeed most human concepts, just do not have reductive sufficient conditions at all (or reductive sufficient and necessary conditions), not even vague ones; this general claim about the structure of human concepts is strongly suggested by work in cognitive science on concepts and categories.[71]

So sixth, it makes sense to rethink what might count as philosophical "naturalization" of higher-order properties. Maybe there are ways of construing higher-order properties which (i) do not provide reductive sufficient conditions, but nevertheless (ii) render the physical supervenience of these properties materialistically explainable anyway. If so, then such accounts would still make room for the higher-order properties as part of the physical world, and thereby would naturalize them. (Rethinking naturalization would go hand in hand with investigating the standpoint, target, and resource questions mentioned above.)

But seventh, we should be sensitive to the possibility that for many kinds of higher-order discourse, it will not be possible to give an account of putative higher-order properties under which their ontological supervenience on the physical could be successfully explained. Consider mental properties, for example. With respect to the target problem, a fairly plausible-looking contention is that for any creature that instantiates mental properties, the generalizations of common-sense intentional psychology must be by-and-large true of that creature. With respect to the standpoint problem, it seems fairly plausible that the constraint just mentioned reflects the very *nature* of mental properties, and thus can be legitimately cited in explaining psychophysical supervenience relations. But now the resource problem arises: since there evidently will always be vastly many incompatible ways of assigning propositional attitudes to someone over the course of his lifetime, all of which satisfy the given constraint, it appears that the constraint does not suffice to yield *determinate* supervenience connections between physical properties and facts and mental ones.[72,73]

Eighth, we should keep well in mind the reasons for metaphysical scepticism about in-the-world *normative* facts, a kind of scepticism which after all has been very prominent in meta-ethics throughout this century. One important reason is the difficulty of seeing how one could possibly give materialistic or naturalistic explanations for putative ontological supervenience-relations between natural properties and facts and putative normative properties and facts. Objective moral values do not appear to be part of the natural order.

But ninth, certain important supervenience relations, including but not limited to those that figure in ethics, evidently involve normativity—and thus an is-ought gap. In particular, there is arguably a normative element involved in intentional content—both the content of public-language expressions and the content of intentional mental properties. The "Kripkenstein problem,"[74] for instance, can be seen as a sceptical challenge about whether there are any objective facts or properties, there in the world, that could ground semantic *correctness* (like the putative correctness of answering "125" to the query "68 + 57"). And a parallel problem can be raised about the objective groundability of the correct/incorrect distinction for the putative intentional content of people's mental states. The task of explaining supervenience facts, including perhaps psychological supervenience facts, therefore apparently includes the task of explaining how certain objective, in-the-world, is-ought gaps get bridged. Metaphysical scepticism about in-the-world normative facts now threatens to spill over into philosophy of mind and philosophy of language (not to mention epistemology, since *epistemic warrant* is a normative concept too.)

Tenth, given the apparent difficulty of materialistically explaining ontological supervenience connections in a way that simultaneously handles the target, stand-point, and resource problems, and given that the challenge becomes all the greater insofar as normativity is involved, materialistically-minded philosophers should be exploring *irrealist* ways of accommodating higher-order discourse. They should keep in mind that one can be an irrealist about a given body of discourse (e.g., moral discourse, or mental discourse) without being an eliminativist—someone who regards the discourse as defective, and needing replacement or elimination. Another broad option is preservative irrealism, which would treat higher-order discourse as quite legitimate and perhaps indispensable, while also repudiating its apparent ontological commitments. Instrumentalism, of course, is one form of *preservative* irrealism; instrumentalist views typically attribute utility to the given body of discourse, but deny that it expresses genuine truths. But the intellectual landscape includes other possible versions of preservative irrealism too— for instance, versions that treat truth itself as a normative notion, and which allow for higher-order discourse to be genuinely true even in the absence of any corresponding properties or facts.[75]

Superdupervenience would render higher-order properties metaphysically respectable. But it is not a relation that comes cheap. Explaining ontological supervenience relations in a materialistically acceptable way looks to be a very daunting task, whose difficulty suggests the need for materialists to consider seriously the prospects for preservative irrealism about much of our higher-order discourse. It is not easy formulating a metaphysical position that meets the demands of a material world; there is still a lot of philosophical work to do.[76]

Notes

1 R.M. Hare, *The Language of Morals* (Oxford: Clarendon Press, 1952), 80-81.

2 R.M. Hare, "Supervenience," *The Aristotelian Society* Supplementary Volume 58 (1984), 1.

3 G.E. Moore, "The Conception of Intrinsic Value," in *Philosophical Studies* (New York: Harcourt, Brace, and Co., 1922), 253-75.

4 Ibid., 261.

5 David Lewis, *On the Plurality of Worlds* (Oxford: Basil Blackwell, 1986), 15.

6 For example, Jaegwon Kim, "Supervenience as a Philosophical Concept,"

Metaphilosophy 21 (1990), 1-27; *Supervenience and Mind* (Cambridge: Cambridge University Press, 1993), ch. 9.

7   Several other papers that usefully overview recent issues and discussions are Paul Teller, "A Poor Man's Guide to Supervenience and Determination," in Terence Horgan, ed., *The Concept of Supervenience in Contemporary Philosophy*, Spindel Conference Supplement, *Southern Journal of Philosophy* 22 (1984), 137-62; Jaegwon Kim, "Supervenience as a Philosophical Concept," op. cit.; and Ansgar Beckermann, "Reductive and Nonreductive Physicalism," in Beckermann et al., eds., *Emergence or Reduction? Essays on the Prospects of Nonreductive Physicalism* (Berlin: Walter de Gruyter, 1992), 1-21, "Supervenience, Emergence, and Reduction," in Beckermann et al., op. cit., 94-118.

8   It is also a philosophical question what constitutes a broadly *naturalistic* worldview, and how (if at all) metaphysical naturalism might differ from materialism.

9   I will occasionally employ talk of possible worlds, in connection with modal locutions used to express supervenience theses. The remarks just made about properties and facts apply, mutatis mutandis, to possible worlds too.

10   Brian McLaughlin, "The Rise and Fall of British Emergentism," in Beckermann et al., op. cit., 49-93.

11   John Stuart Mill, *System of Logic* (London: Longmans, Green, Reader & Dyer, 1872).

12   Alexander Bain, *Logic*, Books I and II (London: Longmans, Green, Reader & Dyer, 1870).

13   Henry Lewes, *Problems of Life and Mind*, Volume 2 (London: Kegan Paul, Trench, Turbner, & Co., 1875).

14   Samuel Alexander, *Space, Time, and Deity* (London: Macmillan, 1920).

15   Lloyd Morgan, *Emergent Evolution* (London: Williams & Norgate, 1923).

16   C.D. Broad, *The Mind and Its Place In Nature* (London: Routledge & Kegan Paul, 1925).

17   Does this mean that the laws of physics are abrogated when emergent properties are instantiated? According to the emergentists, no. For, the laws of physics do not actually assert that physical forces are always the *only* operative forces in a physical system. So the laws of physics remain true when an emergent property is instantiated: the usual physical forces are present, and these physical forces are still additive in the usual way. It's just that the physical forces are not the only forces present, and hence the total net force in the system is not identical to the net *physical* force.

18   When Broad wrote, "Nothing that we know about Oxygen by itself or in its combinations with anything but Hydrogen would give us the least reason to suppose that it would combine with Hydrogen at all. Nothing that we know about Hydrogen by itself or in its combinations with anything but Oxygen would give us the least reason to expect that it would combine with Oxygen at all" (*The Mind and its Place in Nature*, op. cit., 62-63), his claim was true. Classical physics could not explain chemical bonding. But the claim didn't stay true for long: by

the end of the decade quantum mechanics had come into being, and quantum-mechanical explanations of chemical bonding were in sight. Within another two decades, James Watson and Francis Crick, drawing upon the work of Linus Pauling and others on chemical bonding, explained the information-coding and self-replicating properties of the DNA molecule, thereby ushering in physical explanations of biological phenomena in general. (These kinds of advances in science itself, rather than any internal conceptual difficulties, were what led to the downfall of British emergentism—as McLaughlin ["The Rise and Fall of British Emergentism," op. cit.] persuasively argues.)

19   Morgan, op.cit., 15-16.

20   Kim ("Supervenience as a Philosophical Concept," op. cit., 4) goes so far as to say, "Lloyd Morgan, a central theoretician of the emergence school, appears to have used 'supervenient' as an occasional stylistic variant of 'emergent', although the latter remained the official term associated with the philosophical position, and the concept he intended with these terms seems surprisingly close to the supervenience concept current today."

21   Broad, op. cit., 67-68.

22   Arthur Lovejoy ("The Meanings of 'Emergence' and Its Modes," in Edgar Sheffield Brightman, ed., *Proceedings of the Sixth International Congress of Philosophy, Harvard University 13-17 September 1926* [New York; also in Krause Reprint, Nendeln, Liechenstein, 1968], 25-26) distinguished two kinds of emergentism:

> [W]e must first of all distinguish between indeterminist and determinist theories. The former declare that there are instances of emergence which are reducible to no causal law; no fixed occasions can be formulated upon which they invariably occur. The hypothesis of "undetermined evolution" to which Professor Dreisch has referred is, I take it, a theory of this sort.... The determinist kind of theory declares that whenever certain specific occasions appear a specific variety of emergent uniformly arises.

Determinist emergentism, I take it, in effect says that emergent properties are supervenient on lower-level properties; indeterminist emergentism in effect denies this. I have been suggesting that Broad and the other British emergentists are best interpreted as advocating determinist emergentism. Beckermann ("Supervenience, Emergence, and Reduction," op. cit.) interprets Broad this way too.

23   Cf. also Terence Horgan and Mark Timmons, "Troubles on Moral Twin Earth: Moral Queerness Revived," *Synthese* 92 (1992), 223-60.

24   G.E. Moore, *Principia Ethica* (Cambridge: Cambridge University Press, 1903).

25   J.L. Mackie, *Ethics, Inventing Right and Wrong* (New York: Penguin Books, 1977), 37-40.

26   Ibid., 44.

27   This passage from Mackie is sometimes interpreted (e.g., in David Brink, "Moral Realism and Skeptical Arguments from Disagreement and Queerness," *Australasian Journal of Philosophy* 62 [1984], 111-25) as presupposing ethical

"internalism," the view that if there were objective, non-natural, moral properties or facts, then they would have to be intrinsically motivating or reason-providing. But it seems to me that in context, the phrases "to-be-pursuedness" and "to-be-doneness" are more plausibly construed as adverting to a *demand* that is supposed to be somehow built into moral properties and facts, rather than to some kind of desirability or reason-generation. On this interpretation, Mackie is not assuming internalism. (It is possible to judge that I am confronted by a demand without thereby having either a motive or a reason to do what is demanded of me, even if I do not consider the demand illegitimate.) So on this interpretation, Mackie's objection applies to Moore even if, as is often claimed, Moore himself was not an internalist.

28 Cf. Horgan and Timmons, "Troubles on Moral Twin Earth: Moral Queerness Revived," op. cit.

29 Hare, *The Language of Morals*, op. cit., 14.

30 This is not to deny that what is good, right, etc., often depends upon certain specific non-moral situational facts concerning a given person or social group. Such facts, though, would figure among the subvenient facts upon which goodness, rightness, etc., supervene.

31 For an argument that this burden cannot be satisfactorily discharged, see Horgan and Timmons, "Troubles on Moral Twin Earth: Moral Queerness Revived," op. cit.

32 Cf. James Klagge, "Supervenience: Ontological and Ascriptive," *Australasian Journal of Philosophy* 66 (1988), 461-70.

33 Donald Davidson, "Mental Events," in L. Foster and J. Swanson, eds., *Experience and Theory* (Amherst: University of Massachusetts Press, 1970), essay 5 in this volume, 90-91.

34 Ibid., 88, this volume, 90-91.

35 Donald Davidson, "The Material Mind," in P. Suppes et al., eds., *Logic, Methodology, and the Philosophy of Science* (Amsterdam: North Holland, 1973), 716-17.

36 E.g., G. Hellman and F. Thompson, "Physicalism: Ontology, Determination, and Reduction," *Journal of Philosophy* 72 (1975), 551-64, "Physicalist Materialism," *Nous* 11 (1977), 309-45; John Haugeland, "Weak Supervenience," *American Philosophical Quarterly* 19 (1982), 93-101; Terence Horgan, "Token Physicalism, Supervenience, and the Generality of Physics," *Synthese* 49 (1981), 395-413; "Supervenience and Microphysics," *Pacific Philosophical Quarterly* 63 (1982), 29-43; Jaegwon Kim, "Supervenience and Nomological Incommensurables," *American Philosophical Quarterly* 15 (1978), 149-56; "Causality, Identity, and Supervenience in the Mind-Body Problem," in H. Wettstein et al., eds., *Midwest Studies in Philosophy* 4 (Minneapolis: University of Minnesota Press, 1979), 31-49; David Lewis, "New Work for a Theory of Universals," *Australasian Journal of Philosophy* 61 (1983), 343-77; and the papers collected in Horgan, *The Concept of Supervenience in Contemporary Philosophy*, op. cit. Although much of this subsequent literature was influenced, directly or indirectly, by Davidson on supervenience, this

may not be so for Hellman and Thompson, op. cit., who used the word "determination" rather than "supervenience."

37   Stephen Schiffer, *Remnants of Meaning* (Cambridge, MA: MIT Press, 1987), 153-54.

38   Although the definition is mine, the word is borrowed, with kind permission, from Bill Lycan, "Moral Facts and Moral Knowledge," in N. Gillespie, ed., *Moral Realism*, Spindel Conference Supplement, *Southern Journal of Philosophy* 24 (1986), 92. I thank him for it.

39   Cf. Teller, op. cit..

40   David Lewis, "Counterfactual Dependence and Time's Arrow," *Nous* 13 (1979), 455-76.

41   Cf. Horgan, "Supervenience and Microphysics," *Pacific Philosophical Quarterly* 63 (1982); 29-43, "Supervenience and Cosmic Hermeneutics," in Horgan, op. cit., 19-38; "Supervenient Qualia," *Philosophical Review* 96 (1987), 491-520; David Lewis, "New Work for a Theory of Universals," *Australasian Journal of Philosophy* 61 (1983), 343-77.

42   Jaegwon Kim, "Concepts of Supervenience," *Philosophy and Phenomenological Research* 45 (1984), 153-76, essay 22 in this volume.

43   Hare, *The Language of Morals*, op. cit.

44   Ibid., 145.

45   Ibid., 153.

46   David Lewis, *On the Plurality of Worlds*, op. cit., 15-17.

47   Although Davidson uses modal language (and talk of properties) in the passages quoted above, in more recent writings he sometimes resorts instead to starker, metalinguistic, formulations which are presumably motivated—at least in part—by philosophical scruples about modality (and about properties). Here is an example:

> The notion of supervenience, as I have used it, is best thought of as a relation between a predicate and a set of predicates in a language: a predicate *p* is supervenient on a set of predicates *s* if for every pair of objects such that *p* is true of one and not the other there is a predicate of *s* that is true of one and not of the other. (Davidson, "Replies to Essays X-XII," in B. Vermazen and M. Hintikka, eds., *Essays on Davidson: Actions and Events* [Oxford: Clarendon Press, 1985], 242.)

How close does this seemingly non-modal formulation come to his formulations I quoted earlier? That depends. If we interpret it as quantifying only over *actual* objects, then it turns out to be vastly weaker than even so-called "weak" supervenience; it says nothing at all about any non-actual possibilities. However, if we interpret the universal quantifier as quantifying over pairs of objects both actual and merely possible (i.e., quantifying pairwise over objects in all possible worlds, it being neither here nor there whether the two objects in a given pair are in the *same* world), then the new formulation expresses strong supervenience (for predicates). I think the passage is best interpreted the second way, since the first interpretation yields such a pale ghost of the pre-theoretic notion of supervenience.

48 Simon Blackburn ("Moral Realism," in J. Casey, ed., *Morality and Moral Reasoning* [London: Methuen, 1971], 101-24; *Spreading the Word* [Oxford: Oxford University Press, 1984]; "Supervenience Revisited," in I. Hacking, ed., *Exercises in Analysis: Essays by Students of Casimir Lewy* [Cambridge: Cambridge University Press, 1985], 47-67) has given an argument against moral realism that goes roughly as follows. A certain supervenience claim, connecting the moral realm to the natural, is true; another stronger claim is false; the moral realist cannot explain why the weaker connection should hold, given that the stronger one does not, whereas the irrealist can easily explain this; so realism accrues an explanatory debt it cannot discharge. Blackburn's argument is sometimes construed as involving weak and strong supervenience, in Kim's sense. But James Dreier ("The Supervenience Argument Against Moral Realism," *Southern Journal of Philosophy* 30 [1992], 13-38) argues persuasively that the argument is better reconstructed as citing two kinds of strong supervenience, involving metaphysical necessity and analytic necessity respectively. (Dreier also replies to Blackburn's argument on the moral realist's behalf—quite persuasively in my view, even though I myself, like Blackburn, am no friend of moral realism.)

49 The issue gets further complicated, unfortunately, by Professor Hare's recent remark that "what I have always had in mind is not what Kim now calls 'strong' supervenience. It is nearer to his 'weak' supervenience." (Hare, "Supervenience," op. cit., 4). Consider however the *reason* Hare gives for this claim. Concerning the judgement "This is a nice room," he says, "I did not have to like that kind of room or call it nice .... My tastes might have been different" (Ibid., 5). But the fact that one's tastes might have been different is quite compatible with the strong-supervenience use of the modal statement "No room exactly like this one could fail to be nice." For, this statement, even though it quantifies over non-actual scenarios, is firmly tethered to the speaker's *actual* evaluative standards—notwithstanding any differing evaluative standards the speaker himself may have in some of those non-actual scenarios. When one claims that there could not be a room that is just like this one except that it fails to be nice, one is talking modally about rooms *under one's actual-world standards of niceness,* even though one may not have *those* standards in certain other possible worlds in which there is a room just like the room under discussion. (Compare: When one claims that water could not have failed to be H_2O, one is talking modally about water *under the actual-world meaning of "water"*, even though "water" may not have that meaning in certain other possible worlds. A possible world in which "water" means beer would not be a possible world in which *water* fails to be H_2O.)

50 Jaegwon Kim, "Concepts of Supervenience," *Philosophy and Phenomenological Research* 45 (1984), 153-76, essay 22 in this volume, "'Strong' and 'Global' Supervenience Revisited," *Philosophy and Phenomenological Research* 10 (1987), 315-26.

51 For example, Horgan, "Supervenience and Microphysics," op. cit.; Kim, "Concepts of Supervenience," op. cit., essay 22 in this volume; "'Strong' and 'Global' Supervenience Revisited," op. cit.

52 Horgan, "Supervenience and Microphysics," op. cit.

53 Cf. ibid.

54 For instance, we could let G be a triply conjunctive property G^*, constructed as follows. Given some physically possible world w^* in which some individual i^* instantiates property F at time t, let the first conjunct of property G^* be some physical property instantiated by i^* in w^* at t (and not instantiated, in w^* at t, by any individual that is distinct from i^* but coincides spatially with i^*). Let the second conjunct of G^* be the property *being at spatiotemporal location L*, where L is the specific spatio-temporal location of i^* in w^* at t. And let the third conjunct of G^* be the property *being such that O*, where O is a "maximal" physical property that has built into it the entire physical history of the world w^*.

55 Horgan ("Supervenience and Microphysics," op. cit.) is often cited as one source of the idea of global physical supervenience. But for some reason the notion of regional supervenience, which was also broached in that paper, has gone virtually unnoticed in the subsequent philosophical literature.

56 Terence Horgan, "Mental Quausation," *Philosophical Perspectives* (1989), 47-76.

57 The issue has a longer history, though. As is pointed out in McLaughlin ("Type Epiphenomenalism, Type Dualism, and the Causal Priority of the Physical," *Philosophical Perspectives* 3 [1989], 109), it was well articulated by Broad (op. cit., 472).

58 There seems to be no fully non-tendentious way of formulating the issue, unfortunately. I use the term "efficacy" rather than "relevance" because the latter seems too weak to capture the kind of *oomph* that higher-order properties ought to have if they are not epiphenomenal. I use the modifier "causal/explanatory" at the risk of being accused of conflating two categories that ought to be kept distinct, in order to emphasize that causal connections among token events, and thus causal efficacy too, involve systematic general relations among the event types instantiated—relations that also figure in causal explanation.

59 Jaegwon Kim, "Epiphenonenal and Supervenient Causation," *Midwest Studies in Philosophy* 9 (1984), 257-70, essay 23 in this volume; "Supervenience and Supervenient Causation," in Horgan op. cit., 45-56.

60 For example, Stephen Stich, "Autonomous Psychology and the Belief-Desire Thesis," *Monist* 61 (1978), 573-91; Jerry Fodor, *Psychosemantics: The Problem of Meaning in the Philosophy of Mind* (Cambridge, MA: MIT Press, 1987); "A Modal Argument for Narrow Content," *Journal of Philosophy* 88 (1991), 5-26.

61 The notion of physical realization, which has been widely employed in philosophy of mind for some time, obviously deserves philosophical investigation in its own right. To my knowledge, as yet this project remains to be undertaken in a systematic way. Meanwhile, philosophers certainly should not assume (as I think they sometimes do assume) that realization is just the converse of super-

venience. The supervenience base is frequently broader than the realizing property.

62 For example, Horgan, "Mental Quausation," op. cit., "Nonreductive Materialism and the Explanatory Autonomy of Psychology," in S. Wagner and R. Warner, eds., *Naturalism: A Critical Appraisal* (Notre Dame: Notre Dame University Press, 1993).

63 For example, Davidson, "Mental Events," op. cit., essay 5 in this volume; "The Material Mind," op. cit.; Fodor, "A Modal Argument for Narrow Content," op. cit.; Ronald Endicott, "On Physical Multiple Reailzation," *Pacific Philosophical Quarterly* 70 (1989), 212-24; "Species-Specific Properties and More Narrow Reductive Strategies," *Erkenntnis* 38 (1993), 303-21; David Owens, "Levels of Explanation," *Mind* 98 (1989), 59-79; Robert Van Gulick, "Nonreductive Materialism and the Nature of the Intertheoretical Constraint," in Beckermann et al., op. cit., 157-79; Horgan, "Nonreductive Materialism and the Explanatory Autonomy of Psychology," op. cit.; Ausonio Marras, "Psychophysical Supervenience and Nonreductive Materialism," *Synthese* 95 (1993), 275-304; "Supervenience and Reducibility: An Odd Couple," *Philosophical Quarterly* 43 (1993), 215-22.

64 For example, Patricia Smith Churchland, *Neurophilosophy* (Cambridge, MA: MIT Press, 1986); Jaegwon Kim, "The Myth of Nonreductive Materialism," *Proceedings and Addresses of the American Philosophical Association* 63 (1989), 31-47; "Downward Causation," in Beckermann et al., op. cit., 119-138; "Multiple Realization and the Metaphysics of Reduction," *Philosophy and Phenomenological Research* 70 (1992), 1-26; "The Nonreductivist's Troubles with Mental Causation," in J. Heil and A. Mele, eds., *Mental Causation* (Oxford: Clarendon Press, 1993), 189-210; Andrew Melnyk, "Physicalism: From Supervenience to Elimination," *Philosophy and Phenomenological Research* 51 (1991), 573-87; John Bickle, "Multiple Realization and Psychophysical Reduction," *Behavior and Philosophy* 20 (1992), 47-58.

65 For some useful sorting of issues, see Beckermann, "Supervenience, Emergence, and Reduction," op. cit., and McLaughlin, "The Rise and Fall of British Emergentism," op. cit., §5.

66 Kim, "Supervenience as a Philosophical Concept," op. cit., 19-20.

67 For example, Bickle, op. cit.; Kim, "Multiple Realization and the Metaphysics of Reduction," op. cit.

68 Cf. Horgan, "Supervenience and Cosmic Hermeneutics," op. cit.

69 Cf. Horgan, "Supervenient Bridge Laws," *Philosophy of Science* 45 (1978), 227-49; Beckermann, op. cit.; McLaughlin, "The Rise and Fall of British Emergentism," op. cit.

70 E.g., Fodor, *Psychosemantics*, op. cit., *A Theory of Content and Other Essays* (Cambridge, MA: MIT Press, 1990); Fred Dretske, *Knowledge and the Flow of Information* (Cambridge, MA: MIT Press, 1981).

71 For further adumbration of these kinds of considerations, including discussions of relevant psychological literature, see Stephen Stich, "What is a Theory of Mental Representation?" *Mind* 101 (1992), 243-61; Michael Tye, "Naturalism

and the Mental," *Mind* 101 (1992), 421-41; and Stich and Laurence, "Intentionality and Naturalism," in H. Wettstein et al., eds., *Midwest Studies in Philosophy* (Minneapolis: University of Minnesota Press, 1994).

72 Cf. W.V.O. Quine, *Word and Object* (Cambridge, MA: MIT Press, 1960).

73 There are also the "phenomenal" or "what-it's-like" mental properties to deal with, the so-called "qualia." Prima facie, it is enormously hard to see how one could possibly explain why any particular physical or neurobiological property always gets co-instantiated with (or why it *necessarily* always gets co-instantiated with) a particular phenomenal property—or with any phenomenal property at all. (Appeals to type/type identity seem only to shift the mystery, rather than eliminating it: why should any given physical or neurobiological property be identical to a particular experiential what-it's-like property—e.g, the property *experiencing phenomenal redness*—rather than to some other phenomenal property or to none at all?) This "explanatory gap" problem is well described, specifically in relation to type-identity treatments of qualia, by Joseph Levine, "Materialism and Qualia: The Explanatory Gap," *Pacific Philosophical Quarterly* 64 (1983), 354-61. The supervenience version of the problem is given a thorough and detailed treatment by David Chalmers, *Toward a Theory of Consciousness*, unpublished dissertation (Bloomington: Department of Philosophy, Indiana University, 1993); he argues that the explanatory gap cannot be bridged, and he defends a positive theory of consciousness which in some ways resembles Broad's emergentism.

74 Saul Kripke, *Wittgenstein on Rules and Private Language* (Cambridge, MA: Harvard University Press, 1982).

75 Cf. Paul Horwich, *Truth* (Oxford: Basil Blackwell, 1990); Terence Horgan, "Naturalism and Intentionality," *Philosophical Studies* 76 (1991), 327-38; Crispin Wright, *Truth and Objectivity* (Cambridge, MA: Harvard University Press, 1992); Horgan and Timmons, "Metaphysical Naturalism, Semantic Normativity, and Meta-Semantic Irrealism," in E. Villanueva, ed., *Philosophical Issues* (Ridgeview, CA: Atascadero, 1993).

76 I thank David Henderson, Jaegwon Kim, John Tienson, and Mark Timmons for helpful comments and discussion.